THE BIBLICAL DANTE

V. STANLEY BENFELL

The Biblical Dante

UNIVERSITY OF TORONTO PRESS
Toronto Buffalo London

© University of Toronto Press Incorporated 2011
Toronto Buffalo London
www.utppublishing.com

ISBN 978-1-4426-4274-4

∞

Printed on acid-free, 100% post-consumer paper with vegetable-based inks.

Toronto Italian Studies

Library and Archives Canada Cataloguing in Publication

Benfell, V. Stanley, 1962–
The biblical Dante / V. Stanley Benfell.

(Toronto Italian studies)
Includes bibliographical references and index.
ISBN 978-1-4426-4274-4

1. Dante Alighieri, 1265–1321 – Religion.   2. Dante Alighieri, 1265–1321 –
Criticism and interpretation.   3. Bible in literature.   I. Title.   II. Series:
Toronto Italian studies

PQ4419.B5B45 2011   851'.1   C2011-902655-4

This book was published with the aid of a grant from the College of
Humanities at Brigham Young University.

University of Toronto Press acknowledges the financial assistance to its
publishing program of the Canada Council for the Arts and the Ontario
Arts Council.

 Canada Council   Conseil des Arts
for the Arts   du Canada   ONTARIO ARTS COUNCIL
CONSEIL DES ARTS DE L'ONTARIO

University of Toronto Press acknowledges the financial support for its
publishing activities of the Government of Canada through the Book
Publishing Industry Development Program (BPIDP).

For Leslie

Contents

Acknowledgments

This book has taken far too long to write. As early as 1995, I published an article that formed the basis for chapter 3, but I soon left the topic of Dante's biblicism to pursue other scholarly projects. But I returned to it, brought back by my interest in the literary qualities of biblical texts and in the ways in which the Bible has served as a central influence throughout Western literary history. Since that time, work has been slowed by administrative assignments, especially by a term as department chair and stints on three Study Abroad programs.

In the long course of finishing this book, I have incurred numerous debts, both intellectual and personal. My greatest intellectual debt is to Teodolinda Barolini. The project ultimately had its origins in a year-long graduate course on Dante's *Commedia* that I took from Professor Barolini at New York University. Part of my work from that course eventually developed into a substantial portion of my dissertation, which she directed. Since that time, she has helped me on numerous occasions with advice and encouragement. Many other colleagues have read through parts of the book at various stages and have provided useful analysis and discussion. Particular thanks are due to Madison Sowell, Christopher Kleinhenz, Santa Casciani, Richard Newhauser, Joseph Parry, George Tate, Mark Wrathall, and Dallas Denery. When I first considered the project as a book, Peter Hawkins kindly offered encouragement as well as a pre-publication look at his *Dante's Testaments*. Jim Faulconer's work on the meaning and function of scripture helped me to reconsider my conceptions of the pre-modern Bible. Kyle Anderson (now finishing his PhD in Comparative Literature at Penn State) very ably served as my research assistant at a crucial time, and his MA thesis on Dante's Earthly Paradise helped me to see that part of the poem in a new light. Scott Miller suggested the title. The Humanities Publication Center at BYU (Mel Thorne, director) helped compile the index. The two anonymous readers for University of Toronto Press have helped me to improve the book in ways too numerous to detail and have saved me from many errors. Ron Schoeffel has been an ideal editor in shepherding the book through the publication process, and I am grateful to him as well as to Anne Laughlin, Margaret Burgess, and the others at the Press who have worked hard to improve the final book. Of course, all remaining mistakes of fact and judgment are my own.

Brigham Young's University College of Humanities offered financial support at important moments, including the subvention necessary for publication. My department chair, Michael Call, and dean, John Rosenberg, arranged on short notice for the research leave that enabled me to complete the original manuscript. More personal debts are due to many colleagues at Brigham Young University and elsewhere, who offered invaluable encouragement and support, particularly Roger Macfarlane, Joseph Parry, George Handley, Matthew Ancell, Kerry Soper, and, especially, David Hamblin. Mark Wrathall, with his formidable argumentative skills, talked me out of abandoning the project at a key moment. My greatest, and most intangible, debt is due to my family, especially to my wife, Leslie, and our three children, Jacob, Matthew, and Frances. The dedication of this book to Leslie is a small gesture but gives some indication of how much I owe her that can never be repaid.

Some portions of this book appeared previously. Parts of chapters 2 and 3 appeared in rather different form as 'Biblical Truth in the Examination of Cantos of Dante's *Paradiso*,' *Dante Studies* 115 (1997): 89–109; and 'Prophetic Madness: The Bible in *Inferno* XIX,' *MLN* 110 (1995): 145–63. Part of chapter 4 appeared in somewhat different form as 'Blessed Are They That Hunger after Justice: From Vice to Beatitude in Dante's *Purgatorio*,' in *The Seven Deadly Sins: From Individuals to Communities*, ed. Richard Newhauser (Leiden: Brill, 2007), 185–206. I am grateful to the editors of these publications for permission to reprint the material here.

A Note on Texts

Citations of Dante refer to the following editions:

'La Commedia' secondo l'antica vulgata, ed. Giorgio Petrocchi, 4 vols. (Milan: Mondadori, 1966–67), as reproduced in Dante, *The Divine Comedy*, trans. Charles S. Singleton (Princeton: Princeton University Press, 1970–75).

Convivio, ed. Cesare Vasoli and Domenico de Robertis, in *Dante Alighieri: Opere minori*, vol. 2, pts. 1 and 2 (1988; Milan: Ricciardi, 1995).

De vulgari eloquentia, ed. Pier Vincenzo Mengaldo, in *Dante Alighieri: Opere minori*, vol. 3, pt. 1 (1979; Milan: Ricciardi, 1996).

Epistole, ed. Arsenio Frugoni and Giorgio Brugnoli, in *Dante Alighieri: Opere minori*, vol. 3, pt. 2 (1979; Milan: Ricciardi, 1996.)

Monarchia, ed. Bruno Nardi, in *Dante Alighieri: Opere minori*, vol. 3, pt. 1 (1979; Milan: Ricciardi, 1996).

All citations and translations of Saint Thomas Aquinas's *Summa theologiae* refer to the Blackfriars edition, 61 vols. (New York: McGraw Hill, 1964–81); I occasionally modify the English translation. Citations take the form *Summa theologiae* 2a.2æ.4.1 = pars secunda, secundae partis, questio 4, articulus 1.

Latin citations of the Bible are taken from *Biblia Sacra iuxta vulgatam versionem* (Stuttgart: Deutsche Bibelgesellschaft, 1969), and the online version at http://www.drbo.org/ may also be of help to readers; all English translations of the Bible are cited according to the Douay-Rheims version (London: Baronius Press, 2003).

Citations of the *Glossa ordinaria* refer to *Biblia Latina cum glossa ordinaria: Facsimile reprint of the Editio Princeps Adoph Rusch of Strassburg 1480/81*, 4 vols. (Turnhout: Brepols, 1992).

Citations of commentators on the *Commedia* without bibliographic information refer to their commentaries as presented in the online archive, the Dartmouth Dante Project (http://dante.dartmouth.edu).

All unattributed translations, including those of Dante, are my own.

Abbreviations

The following abbreviations are used throughout:

CCSL   *Corpus Christianorum: Series Latina*
CSEL   *Corpus Scriptorum Ecclesiasticorum Latinorum*
DE   *Dante Encyclopedia,* ed. Richard Lansing (New York: Garland, 2000).
ED   *Enciclopedia Dantesca,* gen. ed. Umberto Bosco, 6 vols. (Rome: Istituto dell'Enciclopedia Italiana, 1970–78).
PL   *Patrologiae cursus completus: Series Latina,* ed. Jacques-Paul Migne, 222 vols. (Paris, 1844–64); cited by volume and column nos., e.g., *PL* 176: 801a–b.
SC   *Sources Chrétiennes*

Additionally, the following abbreviated forms have been used in references to titles of works by Dante.

Conv.   *Convivio*
Inf.   *Inferno*
Purg.   *Purgatorio*
Par.   *Paradiso*

THE BIBLICAL DANTE

Introduction

O santo padre, e spirito che vedi
ciò che credesti sì, che tu vincesti
ver' lo sepulcro più giovani piedi . . .   (*Par.* 24.124–6)

(O holy father, spirit who sees what you believed to such an extent that
you vanquished younger feet toward the sepulchre . . .)

In the heaven of the fixed stars, Saint Peter subjects Dante the pilgrim
to a test on faith, which takes the form of rigorous questioning in the
manner of a university examination, with Dante explicitly comparing
himself to a degree candidate who anxiously waits for the master to ask
the first questions. Peter's interrogation begins with the proper definition of faith but goes on to probe the source and nature of Dante's own
faith. It is perhaps not surprising that these last questions centre around
the Bible – its truth value, authority, and impact on Dante as a reader
and a Christian. Immediately following Dante's lengthy justification of
the truth of the Bible and of its legitimacy as the source of faith, however, Dante the pilgrim directs to Peter the *captatio benevolentiae* cited
above, in which he mistakenly refers to a key passage in the Gospel of
John, a passage to which Dante refers correctly elsewhere.[1] The episode
is an intriguing and puzzling one that raises several questions: how can
Dante 'prove' the truth of the Bible? If the Bible is indeed true for Dante,
why does he immediately rewrite it, in the very face of his proof? And
if his acceptance of biblical truth can be reconciled with his rewriting
of the Bible, here and elsewhere in the *Commedia*, what does he think
about how we should read the Bible? The purpose of this study is to
address these and other questions related to Dante's use of the Bible.

The Bible and the *Commedia* are very different books – in length, composition history, language, style, and many other ways. Dante scholars have nevertheless frequently linked the two, and not just because the Bible obviously provides one of the key influences on the poem, with some scholars arguing that Dante's works contain more direct and indirect citations of the Bible than of any other work.[2] For many critics, Dante's intertextual relationship to the Bible differs from his relationship to any other text, including Virgil's *Aeneid*.[3] Much of his interest is due to the tremendous cultural and religious prestige that the Bible enjoyed in the late Middle Ages, but it also seems that Dante is drawn to the Bible as a *literary* work; this collection of often disparate ancient texts written in Hebrew and Greek and translated into Latin had a formative influence over how this poet wrote his vernacular poem more than a thousand years after the last of the biblical texts was composed and hundreds of years after the Bible as a whole was given its final, canonical form. Charles Singleton, to take perhaps the most prominent example, has argued that Dante imitated the Bible, imitated, that is, 'God's way of writing' in the *Commedia*.[4] In brief, many scholars have sensed that the Bible has something crucial to do with the composition and meaning of the *Commedia*, beyond its status as one of its most frequently cited and influential sources.

Given the place of the Bible in thinking about the meaning of the poem, it is somewhat surprising that, although there are numerous studies of Dante's intertextual relationship to his poetic predecessors, systematic examination of what is demonstrably the most important subtext of the poem has been missing until comparatively recently; only in the last several years have a few studies appeared that explore various aspects of the biblical presence in Dante's work.[5] What is still lacking, though, is a sustained reading of the Bible in the poem, not in terms of allusions and citations and their importance for the meaning of particular passages, but rather in terms of the ways in which the Bible serves as a model text for Dante, hovering over the poem like God's spirit over the waters of creation. We can best understand this biblical presence by turning to those moments in the *Commedia* where Dante explicitly evokes the status of the Bible as the Word of God. In these passages – which include *Inferno* 19 and the Earthly Paradise cantos (*Purgatorio* 28–33), as well as the so-called examination cantos (*Paradiso* 24–26) mentioned above – Dante not only draws on the scriptures as source material for the poem, he also interrogates the Bible as scripture, questioning its truth value and authority. Ultimately, the Bible proves crucial to Dante both because it helps to frame his own ideas regarding history, ethics, and the fate of the human soul, and because it is the text through which he comes to understand the world and his place in it. Dante, that is to say, draws on an array of interpretive strategies in order to appropriate the Bible and its message for his own time and purposes – to understand the Bible in terms of his own historical moment; or, to state it another way, to understand his historical moment in the light of the Word of God.

How Should We Read Dante Reading the Bible?

My thinking about Dante's use of the Bible has been shaped by my interest in what is often called 'the Bible as literature.' Scholars such as Robert Alter, who draws freely on medieval Jewish exegetes in his work on the literary qualities of the Hebrew Bible, offer convincing evidence that pre-modern readers of the Bible were frequently more in tune with the *literary* features of biblical texts than are most contemporary, 'scientific' biblical scholars.[6] That is, Alter and other literary scholars who have used the tools of modern literary criticism[7] in approaching biblical texts often find sensitive readers among pre-modern exegetes. On the other hand, many modern biblical scholars dismiss pre-modern biblical interpretation out of hand as unscientific. When they do approach these interpreters, however, they often do so only as a historical curiosity. Given our distance from Dante and other pre-modern readers of the Bible, it may prove helpful to bring our own modernist interpretive assumptions into view and so help us to a greater awareness of how they may influence our approach to earlier readers of the Bible.

We can find a telling example of this contemporary disdain for pre-modern biblical interpretation in the Introduction to the respected biblical scholar James Kugel's book, *The Bible As It Was*. In this lengthy work, Kugel details interpretations of key episodes from the Hebrew Bible that were common in late antiquity (and which therefore often had an afterlife that endured well into the Middle Ages), but which seem strange to modern readers. He introduces this largely historical work with an extended attempt to spell out the major differences between a modern understanding of the Bible and that of the ancient interpreters he treats.

More than anything ... these [ancient] interpretations tried to bring out the universal and enduring messages of biblical texts, for the interpreters considered Scripture to be a sacred guidebook for human existence. Interpreters therefore tried to look beyond the obvious content of what was said to find some relevant, usable lesson, even if it was less than obvious at first glance. And so, whatever their particular form or purpose, these interpretive traditions all tended to *transform* the apparent meaning of biblical texts.[8]

Kugel's elucidation of these foreign interpretive practices stems from commonly accepted modernist assumptions of biblical interpretation, which are threefold. First, the Bible is not a 'sacred guidebook' but a text like any other; assuming otherwise leads us to search for 'universal and enduring messages' that '*transform* the apparent meaning' of what we read. Second, the Bible therefore possesses 'obvious content'; we like to think, after all, 'that the Bible, or any other text, means "just what it says"' (xv). Any interpretation that deviates from this obvious, literal sense 'transforms' the meaning of the Bible. Ancient Jews and Christians did not, read *the* Bible, which we are now only able to recover from the centuries of interpretation that have obscured it; they read an '*interpreted* Bible – not just the stories, prophecies, and laws themselves, but these texts as they had, by now, been interpreted for centuries' (xv; emphasis Kugel's).

This second assumption reveals an underlying split in how we often consider medieval interpretive practices, an implicit theory that we may call 'hermeneutic dualism': there is the plain, obvious meaning (just what the text says), and then anything that departs from it. This dualism leads us to reject out of hand virtually all pre-modern interpretations as fanciful, often a synonym for allegorical. While most literary critics would not state this hermeneutical theory as naively as Kugel does, our impatience with pre-modern interpretive methods such as allegory betrays our similar views.[9] Indeed, at least since Coleridge and Goethe famously disparaged allegory in favour of the more 'organic' symbol, literary critics have tended to view the use of allegory as an exercise in hermeneutic dualism: misguided interpreters forcing preconceived ideas onto texts in defiance of the literal sense.[10] This hermeneutic dualism is exacerbated in biblical studies by the common assumption that the literal sense of the Bible is something separable from its historical reference, and that it is the historical events underlying the biblical narrative, rather than the text itself, that should receive the attention of the scholar. Medieval estimations of the literal sense, as I will argue in chapter 1, differ from our modern sense. For the pre-modern reader, to read 'literally' was usually to read *ad litteram*, according to the letter – to devote careful attention to the words themselves. Modern reading practices, however, have resulted in a 'split between the explicative meaning and the historical estimation of biblical narratives,' as Hans Frei has phrased it, an assumption that has a determining influence over both how we interpret the Bible and whether we judge it as true.[11]

The third assumption of modernist exegesis has to do with how we think of biblical truth; we accept the truth of biblical texts insofar as they accord with the 'actual' historical past – to the events transpiring in Palestine during the time period (roughly) of 1500 BCE to 100 CE, or rather to what we are able to reconstruct of those events using the modern disciplines of history, archaeology, anthropology, and so on.[12] Consequently, the 'literal text' (in the ancient sense) is discarded in favour of a reconstructed history that takes the text as its point of departure but leaves it behind to consider the historical reality underlying the biblical narrative, which is taken to constitute the final, irreducible meaning of the text. Parts of the narrative not deemed historically true are considered embellishments, revisions, and accretions that distort and obscure the underlying historical meaning, which is the proper object of disinterested scholarly inquiry. Scriptural meaning, in other words, is limited to reference.[13]

Kugel goes on to provide a very useful overview and summary of many ancient accounts of biblical narratives; however, his condescending curiosity about their practices shows through and colours his account, illustrating how our modern assumptions about textual interpretation, and about biblical interpretation in particular, tend to creep in and influence our reading of Dante and other pre-modern readers of the Bible without our fully being aware of them. If we turn to Beryl Smalley's important, groundbreaking *The Study of the Bible in the Middle Ages*, to provide another example, we can see these assumptions working in the basic narrative thrust of the book. Smalley limits her definition of biblical 'scholarship' to those who privilege the 'literal sense' and find the purpose of exegesis to lie in 'entering into the mind of the author,' and she goes on in her conclusion to characterize those medieval interpreters who did not follow this ideal form of scholarly inquiry to have 'subordinated scholarship . . . to mysticism and propaganda.'[14] In brief, Smalley and Kugel do not, in my view, teach us the way to read Dante reading the Bible. There are recent scholars, however, who have studied the biblical exegesis of Augustine and other pre-modern exegetes, and while noting that these early biblical readers have frequently been read according to our own modern assumptions and so misunderstood, they have proposed some more sympathetic ways of approaching Augustine and other pre-modern interpreters, methods that also shed light on Dante's use of the Bible, as we will see in chapter 1.[15]

My doubts about our traditional views of literal and allegorical interpretation were confirmed when I was asked to write the entry on symbolism for the *Dante Encyclopedia.* The obvious way into the issue seemed to be through the traditional Romantic distinction between allegory on the one hand (bad, artificial, contrived) and symbol on the other (good, organic). Knowing the famous passages where Dante employs the word 'allegory' (e.g., the opening of *Convivio* 2), and but with no instances of his use of 'symbol' coming to mind, I searched the concordances of Dante's Italian and Latin works, only to find that he never used the word either in Italian or Latin (in Italian, at any rate, the first use of *simbolo* postdates Dante),[16] thus suggesting that Dante did not make the distinction between allegory and symbol dear to post-Romantic literary critics.[17]

Dante, that is to say, not only thought of allegorical and literal interpretation in another way than we do – according to pre-modern, rather than modernist, theories of meaning; he also conceived of the Bible, its meaning, and its truth value, differently than we do – differently even than those of us who continue to believe that it is an inspired, sacred text. As I have suggested, for most modern readers, a text is deemed 'true' to the degree to which it conforms to external reality, or at least to what we can determine about the reality external to the text through modern scientific methods. For Saint Augustine, Dante, and others, though, such a conception of textual truth seems to have been foreign. The gap between modernist and pre-modern assumptions of interpretation does not, however, mean that there are no contemporary theories of meaning that may help us to read Dante reading the Bible. The thought of Hans-Georg Gadamer, which he characterized as 'philosophical hermeneutics,' may provide a conception of textual truth that is closer to what Saint Augustine and Dante expected when encountering a text.[18]

For Gadamer, textual truth arises not through a disinterested study of how a text does or does not correspond to external reality, but through the encounter of a reader with the text. For the historically minded critic, the only meaning that need concern us is the original meaning – that intended by the author in his or her original historical context. Gadamer points out, however, that this view of interpretation assumes a remarkably naive faith in the ability of the interpreter to escape from his or her own historical context, as if the interpreter read the text from some timeless space outside of history itself. Gadamer insists, rather, on what he calls the 'historicality of understanding'; interpretation is always caught up in a given moment. Some critics, for example, make a distinction between exegesis and interpretation, in which 'exegesis' represents a systematic attempt to understand a given text historically, in terms of how it would have been understood when it was first written down, while a critic concerned with 'interpretation,' on the other hand, endeavours to understand what a text means *now* – how is it true for us today? From Gadamer's perspective, however, such a distinction is false, as both the concerns of the present-day critic and the pull of the past inevitably exercise an influence over scholarly work on texts from the past. Indeed, viewed from Gadamer's perspective, it is the concerns of interpretation – that is, the concerns of the present-day interpreter – that motivate the approach to the past. For if the past had no claim on us, why would we seek to understand it? As Christine O'Connell Baur has stated it, 'for the hermeneutics of historicality, the interpreter's present concerns, far from being an obstacle to understanding the past, are the very conditions of such understanding.'[19]

The possibility that I as a reader in the early twenty-first century can simply abandon my own historical horizon and inhabit another (such as that of, say, the author of the fourth Gospel in the late first century CE) is illusory. Neither, however, is it accurate to say that the only kind of understanding possible is a contemporary one divorced from the past in which the text was created. For Gadamer, understanding occurs within the fusion of the horizons of both the text and the reader. As he states the idea in *Truth and Method:*

> In fact the horizon of the present is continually in the process of being formed because we are continually having to test all our prejudices. An important part of this testing occurs in encountering the past and in understanding the tradition from which we come. Hence the horizon of the present cannot be formed without the past. There is no more isolated horizon of the present in itself than there are historical horizons which have to be acquired. *Rather, understanding is always the fusion of these horizons supposedly existing by themselves.*[20]

Understanding, then, involves both 'exegesis' and 'interpretation,' with the reader attuned to the past out of which the text emerges as well as the present in which he or she confronts the text. As Gadamer goes on to argue, 'understanding does not consist in a technical virtuosity of "understanding" everything written. Rather, it is a genuine experience (*Erfahrung*) – i.e., an encounter with something that asserts itself as truth.'[21] Joel Weinsheimer explains Gadamer's thought in this way:

> The truth is something we neither possess nor make, a product of consciousness, but rather something that happens to us and in which we participate, as when we get caught up in a game. Truth happens when we lose ourselves and no longer stand over against it as a subject against an object. When we are caught up in the game that is played with us, it is then, even before we are aware of it, that we have joined in the continuing event of truth.[22]

This notion of textual truth – that a reader encounters it as an event that emerges during the engagement with the text – seems to me closer to Dante's understanding of the truth of a text like the Bible than does our modern notion of external correspondence. The problem with this latter notion is that it separates questions of textual understanding from questions of truth, a divorce that Gadamer sees as the natural result of 'historical objectivism.'

> The text that is understood historically is forced to abandon its claim to be saying something true. We think we understand when we see the historical situation and try to reconstruct the historical horizon. In fact, however, we have given up the claim to find in the past any truth that is valid and intelligible *for ourselves*. Acknowledging the otherness of the other in this way, making him the object of objective knowledge, involves the fundamental suspension of his claim to truth.[23]

For many of us, the Bible (or any other ancient text) cannot affect us existentially and make a claim on us, because we refuse the possibility that it communicates truths not available in our own conception of the world and our historical place in it. We separate it from us through our determination to examine it 'objectively.' Of course, the situation differs with Dante, who, if anything, looked to the Bible to find truth *for himself*. Indeed, Saint Augustine's description in book 11 of the *Confessions* of being led to the truth similarly seems to describe a truth that emerges in the event that occurs when a reader encounters the text: 'Who is our teacher except the reliable truth? Even when we are instructed through some mutable creature, we are led to reliable truth when we are learning truly by standing still and listening to him. We then "rejoice with joy because of the voice of the bridegroom," and give ourselves to the source whence we have our being.'[24]

With this understanding of textual truth, Dante's use of the Bible needed to be rethought. It now seemed to me that Dante's frequent creative use of the Bible was due to his conception of biblical truth, which had much less to do with a modern sense of textual truth than with an idea of the Bible's truth as one that orders the world, framing the very ways in which individuals such as Dante saw things. Dante was less concerned, therefore, with unswerving accuracy to the details of the biblical text than with fidelity to the larger truths revealed through the Bible. Dante and other medieval readers did not make the Bible the 'object of objective knowledge,' but instead treated it as an authority, as a text that ordered the world. Certainly, Dante accepted the Bible as historically true, but he thought of the historical nature of the Bible differently than we do. The text's historical meaning was not relegated to the past in such a way that it was cut off from his life. The text's historicity, in other words, did not prohibit other meanings, especially those relevant to the reader's own life, from existing within the text (in fact, as we shall see, it produced them). As Dante cites the Bible within his poem, therefore, he engages in a particular kind of intertextuality.

Intertextuality

Intertextuality occasionally has the undeserved reputation of being strictly 'formalist' in its attention to the literary engagements of poets, but if the history of reception has taught us anything it is that, as Teodolinda Barolini has phrased it, 'there is no such thing as "mere form."'[25] A poet's choice of which texts to cite and how to cite them has implications not only for the form of the poem but also for its ideology, where that word is understood in its broadest sense. Given the tremendous cultural authority of the Bible, the decision to incorporate a given biblical passage into a poem involves more than just the cited subtext; the passage will frequently invoke its interpretive subtext as well. Indeed, the hermeneutic traditions surrounding all of the texts that Dante cites help to elucidate why Dante chooses a particular text and how he transforms it so that it functions as a part of his own poem. His allusions to Ovid's *Metamorphoses*, for example, where he uses Ovid's images of transformation in the service of illustrating Christian conversion, are no doubt due in large part to the long tradition of reading Ovid allegorically, revealed most fully in the *Ovidius moralizatus* of Pierre Bersuire.[26] Nevertheless, as heavily glossed as Ovid's poem was, no text in Western culture possesses a more extensive interpretive history than the Bible.

This history was available to Dante in a variety of ways; indeed, it would have been nearly impossible for him to encounter the 'bare' text of the Bible, without any interpretive apparatus. It served as a foundational university text, on which masters lectured and wrote commentaries; it was the default source of the majority of sermons delivered in church; and it also provided the most frequent subjects for visual art, especially religious art. Many scholars have attempted to detail the influence of specific texts or works of art from this tradition on Dante's poem,[27] but given how little we know of Dante's life, especially following his exile from Florence in the early fourteenth century, it would be impossible to trace every possible source for his understanding of a given biblical passage. Though I have attempted to identify some of the commentaries that Dante specifically mentions or that he most likely would have encountered, for reasons of practicality I have attempted primarily to gauge the general interpretive context in which biblical passages were read in his day. I therefore make frequent recourse to standard commentaries such as the *Glossa ordinaria*; even if Dante did not know the *Glossa* directly on a particular passage, it seems likely that he would have been familiar with the interpretive tradition that it represents. Thus, attempts to flesh out the exegetical context of a given biblical passage are meant to provide a general sense of how the passage was read in Dante's day, not to make the case that he necessarily knew the specific commentaries or works cited in this study.

This interpretive context proves crucial in considering the intertextuality of Dante's poem, because intertextuality is inescapably hermeneutic, and it is so in at least two ways. First, and in its broadest sense, intertextuality refers to the vast tapestry of prior texts and speech-acts that make the poem as a particular act of signification possible. As Jonathan Culler has noted, it 'leads us to consider prior texts as contributions to a code which makes possible the various effects of signification.'[28] When considered more narrowly, however, as a text's explicit use – through citation, allusion, etc. – of other texts, intertextuality invariably requires interpretation. By choosing another text and using it in one's own poetic construction, one necessarily interprets it, as the subtext takes on new meaning when placed into a new context and is subordinated to the demands of a new poem. Grasping the meaning that a given text held in Dante's day thus helps us to understand both why Dante selected a given passage for imitation or citation, and how he transforms it within the text of his poem. There have been several excellent studies of Dante's intertextual practice with respect to his classical predecessors in particular, studies that have influenced my own intertextual analysis here.[29] Nevertheless, Dante's relationship to the Bible differs from his relationship to all other poetic predecessors, at least in part because of the inescapably intertextual nature of the biblical books themselves.

Scriptural texts are filled with citations of other works – Hebrew prophets cite Mosaic law, later prophets quote earlier prophets, and New Testament authors continually refer to the 'Scriptures,' which for them meant the Hebrew Bible, usually in the Septuagint translation. Intertextuality is also characteristic of Virgil, Ovid, and the other Roman poets who influenced Dante, but the Bible presents a different situation than do the Roman poets, because, for the most part, the texts that Jeremiah or Saint Paul cite were texts sacred to them and to their audience. Homer certainly had a tremendous prestige for Virgil's audience, but the status of the *Odyssey* was not quite on a par with that of Genesis, say, for the readers of Saint Paul's letter to the Galatians. Similarly, when Dante cites the Bible as opposed to *The Aeneid*, the status of the two citations is fundamentally different; whereas the truth of Dante's pagan predecessors (even of an author such as Virgil who gained the reputation of a *magus* in the Middle Ages) was inevitably suspect, the Bible defined truth itself. Though, again, this is not to say that Dante never alters the biblical text in his poem; as it happens, he does so with some regularity. In fact, he may well have turned to the Bible itself for models of intertextuality in which an author intent on truth-telling can alter the sacred texts of his tradition while also preserving the authority and truth of those very texts.

Michael Fishbane's work on what he has called 'inner-biblical' exegesis is illuminating as he details the ways in which authors in the Hebrew Bible refer to and comment upon legal and other texts sacred to them and to their audience. In confronting legal texts, for example, biblical authors revered the law delivered by God to Moses on Mount Sinai, and yet in attempting to understand the law and its relevance to their own day, they inevitably confronted gaps in the legal code, or new situations created by evolving historical circumstances that the law did not cover. They were therefore drawn to 'interpret' the biblical code in such a way that it could be understood as meeting the contingencies of the contemporary world: 'Inner-biblical legal exegesis . . . is distinctively concerned with making pre-existent laws applicable or viable in new contexts.'[30] Hebrew prophets also employed previous scriptural texts in ways that would have a similar force in reinterpreting or extending the Mosaic law to make it relevant and compelling for the prophet's audience.[31] We will return to Fishbane's analysis of biblical intertextuality at greater length in chapter 3; here it is important only to note the parallel between the intertextual practices of biblical prophets and those of Dante. He, too, employs sacred texts in new or even creative ways, a practice he follows not to undermine or discredit these texts, but to show their relevance to his own age.

Indeed, like most interpreters in the Middle Ages, Dante's reading of scripture strikes modern readers as focused solely on the Bible's significance for him in his own day rather than on what it meant for the original readers. As I have argued, though, this distinction between the 'interpretation' supposedly characteristic of Dante as opposed to the 'exegesis' of a modern biblical scholar is problematic. As Gerald Bruns has observed, 'The point is that once you take seriously Gadamer's analysis concerning the historicality of all understanding, you have to begin rethinking your ideas about allegorical interpretation, because allegorical interpretation (I mean allegoresis that is aware of itself as such) is simply the tradition of understanding that doesn't try to repress or conceal or get "beyond" its historicality, its belongingness or finitude, but rather asserts it.'[32]

Dante's interpretive interest in what the text meant for his own time does not mean that he ignored 'exegesis.' As we will see in chapter 1, Dante's discussion of biblical passages in book 3 of the *Monarchia* begins with careful exegesis even though his ultimate interest is in interpretation, as he asks what these scriptural passages tell him about the proper relationship of the papacy to the temporal order in his own day. He thus rejects the common papal reading of the 'two lights' that God creates in Genesis 1.16 – with the 'greater light' signifying the papacy and the 'lesser light' referring to the empire – since that interpretation does not represent the 'intention of Moses.'[33] He nevertheless in the *Commedia* transforms this scripture, referring to 'two suns of earthly life' (see *Purg.* 16.106–14) in order to provide a biblical image consonant with his own sense of the proper ordering of the temporal world. The truth of the Bible, then, is key to Dante's use of it, but his citation of it need not be exact, in the manner of a modern biblical literalist. In fact, his determination to speak to his contemporaries virtually requires his freedom in citing scripture. In order to understand why, we must begin by trying to comprehend more fully how pre-modern men and women read the Bible.

The Argument

In the first chapter, I attempt not to provide a detailed reconstruction of the sources of Dante's biblical knowledge, but to explore the poet's conceptual understanding of the scriptures, as, in my view, this is more important for understanding the passages where Dante explicitly evokes the Bible as a sacred text in his poem. The former task, in any event, has been already been ably treated by others.[34] There are, thus, two tasks I undertake in the opening chapter. The first is to delineate, in general terms, how medieval readers approached the Bible. In the chapter's first major section, therefore, I consider the hermeneutics of Saint Augustine – the most influential of the Latin church fathers – in an attempt to show how the hermeneutic sense of textual truth delineated above may account for Augustine's sense of the Bible as a true text. Specifically, there are two main issues: first, Augustine did not understand the Bible as a 'descriptive' text, at least not in our terms; rather, he saw it as what might be described as a symbolically ordering text. Instead of describing the world, it told him how to see that world. The scriptures' meaning emerged out of an individual's existential situation, out of what the Bible meant in his or her life. Second, given that this is the case, the modern assumption of the superiority of the literal sense and the consequent artificiality and inferiority of the allegorical or spiritual sense results in a hermeneutic dualism foreign to Augustine's and other pre-modern theories of biblical meaning. That is, the pre-modern sense of biblical truth relies less on a correspondence between the literal text and its underlying historical reality than on an intensely contemporary sense of the text's veracity; the Bible becomes true as it is true precisely *for us*. The second half of the chapter is more historically minded, as I explore the range of interpretive possibilities open to Dante as a reader of the Bible in the early fourteenth century, which then can prepare a way to explain Dante's biblical hermeneutics as they are revealed in his minor works. Through a close analysis of parts of these texts, I argue that Dante's pre-modern notion of biblical meaning follows the models of Augustine, Aquinas, and others in both eschewing a hermeneutic dualism and in finding biblical truth in its impact on the individual reader, while he also engages with contemporary interpretive strategies, especially when critiquing biblical exegesis with which he disagrees. This section focuses on readings of book 3 of the *Monarchia*, section 2.1 of the *Convivio*, and Dante's letters to the Italian Cardinals and to Henry VII.

In the second chapter, we turn from this conceptual understanding of the Bible and the way it orders Dante's perception of the world to the *Paradiso*, the canticle in which Dante most fully examines what textual truth means in the case of the scriptures. How the Bible is true is a question vitally important not only for Dante as a Christian, but also as a poet, since he, too, is trying to write a poem that is true in some crucial sense. In chapter 2, therefore, we begin by considering how fully Dante ties himself as poet to biblical authors – particularly David and Paul – in the final canticle, as well as by examining Dante's encounter with Cacciaguida, from whom he receives a prophetic commission to write the truth. We then turn for the bulk of the chapter to the 'examination cantos' (24–26), where Peter, James, and John question the pilgrim on faith, hope, and charity, and where the Bible's status, truth value, and authoritative status are explicitly addressed. In canto 24, Dante ends up defending the Bible's truth in existential terms; it is true because it influences its readers to turn to God and abandon sin. As suggested above, the Bible's truth value lies not in its proved correspondence to an external reality, but in the encounter a reader has with the sacred text, in which understanding and truth emerge, which ultimately change the reader. It soon becomes clear, however, that Dante feels that in his time readers no longer read the Bible in this way. He writes his poem, at least in part, to bring readers back to an encounter with the Bible, to help them see it again as key to a proper understanding of the world.

In chapter 3, we begin our exploration of passages in the first two canticles that are specifically and crucially informed by biblical texts, starting with the *Inferno*. At the very beginning of the poem, Dante recounts his story in what can only be called a biblical landscape – an environment derived from, and interpreted through, the Bible. While this landscape quickly recedes, as we journey through hell the Bible's status as a symbolically ordering text is evident, if only in a negative sense. The Bible, while explicitly cited only rarely for most of the *Inferno*, nevertheless helps to order hell's moral landscape. Multiple sinners reveal not only their wickedness but also their ignorance of the proper way of understanding the world, of seeing things as God sees them. In a crucial moment in the *Inferno*, however, in canto 19, Dante turns to the Bible in order to critique the pervasive corruption at the highest levels of church leadership. He uses the Apocalypse to provide an image of the primitive church that Dante hopes will revitalize the contemporary church, as well as to furnish the materials for a devastating criticism of papal simony. He, in fact, manipulates the details of the Apocalypse in order to make his criticism of contemporary popes more pointed, so that the wickedness of the papacy of his day was specifically foreseen and condemned by John the Revelator. Dante's use of scripture does not distort the underlying truth of John's vision; rather, in a prophetic manner, it revitalizes the vision by making it directly relevant for Dante's own day.

In the final two chapters we turn to the *Purgatorio*, where Dante's vision for a just society is made more plain, and his use of the Bible is key to revealing that vision. Chapter 4 addresses the role of the Bible in the pilgrim's ascent toward the Earthly Paradise. After a consideration of the version of the Lord's Prayer that opens canto 11, we turn to the Beatitudes, which punctuate the pilgrim's ascent of Mount Purgatory. The Beatitudes became a text of particular interest in the Scholastic period, as many moral theologians compared traditional Christian notions of happiness (the Beatitudes were taken to be foundational in addressing this question) with the newly discovered Aristotelian understanding of happiness as found in the *Nicomachean Ethics*. A detailed analysis of Dante's Beatitudes against this background reveals that Dante adapts these brief, biblical sayings so as to comment on central questions of moral philosophy while also implying that some of the virtues that the blessed learn on the terraces of Purgatory are crucial not only for *their* eventual *celestial* beatitude, but also for *our* hope for *temporal* happiness in a just society here on earth.

In the final chapter, we take up Dante's vision of contemporary history as revealed in the Earthly Paradise at the summit of Purgatory, a vision informed by and made explicit through the lens of the Apocalypse. Dante uses the narrative framework of the Bible's final book so as to consider contemporary history within a biblical light and a temporal context defined by an end time. Of course, Dante had first extensively drawn on the Apocalypse in *Inferno* 19, but he greatly extends this vision of history in the Earthly Paradise cantos. Eden both stands for human origins and points to our eventual destiny, as the human souls, purged from sin, return to the Earthly Paradise before ascending to heaven. Similarly, the fall inaugurated human history and moved it toward the consummation of that history with the final judgment. Dante understands both his own life and the larger movement of human history within the biblical narrative of creation, fall, and redemption. This overarching narrative also motivates his portrayal of the history of the church and its eventual fate in cantos 32 and 33; in spite of the rampant corruption in both church and state, Dante asserts a fundamentally biblical narrative teleology in which God's purposes eventually triumph. This does not imply the imminent end of the world, but rather a restoration of a just society governed temporally by the Roman emperor and spiritually by a poor church, a temporal embodiment of the order of the world that Dante finds in the Bible.

Through his use of the scriptures, then, Dante interrogates the question of what it means for a text to be sacred as well as true, and how one can use a sacred and true text to revitalize a corrupt society and turn it toward justice. Given the rampant violence of our own day, much of it motivated through a violent reading of sacred texts, the questions that Dante asks of the Bible, as well as the answers he proposes, are of some moment. Given that the concerns of the present are never absent from our efforts to interpret the past, one hope of this author is that Dante may help point the way toward a less violent reading of sacred texts.

1 Dante's Idea of the Bible

When Saint Augustine first decided to examine the holy scriptures as a young man of eighteen, he did not like what he found, as they 'seemed to [him] unworthy in comparison with the dignity of Cicero.' Writing after his conversion, though, he characterized them much more positively as 'something neither open to the proud nor laid bare to mere children; a text lowly to the beginner but, on further reading, of mountainous difficulty and veiled in mysteries.'[1] Augustine describes a text – humble in style but containing the most sublime truths – that seems foreign to most of us, distant from the collection of the books we know as the Bible. Take Augustine's sense of a text 'veiled in mysteries,' for example; those of us trained in post-Romantic literary criticism, especially before the rise of deconstruction, very early on learned from Coleridge, Goethe, and others to disdain allegory – the most common way that medieval exegetes revealed scripture's mysteries – as an artificial and abstract interpretive practice, in which ideologically motivated interpreters foist subjective meanings onto innocent, literal texts.[2] And even with the rise of deconstruction, allegory – while seen more sympathetically – is still understood as an arbitrary imposition of meaning; it is simply that for critics such as Paul de Man, *all* interpretation is arbitrary, that is to say, allegorical.[3] This view of allegory, which method was, after all, a mainstay of ancient and medieval biblical exegesis, may blind us to what these earlier interpreters saw as a coherent interpretive practice. In discussing Dante's idea of the Bible, therefore, we need to abandon these notions of the inferiority of allegorical interpretation in order to gain a sympathetic understanding of the range of interpretive possibilities that were open to an educated lay reader of the Bible in the early fourteenth century.

A closer look at the biblical hermeneutics of Saint Augustine, the most influential church father in the Latin west, may help to bring into focus some basic assumptions about the meaning of the Bible that medieval readers shared. Our primary interest in this discussion of Augustine is to come to grips with his underlying hermeneutic presuppositions, and not in providing an exhaustive account, or even much of a sketch, of Augustine's development as an exegete, which many scholars have argued is characterized by an increasingly restrained use of allegory.[4] While it is true that his views developed in the course of his long career, here we will look for continuities in the underlying assumptions that he made about the scriptures.[5] With these assumptions in mind, we can then approach Dante's moment in the history of biblical interpretation with an improved grasp of the hermeneutic assumptions that animate the interpretive choices that Dante faced in reading the scriptures.

Saint Augustine and the Bible

James J. O'Donnell has argued that, 'Augustine never saw a Bible,' as the collection of writings we know today as 'the Bible' came to Augustine 'in manuscripts of individual books and groups of books';[6] he nevertheless conceived of these seemingly disparate volumes together as *scripturae* – writings that together constituted a unified work both authoritative and truthful. Augustine, in fact, argued that a Christian reader should gain knowledge of all canonical scripture, as the group of writings when considered as a whole are self-interpreting, with the clearer passages commenting on and elucidating the more difficult sections: 'Hardly anything may be found in these obscure places which is not found plainly said elsewhere.'[7] He thus goes on in the *De doctrina christiana* to list 'the whole canon of the Scriptures' that the student should study (see 2.8.13). He possessed, in other words, a conception of the Bible as a unified text, in spite of the fact that he rarely if ever saw a single codex containing all of the canonical books of scripture.

His expression of belief in the unique truth value of scriptural texts may surprise us in how widely it differs from our modern notion of biblical truth. In the *Confessions*, for example, he writes:

> Who but you, O God, has made for us a solid firmament of authority over us in your divine scripture? . . . We have not come across any other books so destructive of pride, so destructive of 'the enemy and the defender' who resists your reconciliation by defending his sins. I have not known,

Lord, I have not met with other utterances so pure, which so persuasively move me to confession, make my neck bow to your yoke, and bring me to offer a free worship. (13.15.16–17)[8]

Augustine's belief in the uniqueness and authority of the scriptures does not rest on their unparalleled historical accuracy, but rather on the impact that the book and the words have had on his life. The Bible is true for Augustine precisely in the sense delineated by Hans-Georg Gadamer: it presents truths 'valid and intelligible for himself.'[9] In other words, the Bible's truth value for Augustine is not only, or not even primarily, *referential*. Its precision in representing historical events is not at issue, at least not in ways we would recognize as corresponding to the concerns of modern historiography. The history recounted by the Bible does not exist in some distant and utterly different past but instead has direct relevance to the Bible's reader today.

We can gain a better sense, perhaps, of what 'literal' interpretation meant for Augustine if we turn to one of his exegetical works specifically devoted to elucidating that sense: *De Genesi ad litteram*. Recently translated as *The Literal Meaning of Genesis*,[10] the Latin is more accurately rendered as *On Genesis according to the Letter*. As I briefly suggested in the Introduction, this attention to the letter, to what the words say, provides a better sense of what the ancients meant by the literal sense than something like the 'historical sense,' even though this is a phrase that Augustine (and many other ancient and medieval exegetes) himself uses.[11] Thus, while he characterizes his literal interpretation of Genesis as treating the Bible's first book 'not according to allegorical meaning but according to an understanding of things that were done,' as he states it retrospectively in his late work the *Retractiones*,[12] he proceeds in a way that often seems remote from a historical view of the book. Michael Fiedrowicz observes that the interpretation offered by Augustine 'as the literal meaning of the biblical text seems in fact to be often the result of an allegorical and figurative interpretation.'[13] It turns out that Augustine pays more attention to the words, the letter of the text, than he does to the history that we would suppose to underlie them. For example, in considering the light and darkness in Genesis 1.4, he suggests that they mean not the material light and darkness of a physical night and day, but spiritual light and darkness. He leaves open the possibility of improving upon his exegesis by finding an interpretation that better accords with the words of the passage: 'for it could come about that even I may perhaps find another interpretation *more fitting with the words* of the divine Scriptures.'[14] This statement finds a later parallel in Hugh of Saint Victor's discussion of the historical sense of scripture:

> But if we take the meaning of the word more broadly, it is not unfitting that we call by the name 'history' not only the recounting of actual deeds but also *the first meaning of any narrative which uses words according to their proper nature.* And in this sense of the word, I think that all the books of either Testament . . . belong to this study in their literal meaning.[15]

If we compare Hugh's and Augustine's notion of the historical sense with Frank Kermode's attempt to disentangle the history underlying the New Testament Passion narratives from the accounts contained in the Gospels, we can sense the distance between these pre-modern and modernist attempts to get at the 'historical' sense of the work.

> We may ask two questions of these pieces of historical writing: how intimately are they related to Old Testament testimonies? How well do they conform with what may be plausibly said to have occurred? The answer to the first may be such as to suggest that parts of the narratives were generated from Old Testament texts, and are therefore interpretations of those texts, and so fictive. The answer to the second may suggest there is a difference between being able to make a text sound as if what it reports had occurred, and making it report what had occurred.[16]

Kermode's analysis reveals certain unquestioned assumptions, such as, for example, that similarities between Gospel accounts and Old Testament texts imply that those accounts 'were generated from Old Testament texts,' and that therefore they are 'fictive.' For Augustine, the similarities between Gospel accounts and passages from the Old Testament are, if anything, proofs of the historical truth of those accounts, as well as evidence for the divinity of Jesus' life. In fact, the central question of Kermode's query – how accurately referential are the Gospel accounts – never comes to issue for Augustine beyond his insistence at the beginning of his work on the reality of the events described in Genesis. For Augustine, the historical narrative of Genesis is historically true, but that truth is not to be separated from the narrative that reports it.

Augustine's view of the Bible's literal sense, then, does not limit the meaning of the scriptures but views them as open to a plurality of meanings, a hermeneutic openness that has its roots in Augustine's conception of language, especially as language is used in scripture. The truism that Augustine believed the Bible to contain the word of God is complicated by the fact that for Augustine God did not simply dictate the words contained in the Bible; instead, He inspired human writers who were obliged to transmit His word according to their own human language and understanding. The 'signs' that are found in the Bible are not natural (signs that convey meaning 'without any intention or desire of signifying') but conventional (signs that signify intentionally) and thus function like other conventional signs used by humans when speaking.[17] Augustine distinguishes between the Word of God and those words of God written down by humans and gathered in the Bible. The signs found in the Bible are primarily human. When God the Father spoke at Christ's baptism (recounted in Matthew 3.17) he spoke in human language – a temporal medium – so that God's words sounded in time, began and ended. We know, however, that God is not created and is not, therefore, subject to temporality. He must have employed some created thing to speak temporally, and God's words – spoken through a created medium – at Christ's baptism must be distinguished from his uncreated, eternal Word: 'that mind would compare these words, sounding in time, with your eternal word in silence, and say: "It is very different, the difference is enormous. The sounds are far inferior to me, and have no being, because they are fleeting and transient. But the word of my God is superior to me and abides forever"' (*Confessions* 11.6).[18]

Augustine makes a similar distinction between 'inner' and 'outer' human words. The inner word exists independently of any particular human language. We speak when we wish to communicate this inner word to another, and so we must *translate* that inner word into the outer signs that form human language.[19] As he writes in the *De Trinitate*, 'It is the thought formed from the thing we know that is the word which we utter in the heart, a word that is neither Greek nor Latin nor any other language; but when it is necessary to convey the knowledge of those we are speaking to, some sign is adopted to signify the word.'[20] The inner word thus exists prior to 'all the signs that signify it,' but when it is translated into a sign, it undergoes some change: 'it is not uttered just exactly as it is, but as it can be seen or heard through the body' (15.11.20).[21] With Augustine's delineation of both the divine Word and the human inner word, then, we sense a gulf between the intelligible truth and its temporal manifestation in language.

Augustine, however, avoids the Neoplatonic implications of this position (that the physical world degenerates from the timeless truths of the intelligible realm and so language, part and parcel of the physical world, is also to be distrusted as inferior) by bridging the space between inner and outer words through an analogy with the incarnation of Christ. 'How did He come except that "the Word was made flesh, and dwelt among us"? It is as when we speak.'[22] Just as Christ, the eternal, atemporal *logos* of God that existed unchanging from eternity, became flesh and subjected himself to time, so our own temporal words are a translation of the inner word.[23] Augustine explains this notion most clearly, perhaps, in the final book of the *De Trinitate:*

> The word which makes a sound outside is the sign of the word which lights up inside, and it is this latter that primarily deserves the name of 'word' ... thus in a certain fashion our word becomes a bodily sound by assuming that in which it is manifested to the senses of men, just as the Word of God became flesh by assuming that in which it too could be manifested to the senses of men. (15.11.20)[24]

This difference between inner word and outward sign is similar, then, in both human language and in the Incarnation. Just as, because of Adam's fall, God took on flesh in order to reconcile God and man, so language is used by God in order to communicate with man, who, after the fall, can only perceive things through the senses of the body. As Augustine writes in the *De Genesi ad litteram*, 'Perhaps, however, God was [prior to the fall] accustomed to speak with [Adam and Eve] inwardly by other ways, either effable or ineffable, just as He speaks with the angels, enlightening their minds with this unchangeable truth.'[25] After the fall, however, God needed to speak to Adam and Eve in human language, for now he could only communicate with them through their senses. Brian Stock notes that human language, reading and writing in particular, 'were the consequences of human curiosity and pride. Before the fall there was no need of such cumbersome instruments of communication. God spoke to Adam and Eve directly, as he did to the Hebrew prophets, or made his will known without use of language.'[26] For Augustine, then, language comes about because of the fall, but, as Harrison argues, 'it is also *needed* by fallen man' (60; emphasis Harrison's), a point that Augustine makes in his exegesis of Genesis 1.22 in the *Confessions*, where God commands marine creatures to 'increase and multiply, and fill the waters of the sea.' For Augustine, 'signs given corporeal expression are the creatures generated from the waters, necessary because of our deep involvement in the flesh' (13.24).[27] Harrison goes on to suggest that while the details and language of scripture are indeed *signa* or signs, the Latin word may perhaps be better translated as 'sacrament' or 'symbol' – 'that is, a visible representation and bearer of spiritual truth' (85) – than as the neutral 'sign,' often understood by modern readers in the sense of a Saussurian signifier. Language incarnates (rather than refers to) the divine Word in a way that makes it accessible to humans, who then in turn are to seek the spiritual truth incarnated within the *signum*.[28]

Scriptural language, therefore, is particularly adept at communicating truths to us, at forcing us to discover the truth that exists beyond its physical representations.

> This [eternal] reason is your Word, which is also the Beginning in that it also speaks to us. Thus in the gospel the Word speaks through the flesh, and this sounded externally in human ears, so that it should be believed and sought inwardly, found in the eternal truth where the Master who alone is good teaches all his disciples. There, Lord, I hear your voice, speaking to me . . . Who is our teacher except the reliable truth? Even when we are instructed through some mutable creature, we are led to reliable truth when we are learning truly by standing still and listening to him. We then 're-joice with joy because of the voice of the bridegroom,' and give ourselves to the source whence we have our being. (*Confessions* 11.8)[29]

As noted in the Introduction, Augustine presents the truth not as something determined through external verification but as emerging from an encounter with the biblical text. The carnal word (the *verbum* or *signa*) written in the scriptures leads us to an eternal truth (*aeterna veritas* or *Verbum*) that exists behind the outward forms we see around us. It reveals to us the underlying structure of things, the laws that God writes into creation itself. This truth is higher than history or any other material or fleshly manifestation of it. As Hans Frei remarks of medieval biblical exegesis, it 'became an imperative need, but its direction was that of incorporating extra-biblical thought, experience, and reality into the one real world detailed and made accessible by the biblical story – not the reverse.'[30] It may be more accurate, however, to state that from the perspective of Augustine and his medieval followers the scriptures opened up the world or revealed it to them in such a way that they could not help but see the world and everything in it in the ways disclosed by the Bible. The scriptures disclose the world to us and teach us to read it; for Augustine, the scriptures are a symbolically ordering text, rather than a referential one.

The implication of Augustine's rich view of human language is that scriptural *signa* do not refer unmistakably to one literal meaning; rather, they possess many meanings. In book 12 of the *Confessions*, for example, Augustine reviews several possible interpretations of the Bible's opening sentence. He then advocates a position in which *all* of the proposed interpretations are true, even though any particular one may not be the meaning that Moses had in mind when he wrote the words down. 'As long as each interpreter is endeavouring to find in the holy scriptures the meaning of the author who wrote it, what evil is it if an exegesis he gives is one shown to be true by you, light of all sincere souls, even if the author whom he is reading did not have that idea?' (12.18).[31] Augustine later states that if he were entrusted with the task of writing a book that was to gain the highest possible authority he would hope to be able to write in such a way as to encourage many meanings, so that each reader could perceive a truth, even if those truths were different from what he originally intended. 'I would choose to write so that my words would resonate with whatever diverse truth in these matters each reader was able to grasp, rather than to give a quite explicit statement of a single true view of this question in such a way as to exclude other views' (12.31).[32]

Contrast Saint Augustine's theory of scriptural interpretation and its dependence upon the opaque *signum* to that of Matthias Flacius Illyricus (1520–75), the author of perhaps the most fully developed early Protestant theory of scriptural interpretation. In his *Clavis scripturae sacrae*, Flacius supports the Lutheran doctrine of the fundamental intelligibility of scripture; obscurity arises not out of difficulties in the text, but from the ignorance of the interpreter. Once an interpreter becomes educated in the language and grammar of the Bible, interpretive difficulties disappear. Underlying this optimistic assessment of biblical meaning is a fundamentally sanguine assessment of language and its ability to communicate: 'Language (*sermo*) is a sign (*nota*) or an image of things, and like spectacles (*perspicilla*) through which we see the things themselves. By which means if language is obscure in itself or for us, we come with difficulty from language to know the things themselves.'[33] Although Flacius notes that it is only with difficulty that we come to pierce through obscure language, his analogy of a pair of spectacles is striking, as it points to the modernist sense of the ability of the interpreter to penetrate through the single, unambiguous meaning of the Bible provided that he or she knows the language, grammar, and historical context of the passage in question,[34] while also affirming the modernist assumption that language is a transparent medium that allows us nearly unmediated access to the 'things' communicated through it.

Augustine's notion of scriptural truth, therefore, is far removed from that of a modern biblical scholar on the one hand and a modern biblical fundamentalist on the other. The language of the Bible does not refer unambiguously to one sense that precludes other meanings, which must then be viewed as ideologically motivated distortions of the text or, at best, allegories imposed upon a clear, literal, historical sense. His turn to allegorical or spiritual meaning is not a refusal to recognize what the text obviously says but grows out of a conception of meaning that views language not as a transparent medium but as a sacrament that reveals the divine through sensible means, a conception of language that undermines the kind of hermeneutic dualism that we often assume in radically splitting the literal and spiritual senses.[35]

Saint Gregory the Great provides a useful analogy in thinking about the relationship between spiritual and literal senses:

> If in this place we understand the door as the Holy Scripture, this also has two thresholds, an exterior and an interior, because it is divided into literal and allegorical. The exterior threshold is the literal; its interior threshold truly is the allegorical. Thus, when we move from the literal to the allegorical, it is as if we come from the threshold that is outside to that which is inside.[36]

In this image, while Gregory exalts the allegorical sense as somehow 'inside' and thus superior from a Neoplatonic perspective to the exterior literal sense, the continuity between the two senses is striking. Both senses form adjoining thresholds and both are necessary for the reader who wishes to enter the door. The allegorical sense is part of the same door as the literal sense; it is not imposed on it or opposed to it.

While Augustine linked the literal sense much more closely to the spiritual or allegorical sense than we assume, it is also true that he became uncomfortable with an unchecked allegorical interpretation and so attempted to define how figurative meaning arose in the scriptures in the *De doctrina christiana*. Recognizing that biblical texts necessarily had many meanings, he nevertheless sought to constrain the proliferation of allegorical readings that were employed by heretical readers. Thus, for Augustine, it is not that figurative signs themselves have a double meaning; rather, 'figurative signs occur when that thing which we designate by a literal sign is used to signify something else' (2.10.15).[37] It is not, then, that any meaning may be assigned to any *signum*. Rather, *signa* refer to *res*, which in turn refer to other *res*, producing in this way a proliferation of meanings. Augustine's understanding of figurative meaning parallels the 'figura' delineated by Erich Auerbach in his classic essay of that title, where the *figura*

> establishes a connection between two events or persons, the first of which signifies not only itself but also the second, while the second encompasses or fulfills the first. The two poles of the figure are separate in time, but both, being real events or figures, are within time, within the stream of historical life. Only the understanding of the two persons or events is a spiritual act, but this spiritual act deals with concrete events whether past, present, or future, and not with concepts or abstractions.[38]

Auerbach's definition, which delineates 'the strangely new meaning of *figura* in the Christian world' (28), helps us to think about the multiplicity of meaning that Augustine, Dante, and others found in biblical texts. It is not, for Augustine, that the text means something other than what it says (the root meaning of 'allegory'); as R.A. Markus summarizes Augustine's thought on this issue, 'it is what the text is literally referring to that itself has a further meaning.'[39]

This basic assumption of the multiple senses of the biblical text will be embraced by Aquinas and by Dante. By that time, a division of biblical meaning into four different senses had become common, a convention expressed in a succinct, pneumonic Latin couplet attributed to Augustine of Dacia (d. 1282):

Littera gesta docet; quid credas allegoria;
Moralis quid agas; quo tendas anagogia.[40]

The literal sense or 'letter' (*littera*) teaches us the 'deeds,' or emphasizes the historical occurrences recounted in scripture; the allegorical sense (*allegoria*) shows us what we should believe, or the spiritual doctrines revealed through a figurative understanding of the literal sense; the moral sense (*moralis*; also called the 'tropological') informs us of how we should act; the anagogical sense (*anagogia*) teaches us, literally, about where we 'tend [*or* aim *or* are directed],' and thus concerns both the eschatological future of human history and our reward in heaven after this life. Of course, in practice, medieval exegesis was not so schematic and did not typically detail four different meanings for each scriptural passage. This specification of multiple meanings, which draws on a long tradition, simply points out the importance and ubiquity of the idea of scripture's hermeneutic richness, while also tying the three 'spiritual' senses together to the literal sense, and ultimately making for a much closer relationship between literal and figurative meaning than modern readers often understand.[41]

Some scholars, however, have made a determined effort to separate Auerbach's *figura*, also called 'typology,' out from allegory, and so to spare it the opprobrium often directed towards the latter term. A.C. Charity, for example, in his useful study of typology in the Bible and Dante, carefully notes the distinction that 'was rightly drawn between allegorism and typology.'[42] But for Augustine and other patristic and medieval exegetes, we look in vain for a terminological consistency that makes this distinction. As de Lubac and Pépin have shown, what we often call 'typology' was most frequently termed 'allegory' in the Latin patristic tradition. In fact, the terms 'type,' 'allegory,' and 'figura' are frequently interchangeable.[43] Even Origen, for example, the exegete most fully associated with the Alexandrian school of biblical interpretation – one devoted to *allegoresis*, and one who attributed the disbelief of Jews and the mistaken beliefs of heretics to the fact that 'the Holy Scripture is not understood by them in its spiritual sense, but according to the sound of the letter' – uses the term 'type' to refer to what, in terms of the modern distinction between typology and allegory, we would call allegory.[44] Of course, Dante himself, when he argues for a distinction similar to the one assumed by our use of the terms 'allegory' and 'typology,' did so by distinguishing between different allegories – the allegory of the poets and the allegory of the theologians (see *Convivio* 2.1). I do not mean to suggest that there were not differences of emphasis and application among the patristic exegetes, differences that often led to fierce debates, even in terminology. I am instead arguing for the realization that there is an underlying unity in pre-modern biblical interpretation, with Origen recognizing the necessity and validity if also insufficiency of literal exegesis, and more literal-minded exegetes likewise noting the importance of what we would call spiritual interpretation. As Henri de Lubac argued, the major patristic and medieval exegetes did not disregard the letter: 'it is not at all the *littera* that bothered them, but the *littera sola*, the *sola superficies litterae . . .* '[45]

The continuity among ancient exegetes arose because of a shared assumption about the biblical text and its unity; for Augustine and other patristic and medieval exegetes, the various books of scripture accord with one another. Because of this underlying harmony, Augustine suggests in the *De doctrina christiana*, as we have already noted, that a first step for the would-be exegete is to gain a broad familiarity with all scriptural writings: 'the first rule of this undertaking and labor is, as we have said, to know these books even if they are not understood, at least to read them or to memorize them, or to make them not altogether unfamiliar to us.' This broad familiarity is essential because through it we gain an understanding of the 'open' passages of scripture, which can then aid us in understanding the scriptures as a whole, 'so that we may take examples from those things that are manifest to illuminate those things which are obscure' (2.9.14).[46] While Augustine recognizes the human element in the composition of the biblical books,[47] he also assumes their underlying unity because of the determining influence of the Holy Spirit in their authorship, which provides for a group of writings that interpret each other, the clearer writings coming to the aid of the interpreter when confronted with an obscure passage.[48] Hans Frei sees in this procedure the key to understanding pre-modern spiritual readings of scriptural texts; in his view, 'figural reading [was] literalism extended to the whole story or the unitary canon containing it' (7).

Many scholars, in fact, have recognized the force of allegorical biblical reading and have argued for a more sympathetic understanding of it. Andrew Louth, for example, has turned to patristic allegory as a way of opening up the biblical text to what he sees as the mystery proper to biblical Christianity: 'It is important to realize this: that the traditional doctrine of the multiple sense of Scripture, with its use of allegory, is essentially an attempt to respond to the *mira profunditas* of Scripture, seen as the indispensable witness to the mystery of Christ. This is the heart of the use of allegory.'[49]

Augustine's underlying assumptions concerning biblical meaning thus reflect the hermeneutic depth and richness he encountered in reading the scriptures. The signs employed by biblical authors are not transparent conveyers of a single unambiguous meaning, but dense, opaque bearers of truth – sacraments rather than 'mere' signs. Because these signs are dense and allusive, they mean different things to different readers, allowing for a much closer relationship between literal and spiritual senses than modern readers typically understand or accept. These assumptions – bolstered no doubt by Augustine's influence – carried over into the Middle Ages and into Dante's own day, and they can be helpful in understanding the array of interpretive practices and methods that Dante would have confronted as he studied the Bible.

The Bible in Dante's World

We will now turn to the later Middle Ages, a period that saw debates and controversy over the study of the Bible and the method required to understand it.[50] It is common to see in the advent of Scholasticism the rise of a new, more systematic study of the Bible, one that was opposed to (and was often opposed by) advents of traditional, more 'spiritual' methods of interpretation. This conflict is located in the institutions that seemed to support the competing methods: the cathedral schools and then universities where more rational methods were taught on the one hand, and monasteries where traditional 'contemplative' methods of study often flourished to the exclusion of newer methods on the other. While this hard and fast dichotomy is often overstated, and there may well be greater continuity between the two methods than is often supposed, there is value in noting the varying emphases of these contemplative and rational approaches.[51]

In the monasteries biblical study was often considered divine, and as part of the *lectio divina* the reader was encouraged to learn the scriptures by heart in the hope that they would become a prominent part of his mind and heart, changing both as a result of his contemplative study of the Bible.[52] When Saint Bernard of Clairvaux, for example, begins his series of sermons on the Song of Songs, he remarks that he will say 'different things than the words addressed to those in the world,' since the monks are spiritually mature, as they 'have for a long time been occupied with the study of heavenly teachings, have mortified the senses, and meditated on the law of God day and night. Prepare then,' he concludes, 'to feed not on milk but on bread.'[53] This contemplative form of reading continued more or less unabated during the Scholastic period; we can, indeed, see evidence of it in the governing 'banquet of learning' metaphor of Dante's *Convivio*, a frequent image in the monastic tradition of the *lectio divina* (as Bernard's introductory comments illustrate).

Aristotle's reintroduction into western Europe during the twelfth century, however, coincided with a new, more systematic method of studying the Bible, which became common first in the cathedral schools and then later in the universities. The cathedral schools, for example, were frequently the site of a synthesis of important commentary, usually patristic, that was combined with the biblical text and some twelfth-century refinements into a single book or books of the Bible. The result was the *Glossa ordinaria*, an 'edition' of books of the Bible that contained a compendium of interpretive commentary surrounding the biblical text.[54] This summary of the commentary tradition joined together 'three historical moments of Latin biblical interpretation, the late antique world of the Latin fathers, the monastic world of the Carolingian period, and the twelfth-century schools.'[55] The commentary represented, then, both continuity with the long tradition of biblical interpretation and a determination to treat that past more systematically.[56]

Aristotelian philosophy – with its own emphasis on systematic understanding – reinforced this trend in biblical studies, as Aristotle's devotion to the concrete and physical led to a renewed interest in the scripture's literal sense (its 'body') with respect to its allegorical sense (or 'spirit').[57] Scholastic exegesis proved to have an important effect, shifting the emphasis of some biblical exegesis even while *lectio divina* continued to flourish. Minnis and Scott, for example, illustrate this shift by contrasting two readings of the Psalms, the first by Peter Lombard, which dates from around 1159, and the second from Nicholas of Lyre, which dates from nearly two centuries later (c. 1322–30). In his commentary, Peter Lombard views the names placed over many of the Psalms as appearing there 'for the sake of the mysterious significance, which is obtained from the interpretation of the names.' Far from being markers of the varied authorship of the Psalms, they were placed there by the sole author of the book (David himself), who received his prophecies 'by direct inspiration of the Holy Spirit.'[58] Nicholas, however, prefaces his commentary with what had by then become a standard form of introduction: the 'Aristotelian prologue,' in which he details the 'causes' of the biblical book. Its 'efficient cause' is twofold: God, who is the 'principal efficient cause,' and David, 'the instrumental efficient cause.' In contrast to Peter Lombard, Nicholas understands the names over the individual psalms as referring to specific, historical individuals (other than David) who authored many of the psalms. Nicholas even goes on to consider the effects of Ezra's post-exilic editing on the book.[59] There resulted, in other words, an increased emphasis on the human authorship of scriptural texts, with exegetes examining the historical circumstances of the Bible's human authors while simultaneously continuing to insist on the inspiration received by these authors, a view that retained the notion that God is the ultimate author of the Bible. Nevertheless, as Minnis characterizes the resulting shift, Aristotle's influence brought about 'a new awareness of the integrity of the individual human *auctor.*'[60] As we will see, Dante's own treatment of the Bible reflects this dual conception of biblical authorship.

This shift in the emphasis of biblical exegesis is also apparent near the opening of Aquinas's *Summa theologiae,* where, while recognizing the validity of allegorical interpretation (and making what had become by his time the standard identification of three principal spiritual senses), he nevertheless asserts that all meaning for theology depends upon the literal sense:

> These various readings (*multiplicitas horum sensuum*) do not set up ambiguity or any other kind of mixture of meanings, because, as we have explained, they are many, not because one term may signify many things, but because the things signified by the terms can themselves be the signs of other things. Consequently holy Scripture sets up no confusion, since all meanings are based on one, namely the literal sense. From this alone can arguments be drawn and not, as St. Augustine remarks in his letter to Vincent the Donatist, from the things said by allegory (*secundum allegoriam*). Nor does this undo the effect of holy Scripture, for nothing necessary for faith is contained under the spiritual sense that is not openly conveyed through the literal sense elsewhere. (1a.1.10)[61]

Thus, though it is common to see Aquinas arguing for a new, literal-minded exegesis in this passage, he nevertheless draws on patristic tradition in order to make his case. His insistence on the importance of the literal sense, that it must be used exclusively for theological argument, was anticipated in Augustine's letter in which he, attempting to undermine a Donatist argument buttressed by an allegorical reading of the scriptures, asks 'who, however, endeavours without shame to expound something allegorically for his own purposes unless he also has clear witnesses, whose light illuminates the obscure passages?'[62] The basic exegetical principle of understanding obscure passages with the aid of clear ones, we recall, was also put forward by Augustine in the *De doctrina christiana.* Thus, we must qualify Robert Grant's assertion of Aquinas's insistence on the unique value of the literal sense for theology – 'This marks theology's declaration of independence from the allegorical method' – with Aquinas's equal claim of continuity with patristic authority.[63] Given the innovative aspects of Scholastic approaches to the Bible, the Scholastic hermeneutic shift should be understood as a development in emphasis rather than a revolution in the assumptions medieval exegetes made regarding biblical meaning. We can, in fact, see the same assumptions at work in Aquinas that we discerned in Augustine.

First, for Aquinas as for Augustine, the Bible is a uniquely authoritative text. When Thomas considers whether Christian theology is a science, he argues in the affirmative by making a distinction between those sciences that 'work from premises recognized in the innate light of intelligence' and those that 'work from premises recognized in the light of a higher science.' Theology is a science of the latter sort, as 'Christian theology takes on faith its principles revealed by God' (1a.1.2), principles revealed in the scriptures.[64] Second, although Aquinas places renewed emphasis on the literal sense, he does not equate it with a single, unambiguous, historical meaning. Indeed, he suggests, like Augustine, that several senses may be present within the literal sense itself: 'Now because the literal sense is that which the author intends, and the author of holy Scripture is God who comprehends everything all at once in his understanding, it comes not amiss, as St. Augustine observes in book twelve of the *Confessions*, if many meanings are present even in the literal sense of one passage of Scripture' (1a.1.10).[65] He defines the literal sense simply as that sense intended by the author, but he opens up the range of authorial meanings by identifying the author with God, citing Augustine once again as an authority. His view of the literal sense is thus much closer to Augustine's than it is to a modern view of the literal sense containing a single, unambiguous meaning. While Aquinas privileges the literal sense, he recognizes the validity of the spiritual sense and reaffirms the close tie between literal and spiritual senses, 'since all meanings are based on one, namely the literal sense.' As with Augustine, spiritual meanings are produced by the fact that the scriptural words refer to things, which in turn refer to other things. Finally, he too finds a profound unity in the Bible. While, as some scholars have argued, there was a tendency to fragment the Bible in its editions (with the major exception of the widespread 'Paris' Bible, which began to be produced in the twelfth century), paraphrases, and commentaries,[66] there was also the compulsion to unify it exegetically. This is not to say, however, that medieval readers recognized only the Latin Vulgate as 'the Bible.' Several scholars have argued that many medieval readers and writers had a 'much more fluid understanding of what constitutes "the Bible,"' as one reviewer has put it, 'one that could comprehend paraphrase, translation, partial texts, a wide range of apocrypha and elaborations of the biblical text, glosses, exegesis, history, and illustration.'[67] There is reason to believe, however, that not all medieval thinkers took so liberal a view of what constituted scripture. James Morey notes that there were both liberal and conservative theologians, and that the latter group tended to reject paraphrases, translations, and reworkings of the sacred text.[68] Nevertheless, the 'Bible,' in whatever form it took, carried with it an unequalled cultural authority.

Before moving on to Dante, we should take note of another crucial interpretive movement of the later Middle Ages, one important to Dante and perhaps best represented in the person of Saint Francis. The contemplative and Scholastic methods we have briefly examined thus far both found their home in elite settings – monasteries and schools, including universities – and were the product of individuals who were highly educated. Francis, however, came to the Bible first as a layman. As the son of a successful merchant, he would have had a good education and, as Théophile Desbonnets points out, would have had the 'feeling that he could have direct access to the gospel, without accepting the barrier set up against him by the privileged status which the clergy had arrogated to themselves concerning the word of God.' Francis's use of the Bible generally eschewed the allegorical exegesis of the contemplative style and the theological interest shown by Scholastic interpreters, opting instead for a direct grasping of the gospel text, which contained 'honest words, without a mask, which had a weight of meaning accessible to all.'[69] There seems to be in this Franciscan biblicism a dissatisfaction with intellectualizing attitudes about the scriptures, whether they were found in the schools or in the monasteries, and a determination to get people to engage with the scriptures directly.

This more direct approach to the scriptures, anticipating the developments that would come about during the Reformation, was also mirrored by the first translations of the Bible into the vernacular. There is evidence that as early as the thirteenth century anonymous translators were rendering parts of the Vulgate Bible into the regional Italian dialects, especially those of Venice and Tuscany. The process of translation took longer to get started in Italy than in other western European countries, and the resulting vernacular translations spread less widely.[70] The translations seem to have been largely directed to the audience out of which Saint Francis originally came – members of the educated merchant class, much as Dante's unfinished vernacular philosophical treatise, the *Convivio*, was directed to those who sought learning but were prevented from pursuing it by the cares of domestic and civic responsibilities (see *Conv.* 1.1.4).

The age in which Dante lived was, therefore, biblical, but it was also one in which there were competing approaches to reading the scriptures. Nevertheless, all of these methods shared assumptions about the nature of the Bible. This basic continuity in the fundamental presuppositions about biblical meaning, truth value, and unity – despite changes in emphasis and individual variations – suggests that these assumptions form the basis for a medieval idea of the Bible.[71] Dante, as we shall see, shares these basic assumptions, a fact that is evident in all of his writings; we will limit our discussion in this chapter to a few passages in his minor works, in which Dante presents his ideas concerning biblical meaning, truth, and authority.

Dante and the Medieval Bible: *Monarchia, Convivio*, and Epistles

The methods and texts by means of which Dante came to study and know the Bible are to a large extent unknown, but his works show evidence that he came to possess a very detailed and 'current' notion of biblical meaning, understanding both the new systematic, scholastic approach to the Bible and the contemplative tradition of the *lectio divina*, perhaps through his frequenting of the 'schools of the religious and the disputations of the philosophers' both in Florence in the 1290s and in Bologna and elsewhere following his exile.[72] Dante most likely read and studied the edition of the Vulgate known as the 'Paris' Bible, a text produced commercially in Paris scriptoria for university use. It was similar to a modern Bible, in that it contained the entire Bible in one volume, written with a small hand on thin parchment.[73] This Bible would have been the one most likely to be available to an educated layman such as Dante; as one historian of the Bible has written, these compact Bibles were 'the first Bibles to be easily available across a wide social spectrum: to the wealthy bourgeoisie as much as to professional clerics and religious.'[74] Most copies of the Bible contained exegetical material, usually patristic, that aided in framing biblical interpretation, even when they lacked the full interpretive apparatus of the *Glossa ordinaria;* prefaces and prologues to individual books, usually by Jerome, were very common, as were chapter summaries.[75]

The degree to which Dante would have known (or even helped to produce) the vernacular scriptures that began to appear as early as the thirteenth century is a matter of some debate. Dante did in fact translate individual passages of the Bible numerous times in the course of his works. Kenelm Foster, for example, has counted in the *Convivio* fifty-two Italian citations of the Bible, which appear to be Dante's own work.[76] Dante himself explicitly mentions biblical translation only twice, and in each case he does not refer to Italian versions.[77] As we will see, in the *Commedia*, Dante refers to the Vulgate text of the Bible on numerous occasions in the *Purgatorio* and *Paradiso*, as he does in the *Monarchia*, particularly in book 3. Thus, while Dante was well aware of biblical translations, Kenelm Foster's judgment, made now forty years ago, still seems accurate: 'any direct influence on a large scale is most improbable.'[78]

While Dante's writings are full of biblical citations and allusions, he explicitly considers the meaning of the Bible, its authority and interpretation, only in comparatively rare circumstances. The most complete and straightforward of these is found in the third book of the *Monarchia*, where he addresses the third and final question of the treatise: whether the world monarch derives his authority directly from God or through an earthly intermediary, namely the pope. Dante will argue for the former of these possibilities, and to do so he first seeks to undermine arguments supporting the view that the emperor derives his political power from the pope, arguments based on allegorical readings of the scriptures. Before he explicitly turns to debate these exegetical proofs, however, he first works to lay down some basic assumptions for the argument. He begins by attempting to exclude the 'Decretalists,' those who accept the Decretals (especially those written after Gratian's compilation made in 1140) as authoritative documents for determining church doctrine. He links the Decretals with the traditions of the church and then seeks, not to discredit them completely, but to show that their authority is inferior to that of the Bible and the fathers of the church. He begins, therefore, by providing a broad overview of the various writings that are – at least to some degree – accepted as authoritative in the church, and he creates a temporal hierarchy among them, with the greatest authority granted to the earliest writings.[79] He separates them into writings 'before' the church (*ante Ecclesiam*), writings 'with' the church (*cum Ecclesia*), and writings 'after' the church (*post Ecclesiam*) (3.3.11), in a passage that has vexed many commentators, not least because of what Philip Wicksteed has termed its '"Protestant" tone.' What, after all, are we to make of his assertion that certain writings come *after* the church?[80] However we understand his terminology, Dante importantly limits the writings that precede the church to those contained in the Bible, that is the 'vetus et novum Testamentum,' which he characterizes, quoting the Psalms, as 'sent from all eternity' (*in ecternum [sic] mandatum est* [3.3.12]). This passage reveals several important aspects of Dante's conception of the Bible. First, although he goes on to recognize the limited authority of non-biblical writings (especially those of the early councils and the fathers), he sees the Bible as uniquely authoritative, superior to the church itself, since it both preceded the church in time and helped to create it. Second, Dante conceives of the two testaments as forming a unified text. As Richard Kay notes in his commentary on this passage, Dante's unusual use of the singular *testamentum* to refer to both the Old and New Testaments is mandated by the Psalm (the 110th) to which he alludes: 'mandavit in aeternum testamentum suum.' The *Glossa ordinaria*, however, reads 'testamentum' as not referring to the Bible as a whole, but to the *New* Testament only.[81] Further, the *Glossa* interprets 'aeternum' as endless duration, 'because no other will follow it' (*quia nullum huic succedet* – interlinear gloss). Given, however, that Dante cites the psalm in order to support his argument that the Bible has temporal priority, we must assume that for him the Bible was sent or commanded from before the foundation of the world.[82] Dante seems to understand 'eternal' in Augustine's sense; God's Word, outside of time, sends scriptural words to us in time.

Dante's exaltation of biblical authority has a purpose, which emerges when he moves on to discuss those writings that arose 'with' or 'after' the church. Those arising with the church refer to both the main councils (*concilia principalia*), which were inspired by Christ himself, and the writings of the fathers (*Scripture [sic] doctorum]*), whom Dante names as 'Augustine and others.' Finally, we have the Decretals, which came 'after' the church and whose authority, therefore, is to be placed after that of the 'fundamental writings' of the church (*fundamentali tamen Scripture postponendas esse dubitandum non est*). He then concludes this section of book 3 by once again asserting the superiority of the scriptures over 'tradition' (here referring to the writings of the Fathers and the Decretals) by referring to Matthew 15.2–3, where Christ criticized, in Dante's reference to the scriptural passage, the 'priests': 'Why do you also transgress the commandment of God for your tradition?' The Decretalists, therefore, are to be excluded from the debate, 'for it is necessary, in coming to the truth, to proceed by investigating those things from which authority flows to the Church' (*oportet enim, hanc veritatem venantes, ex hiis ex quibus Ecclesie manat auctoritas investigando procedere* [3.3.13–16]). Indeed, Dante alters the biblical reference in having Christ interrogate the *sacerdotes* (rather than the *scribae et Pharisaei* mentioned in Matthew) in order to make the passage more pointedly relevant to his time. Dante evidently came to the conclusion that Christ would address the same words that he spoke to the religious leaders of his day to the leaders of Dante's day, and so Dante alters the biblical passage accordingly. As we will see, in the *Commedia* Dante commonly alters biblical passages so that they speak more directly to his contemporaries.

Dante, then, makes a stronger case for the Bible's unique authority than do many other late medieval thinkers. Two centuries earlier, for example, Hugh of Saint Victor (writing in the late 1120s) divided each of the testaments into three parts: the Old Testament into 'the Law, the Prophets, and the Hagiographers (*agiographos*),' and the New into 'the Gospel, the Apostles, and the *Fathers*.' He further subdivides 'the Fathers' and organizes those subdivisions hierarchically as follows: 'first place is held by the Decretals, which we call canons, or rules, the second, by the writings of the holy Fathers and Doctors of the Church.'[83] Vincent of Beauvais, in the general prologue to the widely disseminated *Speculum naturale* (written in the mid-thirteenth century), distinguishes among the authoritative writings as follows (in descending order): Holy Scripture; Decretals, Canons (following papal confirmation), and the writings of the church fathers (these all occupying about the same rank in authority); Catholic doctors; and the works of pagan philosophers and poets.[84] Each of these writers is noteworthy both for placing the Decretals before the writings of the church fathers, something Dante explicitly argues against, and – in Hugh's case – for expanding the canon of scripture to include many things that Dante labels 'tradition.'

It is not surprising that Dante endorses the Bible as the single most authoritative text in his culture, but he pushes that idea further, as he describes the scriptures as existing from eternity and thus as both temporally and ontologically prior to the Church, seemingly undermining the human aspect of the scriptures that, as we have seen, Scholastic theologians were exploring in his day. This assertion of the Bible's heavenly authority is also supported by a passage in chapter 4 of book 3, where Dante inveighs against those who twist the scriptures for their own advantage, calling their actions the 'worst of crimes ... to abuse the intention of the eternal Spirit.' Their sin is not against Moses, David, Paul, and other human biblical writers, but against the 'Holy Spirit, who speaks in them. For while there are many scribes of the divine word, the only dictator is God, who has deigned to explain his will to us through the pens of many' (3.4.11).[85] We must qualify this passage,

however, with Dante's criticism later in book 3 of the pro-papal interpretation that deviates from Moses' intention (see 3.4.16). Dante proposes the dual conception of biblical authorship discussed above and
seen in Aquinas and Nicholas of Lyre: God and the inspired but human
biblical writer are both responsible for the resulting texts.

In the following chapters of book 3, having dealt with the preliminar-
ies to the argument (*Hiis itaque prenotatis*), Dante systematically undermines arguments for papal supremacy based on the scriptures. He treats
three arguments from the Old Testament (the 'two lights' of Genesis 1;
the superiority of Levi over Judah; and Samuel's 'unmaking and making'
kings) and three from the New (the gifts of the Magi, the keys given to
Peter, and – the most common of the papal arguments – the two swords
mentioned by Peter to Christ). Through his criticisms of papal exegesis,
his own underlying hermeneutic principles become apparent. He begins
with an attempt at demolishing the papal argument that the two lights
referred to in Genesis 1.16 signify, when interpreted figuratively (*typice
importare*), the papacy and the empire, with the implication that the papacy is represented by the 'greater light.' His argument opens with the
observation that these luminaries were created before man himself, and
it would have been impossible for God to follow the perverse ordering
of creating the 'accidents' that pertain to man (*accidentia quedam ipsius
hominis*) before creating him. Furthermore, the papacy and the empire
are institutional remedies put in place to help man in his fallen condition following Adam and Eve's transgression in the Garden of Eden. It
would therefore make no sense, he concludes, for God to have created
the governing powers of the postlapsarian world on the fourth day of
creation; this interpretation is not what Moses intended.[86]

This is not to say, however, that Dante invalidates the use of the
spiritual sense; instead, he criticizes particular uses of it. Earlier in the
same chapter he noted that there are two ways in which one can enter
into error with respect to the 'mystical sense': 'concerning the mystical
sense one comes to err in two ways: either seeking it where it is not, or
accepting something other than what one ought to accept' (3.4.6).[87] In
explaining the first error, he refers to Augustine's *De civitate Dei* (16.2),
where Augustine argues that not all events narrated in the scriptures
can or ought to be taken to mean something other than the literal sense.
For the second error, he turns again to Augustine, this time to the *De
doctrina christiana* (1.36.40), where Augustine warns against finding
meanings that deviate from the author's intention.[88] Dante, therefore,
sees the mystical sense as legitimate provided that it can be linked to

authorial intent. Indeed, in his consideration of the 'gifts of the Magi' (Matthew 2.1–12), he admits that the common reading of the passage (the gifts of gold and frankincense signify that Christ is lord and governor over temporal *and* spiritual things) is correct ('Ad hoc respondens, licteram [*sic*] Mathei et sensum confiteor' [3.7.2]), objecting instead to the conclusions that his opponents draw from the reading. Indeed, his manner of phrasing this acknowledgment is telling: he confesses the truth of both the 'letter' and the 'interpretation' (*sensus*) of Matthew.

All of these assumptions and methods are at work in his most extensive attempt at biblical exegesis: the 'two swords' scripture (found in Luke 22.38). In his debunking of this common papal proof text at *Monarchia* 3.9, used by the despised Boniface VIII himself in his bull *Unam sanctam* to claim papal supremacy over temporal power, Dante devotes his attention to the context of the scriptural passage and to a careful examination of the meaning of words. He continues to assert the authority of the scriptures, and he comes to accept both literal and spiritual readings, provided that the spiritual readings are properly derived from the letter of the text. Dante begins with a summary of the papal argument; Peter's response – 'Lord, behold here are two swords' – to Christ's injunction that 'he that hath not, let him sell his coat and buy a sword,' refers to the two governing powers of Church and Empire that Peter and his successors possess by right.[89] Dante claims that he will invalidate this argument by showing that the pro-papal argument provides a false reading of the biblical verse: 'And I will respond to this through the demolition of the interpretation (*sensus*) on which they found their argument' (3.9.2).[90] In considering Dante's use of *sensus*, we would do well to recall his use of it at 3.7.2, discussed above, where he makes an implicit distinction between the 'letter' of a text and its 'interpretation.' It is nevertheless interesting that virtually all modern translations of the treatise are anxious to identify Dante's *sensus* with allegory, thereby implying that Dante attacks the very idea of allegorical interpretation.[91]

Sensus is an important word in medieval writing about the Bible; Hugh of Saint Victor makes an interesting use of it in his discussion of biblical interpretation in the *Didascalicon*, where he identifies three steps to an exposition (*expositio*) of a biblical text: 'exposition includes three things: the letter (*litteram*), the sense (*sensum*), and a deeper meaning (*sententiam*).'[92] In his analysis of this passage, Dahan argues that Hugh here identifies the three steps of a literal exegesis, which included a recognition of the complexity, or 'thickness' (*épaisseur*) of the literal sense. In his reading, the *littera* represents 'textual analysis; the *sensus*, a study of the historical and archaeological context; the *sententia*, a philosophical and theological approach.'[93] Of course, it is impossible to say that Dante knew Hugh's discussion and drew on it here,[94] but Dante's use of *sensus* (and its Italian equivalent, *senso*) elsewhere in his works, which support a more general understanding of the word's meaning, makes problematic any simple alignment of the word with allegorical interpretation. It seems best, then, to interpret it in a much more general sense.[95]

This propensity to read book 3 of the *Monarchia* as critical of all allegorical interpretation may be informed by Beryl Smalley's brief but influential reading of Dante's biblical exegesis in this passage, as Smalley is anxious to find a Dante who is hostile to *allegoresis*. Indeed, she reads Dante's use of *typice* (from *Monarchia* 3.4.12, cited earlier) differently from my own translation ('figuratively'): '*typice* for [Dante] has the sense of "metaphorically." Hence it is part of the literal interpretation.'[96] Dante, however, actually uses *typice* and *allegorice* interchangeably, as two passages from this chapter of the *Monarchia* make clear. He discusses the interpretation of many 'adversaries of the Empire' of Genesis 1.16, which is that the two heavenly luminaries, understood allegorically, are to be read as the two governing powers of the world ('que *allegorice* dicta esse intelligebant ista duo regimina' [3.4.2; emphasis mine]). In the passage previously considered, however, Dante makes virtually the same statement, this time through the use of the word *typice*; he will invalidate the figurative meaning that his opponents find in this verse ('dicunt illa duo luminaria *typice* importare duo hec regimina' [3.4.12]). Smalley endeavours in her reading of the passage to make the kind of hard and fast distinction between literal and allegorical that was foreign to Dante, as his own biblical exegesis makes clear.

Dante goes on to provide a very careful reading of the 'two swords' passage in Luke according to the letter and the context. Peter's words, Dante argues, cannot mean what his opponents say they mean because, first, Christ's statement to which Peter responds has a very specific contextual meaning – he was warning his disciples of their future trials[97] – and we must understand Peter's response in the light of Christ's statement. Second, if Peter had mistaken Christ's meaning in his response and answered by pointing to the governing powers that he and his successors would have, Christ would have rebuked him. Third, his reply makes much more sense if we interpret Peter's question as referring to two actual swords, and so interpreted it is also very much in character, since Peter was speaking to the obvious, surface meaning of Christ's words, as was his wont ('Petrus de more ad superficiem loqueretur' [3.9.9]). Dante then goes on to list a dozen instances of Peter's similar behaviour as reported in the Gospels. His argument here indeed seems to be based solely on the letter of the text; he does, however, return to the possibility of a figurative meaning at the chapter's conclusion, and his method of arriving at his own figurative interpretation is instructive. 'But if,' he writes, 'it is necessary to interpret these words of Christ and Peter figuratively (*typice*),' then they must be read differently, according to the interpretation (*sensus*) of the sword that is implied by Christ's use of the word *gladius* at Matthew 10.34–5: 'I came not to send peace but a sword.' One accomplishes the spreading of Christ's gospel through word and deed (based on scriptures such as Acts 1.1), and this 'word and deed' was the sword to which Christ referred. Peter's response, therefore, showed that he and the apostles were ready to do that which Christ had come to do by means of the 'sword' of word and deed (3.9.18–19).[98] Dante justifies this allegory by deriving the interpretation or *sensus* of the key word in the scriptural passage from its broader context – other passages that employ the same word. He thus uses one part of the Bible to interpret another, as Augustine had advocated, tying the figurative reading closely to the letter of the text. It seems that Dante provides this figurative reading in order to demonstrate that such readings may be valid when the exegete pays close attention to the context and draws on other parts of the scriptures to help provide the meaning of disputed words; in this way, legitimate spiritual interpretations can be derived from the letter of the text.

Dante's earlier exploration of the multiple senses of texts, found at the beginning of the second book of the *Convivio*, also supports this understanding of Dante's biblical hermeneutics found in book 3 of the *Monarchia*. Following book 1 of the *Convivio*, in which he lays out the basic organization of the philosophical treatise, Dante opens the second book as he does books 3 and 4, by citing one of his own canzoni – in this case 'Voi ch'ntendendo il terzo ciel movete' – before proceeding to literal and allegorical expositions of the poem, which will provide the materials for his philosophical discussion. Book 2, however, differs from the two following books by treating further material that is preliminary to the remainder of the treatise: the method and justification of proper reading. For if, continuing the governing metaphor of the banquet, one is to eat profitably, one must – before the first course arrives – know *how* to eat ('Ma però che più profittabile sia questo mio cibo, prima che vegna la prima vivanda voglio mostrare come mangiare si dee' [2.1.1]). Feasting on a text requires both literal and allegorical reading; writings, in fact, must be interpreted according to the standard four senses. The first of these is called literal and the second allegorical, which is 'quello che si nasconde sotto 'l manto di queste favole, ed è una veritade ascosa sotta bella menzogna' ('hidden under the veil of these stories, and it is a truth hidden beneath a beautiful lie' [2.1.3]). The example Dante provides to illustrate these two senses is Ovid's version of the story of Orpheus (found in *Metamorphoses* 11.1–2), where Orpheus tames wild beasts with his *cetera*. Dante finds in this narrative a story of how the wise man can with his voice tame and humble cruel hearts. After illustrating and defining this allegorical sense, however, Dante notes that theologians understand it differently. 'Veramente li teologi questo senso prendono altrimenti che li poeti; ma però che mia intenzione è qui lo modo de li poeti seguitare, prendo lo senso allegorico secondo che per li poeti è usato' ('Theologians truly understand this sense differently than do the poets; but since my intention here is to follow the manner of the poets, I understand the allegorical sense as it is used by the poets' [2.1.4]). Dante does not elaborate on the different understanding that theologians possess of the allegorical sense, though critics frequently identify an 'allegory of the poets' and an 'allegory of the theologians' based upon the distinction Dante makes in this passage. Most commonly, the distinction is seen to derive from the truth value of the literal sense: theologians view the literal sense of the Bible as true and not, therefore, as a 'bella menzogna,' as Dante defines the literal sense of poetry. The allegory of the theologians is based on a text that is literally true, while the allegory of the poets is derived from the beautiful lie that must be stripped away in order to reveal the truth that lies beneath it.[99] Indeed, Dante's 'bella menzogna' seems similar to the term 'integumentum,' often used in the Middle Ages to describe the covering that poets employ to wrap the truths that are found underneath the surface of their works.[100]

And indeed, the traditional interpretation finds support in Dante's discussion of the remaining two senses. Though he claims to discuss 'lo modo de li poeti,' when he goes on to consider the moral (*morale*) and anagogical (*anagogico*) senses he illustrates them through scriptural rather than poetic examples, interpreting the Transfiguration on the Mount morally and the exodus anagogically. His discussion of the anagogical sense in particular reveals his assumptions about what we typically call the 'allegory of the theologians,' as he follows it up with an example of spiritual biblical interpretation:

Lo quarto senso si chiama anagogico, cioè sovrasenso; e questo è quando spiritualmente si spone una scrittura, la quale ancora [sia vera] eziandio nel senso litterale, per le cose significate significa de le superne cose de l'etternal gloria: sì come vedere si può in quello canto del Profeta che dice che, ne l'uscita del popolo d'Israel d'Egitto, Giudea è fatta santa e libera. Che avvegna essere vero secondo la lettera sia manifesto, non meno è vero quello che spiritualmente s'intende, cioè che ne l'uscita de l'anima dal peccato, essa sia fatta santa e libera in sua potestate. E in dimostrar questo, sempre lo litterale dee andare innanzi, sì come quello ne la cui sentenza li altri sono inchiusi, e sanza lo quale sarebbe impossibile ed inrazionale intendere a li altri, e massimamente a lo allegorico. (2.1.6–8)

(The fourth sense is called anagogical, that is overmeaning; and this is when a writing [or scripture] is explained spiritually, which is nevertheless true in the literal sense, by which the things signified themselves signify the highest things of eternal glory: just as one can see in that song of the Prophet who says, in the exodus of the people of Israel from Egypt, that Judah was made holy and free. That this is true according to the letter is obvious, while no less true is that which is understood spiritually, that is, in the exodus of the soul from sin, it is made holy and free in its turn. And in demonstrating this [interpretation], the literal sense must always go before, as it is in this sense that the others are included, and without this sense it would be impossible and irrational to understand the others, and especially the allegorical.)

Allegorical interpretation of scripture depends upon the truth of the literal sense; instead of a fictional veil to be taken away so that the truth below it can be uncovered, we have a true narrative in which the things signified in turn signify other things. Indeed, the closeness of this description to Aquinas' discussion in *Summa theologiae* 1a.1 is striking.[101] In stating that for purposes of *dimostrar* the literal sense must always be considered first, Dante parallels Aquinas's contention that only the literal sense can be used for theological argument. Nevertheless, also paralleling Aquinas, Dante asserts the *continuity* between the literal and the other senses, since the 'spiritual senses' are included within the literal. And while it thus seems true that for Dante an important difference between the allegory of the poets and the allegory of the theologians lies in the truth of the literal sense, an equally important distinction is found in the relationship between the literal and figurative senses. While the allegory of the poets seeks a 'truth hidden beneath a beautiful lie' and thus posits a duality between the literal lie and the allegorical truth, the allegory of the theologians (which seems a synonym for a theory of scriptural meaning) sees continuity between the truth of the literal sense and the truth of the spiritual meanings included within the letter of the text. Hans Frei's characterization of pre-critical figurative exegesis, 'literalism extended to the whole story or the unitary canon containing it' (7), aptly summarizes Dante's theory of the 'allegory of the theologians' in the *Convivio*.

This examination of Dante's theory and practice of biblical exegesis in the *Monarchia* and the *Convivio* reveals the same fundamental assumptions regarding biblical interpretation that we found in Augustine and Aquinas.[102] First, Dante sees the Bible as a uniquely authoritative text, true in a way that other texts are not, since it has been proclaimed from the foundation of the world. Dante's understanding of biblical uniqueness, however, may also be somewhat less rigid than we assume. As noted above, some scholars have argued that medieval readers and writers possessed a 'much more fluid understanding of what constitutes "the Bible."'[103] There is some reason to believe that in Dante's case, at any rate, he was fully conscious of the difference between the Bible per se and the more flexible 'Bible' that was found throughout medieval culture and even the Latin translation that was used in his culture.[104] Second, while Dante asserts the importance of the literal sense in both practice and theory, he does not see the literal and spiritual senses as opposed but as complementary. In fact, the figurative senses grow out of and are included within the literal. Third, he does not limit the literal sense to a single unequivocal meaning reducible to historical reference. Even when critiquing the pro-papal exegetes in book 3 of the *Monarchia* by insisting on a more literal and historical reading, Dante continues to find meaning in the scriptures 'that is valid and intelligible for himself.' He does not reject the 'spiritual' reading of the Bible to understand Church and Empire but objects only to particular readings.

This tendency to read the Bible as directly relevant to himself and his time is most readily apparent, perhaps, in Dante's epistles, especially those written to Henry VII and to the Italian cardinals. Dante dated the first of these letters 17 April 1311, and it is actually the third in a series of three letters concerning the Holy Roman Empire. In the first (letter 5 in the Frugoni and Brugnoli edition of the epistles), he wrote a public letter to the people of Italy, exhorting them to open their arms to

Henry VII, their rightful ruler. In the second epistle (letter 6), he wrote more specifically to the Florentines in order to scold them for their intractability in refusing to welcome Henry. In his final letter of the three, he wrote directly to Henry and – having grown anxious over Henry's delay – asked him to descend through Italy more quickly. In all of these letters, Dante repeatedly portrays the events of his day within a biblical framework, evoking that framework to convince his readers (including Henry himself) of Henry's divinely appointed role. In the second paragraph of his letter to Henry, for example, Dante compares the emperor to Christ himself, addressing him with the words of John the Baptist to Jesus: 'Art thou he that art to come, or look we for another?' (7.2.8; see Matt. 11.3 and Luke 7.19).[105] Dante looks to the emperor as a political messiah, convinced that he can conquer Italy and restore order if only he will recognize God's hand upon him. Dante sees himself as exercising the role of forerunner in this biblical scenario; as the new John the Baptist, he in turn points to Henry and proclaims, 'Behold the Lamb of God. Behold him who taketh away the sins of the world' (7.2.10; see John 1.29).[106] Dante in fact multiplies the biblical parallels to Henry's mission; Henry is Saul, God's anointed king, 'that you may strike Amalech and not spare Agag,' which names signify the 'brutal people' and their 'hasty celebration' (7.5.19).[107] He is the new offspring of Jesse and thus a king in the Davidic line; he will fight Goliath with the sling of his wisdom and the stone of his strength, and when the giant falls, it will strike fear into the camp of the Philistines; they will flee Israel, which will be liberated. Just as the children of Israel returned to Jerusalem with rejoicing after the misery of captivity, so too will Italians revel in freedom after their own Babylonian captivity.[108] This kind of biblical rhetoric, though it may seem extreme to us, was not unique to Dante. John Larner has noted how Frederick II had his panegyrists speak of him through biblical parallels, with Niccolò of Bari, for example, portraying him as born in the house of David.[109] Similarly, Joachim of Fiore's disciples saw in the condemnation of his doctrine of the Trinity at the Fourth Lateran Council a fulfilment of Jeremiah's persecution, and they compared Pope Innocent III to Herod and Caiaphas.[110]

Dante begins his letter to the Italian cardinals (letter 11 in the Frugoni/Burgnoli edition) – written in the spring or summer of 1314[111] – with a citation from Jeremiah, 'How doth the city sit solitary' (Lamentations 1.1). Jeremiah's lament for the destruction levelled on Jerusalem matches Dante's grief over the widowed state of Rome itself, which has been devastated through the avarice of the pope, whom Dante calls the prince of the Pharisees. Dante's grief results in an extended lamentation over the state of the city and a thorough-going criticism of the cardinals and their complicity in the pope's corruption. They have become similar to the money changers who made merchandise of the sacred, and whom Jesus expelled from the temple. And while Dante identifies himself with Jeremiah – a prophetic figure constrained to lament over the fallen state of a holy city – and with Paul,[112] he realizes that the cardinals may associate him with another biblical figure: the presumptuous Uzzah, who dared to steady the ark and so was struck dead by God. Dante rejects the terms of the analogy, though not the analogy itself, distinguishing between Uzzah's ark-steadying and his own attempt to lead back recalcitrant and straying oxen that are dragging the ark off into the wilderness.[113] But the prophetic model is paramount; as Dante attempts to speak a brave but unpopular truth to those in power, he finds a model in the biblical prophets, and he correspondingly links his own purpose and authority to theirs.

In both of these letters, Dante turns to the Bible because he finds precise parallels between the events portrayed there and the problems and challenges of his own day. For Dante the Bible is not true because it is historically accurate (though it is that, of course), but because it is true *for us*; it provides the lenses through which we are to understand earthly reality and respond to it. Above all he turns to the Bible because in it he finds the proper order of the world, and in explaining how the world has gone out of joint, he inevitably sees it against the background of the scriptures. The *sacerdotes* of the papal curia resemble the *scribae et Pharisaei* of Matthew's account so that Dante comes to see them as the antitypes of those biblical types, recapitulating in his own day what occurred in the New Testament. The Pope is the prince of the Pharisees because that is how one comes to see a corrupt church leader in a world ordered by the Bible.

In this brief analysis of Dante's epistles, *Convivio*, and *Monarchia*, we have seen Dante use the Bible in a number of ways, corresponding to the variety of exegetical methods he learned in the late thirteenth and early fourteenth centuries. In the *Monarchia*, he treats the Bible systematically, carefully laying out principles of exegesis and patiently working through passages of scripture in order to discredit mistaken interpretations. In the epistles, however, he uses the Bible much more freely, associating contemporary figures and events with biblical types in order to view those events within a scriptural framework, one that, Dante is convinced, provides the moral and historical vision necessary to understand how society and the church must be reformed. This usage, too, seems to derive from recent developments in the understanding of human history and the Bible's relationship to it. Augustine had seen the Incarnation of Christ as in some ways the 'end' of history. What was left was simply a period in which, as Marjorie Reeves has stated it, 'nothing significant would happen except the garnering of souls.'[114] As the time following the Incarnation lengthened many modified Augustine's sense of history and saw in biblical types and figures foreshadowings of the more recent past. As we will see in the final chapter, this reconsideration of Christian history developed into full-blown theories of the history of the church that were rooted in biblical narratives, with Joachim of Fiore's Trinitarian conception of history as perhaps the most prominent example. This re-conception of the meaning of history in biblical terms is something Dante himself attempts in the Earthly Paradise cantos of the *Purgatorio*. In his epistles, however, his use of biblical figures to describe and comment upon more recent events has a narrower scope, illuminating particular, contemporary events in the light of biblical predecessors.

Hans Frei has argued that the beginnings of modern biblical interpretation resulted in the complete reversal of traditional interpretive practices. Even for those modern commentators who implicitly accepted the historical accuracy of biblical narrative, the meaning of those narrated events now became 'referable to an external more general context, and the story now ha[d] to be interpreted into it, rather than that external pattern of meaning being incorporated – figurally or in some other way – into the story' (6). As we have seen, Dante's approach to contemporary history provides an apt illustration of Frei's point, as the trials of his day are seen as part of the story told by the scriptures. Indeed, as we have seen, Dante's understanding of the Bible is 'pre-critical' in precisely Frei's sense. While Dante bends his considerable acumen to unravelling the mysteries of the Bible and takes issue with those who, in his view, twist the scriptures for their own ends, he ultimately treats the Bible not in the manner of modern objectivism but as the word of God through which he comes to understanding. He is open to either a systematic, literal exegesis, or to a more subjective, contemplative form of interpretation – if that is what will bring about the comprehension he seeks. The framework of God's truth revealed by the scriptures, in other words, provides the context in which he understands his own life and poetry. Auerbach's *Mimesis* states it in this way: '[the Bible] seeks to overcome our reality: we are to fit our own life into its world, feel ourselves to be elements in its structure of world history.'[115] If we turn to the *Commedia*'s final canticle, we can see Dante nevertheless interrogating the Bible's authority and truth, and how it guides not only his understanding of history, but also the writing of his poem.

2   Biblical Truth in the *Paradiso*

[But let us] assume, then, that with regard to the Bible there has been a successful demonstration of whatever any theological scholar in his happiest moment could ever have wished to demonstrate about the Bible. These books, no others, belong to the canon; they are authentic, are complete; their authors are trustworthy – one may say that it is as if every letter was inspired ...

Thus everything is assumed to be in order with regard to the holy scriptures – what then? Has the person who did not believe come a single step closer to faith? No, not a single step. Faith does not result from straightforward scholarly deliberation, nor does it come directly; on the contrary, in this objectivity one loses that infinite, personal, impassioned interestedness, which is the condition of faith, the *ubique et nusquam* in which faith can come to existence.

– Søren Kierkegaard[1]

In the first two canticles of the *Commedia,* Dante's assumption of the Bible's truth and its crucial role in informing his conceptions of history, of moral theology, and of the necessity of ecclesiastical and societal reform are implicit throughout. Having explored Dante's conceptual understanding of the Bible in his minor works, in this chapter we will carry this investigation into the *Commedia.* To do so, however, we must first consider the final third of the poem; only in the *Paradiso* does the question of *how* the Bible is true, and how its truth relates to the truth of Dante's poem, move into the foreground.

As early as the first heaven Dante explicitly has Beatrice address the relation of the Bible's truth to its representational strategies and also link them to the strategies of the poem. In canto 4, she explains to the pilgrim that the souls he sees and speaks to in the heaven of the moon do not actually reside there; they appear there temporarily for his sake in order to provide a sign that their degree of beatitude is less than that of the other blessed in heaven ('per far segno / de la celestïal c'ha men salita' [38–9]). This accommodation is necessary because of Dante's body, which requires him to learn through the medium of the senses.

> Così parlar conviensi al vostro ingegno,
> però che solo da sensato apprende
> ciò che fa poscia d'intelletto degno.
>   Per questo la Scrittura condescende
> a vostra facultate, e piedi e mano
> attribuisce a Dio e altro intende.   (*Par.* 4.40–5)

(Thus it is fitting to speak to your mind, since it learns only from sensible things what it then makes worthy of the intellect. For this reason the scriptures condescend to your faculties, and attribute foot and hand to God but mean something else.)

Given the long Christian theological tradition of recognizing the inadequacy of sensible human language to represent the ineffable realities of heaven, Dante's use of the principle of accommodation is only to be expected. What is striking, however, is how he works to link the signifying practices of his poem with those of the scriptures. Both the Bible and the *Commedia* represent God, and both must adapt their messages to the limitations of the human condition. For it is from our senses, as Dante himself says, echoing scholastic theologians in the *Convivio*, that our knowledge begins ('comincia la nostra conoscenza' [2.4.17]). Indeed, Dante will tie his poem to the scriptures thoroughly in this final canticle, and he will repeatedly associate himself as poet with biblical authors, Saint Paul in particular.

As Dante begins the poem's final canticle, he spends much of his time lamenting his inability to describe his transcendent experience in that part of God's creation that 'receives more of his light.' Faced with such a daunting task, Dante turns to a biblical figure – Saint Paul – whom he had evoked at the beginning of the poem by telling Virgil that he was *not* Paul (*Inf.* 2.32). Of course, the parallel between the two turns out to be all too apt, as Paul also made a journey to paradise; at least that is how medieval exegetes commonly read Paul's somewhat oblique description of a man 'caught up (*raptum*) to the third heaven. And I know such a man (whether in the body, or out of the body, I know not: God knoweth): That he was caught up into paradise (*raptus est in paradisum*) and heard secret words (*arcana verba*) which it is not granted to man to utter (*loqui*)' (2 Cor. 12.2–4).[2] Dante similarly draws an implicit parallel between Paul as apostle and himself as poet in the invocation to the muses that prefaces his account of the mystical procession in *Purgatorio* 29. Dante's suffering of 'fami, / freddi o vigilie' ('hunger, cold, and vigils' [*Purg.* 29.37–8]) for his art recalls Paul's claim that he has been 'in much watchings (*vigiliis multis*), in hunger and thirst (*in fame et siti*), in cold and nakedness (*in frigore et nuditate*)' (2 Cor. 11.27) for the sake of Christ. Given that Paul can be viewed as Dante's forerunner, it is not surprising that Dante makes several references to him in the first canto of the *Paradiso*, bringing the similarities to the surface.

Dante puts forward, for example, the request that Apollo make him a 'fitting *vessel* of [his] worth' ('del tuo valor sì fatto vaso' [*Par.* 1.14]), a word that recalls the Lord's description of Paul to Ananias as a 'vessel of election' (*vas electionis* [Acts 9.15]). The connection becomes clearer when Dante attempts to describe his experience of transcendence, or – in his neologism – *trasumanar*, and retrospectively wonders if he took his body with him.

> Nel suo aspetto tal dentro mi fei,
> qual si fé Glauco nel gustar de l'erba
> che 'l fé consorto in mar de li altri dèi.
> Trasumanar significar *per verba*
> non si poria; però l'essemplo basti
> a cui esperïenza grazia serba.
> S'i' era sol di me quel che creasti
> novellamente, amor che 'l ciel governi,
> tu 'l sai, che col tuo lume mi levasti.   (1.67–75)

(In looking at her I was made within such as Glaucus was in tasting the grass that made him a companion of the other gods in the sea. Signifying the transcending-the-human *per verba* cannot be done; therefore let the example suffice to whom grace destines the experience. If I carried with me only that which you created last, you know, love who governs the heavens, as you raised me with your light.)

His echo of Paul's 'in the body or out of the body' is prefaced by an Ovidian allusion to transfiguration in the figure of Glaucus, the fisherman who ate enchanted grass and found himself transformed into a sea god. As Paola Rigo has observed, however, Dante's description of Glaucus's tasting of the grass, 'nel gustar de l'erba,' anticipates Adam's description (in *Par.* 26.115) of his original sin in Eden, 'il gustar del legno,' and thus suggests that Dante here echoes both the deified Glaucus and our fallen progenitor, whom the Lord God himself pronounced as becoming almost one of the gods: 'Behold Adam is become as one of us, knowing good and evil' ('ecce Adam factus est quasi unus ex nobis, sciens bonum et malum') (Gen. 3.22).[3] The pilgrim's role as a redeemed Adam seems to be based on Paul's descriptions of Christ as a new Adam, who reverses the effects of the fall. This parallel illustrates, as Giuseppe Di Scipio has argued, that here and elsewhere Dante draws on the Pauline belief in the new life given to Christians through the putting off of the 'old man' (*vetus homo*) in repentance and baptism.[4] And of course Paul understood this conversion from old man to new, from Adam to Christ, from its occurrence in his own life, as he turned away from his earlier self, a persecutor of Christians, and became a new man and an ardent apostle. Dante in turn applied this narrative trajectory to his experience; waking in the dark wood of sin, having lost the path that does not stray, he too turns back toward God and becomes a new man in Christ.[5]

Dante continues to portray himself as a Pauline 'new man' sent on God's errand at several places in the *Paradiso*, most clearly perhaps at the end of canto 25 and the beginning of 26, when Dante becomes blind through his overly intense gaze at the apostle John, as he seeks to discern whether John's brilliant light conceals his body. John reassures Dante that his sight will return, since Beatrice 'ha ne lo sguardo / la virtù ch'ebbe la man d'Anania' ('has in her gaze the virtue that the hand of Ananias possessed' [26.11–12]), with Beatrice thus playing Ananias to Dante's Paul. While Dante frequently spells out similarities between Paul and himself, he does, however, differ from Paul in one crucial respect; unlike the early apostle, Dante will spend thirty-three cantos delineating his vision, he *will* speak the words that Paul thought unlawful to utter.[6] Dante's aligning himself with Paul is strategic; Paul's vision was widely discussed by patristic and medieval theologians, who debated the precise nature of Paul's vision, whether it occurred 'through a glass darkly' (*per speculum in enigmate*) or 'face to face' (*facie ad faciem*), to use Paul's own terminology from 1 Corinthians 13.12. Dante's self-identification with Paul created a link to a man who was both biblical author and mystic,[7] thus providing an authoritative precedent for both his vision and his poem.

The implications of this link become clearer in canto 24 (a canto to be discussed at some length below), where the pilgrim defines faith according to its most common, Pauline definition – that found in Hebrews (11.1), an epistle attributed to Paul in Dante's time. In introducing the definition, the pilgrim carefully attributes it to its apostolic source, 'Come 'l verace stilo / ne scrisse, padre, del tuo caro frate / che mise teco Roma nel buon filo' ('As the truthful pen wrote of it, father, that of your dear brother who with you placed Rome onto the good path' [*Par.* 24.61–3]). As we will see below, Paul is more than once associated with Peter in this canto as an apostle who played a key role in establishing the church after the death of Christ. But here Dante is also interested in Paul's status as an author who writes with a truthful pen. In this context, we may recall a passage from the *Monarchia* that we discussed in the previous chapter, where Dante inveighs against those who deliberately misread the scriptures, since they sin not only against the human, biblical authors, but also against the 'Holy Spirit, who speaks in them. For while there are many scribes of the divine word, the only dictator is God, who has deigned to explain his will to us through the pens of many' (3.4.11).[8] Dante's consistent attempts to link Paul as a voyager to the afterlife with himself as pilgrim also extend, I suggest, to Dante's identity as an author who possesses a truthful pen, and who therefore may likewise be described as a scribe of the divine word.

Dante's reference to and portrayal of David has a similar force; the Old Testament king and psalmist frequently provides a parallel to Dante as both pilgrim and poet, both because David was an inspired poet and because his own life – like Paul's – offers similarities to Dante's, as portrayed through the character of the pilgrim within the poem. David sinned by committing adultery with Bathsheba and then arranged for the death in battle of her husband Uriah. When confronted with his sin by the prophet Nathan, David repented, writing the great penitential Psalm – the fiftieth – in which he asks for God's forgiveness: *Miserere mei* ('Have mercy on me'). The pilgrim's first spoken words in the *Commedia* cite this psalm, '*Miserere* di me' (*Inf.* 1.65), and thus draw a parallel between his own turning from the dark wood of sin in which he finds himself at the poem's opening and David's seeking for forgiveness. In chapter 4, we will consider how David's humble dancing before the ark provides a model for Dante's relationship to the scriptures. In the *Paradiso*, Dante refers to David several times, usually in ways that emphasize once again his similarities to Dante, thus creating the image of the biblical king and psalmist as a kind of alter-ego for the Italian poet. In the heaven of Jupiter, for example, Dante identifies David as the soul occupying the pupil of the eagle's eye; but whereas we would expect the emphasis in this heaven devoted to justice to fall on David's righteous kingship, Dante instead identifies him as an inspired poet.

> Colui che luce in mezzo per pupilla,
> fu il cantor de lo Spirito Santo,
> che l'arca traslatò di villa in villa:
>   ora conosce il merto del suo canto,
> in quanto effetto fu del suo consiglio,
> per lo remunerar ch'è altrettanto.   (*Par.* 20.37–42)

(He that shines in the middle of the pupil was the singer of the Holy Spirit, who transported the ark from town to town: now he knows the worth of his song, inasmuch as it was the effect of his counsel, by the remuneration that is proportioned to it.)

David's song – and not, seemingly, only his actions as king – merits his privileged place in the eye of the eagle of justice. Similarly, toward the end of the poem, Dante identifies David's ancestor Ruth as one of the blessed in the heavenly rose, and he does so through a periphrasis that emphasizes both her relationship to David and David's identity as poet – 'bisava al cantor che per doglia / del fallo disse '*Miserere mei*' ('great-grandmother to the singer who through grief for his sin said "*Miserere mei*"') (*Par.* 32.11–12) – a characterization that, as Teodolinda Barolini has pointed out, recalls both David's psalm and Dante's first spoken words.[9] It is not simply the fact that David was a poet, however, that seems worthy of merit in the heaven of justice, but that he was a particular kind of poet: 'il cantor de lo Spirito Santo.'[10] David, that is to say, was inspired by the Holy Spirit in his Psalms. Nevertheless, the merit of his song seems to derive not only from the fact of his inspiration, but also from his own 'consiglio,' a word that may be translated as 'counsel' (as I have done here), but also as 'decision' or 'will.' It seems to refer to the degree to which David's artistic efforts were the result of his own will, at least insofar as he willingly accepted the inspiration of the Holy Spirit. These two tercets assume the model of biblical authorship that we encountered in the previous chapter, in which both the human author and the Holy Spirit are responsible for the biblical texts that they jointly produce. Inspiration is crucial, but the poet must accept it and write according to it. The ties between this characterization and Dante's self-definition as poet in *Purgatorio* 24 are striking. In this earlier canticle, Dante describes the process of poetic composition in the following terms: 'I' mi son un che, quando / Amor mi spira, noto, e a quel modo / ch'e' ditta dentro vo significando' (52–4) ('I am one who, when Love inspires me [breathes into me], I note it, and in the manner in which it is spoken within, I go signifying'). Dante accounts for his creation of poetry through a process of inspiration. Love in-spires him, dictates to him within; nevertheless, his own will must also be engaged, as he notes the inspiration and then creates poetry as a result through the active process of signification (*vo significando*). He echoes this process of inspiration at the beginning of the *Paradiso*, when he asks Apollo to in-spire him ('Entra nel petto mio, e spira tue' ['Enter into my breast, and you breathe (or inspire) there'] [1.19]). Dante's characterization of his own inspired writing process thus resembles that of David and other biblical authors. Dante, too, may be a 'singer of the Holy Spirit.'

One other significant mention of David and his writings occurs in the second of the three examination cantos. In a passage we will consider further below, Saint James queries Dante regarding the source of his hope, and Dante identifies David's writings in particular as providing him with this virtue:

> Da molte stelle mi vien questa luce;
> ma quei la distillò nel mio cor pria
> che fu sommo cantor del sommo duce.
>   'Sperino in te,' ne la sua tëodia
> dice, 'color che sanno il nome tuo':
> e chi nol sa, s'elli ha la fede mia?   (*Par.* 25.70–5)

(This light came to me from many stars, but the one who first distilled it in my heart was the highest singer of the highest lord. 'They hope in you,' he says in his godsong, 'who know your name': and who does not know it if he has my faith?)

Dante's characterization of David (Dante cites the ninth Psalm in lines 73 and 74) as the 'highest singer of the highest lord' recalls his earlier reference to David as the 'singer of the Holy Spirit,' and matches the neologism that Dante coins, *tëodia*, to refer to David's divine poetry, a term that we may equally well apply to Dante's poem, especially since Dante refers to the *Commedia* as "l poema sacro' ('the sacred poem' [see 25.1]) at the beginning of this same canto. Both David and Dante write godsongs, poetry inspired by and leading men to God. David's life and poetry, then, come to prefigure both Dante's turning from the dark wood of sin and his writing of the *Commedia* itself, as he consistently links David to himself and David's biblical poetry to his own poem.[11]

In addition to this thick presence of biblical authors in the *Paradiso*, Dante – more frequently than in the other two canticles – alludes to and draws on the scriptures, often tying his poem to them in order to reinforce the truth and authority of his message. An important instance of this practice occurs in the heaven of Mars, in the canticle's central canto. After Cacciaguida has clarified Dante's destiny, the pilgrim asks Cacciaguida if he should deliver such a strong and unpopular message. His ancestor responds that his message will indeed cause the guilty to scorn his bitter words, but his task is nevertheless to speak the truth forcefully and fully.

> Ma nondimen, rimossa ogne menzogna,
> tutta tua visïon fa manifesta;
> e lascia pur grattar dov' è la rogna.
>   Ché se la voce tua sarà molesta
> nel primo gusto, vital nodrimento
> lascerà poi, quando sarà digesta.
>   Questo tuo grido farà come vento,
> che le più alte cime più percuote;
> e ciò non fa d'onor poco argomento.   (*Par.* 17.127–35)

(But nevertheless, push aside every falsehood, make your whole vision clear; and let whoever has a scab scratch it. For if your voice will be bitter at the first tasting, it will leave sustaining nourishment once it has been digested. This cry of yours will act as does the wind that most strikes the highest peaks; and this makes no small argument for honour.)

Many commentators have pointed to Boethius as the source for Dante's image of his word as being digested: 'Those remedies that are left now are like those that sting on the tongue, but sweeten once taken within.'[12] There is a biblical source here, however, that is at least equally plausible and that better fits the context of the passage; in both the Old and New Testaments, God's word is portrayed as a book that the biblical author eats.[13] When the prophet Ezekiel is commissioned to deliver the Lord's word to the children of Israel, for example, he is given a book:

> But thou, O Son of man, hear all that I say to thee: and do not thou provoke me, as that house provoketh me: open thy mouth, and eat what I give thee. And I looked, and behold, a hand was sent to me, wherein was a book (*liber*) rolled up: and he spread it before me, and it was written within and without: and there were written in it lamentations, and canticles, and woe. And he said to me: Son of man, eat all that thou shalt find: eat this book (*comede volumen istud*) and go speak to the children of Israel. And I opened my mouth, and he caused me to eat that book: And he said to me: Son of man, thy belly shall eat, and thy bowels shall be filled with this book, which I give thee. And I did eat it: and it was sweet as honey in my mouth (*et comedi illud et factum est in ore meo sicut mel dulce*).[14] (Ezek. 2.8–3.3)

The parallels between this passage and Cacciaguida's exhortation become clearer when considered in the light of the exegetical tradition. Gregory the Great, for example, identifies the book Ezekiel receives as 'the pages of the holy Scriptures,' and notes that it contains lamentations because 'in it is written penitence for sins.'[15] When Ezekiel is instructed to eat the book, Gregory notes that this is because 'holy scripture is our food and drink' (1:10.3)[16], observing that the Lord himself draws on the same metaphor when he prophesies through Amos 'not a famine of bread, nor a thirst of water, but of hearing the word of the Lord' (see Amos 8.11). When Ezekiel eats the book it is sweet to him, as it is to any 'whose inner life is filled with his commandments,' while it is bitter to those whose conscience reproaches them for their reprobate existence.[17] The situations of Ezekiel and Dante are similar, as both receive commissions from heavenly messengers to write, though the way in which the 'eating of the word' applies to each of them differs. In Ezekiel's case, the book he eats represents the word of the Lord that he receives and that he then must transmit to the 'children of Israel,' while in Dante's case his poem is 'eaten' by his readers. Nevertheless, intriguing parallels emerge; in both instances the words that are eaten refer to inspired words, and in both instances they irritate the digestion of the wicked.

Similarly, in the Apocalypse John receives a book from a 'mighty angel' and is instructed to eat it:

> And I heard a voice from heaven again speaking to me, and saying: Go, and take the book (*librum*) that is open, from the hand of the angel who

standeth upon the sea, and upon the earth. And I went to the angel, saying unto him, that he should give me the book. And he said to me: Take
the book and eat it up (*accipe et devora illum*): and it shall make thy belly
bitter, but in thy mouth it shall be as sweet as honey. And I took the book
from the hand of the angel, and ate it up: and it was in my mouth, sweet
as honey (*et erat in ore meo tamquam mel dulce*): and when I had eaten it, my
belly was bitter (*amaricatus est venter meus*). And he said to me: Thou must
prophesy again to many nations, and peoples, and tongues, and kings.[18]
(Apoc. 10.8–11)

The author of the Apocalypse seems to have had the passage from
Ezekiel in mind when writing this passage, as its basic form matches
that found in Ezekiel 2–3; a heavenly messenger gives a visionary
prophet a book and commands the prophet to eat it; the prophet eats the
book and finds it both bitter and sweet; after he has eaten the book, the
heavenly messenger commands him to prophesy. Medieval exegesis of
this passage also has similarities to Gregory's interpretation of Ezekiel.
The *Glossa ordinaria*, for example, interprets John's going to the angel
to receive the book as going to 'the Scriptures, accomplished by God
and published for the faithful.'[19] Dante draws on this biblical context
in his conversation with Cacciaguida, receiving a commission to write
and comparing his own poem to words that are digested. Given the
medieval practice of allegorizing the entire situation so that the prophet
represents the Christian reader who receives the scriptures and then
'eats' them by studying them and internalizing them and, if he is righteous, finding them sweet, Dante implies that the words of his own
poem function in a way analogous to scriptures. Readers will digest
them, and their reaction to the taste of the words will depend greatly
on the reader's spiritual disposition. Whatever the state of the reader,
however, Dante's poem will leave behind life-sustaining nourishment,
paralleling Gregory's assertion that the scriptures prove to be 'cibus noster et potus.'

In several places in the *Paradiso*, then, Dante works to tie his poem to
the scriptures, asserting their similarities in the way that they signify,
in the source of their inspiration, and in their effects on their readers.
As we turn now to the examination cantos, we will see Dante explicitly
foreground the issue of biblical truth and relate that question to the
vital issue of reader response: what relevance does the truth of the Bible
have for the readers who encounter it? As we will see, Dante addresses
these same questions to his own poem and once again implicitly aligns

his poem with the scriptures, while at the same time subtly suggesting that his poem is necessary precisely because readers do not hear the scriptures in the way they once did.

The Examination Cantos

Critics have long recognized the centrality of *Paradiso* 24–26 to Dante's journey both as pilgrim and as poet. Ugo Foscolo, for example, pointed out that the end of canto 24, where Saint Peter symbolically crowns the pilgrim (see lines 151–4), prepares the way for the well-known opening of canto 25, where the poet expresses his wish to be crowned poet laureate at his baptistery in Florence. Foscolo, in fact, suggested that the final verses of canto 24 represent 'the right of the imposition of hands and the consecration to the Apostolic ministry.'[20] Peter's approval of Dante extends as much to his poetry as to his profession of faith. The examination of the pilgrim on the three theological virtues not only establishes his worthiness to ascend to the Empyrean toward the vision of God, it also justifies the writing of the poem. Immediately following these cantos, Peter – with words that recall Cacciaguida's commission to Dante considered above – instructs the pilgrim to become the poet, to open his mouth and reveal what he has seen. Part and parcel of this ritual of certification is Dante's lengthy discussion of the Bible and its truth value, whose status is intimately linked to that of the *Commedia*.

Canto 23 ends with Dante's words of rejoicing as he reflects back on the things he has seen in the realm of the fixed stars, words whose force derives from biblical imagery, for there, Dante tells us, one enjoys the 'tesoro / che s'acquistò piangendo ne lo essilio / di Babillòn' ('treasure that is acquired through the tears of the Babylonian exile' [*Par.* 23.133–5]). This imagery anticipates the thick presence of the Bible in the following cantos. The first of the examination cantos begins with Beatrice's brief prayer to the apostles to aid Dante, couching her words within the image of the banquet of learning that Dante drew on in the *Convivio*, an image derived from biblical subtexts, including references to the 'great supper of the blessed Lamb' (lines 2–3; see Apoc. 19.9 and also Luke 14.16 and Matt. 22.14), the crumbs 'that fall from your table' (line 5; see Matt. 15.27), and the fountain 'whence comes that which he thinks' (line 9; see John 4.14 and Apoc. 17.16–17). The canto is better known, however, for Dante's examination on the virtue of faith (whether Dante believes well – see line 40), in which, because Dante points to the scriptures as the source of his faith, the question of the Bible's truth is explicitly addressed.

Dante treats the issue of biblical truth following Peter's initial question, which asks the pilgrim to define faith. He replies with a literal translation of Hebrews 11.1, which was frequently taken to be the standard scriptural definition of faith.[21]

> Come 'l verace stilo
> ne scrisse, padre, del tuo caro frate
> che mise teco Roma nel buon filo,
>   fede è sustanza di cose sperate
> e argomento de le non parventi;
> e questa pare a me sua quiditate.   (24.61–6)

(As the truthful pen, father, of your beloved brother who with you put Rome on the good path writes of it, faith is the substance of things hoped for and evidence of those not appearing; and this seems to me its essence.)

As mentioned above, Dante here refers to Paul's truthful pen; interestingly, however, he does not refer to the divine inspiration that in the *Monarchia* guarantees the truth of Paul's words.[22] Instead, he concentrates on the fact that the pen that authored that definition was Paul's, reinforcing the point by describing Paul in historical terms – along with Peter he was instrumental in establishing the Church and directing it toward its proper goal. We have already noted that Dante has linked Paul to himself several times; with that background in mind it seems that Dante's description of the biblical author in terms of his ability to preach, to deliver a divine message effectively, will also prove to be significant.

Peter, however, does not address these issues, and instead questions Dante further regarding his definition, especially regarding his classification of faith as substance and evidence. Dante's response highlights the paradoxical relationship that faith has with reason.

> Le profonde cose
> che mi largiscon qui la lor parvenza,
> a li occhi di là giù son sì ascose,
>   che l'esser loro v'è in sola credenza,
> sopra la qual si fonda l'alta spene;
> e però di sustanza prende intenza.
>   E da questa credenza ci convene
> silogizzar, sanz' avere altra vista:
> però intenza d'argomento tene.   (24.70–8)

(The profound things that allow me sight of them here are so hidden to eyes below that their existence there is solely in belief, upon which is founded the high hope; and therefore it takes the designation of substance. And from this belief it is necessary to reason, without having any other sight: therefore it takes the designation of evidence.)

Dante balances the lexicon between rationality and belief (*credenza* and *spene* are juxtaposed with *intenza, silogizzar,* and *argomento*), and he uses the tools of rationality to explain the irrational belief required by faith. Through belief alone mortals come to know the profound truths that Dante sees, and from this belief they reason. Indeed, according to Aquinas, the objects of faith differ from those of science, because the latter are seen whereas the former are heard.[23] As Paul wrote to the Romans (10.17), 'Faith then cometh by hearing' (*fides ex auditu*),[24] an assertion that matches the definition found in Hebrews that Dante translates into his poem: 'Est autem fides . . . argumentum non apparentium.' It is thus through the scriptures, the hearing of the word of God, Dante asserts, that one comes to faith.[25]

This attribution of faith to hearing the word of God becomes explicit later on in the examination, when Peter – after he has questioned Dante concerning the status of his own faith – queries the pilgrim about his faith's source. Dante responds – as we would expect from the implications of his previous answer – that his faith comes from the Bible:

> La larga ploia
> de lo Spirito Santo, ch'è diffusa
> in su le vecchie e 'n su le nuove cuoia,
>   è silogismo che la m'ha conchiusa
> acutamente sì, che 'nverso d'ella
> ogne dimostrazion mi pare ottusa.   (24.91–6)

(The abundant rain of the Holy Spirit, which is diffused over the old and new parchments, is the syllogism that has proved it to me so sharply that, against it, every demonstration appears to me obtuse.)

To be precise, it is not the Bible that leads Dante to faith, but the 'Spirito Santo' that is manifest within the pages of scripture; not the pages themselves, but the inspiration behind them is Dante's all-convincing syllogism. The Holy Spirit 'covers' the scriptures; to portray the distilling of that inspiration Dante draws on the biblical metaphor of rain, a metaphor to which Dante will return in the following canto.[26] Given his emphasis on the inspiration of the 'Spirito Santo' his description of the scriptures is oddly physical, pointing to the parchment upon which the inspired words are written. Dante's use of a physical metaphor (rain spreading over parchment) in the examination on faith thus marks his description as material, one that emphasizes the leaves of parchment that make up the physical object of the Bible. His faith derives from the Holy Spirit that has inspired the scriptures, but that spirit is only evident within the physical pages of the biblical text. The Bible is crucial not only because it is inspired, but also because it is an object, accessible to humans who learn things through their senses.

Further, Dante combines the discourses of faith and rationality in his response, claiming that the Holy Spirit as manifested in the scriptures forms a 'syllogism' that no other demonstration can disprove. Of course, we know already from Dante's previous definition that faith concerns things unseen and is thus not open to rational demonstration; Dante instead appropriates the language of rationality in order to show the superiority of the scriptures to any rational demonstration. They are the supreme syllogism, not because they present rational proof through the most stringent standards of Aristotelian logic, but because they are inspired. They are, in fact, a remarkable artefact – physical, tangible, earthly, and yet inspired by the Holy Spirit, accessible and true for humans on the earth – or for those of us, at least, who are unable to live through seeing but must rely on faith.

Peter, however, continues the process of rational examination that Dante had assumed at the beginning of the exam, when he compared himself to a degree candidate who waits for the master to pose the first question (see 24.46–51). Peter thus picks up on Dante's use of the language of reason and refers to the scriptures as 'L'antica e la novella / proposizion che così ti conchiude' (24.97–8) ('the old and new premises that have so proved to you'), but he goes on to ask Dante to tell him why, precisely, he believes the scriptures to be inspired and thus to be 'divine speech' ('perché l'hai tu per divina favella?' [24.99]).

> La prova che 'l ver mi dischiude,
> son l'opere seguite, a che natura
> non scalda ferro mai né batte incude.   (24.100–2)

(The proof that discloses the truth to me are the works that followed, for which nature never heats iron nor beats anvil.)

Nature is described as a craftsman with her own tools, all of which are inadequate to create the works or miracles recounted in the scriptures. Dante's response attempts to exploit the dialectic between faith and visual proof that we have already discussed; the scriptures offer – through their accounts of miraculous events unwitnessed in 'Nature' (here understood as a realm governed by law; otherwise how could Dante make claims about what does *not* occur there?) – a kind of proof, which provides evidence that the events described by biblical authors were miraculous and thus could only be brought about by God himself.[27] The miracles, therefore, witness to God's intervention in the story recounted by the Bible and imply that the book recounting those events partakes of the same intervention, this time through divine inspiration.[28]

Dante's reasoning, however, appears circular; in order to demonstrate that the scriptures are true, Dante points to the miracles the scriptures recount. And yet to accept the truth of the miracles, one must accept that these events are narrated truly by the Bible, the text under discussion. Dante's identification of the scriptures as the source of his faith thus highlights the issue of textual truth: how can one accept a scriptural text as true without possessing visual evidence of the miraculous events that it recounts? But this paradox is rooted in the gift of faith. The Word of God, after all, comes by hearing, not seeing, and the faith that Dante draws from the scriptures concerns things unseen. Peter's formulation of his next question emphasizes the logical problem generated by Dante's formulation in terms of proof:

> Dì, chi t'assicura
> che quell' opere fosser? Quel medesmo
> che vuol provarsi, non altri, il ti giura.   (24.103–5)

(Say, who assures you that those works occurred? That which needs to be proved, nothing else, swears it to you.)

We may recall that Dante similarly authenticates the veracity of an incredible occurrence that he recounts in his poem – the appearance of Geryon in *Inferno* 16 – by swearing by the very words that recount the event.

> e per le note
> di questa comedìa, lettor, ti giuro,
> s'elle non sien di lunga grazia vòte,
> ch'i' vidi ...   (*Inf.* 16.127–30)

(And by the notes of this comedy – may they not be devoid of lasting favour – reader, I swear to you that I saw ...)

Even here Dante anticipates his discussion of biblical truth in the *Paradiso* by juxtaposing the visual truth that he possesses as pilgrim ('ch'i vidi') with the textual truth of the poem, which the reader must take on faith. Dante seems to posit a kind of hermeneutic circle in the reading of his poem, in which faith is necessary to accept its truth; the events he narrates are true, but the only 'event' that guarantees the truth of the text that recounts them is the text itself.

Peter, however, will not allow the pilgrim to conclude with this kind of reasoning, which appears to be circular, and so asks him the source of his belief in the scripture's veracity, specifying Dante's source, interestingly, as a 'who' rather than a 'what' ('*chi* t'assicura'). Dante's response turns away from the scriptures themselves and toward their effect within human history.

'Se 'l mondo si rivolse al cristianesmo,'
diss' io, 'sanza miracoli, quest' uno
è tal, che li altri non sono il centesmo:
    ché tu intrasti povero e digiuno
in campo, a seminar la buona pianta
che fu già vite e ora è fatta pruno.'   (24.106–11)

('If the world turned to Christianity,' I said, 'without miracles, this one is such that the others are not one one-hundredth of it: for you entered the field poor and fasting in order to sow the good plant, which was once a vine and now has been made a thorn.')

Saint Augustine makes a similar argument in the *De civitate Dei* for the truth of an event attested in the Bible – Christ's resurrection – and also turns to the miraculous fact of the world's conversion to substantiate the truth of that miracle.

And in order to make credible that one incredible event, Christ's resurrection and ascension, as it is reported, we heap up all evidence for a multitude of incredible events; and yet we still cannot turn them from their hair-raising obstinacy and bring them to believe. Nevertheless, if they do not believe that those miracles were effected through Christ's apostles, to ensure belief in their proclamation of Christ's resurrection and ascension, then this one overpowering miracle is enough for us – that the world has come to believe in it without any miracles at all. (22.5)[29]

Aquinas likewise draws on the miraculous conversion of the world in his discussion, early in the *Summa contra Gentiles,* of why one can submit to the truths of faith without offence to reason, arguing that the world's conversion presents 'the clearest witness of the signs given in the past; so that it is not necessary that they should be further repeated, since they appear most clearly in their effect' (1.6.3).[30] Indeed, the fact that 'minds of mortal men ... assent to these things is the greatest of miracles, just as it is a manifest work of divine inspiration that, spurning visible things, men should seek only what is invisible' (1.6.1).[31]

Faith itself is a miracle; not attributable to natural processes, it must be credited to God's intervention. In the *Summa theologiae,* Aquinas asserts that faith comes through *auctoritas divina:* 'the believer's mind is convinced by divine authority to assent to the unseen (*ad assentiendum his quae non videt)*' (2a.2æ.4.1). He further develops this idea in the first article of section 6 in the same part of the treatise, which considers 'whether faith is infused by God' (*utrum fides sit homini a Deo infusa).* One objection to this proposition is that 'a person comes to faith by seeing miracles and by hearing the faith taught' (*homo pertingit ad credendum et videndo miracula et audiendo fidei doctrinam).* Aquinas answers this objection by noting that there are two causes 'as to assent to matters of faith' (*ad assensum hominis in ea quae sunt fidei);* one is external, such as a miracle or preaching of the sort noted in the objection, but this cause proves insufficient, since even in the scriptures there are varying reactions to the miracles that Christ performed: 'some believe and others do not' (*quidam credunt et quidam non credunt).* We must look for another cause, one that leads to inward assent; Aquinas can only account for this inner movement by a divine infusion of belief. 'Since in assenting to the things of faith a person is raised above his own nature, he has thus assent from a supernatural source influencing (*movente)* him; this source is God. The assent of faith, which is its principal act, therefore, has as its cause God, moving us inwardly through grace.'[32] The ultimate miracle for Aquinas as for Dante is not the outward proof of the visible wonder but the inward movement of the soul towards faith, brought about by God.

When he appeals to the effect of the Bible in the lives of its readers, the miracle of faith that occurs in so many, Dante thus shifts the ground of textual truth, moving from a model of truth dependent on external correspondence and verification to one based on the individual's encounter with the text that changes the individual. Peter asks how it is possible to verify a text's accuracy when the only evidence we have for the events narrated by the text is the text itself. The question pushes us toward external verification, some external source that can substantiate the accuracy of biblical narrative. Dante, however, turns away from the Bible itself, and the history that it recounts, to consider the effect of the Bible on its readers. It is not so much the Bible's accurate representation of past events, its correspondence to an objective reality exterior to the text, that verifies scriptural truth; rather, the text is true as it influences people to convert, literally, to *turn toward* Christianity ('si rivolse al cristianesmo'). Dante sets up a demonstration of biblical truth that reaches a dead end; he can only continue by changing the terms of the proof, by moving beyond rational demonstration based on external verification to the realm of faith. Faith does not arise, as both Aquinas and Kierkegaard saw, through rational demonstrations but through an inner movement as individuals change and repent. The miracle of the Bible is that it becomes true precisely *for us*. As we have seen in chapter 1, this notion of biblical truth was widespread, beginning at least with Saint Augustine, but Dante gives it a peculiar emphasis here by including it in an overt, and often intellectualizing, discussion of the Bible's truth value. The 'event,' then, that guarantees the truth of the Bible is that which occurs in the encounter between reader and text and results in the changing of the reader.[33] The infusion of faith that Augustine experiences in the garden, when he encounters the words of Paul in such a way that the light of confidence floods into him, displacing the darkness of doubt, becomes typical of the way in which the truth of the Bible is proved to individual readers: not through a logical demonstration of the Bible's referential truth but through an encounter with the text.

The Bible's truth, therefore, is primarily existential, and so it is to be expected that Peter continues his interrogation of Dante by asking him to elucidate his own faith and its source, beginning his query with an assertion that the miracle of Dante's faith has been brought about by the grace of God, and not by the rational demonstration that Dante has attempted to carry out:

> La Grazia, che donnea
> con la tua mente, la bocca t'aperse
> infino a qui come aprir si dovea,

> sì ch'io approvo ciò che fuori emerse;
> ma or convien espremer quel che credi,
> e onde a la credenza tua s'offerse.   (24.118–23)

(Grace, which directs your mind, has opened your mouth to this point as it should have been opened, so that I approve what has emerged without; but now it is time to express what you believe, and whence is your belief that shows itself.)

Dante responds with a recitation of his monotheistic and orthodox creed of the triune God, and he accounts for his belief once again by pointing to the scriptures, which have manifested the truths of heaven.

> e a tal creder non ho io pur prove
> fisice e metafisice, ma dalmi
> anche la verità che quinci piove
>   per Moïsè, per profeti e per salmi,
> per l'Evangelio e per voi che scriveste
> poi che l'ardente Spirto vi fé almi.   (24.133–8)

(and for such belief I have not only physical and metaphysical proofs, but also the truth that rains down from here through Moses, the prophets, the psalms, the gospel, and through you who wrote after the ardent Spirit made you holy.)

Dante here combines the images of inspiration that we have previously discussed; the Spirit effects an inner transformation in biblical authors such as Peter so that they can make visible on the page the truths that rain down through them onto the old and new parchments. Dante's belief, then, is supported by 'physical and metaphysical' proofs, but more importantly by the scriptures that transmit the sanctifying Spirit through the biblical authors to readers like Dante, changing them in the process.

Sandwiched within Peter's question regarding Dante's own faith and Dante's response is a *captatio benevolentiae* directed by Dante to Peter in praise of his faith that proves to be as intriguing as anything else in the canto's discussion of the Bible.

> O santo padre, e spirito che vedi
> ciò che credesti sì, che tu vincesti
> ver' lo sepulcro più giovani piedi . . .   (24.124–6)

(O holy father, and spirit who sees what you believed to such an extent
that you vanquished younger feet toward the sepulchre ...)

The pilgrim's words refer to events narrated at the end of the Gospel
of John; following Christ's crucifixion, the apostles hear from Mary
Magdalene that the sepulchre where Jesus was buried has been found
empty. Peter and 'ille alius discipulus' ('that other disciple' – ubiqui-
tously identified as John the Beloved in Dante's time), rush to see the
empty tomb for themselves. John 20.4 reads 'currebant autem duo
simul et ille alius discipulus praecucurrit citius Petro et *venit primus*
ad monumentum' ('and they both ran together, and that other disciple
did outrun Peter, and *came first* to the sepulchre'; emphasis mine). John,
however, does not enter immediately; Peter, arriving later, proceeds into
the tomb first. John finally enters, and he alone, we are told, 'saw and
believed' (*vidit et credidit*): the Gospel tells us nothing of Peter's belief.[34]

The differences between the Gospel account and the pilgrim's version
of it in his address to Peter are immediately apparent: according to the
biblical text, John's 'più giovani piedi' arrived first; according to the pilgrim, Peter outran them.[35] In addition, verse 9 of John 20 tells us that 'as
yet they [Peter and John] knew not the scripture (*nondum enim sciebant
scripturam*) that [Jesus] must rise again from the dead,' whereas Dante
credits Peter's speed to his belief in the Resurrection.

What, then, are we to make of this discrepancy, especially in light of
the fact that it occurs in the midst of a rich discussion and defence of
biblical truth? Many critics have contended that the difference between
the biblical account and Dante's proves trivial, since Dante's point is that
although Peter might not have won the foot race, he won in faith, as he
was the first to enter the tomb.[36] While the biblical text states nothing
concerning Peter's faith, it is nevertheless true that medieval interpreters
frequently read the passage as an allegory of faith in Christ's resurrection. The *Glossa ordinaria*, for instance, interprets John as a symbol of the
synagogue and Peter of the church. Just as John came to the tomb and
refused to enter, so the Jews heard the prophecies of Christ's Passion
but refused to believe that their messiah would be killed. The gentile
church, however, like Peter, arrived late but believed in the Resurrection
and entered into the Promised Land, displacing the Jews who had been
God's chosen people.[37] The liberties that Dante takes with the text are
not resolved here, however, as this interpretation makes much of the
fact that John arrived first; furthermore, the *Commedia* portrays a Peter
whose faith allows him to win a footrace over a younger opponent, not

a contest of faith. The difference may appear negligible, and perhaps the explanation lies in the possibility that Dante simply nods here, misremembering a biblical passage that he in all likelihood did not have in front of him as he wrote. The eighteenth-century commentator Pompeo Venturi, for instance, noted that while 'the commentators exert their ingenuity in order to affirm that Dante has not made a blunder, as it appears at first sight,' he concludes, 'I hold to be ingenious the saying: Dante here has made a mistake.'[38] Working against this possibility, however, is *Monarchia* 3.9, where Dante refers correctly to this same biblical passage. The context is the debate over Luke 22.38 – the two swords scripture – that we discussed in the previous chapter. In order to support his thesis that Peter's response to Christ was superficial and sprung from his own impetuous personality, Dante adduces a number of episodes from the Gospels that illustrate Peter's impulsive nature, including John 20.1–9: 'And John likewise says that Peter entered immediately when he arrived at the sepulchre, seeing the other disciple lingering at the entrance' (3.9.16).[39] Dante, in other words, knew the biblical text and, one can only assume, could have written the tercet in question to conform to the biblical passage. We are faced, then, with a deliberate altering of the biblical text. We will return to this passage at the end of the chapter.

Whereas Saint Peter's questions on faith elicit a discussion of biblical truth, Saint James's queries on hope in the following canto draw out a consideration of the proper interpretation of scripture, which Dante addresses most clearly in his response to James's final question, which concerns 'quello che la speranza ti 'mpromette' ('what hope promises you' [25.87]). Dante responds that he has learned to hope through the Old and New Testaments.

> Le nove e le scritture antiche
> pongon lo segno, ed esso lo mi addita,
> de l'anime che Dio s'ha fatte amiche.
>   Dice Isaia che ciascuna vestita
> ne la sua terra fia di doppia vesta:
> e la sua terra è questa dolce vita;
>   e 'l tuo fratello assai vie più digesta,
> là dove tratta de le bianche stole,
> questa revelazion ci manifesta.   (25.88–96)

(The new and ancient scriptures provide the sign, and it points me to hope, of the souls that God has made his friends. Isaiah said that each

friend will be dressed in a double garment in their land, and their land is
this sweet life; and your brother, more clearly, where he talks of the white
robes, manifests the revelation to us.)

The response begins with a general assertion of the Bible's meaning;
both the Old and the New Testaments provide readers with signs that
point to the hope of the elect, those whom God has made his friends.
These scriptural signs, as Saint Augustine argues, should not be considered 'for what they are but rather for their value as signs which signify
something else.'[40] As in the previous canto, the importance of the Bible
lies in its meaning for readers and its ability to influence them to turn
to God. Dante follows the general statement of an interpretive principle
with two specific examples of how this principle should be applied in
interpreting scripture.

The first example is taken from the Old Testament prophet Isaiah:
'therefore shall they receive double in their land, everlasting joy shall
be unto them' (61.7).[41] Modern scholars often read the passage as an
exilic promise of return to the physical, historical Jerusalem, in which
the children of Israel will receive a double blessing of joy in recompense
'for [their] double confusion and shame' ('pro confusione vestra duplici
et rubore'). Dante, however, in the tradition of medieval exegesis, reads
the passage as pointing beyond its specific historical context to the life
beyond;[42] he thus identifies 'terra sua' with paradise and expands the
unmodified 'duplicia' to read 'doppia vesta,' a reading he most likely
extrapolates by anticipating verse 10 of the same chapter ('for he hath
clothed me with the garments of salvation: and with the robe of justice
he hath covered me').[43] The concrete promise for a double portion of
material blessings in the historical Jerusalem becomes in Dante's hands
a more universal promise for the double garment of body and spirit
at the time of resurrection. This reading follows the exegetical principles for 'spiritual' interpretation that Dante both uses and defends
in book 3 of the *Monarchia*, which we considered in the first chapter;
key words must be interpreted according to their usage in other parts
of the scriptures, which can then be read back into the passage under
consideration. As we saw, furthermore, the guiding principle of scriptural interpretation is to read for the existential truth of the scriptures,
its truth for us. Dante teaches us how to read Isaiah 61.7 in this way by
subtly expanding it so that it is more easily read as a sign that points us
as readers, not back to the historical situation of the Israelites in exile,
but forward to Christian salvation.

The next tercet derives from the New Testament's final book, which, Dante assures James, is clearer in its message. 'After this I saw a great multitude, which no man could number, of all nations, and tribes, and peoples, and tongues, standing before the throne, and in sight of the Lamb, clothed with white robes, and palms in their hands' (7.9).[44] Dante's reference to the *bianche stole* in line 95 is commonly interpreted, probably because of the implicit parallel with the Isaiah passage and Dante's reference to the *due stole* of body and spirit later in the canto (see line 127), as a reference to the resurrected bodies of the blessed. It is certainly a sign of the future glory that Dante claims to hope for in line 69. The image of the *stola alba* found in Apocalypse 7.9, however, was frequently interpreted to refer to the innocent state that comes about through baptism, where our robes or garments are washed in the blood of Christ. This meaning becomes clear later in this chapter of the Apocalypse, when we are told that the saints appearing before the Lamb are those who 'have washed their robes, and have made them white in the blood of the Lamb,'[45] a process that the *Glossa ordinaria* describes as baptism. As an alternate reading, however, the *Glossa* also identifies the *stolas* as the bodies of the blessed,[46] a reading that parallels other medieval uses of the word *stola*. Bonaventure, for example, refers to the glory of the body that the blessed enjoy in paradise as the 'second robe.'[47] In citing the Apocalypse, then, as well as Isaiah, Dante implicitly interprets according to his method of existential interpretation delineated in the *Monarchia*. By placing the apocalyptic image within his discussion of hope, he treats the scriptures as a sign that points beyond itself to the hope of eternal glory.

This emphasis on scriptural interpretation continues at the end of the canto, when Dante is blinded by gazing too ardently at Saint John, an action that is motivated by a misreading of a biblical passage, one that John corrects and has Dante report back on earth.[48] At the end of the Gospel of John, Jesus tells Peter, referring to John, 'So I will have him to remain till I come, what is it to thee?' (John 21.22).[49] This cryptic sentence had elicited varying attempts at elucidation, most prominent among them, perhaps, the assertion that John had been taken up to heaven with his body.[50] John's assertion in *Paradiso* 25 that the interpretation is incorrect, that only Christ and Mary have their bodies in paradise before the end of time, serves only to invalidate a mistaken reading; he does not provide the correct interpretation. This non-answer proves as significant as the correction itself. The kind of information a correct interpretation of this scriptural passage would provide is simply unnecessary. We read the scriptures to help us turn ourselves toward God; speculation over Saint John's fate does not serve to further our existential engagement with the Bible.

In addition to these scriptural references, Dante engages Saint James's own epistle both implicitly and explicitly in canto 25. Thus, when Dante responds to James's query concerning how he came to hope, he mentions the scriptures by referring to two biblical authors, first of all David (see lines 70–5; a passage discussed previously), and then James himself.

> Tu mi stillasti, con lo stillar suo,
> ne la pistola poi; sì ch'io son pieno,
> e in altrui vostra pioggia repluo.   (25.76–8)

(You next instilled in me, with his [David's] instilling, in your epistle; so much so that I am full, and in others I rerain your rain [of hope].)

William Stephany has shown how fully Dante treats James's epistle here, noting in particular the admonition that we should be doers of the word and not hearers only ('Estote autem factores verbi, et non auditores tantum' [James 1.22]). When we consider the multiple connotations of the Latin *facere*, far broader than our English *do*, we realize that James's admonition in the Vulgate can be read to mean that we should be *makers* of the word as well as hearers and doers. Dante's response to the hearing of James's words is to make words in his turn, just as James made his words following hearing those of David.[51] Dante's self-identification with biblical authors thus continues here in the midst of his rich consideration of the Bible, its interpretation, and its truth.

In canto 25, we see an underlying consistency between this and the previous canto, as each places emphasis on the effect of reading on readers, on seeing the Bible as true for us. The final examination canto likewise echoes this conception of biblical truth; John's biblical writings have directed Dante toward charity, just as the Bible led him to faith and hope.

> Sternilmi tu ancora, incominciando
> l'alto preconio che grida l'arcano
> di qui là giù sovra ogne altro bando.   (26.43–5)

(You reveal this to me as well, in beginning your lofty work that cries out the mystery of this place down there over every other proclamation.)

The truth of the Bible throughout the examination cantos, then, resides in its becoming true for the pilgrim and consequently for each individual reader.

The second half of canto 26 is also important for our consideration of biblical truth, since in Dante's discussions with Adam he directly addresses the issue of Adam's language, which Dante had previously defined in the *De vulgari eloquentia* as Hebrew, the language of the Old Testament. Whereas in the earlier treatise Dante characterized Adam's tongue as a language created directly by God and hence incorruptible, in Adam's discourse we learn that God provides the faculty for language, but each language is a human creation; no language, therefore, proves incorruptible. In the earlier treatise, Dante had exempted Hebrew from the usual fate so that Christ could speak a divine rather than a human language.[52] Hebrew's isolation from the fate of all other languages seems to reflect a desire to reserve a divine language for Christ and for God's book. This sacred language would thus be able to transmit truths without contaminating them with the historical accidents that inhere in all other tongues. Dante's revision of this earlier view to one in which Adam's language is as fallible as any other, that even the name of God changed in Hebrew, and that Adam's language had disappeared by the time of the Tower of Babel suggests that even the language of the scriptures is caught up in the accidents of history.[53]

We have already seen how Dante identifies the Bible's truth as existing within the heart of each reader. The miraculous conversion of the world was even more astounding because of the poverty and ignorance of the original apostles, including Dante's interlocutor Peter:

> ché tu intrasti povero e digiuno
> in campo, a seminar la buona pianta
> che fu già vite e ora è fatta pruno.　　　　　　　　　(24.109–11)

(that you entered the field poor and hungry to sow the good plant, which was once a vine and is now made a thorn.)

The effect of the apostolic message is a guarantee of its truth, but the scriptures no longer have the same effect; the vine has become a thorn. Just as the history of early Christianity demonstrates the truth of the Bible as it was embraced and lived, the more recent history of the church in Dante's day – the rise of corruption at its highest levels in particular – suggests that readers no longer respond to the scriptural message in the same way. For the thorn to become a vine once again, Dante must imitate these biblical authors by sowing the good seed, making the biblical message new so that it speaks to his contemporaries. It is for this reason, in fact, that Dante tells us that he writes, 'in pro del mondo che mal vive' ('on behalf of the world that lives badly' [*Purg.* 32.103]). He must turn his readers back to the sacred book so that they may find renewed faith, hope, and charity, as he has.

With this fuller context, we now return to Dante's strange alteration of John 20.4 in the first of the examination cantos.

> O santo padre, e spirito che vedi
> ciò che credesti sì, che tu vincesti
> ver' lo sepulcro più giovani piedi.   (24.124–6)

(O holy father, and spirit who sees what you believed to such an extent that you vanquished younger feet toward the sepulchre.)

We should first acknowledge that this tercet subtly recapitulates Dante's and Peter's dialogue concerning faith and biblical truth; Peter's previous faith ('credesti') contrasts with his present visual knowledge ('vedi'), and his actions (running to the tomb) spring directly from his faith. One of the intriguing ironies of Dante's distortion of the biblical original, however, is that the original scriptural version of the story actually reinforces the formative value that he assigns to the scriptures in creating faith, as the disciples' incomprehension is due to their not knowing 'the scripture, that he must rise again from the dead.' In contrast, therefore, to the suggestion of Bosco and Reggio that Dante alters the passage in order to suit the demands of his poem,[54] it seems that Dante's alteration here does not even serve his immediate purposes. We must instead look to the larger poetic purposes revealed in these cantos, to his conception of biblical truth. Dante's *captatio benevolentiae*, it turns out, does not concern itself with referential accuracy, to what actually occurred according to the Gospel of John, but with portraying the movement of faith within the individual Christian. In Dante's biblical revision, Peter knows the scripture 'that Christ must rise again from the dead,' and this scripture leads him to believe, a belief that affects him so strongly that it overcomes his physical limitations. This is the same faith that led Peter and Paul to sow the good seed as poor and fasting apostles, and that led their hearers to turn toward God. And it is this existential truth that Dante seeks to renew within his poem. For that renewal to take place, however, he must convince his readers that his poem carries biblical authority. This is not to say that Dante would have considered his poem equal to the Bible, produced, as he argued in book 3 of the *Monarchia*, before the church and true from all eternity. Instead, Dante seeks to renew that original, biblical, revelation by transforming it so that it appears new, with a force and immediacy that it possessed when Peter and Paul first set out 'to sow the good plant.' But if we are to take Dante's biblical message seriously, we must accept the authority of his poem, an authority that depends upon biblical texts, to be sure, but also upon a renewal of biblical inspiration.

Proving biblical inspiration is a task of a high order. One way he seeks to accomplish it is, as we have seen, by associating himself with the authors of the Bible. Like Paul, Dante possesses an other-worldly message; like David, he has received the grace to repent of his sins, turn to God, and produce a 'sacred poem,' a godsong. Another way is by adapting, one might even say appropriating, the scriptures so as to renew their message. In the previous chapter, we saw how readily, in his political epistles, Dante adopted biblical events and applied them to the troubled history of his day, even identifying Henry VII as a kind of political messiah, and himself as a political John the Baptist. In the chapters that follow, we will see a number of examples of this intertextual practice of adaptation and appropriation in the first two canticles of the *Commedia*, in which Dante both honours the truth of the Bible and extends the biblical message, showing how it applies to the events and problems of his own day, in many key cases by adapting or even rewriting a biblical passage. For Dante, the scriptures are uniquely true, but they are also physical objects written with a human, material, and corruptible language. Their words or *verba*, therefore, need to be renewed so that the eternal *Verbum* contained within them can be heard once again and become true for Dante's readers. Dante, in other words, feels the need both to assert the unparalleled truth of the scriptures *and* to try and renew that truth in the mind of his readers by adapting key biblical passages so that they speak more directly. This dual focus of Dante's scriptural poetics becomes clear in *Paradiso* 24, where he both defends biblical truth and alters a key scriptural passage.

Peter, in fact, in the canto following the completion of Dante's examination, instructs Dante to imitate the apostles in sowing the good seed by carrying the message of God's approaching intervention back to earth.

e tu, figliuol, che per lo mortal pondo
ancor giù tornerai, apri la bocca,
e non asconder quel ch'io non ascondo.   (27.64–6)

(and you, son, who will yet return again to the mortal world, open your
mouth and do not hide what I do not hide.)

These words, which can only be called a prophetic commission, utilize
visual language reminiscent of the discussion of faith in canto 24. Dante
opens his mouth so as to make something visible, to give sight to things
through speaking – and only when Dante speaks of them does it seem that
they are not hidden. The prophetic urgency of speaking suggests that
Peter's message has been obscured from the sight and hearing of our
erring world. Dante uncovers his knowledge of celestial realities and
places it before our ears, but he writes that knowledge, at times, over
the sacred text so as to preach *here* and *now*. The truths of the Bible, the
divine *Verbum*, must not be limited to the *verba* that reveal them, since
contemporary readers no longer seem to hear those words. Dante, by
adapting and revising the Bible, extends its message, reveals the Word
of God anew. In this way, he may influence readers to return once again
to the Bible, and in the light of his poem, read its words again, now
taking them to heart and finding the faith, hope, and charity that Dante
has found there. Only then, when the individual reader is engaged in it,
will the Bible once again become true in the only way that matters. For
Dante, the Bible should no longer concern solely the ancient Israelites
or the early Christians converted by the preaching of Peter and Paul. It
must speak here, presently, to *you*.

3 The Bible in the *Inferno:* Misprision and Prophetic Appropriation

In the remaining three chapters, we turn back to the *Commedia*'s first two canticles, seeking an understanding of how Dante's notion of biblical truth, which he addresses explicitly only in the final canticle, informs many passages in the first two-thirds of the poem. While these, for the most part, lack the kind of theoretical interrogation to which Dante subjects the scriptures in the final canticle, he nevertheless draws frequently on the Bible, especially in moments in which he addresses questions related to the church, to moral theology, and to the meaning of history. One cannot escape the feeling that when Dante turns to matters closest to his heart, he also turns to the Bible. We open this second exploration of the biblical Dante at the beginning – the first canticle and the opening of the poem.

According to traditional Dante criticism, the *Inferno* is the realm of the problematic. Those things that will appear clearly and positively in the later canticles are only glimpsed incompletely or in a distorted manner. Texts cited or evoked here share the same fate. The quintessential example of infernal intertextuality from this point of view is the opening line of the final canto: '*Vexilla regis prodeunt inferni*' ('the banners of the infernal king come forth' [*Inf.* 34.1]). This line – the sole Latin citation in the *Inferno* – is a miscitation of the well-known Latin hymn by Venantius Fortunatus celebrating the true cross. By simply adding the word *inferni* to the hymn's first line, Dante transforms it to an announcement of hell's king.[1] While not taken directly from the Bible, the hymn's intertextual fate leads us to expect a similarly distorted biblical intertextuality in this canticle – only misunderstood and garbled echoes of biblical texts, inversions and misprisions that distort biblical meaning. In many respects this assumption, as we will see, will prove to be accurate.

The damned often allude to scriptural passages in mistaken and fallible ways, revealing through their lack of biblical knowledge their distance from God. Nevertheless, this 'negative' understanding does not tell the whole story. As we saw in the first chapter, the pre-modern Bible was a text that informed the ways in which Dante and other writers perceived the world, and this 'biblical world' comes through in the *Inferno* as well, underpinning its structure and landscape, something that is especially apparent in the poem's opening. In addition, at a key moment, when the pilgrim becomes disgusted with the corruption of the church manifested in the eighth circle of hell, the poet has him turn to the Bible to offer a devastating critique and denunciation of papal simony, finding in the scriptures a hope for reform that could become actual if only the leadership of the church would hear the biblical truths that Dante, in prophetic fashion, retrieves from the sacred text. The Bible, in other words, has a crucial role to play in the *Commedia*'s opening canticle, a role evident from the poem's opening lines.

The Biblical World and the *Inferno*

When the pilgrim awakens in the dark wood midway through his life, he finds himself in a scriptural landscape. As early as the opening tercet, biblical subtexts proliferate.

> Nel mezzo del cammin di nostra vita
> mi ritrovai per una selva oscura,
> che la diritta via era smarrita.

(In the middle of the journey of our life, I found myself in a dark wood, for the straight road was lost.)

Virtually all modern commentaries point out the implicit reference to Psalm 89.10: 'the days of our years in them are threescore and ten years,'[2] a reference that situates the fictional date of the journey precisely in the midst of Dante's biblical life span, thirty-five years after his birth in 1265. Looking back on the opening tercet from the perspective of the third canto, when the pilgrim arrives at the gate of hell, Isaiah 38.10 – 'in the midst of my days I shall go to the gates of hell (*in dimidio dierum meorum vadam ad portas inferi*)' – also becomes relevant. Isaiah's words are actually a report of those written in thanksgiving by Hezekiah, the King of Judah. When Hezekiah was ill and knew that he was to die, he prayed for the Lord to intervene and lengthen his life, and the Lord responded by prolonging it by fifteen years. As Anthony Cassell has observed, Dante's poem can also be read as a 'song of thanksgiving,' for how the Lord prolonged his life and saved him from the dark wood of sin.[3] The interpretation found in the *Glossa ordinaria* reinforces this moral understanding of the scripture, as it suggests that 38.10 predicts the untimely death of 'impious and deceitful men [who] will not live out their days, since they do not fulfil works of virtue, nor do they correct their faults by repenting.'[4]

Dante's lost 'diritta via' also finds its meaning within the Bible. As Boccaccio noted of these lines of Dante, while there are many roads, there is only one that leads to salvation.[5] We know that Dante's lost road is the straight one leading to life eternal, since Christ himself identified that road as both *angusta* and *arta* (narrow and straight – see Matt. 7.14), and in John's Gospel Christ identifies himself as that way: 'ego sum via et veritas et vita' (14.6). Dante's later admission (in line 11) of ignorance as to how he left the road to salvation because he was so full of sleep ('tant' era pien di sonno') has many analogues in patristic and medieval writers. Cassell points to *Confessions* 8.5 and to Saint Bernard's *De gradibus humilitatis* 21, Bosco and Reggio to Augustine and Boethius. The Bible, however, once again provides the most probable source.

> And that knowing the season; that it is now the hour for us to rise from sleep (*de somno surgere*). For now our salvation is nearer than when we believed. The night is passed, and the day is at hand. Let us therefore cast off the works of darkness (*opera tenebrarum*), and put on the armour of light. Let us walk honestly, as in the day: not in rioting and drunkenness, not in chambering and impurities, not in contention and envy. But put ye on the Lord Jesus Christ, and make not provision for the flesh in its concupiscences. (Romans 13.11–14)[6]

The ties between Paul's exhortation and Dante's description extend beyond the reference to sleep; Dante's *selva oscura* recalls Paul's 'works of darkness,' and Dante's portrayal of the time of his waking – sunrise after a night passed in torment ('la notte ch'i' passai con tanta pieta' [21]) – echoes Paul's assertion that 'the night is passed and the day is at hand.' It is also worth recalling that the closing of this passage is the one read by Saint Augustine in the garden that precipitates his conversion (see *Confessions* 8.12). Dante's escape from the dark wood of sin and his search for a way up the hill of salvation parallels Augustine's turning toward God in his own autobiographical narrative of conversion. Indeed, the hill as a symbol of possible salvation and divine aid finds a parallel in the Psalms (120.1), where the Psalmist exclaims, 'I have lifted up my eyes to the mountains, from whence help shall come to me.'[7]

These biblical allusions could be multiplied further, but as a final example I will make brief mention of Dante's three beasts, almost universally interpreted as besetting sins that inhibit the pilgrim's moral and spiritual ascent. As Cassell notes, 'the metaphor of wild beasts as temptation and punishment occurs in many places in the Bible,' though the most prominent example is in the fifth chapter of Jeremiah. Here, the 'great men' (optimates) have been devoured by a 'lion of the wood' (leo de silva), a wolf (lupus), and a leopard (pardus), which parallels Dante's lonza, leone, and lupa. Jeremiah's beasts were frequently interpreted allegorically as different kinds of sins that beset the citizens of Jerusalem, an interpretation Dante draws on here.[8]

We begin the Commedia, then, in a carefully constructed biblical landscape, one familiar from the lengthy tradition of biblical exegesis and from allegorical composition based on the Bible. The landscape seems abruptly to shift, however, with the appearance of Virgil, who is, naturally, not biblical, and whose self-description undermines any attempt at allegorical identification. He is not Reason or Antiquity, but a pagan poet born at the time of Julius Caesar who wrote the Aeneid. Dante's allegory, as many critics have noted, here makes a turn away from personification allegory toward the 'typological' or 'figural' allegory – what Dante calls the 'allegory of the theologians' in Convivio 2 – of the Bible itself, in which, as we saw in chapter 1, the letter and the spirit are seen to merge together. Characters and events are presented to us as real, but they then come to take on further meaning as these 'things' signify other things.[9] This biblical introduction, then, establishes a background against which we as readers judge the events and characters to follow.[10] Dante and his readers live within the world marked out by the Bible; in the prologue to the poem this world is briefly highlighted for us, but with the appearance of Virgil it recedes (for the most part) into the background. Dante's prologue, however, shows his own understanding of the world as fundamentally biblical. And while Dante has Virgil point to Aristotle's Nicomachean Ethics as the rationale for the organization of hell in Inferno 11, and classical texts such as the Aeneid provide many details of the physical landscape of the infernal realm, the Bible nevertheless provides concrete details of that landscape as well.

The arrangement of the seventh circle seems particularly to have its roots in biblical imagery and events. When the pilgrim, for example, confronts the ruins that characterize the seventh circle, Virgil explains that when he previously descended to the lower circles of hell these ruins did not yet exist; they came about through a great earthquake that occurred just before the harrowing of hell after Christ's death, which Virgil describes as the coming of the one who took the great spoils from the first circle of hell. It was during this earthquake, which was so great Virgil thought that 'l'universo / sentisse amor' ('the universe felt love' [*Inf.* 12.41–2]), that the ruins must have been created. The earthquake refers to the tumult that happened at the time of Christ's crucifixion, recounted in Matthew 27.51. Even Christ's visit to hell to claim the Hebrew patriarchs and other righteous individuals who had died before his death, while elaborated in medieval legends, has a biblical origin (see 1 Peter 3.18–19). Similarly, later in the seventh circle when Dante confronts the sodomites, who are grouped with the violent against nature, they come upon the unnatural sight of fire raining down like snow (see *Inf.* 14.28–30), a detail that Dante no doubt derives from the biblical account of the punishment of Sodom and Gomorrah, when 'the Lord rained upon Sodom and Gomorrah brimstone and fire from the Lord out of heaven' (Gen. 19.24; see also Ezekiel 38.22).

But it is the sinners that the pilgrim encounters who most fully reveal biblical underpinnings. The 'lukewarm' of canto 3, for example, those who reside outside of hell and who 'are envious of every other fate,'[11] are a type identified in the Apocalypse, where the Lord chastises the church of Laodicea for being 'neither cold, nor hot' (3.15–16). Dante's description of these souls as never having been alive (*mai non fur vivi* [3.64]) echoes another part of this same biblical chapter, where the Lord tells the church at Sardis, 'I know thy works, that thou hast the name of being alive: and thou art dead' (3.1).[12] Indeed, the *contrapasso* Dante frames for each damned soul often finds its origins in biblical imagery. The hypocrites in the eighth circle, for example, who appear wearing golden cloaks that turn out to be lined with lead and so are unbearably heavy, may stem from Christ's description of hypocrites in the Gospel of Matthew as 'whited sepulchres, which outwardly appear to men beautiful, but within are full of dead men's bones, and all filthiness' (23.27).[13] Likewise, the false counsellors later in the eighth circle, who are encased in a flame that seems to move 'as if it were a tongue that spoke' (*Inf.* 26.89), may well derive from James's description of the destructiveness of the tongue: 'Behold how small a fire kindleth a great wood. And the tongue is a fire, a world of iniquity' (James 3.5–6).[14] Master Adam, thirsting for 'un gocciol d'acqua' ('a drop of water' [*Inf.* 30.63]), recalls the rich man in the parable of Lazarus, who desires only that Lazarus 'dip the tip of his finger in water, to cool my tongue' (Luke 16.24).[15]

While we recognize the biblical resonance of these and other *contrapassi*, the damned generally do not. Brunetto Latini, for example, seems unperturbed by his place in the seventh circle of hell, wishing only that Dante honour his poem the *Tresor*, 'nel qual io vivo ancora' ('in which I still live' [*Inf.* 15.120]). Off he runs, however, seemingly oblivious, as Dante describes the encounter, to his fate.

> Poi si rivolse e parve di coloro
> che corrono a Verona il drappo verde
> per la campagna; e parve di costoro
>   quelli che vince, non colui che perde.   (*Inf.* 15.121–4)

(And then he turned away, and seemed one of those who run in Verona for the green flag; and he seemed of these the one who wins, not he who loses.)

The image refers to an event contemporary to Dante – the race in Verona that took place on the first Sunday in Lent, but the image of a race also has a biblical force, once again echoing Paul: 'Know ye not that they that run in the race, all run indeed, but one receiveth the prize? So run that you may obtain' (1 Cor. 9.24).[16] Brunetto indeed appears to win the prize, but he is running the wrong race, one for literary immortality ('nel qual io vivo ancora') rather than for the eternal life brought about through Christ. In fact, as we move through Dante's hell, we come to realize fairly quickly that many of the damned, and even, at times, Dante and Virgil, are marked by their inability to grasp or even to see this biblical world that surrounds them, and how they are implicitly judged by it. A brief examination of three episodes in the *Inferno* will provide representative examples.

Misprision in the *Inferno*

Toward the end of their journey through the fifth circle of the *Inferno*, in which the wrathful and sullen are punished, Dante and Virgil board a small boat with a single oarsman to ferry them across the Styx, which separates the first five circles from the gates of the City of Dis, the entrance to the lowest four circles. As they make their way across the river, with the boat unusually weighed down by the pilgrim, one 'full of mud' rises up and addresses Dante, asking who comes before his time. The pilgrim soon recognizes and rebukes him:

> Con piangere e con lutto,
> spirito maladetto, ti rimani;
> ch'i' ti conosco, ancor sie lordo tutto.   (*Inf.* 8.37–9)

(With weeping and with mourning, cursed spirit, remain there; for I know you, even though you are completely filthy.)

Virgil seconds Dante's words by pushing the damned soul, later identified as Filippo Argenti, shoving him away from the boat, telling him to go back 'with the other dogs.' He then embraces the pilgrim around the neck, kissing his face, and praises him: 'Alma sdegnosa, / benedetta colei che 'n te s'incinse' ('Disdainful soul, blessed is she who was pregnant with you' [*Inf.* 8.44–5]). Filippo was a prideful contemporary of Dante (and also a political enemy), who supposedly received his name *Argenti* for having shod his horse with silver horseshoes. Later in the canto he turns his own teeth on himself (see line 62), perhaps illustrating the self-consuming force of wrath.

Interpreters, however, have typically focused not on Filippo, but on Virgil's response in praise of Dante's harsh words to Filippo, especially the biblical echo contained in Virgil's words. Virgil's proclaiming Dante's mother blessed (*benedetta colei che 'n te s'incinse*) recalls Luke 11.27, where a woman in the crowd being taught by Jesus proclaims, 'Blessed is the womb that bore thee' ('beatus venter qui te portavit'). Most commonly, Virgil's words are seen to be an appropriate response to the pilgrim's righteous anger or *buona ira*, what Dante will in Purgatory call *dritto zelo* and *buon zelo* (see *Purg.* 8.83 and 22.9),[17] and Virgil echoes this biblical praise directed toward Jesus in order to make his point. Christopher Kleinhenz, however, has argued that if we examine the biblical words in context, we will come to a different conclusion. Jesus, in fact, responds to the woman's words by correcting her, 'Yea rather, blessed are they who hear the word of God, and keep it' ('quippini beati qui audiunt verbum Dei et custodiunt' [Luke 11.28]). Kleinhenz asks the question, 'If this praise is inappropriate to Jesus, does it not logically follow that, given the parallel context evoked by the reference, such praise should be considered equally inappropriate to Dante the Pilgrim?'[18] May we not, then, conclude that Virgil's response recalls a biblical episode in which the very praise he offers to Dante is criticized for ignoring the actions that alone are praiseworthy – hearing (with the implication of following) the word of God? Dante's response to Filippo should thus be seen as too personally vindictive; the pilgrim remains caught up in the sins he sees, responding with wrath to the wrathful Argenti, just as he reacted in an overly sympathetic manner to Francesca and the lustful in the second circle.[19] Virgil echoes the Bible in a way designed to praise Dante, but he, like many of the rest of the damned in hell, does so ignorant of the larger biblical context in which the words appear, and his words end up having a different force than he intends.

Another example of biblical misprision occurs in the very next circle. As Dante and Virgil move among the tombs that dot hell's sixth circle, they are surprised to hear Farinata degli Uberti suddenly rise up from his sepulchre in order to address Dante:

> O Tosco che per la città del foco
> vivo ten vai così parlando onesto,
> piacciati di restare in questo loco.
>   La tua loquela ti fa manifesto
> di quella nobil patrïa natio,
> a la qual forse fui troppo molesto.   (*Inf.* 10.22–7)

(O Tuscan who, living, pass through the city of fire, speaking honourably, may it please you to stop in this place. Your speech makes it clear that you are native of that noble fatherland, to which I was perhaps too harsh.)

Farinata's words of recognition, 'la tua loquela ti fa manifesto,' are a direct translation of the Vulgate text of Matthew 26.73: 'loquella tua manifestum te facit' ('even thy speech doth discover thee'). The biblical text refers to the last of Peter's three denials of Christ; following his first two declarations that he knew not Christ, he once again was grouped with Jesus, as his Galilean accent betrayed him. Peter immediately, however, 'began to curse and swear that he knew not the man.' These biblical words, therefore, evoke a context of betrayal, important in this canto, concerned as it is with political betrayal. In addition, Kleinhenz has shown that Farinata's use of the word *molesto* recalls another biblical subtext from this very same chapter in Matthew (verse 10), in which Jesus rebukes his disciples, Judas in particular, for troubling Mary Magdalene as she anoints his head with 'precious ointment':

'Quid molesti estis mulieri?' ('Why do you trouble this woman?'). As Kleinhenz notes, 'The sense of betrayal which accompanies the phrase "loquella tua manifestum te facit" and its Dantean analogue is also associated with the term *molesto* because of its direct link with Judas and his treason.'[20]

Furthermore, by linking himself with Peter's interrogators and Dante with Peter, Farinata unwittingly identifies himself as someone who attacks Christ's followers, and identifies Dante as Peter, one who, after denying Christ, turns again to his master in order to devote his life to him and find salvation.[21] Farinata's disbelief or heresy is identified as Epicureanism, which Virgil defines as a denial of the immortality ensured by Christ's sacrifice and resurrection.[22] The heretics are thus imprisoned in tombs that make their sceptical disbelief all too literal. Farinata's simple declaration therefore recalls an entire biblical episode that serves to illustrate his own self-imposed identity of betrayal and mortality.

Moving from Farinata to the final, ninth circle where the treacherous are punished, we find another charismatic sinner, Ugolino, who presents a completely different view to Dante and Virgil. Rather than finding an impassive Stoic who disdains hell itself, Dante comes upon Ugolino as he chews upon the head of Archbishop Ruggieri. In telling his story, moreover, Ugolino insists upon the emotional response of his listeners, though his own recounting of it seems coldly single-minded; he tells the story primarily as a way of wreaking further vengeance upon Ruggieri. But like Farinata, Ugolino misunderstands the words he uses, not sensing the depths of meaning they evoke. Ugolino thus sees in his children's request for bread a simple plea for life-sustaining physical nourishment:

> Quando fui desto innanzi la dimane,
> pianger senti' fra 'l sonno i miei figliuoli
> ch'eran con meco, e dimandar del pane ...
> Io non piangëa, sì dentro impetrai.   (33.37–9, 49)

(When I awoke before morning, I heard my little sons who were with me crying in their sleep and asking for bread ... I did not weep; inside I turned to stone.)

The word 'bread,' however, has profound meaning within the New Testament. When Satan tempts Christ in the wilderness, he suggests that

Christ turn stones into bread and thereby provide a way of satisfying his hunger. Christ's response, 'It is written, that Man liveth not by bread alone, but by every word of God' (Luke 4.4),[23] shows the inadequacy of bread as simply physical nourishment, a point underscored by the interpretation offered in the *Glossa ordinaria*, which explains that Satan appealed to 'cibo corporis' ('food of the body') rather than 'cibo mentis' ('food of the mind'). Later, Christ provides a further spiritual meaning for the word when he identifies himself as the 'bread of life' (*panis vitae*) and the 'living bread come down from heaven' (*panis vivus qui de caelo descendi;* see John 6). When his sons ask Ugolino for bread, therefore, they are seeking far more than breakfast, a fact that becomes apparent later, when his sons see Ugolino biting his hands out of grief, and they offer their own flesh to him:

> Padre, assai ci fia men doglia
> se tu mangi di noi: tu ne vestisti
> queste misere carni, e tu le spoglia. (33.61–3)

> (Father, it would give us less grief if you ate of us; you clothed us in these wretched bodies, and so you strip them off.)

While Ugolino sees in this offer only a pathetic redoubling of his own suffering, the Christian reader sees Christ's willing submission to the cross. Christ's sacrifice is regularly recalled by the Christian faithful at Mass, where, by eating the Eucharist, they literally consume the flesh of Christ. As John Freccero has observed, 'the offer of the children to their father is the same as Christ's offer to his disciples: a spiritual eating of the *living* bread, which absorbs the recipient into the mystical body of Christ.' Ugolino's unbiblical literalism blinds him to the sacrificial meaning of his sons' offer.[24] His children now need spiritual nourishment, the bread of life, much more desperately than they need physical bread.

Further, Ugolino unknowingly betrays his shortcomings in describing his emotional state; his inner petrifaction (described in line 49) recalls Christ's discussion of prayer in the Sermon on the Mount: 'Or what man is there among you, of whom if his son shall ask bread, will he reach him a stone? Or if he shall ask him a fish, will he reach him a serpent? If you then being evil, know how to give good gifts to your children: how much more will your Father who is in heaven, give good things to them that ask him?' (Matthew 7.9–11).[25] The *Glossa ordinaria* finds a spiritual meaning in this verse, reading the *panis* as 'charity or

Christ' in the interlinear gloss and juxtaposing the bread of life with the 'stony' heard-heartedness of those who refuse to become penitent.[26] That is to say, sons ask for the bread of life, and fathers are obligated to provide that bread rather than a stumbling block to their children. When confronted with a request for bread, however, Ugolino can offer only an emotional stone.

Farinata, Ugolino, and even Virgil move within a biblical world, a place charged with spiritual meaning if only they had eyes to see. The damned, however, refer to biblical texts incompletely, as if they remembered them by the same 'bad light' by which, Farinata tells Dante in *Inferno* 10, they are constrained to glimpse the future.[27] Despite their ignorance, they unknowingly bear witness to this world – but how could they not? The Bible, God's written book, defines the world – God's other, fleshly book – and whenever they refer to an object in it – as ordinary an object as bread – or notice someone's identity by his speech, they recall that ignored world. In fact, as Marc Cogan has observed, the very principle of the *contrapasso* exists as an illustration of the Pauline principle enunciated in Galatians, 'for what things a man shall sow, those also shall he reap' (6.8);[28] and it seems to be no accident that Dante has Bertran de Born enunciate and name this principle in the realm that punishes the sowers of discord (see *Inferno* 28.35).

If we return to Master Adam and his biblical thirst for water in the lower reaches of hell, we find that the evocation of the parable of the rich man and Lazarus has implications beyond Adam's *contrapasso*. In that parable, when Abraham tells the rich man that there is a 'great chaos' (*chasma magnum*) that separates the damned from the saved, the rich man then asks that Lazarus be sent to his father's house, to warn his brothers of the torment that awaits them, as Lazarus insists that if 'one went to them from the dead, they will do penance.' Abraham refuses this request as well, since 'if they hear not Moses and the prophets, neither will they believe, if one rise again from the dead' (Luke 16.27–31).[29] We have already seen Dante's frustration, in the *Monarchia*, the Epistles, and the *Paradiso*, with those who ignore biblical warnings, who 'hear not Moses and the prophets.' Similarly, the biblical episode to which Virgil's words to Dante in the Filippo Argenti encounter refer also focuses on those that 'hear the word of God.' Dante believes that, in his day, too few hear the scriptures, and he hopes that his poem can help restore the force of the Bible, can influence his readers to hear them. In addition, while Dante has not risen from the dead, he nevertheless claims to be one who comes 'from the dead,' bringing a biblical message.

As we have seen, for much of the *Inferno* Dante illustrates the nature of sin, and of the sinners the pilgrim encounters, by twisting the Bible, placing garbled and distorted echoes of biblical texts in the mouths of the damned and creating an infernal landscape from misshapen reflections of scriptural imagery. Nevertheless, the biblical message of repentance comes through, usually implicitly, through allusions and reminiscences, and even in the misprisions of hell's sinners.[30] Dante the poet creates in the *Inferno* a world haunted by the memory of the biblical world, which shows through just sufficiently to show us how the damned have misunderstood and warped it. By uncovering for us as readers (as well as for the pilgrim) the 'lost people' (*perdute genti* [see *Purg.* 30.138]), the poet may help us to come to understand sin and to end our wanderings and turn toward God and live. There is, however, one place in the *Inferno* – canto 19 – where Dante asserts his biblical message much more directly. The remainder of this chapter will therefore be devoted to a careful reading of the biblical presence in that canto.

The Bible in *Inferno* 19

This canto, which details Dante's journey through the third *bolgia* of the eighth circle, contains material central to the *Inferno* and to the poem as a whole. The pilgrim's interrogation of Nicholas III constitutes Dante's first extended consideration of the contemporary state of the church; his use of apocalyptic imagery likewise inaugurates a discourse that will become central to the two remaining canticles. As if to signal its importance, Dante works to set this canto off from those that surround it. The opening lines create a distinction between the previous canto, which ends with the portrayal of the damned flatterers – a notably 'comic' episode, in which the linguistic sin of the damned leads to Dante's crudely realistic use of the words *merda* and *unghie merdose* – and the canto of the simonists, which Dante opens with an apostrophe to Simon Magus that signals a new pouch, theme, and tone:

> O Simon mago, o miseri seguaci
> che le cose di Dio, che di bontate
> deon essere spose, e voi rapaci
>   per oro e per argento avolterate,
> or convien che per voi suoni la tromba,
> però che ne la terza bolgia state.   (19.1–6)

(O Simon Magus, o wretched followers that the things of God, which should be brides of goodness, you rapacious ones adulterate for gold and for silver; now it is time that the trumpet sound for you, as you are in the third pouch.)

The new tone is signalled in part through the direct apostrophe of a biblical figure, an anticipation of the numerous biblical citations, references, and echoes that will follow and that make this canto by far the most biblical in the first canticle.[31] The sinners inhabiting this *bolgia* are in fact explicitly identified according to a biblical type; Simon Magus's attempt to purchase the gifts of the Holy Spirit from Peter (recounted in Acts 8.14–24) defines the buying and selling of church offices in which the simonists (named, of course, for Simon) engage. But this biblical type becomes inverted as we proceed; in the episode from the Book of Acts involving Simon, the first pope Peter the apostle rebukes Simon for his attempt to buy the power to confer the Holy Ghost, telling him that he will perish with his money since he thought that 'the gift of God may be purchased with money' ('donum Dei existimasti pecunia possideri' [8.20]). In canto 19, however, Nicholas III – a pope guilty of simony – undergoes examination by a layman.[32] The inversion of biblical roles mirrors the popes' own inverted and perverted use of the things of God, which the popes have transformed from lawful spouses of Christ to whores, set out to serve the highest bidder. Indeed, Nicholas admits that his governing motivation while 'clothed with the highest mantle' was avarice. The poverty of the first pope, however, is a matter of biblical record; Peter explicitly claimed *not* to possess silver and gold, the very substances that Nicholas and his fellow simonists seek in adulterating 'le cose di Dio.'[33] The first six lines of the canto lead us to expect a canto of inversions, in which the appropriate and divinely ordained relationship between the church, her Lord, and the goods of this world is – quite literally – turned on its head.[34]

Dante makes an interesting choice in portraying only popes in the nineteenth canto (while Nicholas III is the only sinner directly portrayed in the canto, the future damnation of both Boniface VIII and Clement V is discussed). Simony was a widespread practice in the late thirteenth and early fourteenth centuries, and Dante's limited portrayal of simonists suggests that he sees the pope as responsible for the corruption of the entire church.[35] As head of the church, he puts the things of God on the selling block; those local leaders who commit simony are simply following the pope's lead. Even the canto's *contrapasso* echoes the specifically papal practice of inverting spiritual and temporal; Nicholas's scorched feet recall the biblical day of Pentecost, when tongues of flame descended onto the apostles. As we should expect, however, the image is inverted; the apostles received the Holy Ghost through the tongues of fire on their heads in order to help them govern and direct the growing church of Christ; for the papal simonist, however, the flames punish the feet of one who has failed to guide the church as Christ ordained.

Nicholas reinforces this emphasis on papal responsibility when he taunts the pilgrim, mistaking him for Boniface:

> Se' tu sì tosto di quell' aver sazio
> per lo qual non temesti tòrre a 'nganno
> la bella donna, e poi di farne strazio?   (19.55–7)

(Have you been so quickly inundated with that wealth for which you did not fear to take the beautiful woman with deceit and then to prostitute her?)

In these lines the main image of the canto – the prostitution of the bride of Christ – is again repeated. This image is, of course, biblical, deriving most immediately from the Song of Songs, which was frequently interpreted in the Middle Ages as a song from the Lord to his bride the church.[36] Dante joins this image to another frequent image of marriage in the Old Testament, that of a straying Israel as an unfaithful spouse who goes 'whoring after other gods.' A typical example is found in Ezekiel 16:8, 14–15:

> And I passed by thee, and saw thee: and behold thy time was the time of lovers: and I spread my garment over thee, and covered thy ignominy. And I swore to thee, and I entered into a covenant with thee, saith the Lord God: and thou becamest mine ... And thy renown went forth among the nations for thy beauty: for thou wast perfect through my beauty, which I had put upon thee, saith the Lord God. But trusting in thy beauty, thou playedst the harlot because of thy renown, and thou hast prostituted thyself to every passenger, to be his.[37]

While several Old Testament prophets employ this image, it is most fully exploited in the opening three chapters of Hosea, where the prophet recounts that God had commanded him to marry a prostitute so that his marriage and offspring would become signs of Israel's infidelity. Dante was drawn to this language when criticizing church corruption; in his bitter letter to the Italian cardinals that was discussed briefly in chapter 1, for example, Dante blames the wretched state of Rome on the corruption of the ecclesiastical hierarchy, as each cardinal 'has taken to himself greed (*cupiditatem*) as a wife, who is the mother, not of piety and equity, as is charity, but of impiety and iniquity.'[38] Dante adapts this image, however, by adding a fourth participant to the Bible's triangular structure; instead of Israel prostituting itself, abandoning her husband for the allure of foreign gods, Dante creates a pimp, who, by all appearances, sells the woman against her own wishes. According to Nicholas, before Boniface sells her, the church is a 'bella donna.'

After Dante corrects Nicholas's mistaken identification, Nicholas quickly sets himself off from the other sinners Dante meets in the *Inferno* in his willingness to blame himself for his sins and recognize his own responsibility for being in hell: 'fui [. . .] /cupido sì per avanzar li orsatti, / che sù l'avere e qui me misi in borsa' ('I . . . was so greedy to advance the cubs that up above, wealth, and here, myself, I placed in a purse' [19.70–2]). And if he, like other sinners, eagerly casts blame on his fellow simonists as he details the anticipated arrivals of Boniface and Clement V, Dante elevates the tone of Nicholas's discourse so that it finishes on a note of biblical, prophetic denunciation:

> ché dopo lui verrà di più laida opra,
> di ver' ponente, un pastor sanza legge,
> tal che convien che lui e me ricuopra.
>   Nuovo Iasón sarà, di cui si legge
> ne' Maccabei; e come a quel fu molle
> suo re, così fia lui chi Francia regge.   (19.82–7)

(and after him will come one of uglier works, from the west, a pastor without law, such that he will suitably cover both him and me. He will be a new Jason, of whom is read in the Maccabees, and as to that one his king was pliant, so to this one shall be he who rules France.)

Nicholas's discourse would sit equally well in the mouth of Beatrice or Peter in their later, biblically inspired diatribes against church corruption. In these lines, Dante has Nicholas criticize a specific pope by aligning him with a biblical figure, just as Dante opened the canto by associating the simonist popes with Simon Magus. Jason, the brother of the high priest in the second century BCE, bought the priesthood from the Seleucid king Antiochus IV, whom he then worked to please by hellenizing Jewish religious practice, including temple worship (the story is recounted in 2 Maccabees 4). Bertran de Got recapitulates this biblical type and thus becomes a 'new Jason' when he is elected pope in 1305 and proceeds to act in the interests of Philip the Fair, condemning and dissolving, for example, the Knights Templar so that Philip could control their considerable assets, and moving the seat of the papacy to Avignon, which, while not in control of the French king, was under the governance of Philip's vassals, the Angevin kings of Naples. In Dante's letter to the Italian cardinals, he similarly accuses Clement of perverting the true religion of Israel in order to gain favour with the secular ruler (and the cardinals for complicity with him) with an allusion to the same period of Israelite history, this time linking Clement with Alcimus and Philip with Demetrius (see 1 Maccabees 7).[39] These allusions, in other words, tie the events of Dante's day to the Bible; in this instance, even the damned Nicholas sees church history in terms of biblical precedents.

Prior to this speech, Dante's use of the Bible had been consonant with that found throughout the *Inferno*, a use characterized by inverted allusions and perverted biblical examples. Nicholas's speech, however, marks a more straightforward use of the biblical text, one that works to introduce a more elevated, biblical tone into the canto. Thus, Nicholas's biblical discourse is, to say the least, unusual in the mouth of one of the damned. It serves, however, to set the stage for the pilgrim, who begins where Nicholas leaves off, denouncing the papal simonists with a flurry of biblical examples. The poet prefaces his account of his words as pilgrim, however, with an aside that retrospectively doubts the decorum of his words: 'Io non so s'i' mi fui qui troppo folle, / ch'i' pur rispuosi lui a questo metro' ('I do not know if I was here too foolish, that I answered him in this way' [19.88–9]). As Umberto Bosco has shown in his classic essay on Dante's 'follia,' Dante's folly or madness here and throughout the poem refers not to a condition of mental instability but to 'a certain spiritual attitude' characterized by a transgressive desire to exceed lawful limits, a meaning reinforced here by the qualifier 'troppo.'[40] Critics have tended to read this 'madness' as referring to Dante's attack on ecclesiastical authority, his regret for having criticized one who was 'vestito del gran manto.' The pilgrim indeed goes on to claim that he refrains from harsher language because of his respect for the authority of Nicholas's earthly office:

> E se non fosse ch'ancor lo mi vieta
> la reverenza de le somme chiavi
> che tu tenesti ne la vita lieta,
>> io userei parole ancor più gravi.   (19.100–3)

(And if the reverence for the highest keys that you held during the happy life did not prohibit it to me, I would use even harsher words.)

Dante's self-proclaimed reticence here may remind us of his ostensible disavowal of being like Aeneas and Paul in canto 2 ('Io non Enëa, io non Paulo sono') (2.32). There, while claiming not to resemble the two most famous voyagers to the afterlife, the pilgrim actually draws attention to the ways in which he resembles Aeneas and Paul. Here, the poet's reservations about speaking serve to focus our attention on the audacity of the words that follow, in which a layman offers a harsh critique of papal leadership.[41]

But Dante's words do not spring simply from his own authority; he draws extensively on the Bible to demonstrate how contemporary popes fail to measure up to their biblical predecessor, the first pope Saint Peter:

> Deh, or mi dì: quanto tesoro volle
> Nostro Segnore in prima da san Pietro
> ch'ei ponesse le chiavi in sua balìa?
> Certo non chiese se non 'Viemmi retro.'
> Né Pier né li altri tolsero a Matia
> oro od argento, quando fu sortito
> al loco che perdé l'anima ria.
> Però ti sta, ché tu se' ben punito;
> e guarda ben la mal tolta moneta
> ch'esser ti fece contra Carlo ardito.   (19.90–9)

(Now, tell me: how much treasure did Our Lord want from Saint Peter before he gave the keys into his keeping? Certainly he asked nothing but 'follow me.' Neither Peter nor the others took gold or silver from Matthias when he was chosen for the place that the guilty soul lost. Stay there then, as you are well punished; and keep well the ill-gotten money that made you bold against Charles.)

The first tercet refers to two different passages in the Gospels: Jesus' consigning of the keys of the kingdom to Peter (found in Matthew 16.13–20) and his earlier invitation to Peter and Andrew to 'come after him' and become his disciples (see Matthew 4.18–19 and Mark 2.16–17); but these two work together to make the central point: in appointing the first pope, the Lord asked nothing but discipleship.

The second example recounts a similar instance of the conferral of priestly office, this time by Peter himself. When Matthias was chosen to replace Judas Iscariot to join the twelve apostles, Peter's sole concern was that the new apostle be an appropriate witness: 'Wherefore of these men who have companied with us all the time that the Lord Jesus came in and went out among us, beginning from the baptism of John, until the day wherein he was taken up from us, one of these must be made a witness with us of his resurrection' (Acts 1.21–2).[42] The contrast between biblical worthiness and present-day wickedness becomes obvious in the light of these scriptures. *Oro* and *argento* only become conspicuous in Acts by their absence, since Peter insists that he has none (Acts 3.6). Indeed, Christ himself told his apostles, including Peter, 'Do not possess gold, nor silver, nor money in your purses' (Matthew 10.9).[43] This biblically inspired rhetoric anticipates the use of the Bible by reformers in the sixteenth century, in that the Bible alone (*sola Scriptura*) – rather than the church and its traditions – is accepted as normative. Thus Nicholas's greedy actions that led to the Sicilian vespers simply cannot be defended in the light of the biblical model of apostolic and hence what should be papal behaviour.[44] Dante's sarcastic reinforcement of Nicholas's damnation fits directly into this biblical context and recalls Jesus' verdict on those who pursue good works for worldly gain, 'they have received their reward,' as well as echoing Peter's rebuke to Simon, 'keep thy money to thyself, to perish with thee,' a statement that is even stronger in the Vulgate: 'pecunia tua tecum sit in perditionem' (Acts 8.20). Dante the lay poet/prophet places himself directly into Peter's shoes and rebukes Peter's successor with language that is very close to Peter's own.

As Peter Hawkins notes, 'this is an extraordinarily confident denunciation,'[45] but Dante effectively masks its boldness through both the disclaimer that the poet provides before reporting the pilgrim's speech and the pilgrim's own assertion that he is restraining his language because of reverence for the papal office. Indeed, one is tempted here to agree with William Franke that Dante as poet steps aside in this address, giving place to the scriptures and therefore 'letting that Other who alone can make the poem truly prophetic be heard in it, not in rhetorically elaborate speech, but in the biblical *sermo humilis*.'[46] But Dante's accusation and, above all, his implicit association of his own judgment with Peter's work against this view. And as we shall see, as the pilgrim finishes with his invective, he returns to the Bible, but in a way that suggests that he is hardly simply letting the scriptures speak while he steps aside.

Dante returns to the New Testament, this time to the Apocalypse of John, as he continues his invective:

> Di voi pastor s'accorse il Vangelista,
> quando colei che siede sopra l'acque
> puttaneggiar coi regi a lui fu vista;
>   quella che con le sette teste nacque,
> e da le diece corna ebbe argomento,
> fin che virtute al suo marito piacque.   (19.106–111)

(The Evangelist saw you pastors, when she who sits on the waters fornicating with kings was seen by him; she who was born with seven heads, and who had strength from the ten horns, as long as virtue pleased her husband.)

Dante's language here recalls the first three verses of chapter 17 of the Apocalypse:

> And there came one of the seven angels, who had the seven vials, and spoke with me, saying: Come, I will shew thee the condemnation of the great harlot, who sitteth upon many waters, With whom the kings of the earth have committed fornication; And they who inhabit the earth, have been made drunk with the wine of her whoredom. And he took me away in spirit into the desert. And I saw a woman sitting upon a scarlet coloured beast, full of names of blasphemy, having seven heads and ten horns.[47]

In traditional medieval exegesis, this passage describes the time of the Antichrist, who is represented by the *meretrix magna*. As the *Glossa ordinaria* reads verse 1, the harlot refers to some yet undetermined Antichrist (*Meretrix ista magna est Antichristus*); the lack of specificity is typical of the mainstream interpretation of the book in the medieval church. While in the early Christian church of the third and fourth centuries, especially before Constantine's edict of Milan, the Apocalypse was read literally and eschatologically, later the book began to be read more generally, as an allegory of the church. Saint Augustine, while certainly accepting the reality of a second coming of Christ in the flesh and a final judgment, followed the lead of the Donatist theologian and commentator Tyconius and argued that the Apocalypse actually refers to the tribulations of the kingdom of God on the earth, that is of the church, and not to a timeline of catastrophic events that will usher in a literal, millennial reign of Christ. Augustine's reading proved formative, as most medieval commentators followed his lead in reading the book.[48] Beginning with Joachim of Fiore, however, a more historical reading of the book became prominent in the Middle Ages, in which the Apocalypse was understood to refer to specific historical events that precede the coming of the Antichrist and, for Joachim, the inauguration of a new, third age of world history – the age of the Holy Spirit – which would be characterized by a millennial period of peace. Joachim had a profound influence, especially on the group normally called the Spiritual Franciscans, who exercised an important but debated influence on Dante.[49] I will leave a more thorough consideration of Dante's apocalypticism and its relation to medieval traditions to the final chapter, referring to medieval tradition here only enough to understand Dante's revisions of the Apocalypse in canto 19.

If we compare, then, the moralized reading of the Apocalpyse that was prominent in the earlier Middle Ages to Dante's use of the book in these six lines, we immediately note that Dante's account of the opening of Apocalypse 17 is specific and literal. The evangelist – John the Revelator – saw Nicholas III and the other corrupt popes of his day. Dante here may be following the Spiritual Franciscans in general and their most famous exegete Peter John Olivi in particular. In his commentary on the Apocalpyse, Olivi too sees in the whore of Apocalypse 17 an image of the corrupt church: 'she is therefore called a great prostitute, because withdrawing from the faithful worship and genuine love and delights of the God Christ her bridegroom, she clings to this age and its delights and riches and the devil and even the kings and magnates and prelates and all other lovers of this world.'[50] Indeed many Franciscans identified the contemporary church, and the pope in particular, with the Antichrist.[51]

Unlike Olivi, however, who while criticizing the church leadership stays close to the biblical text, Dante uses the Apocalypse to indict the simonist prelates in a manner that is surprising. Indeed, it may be that his appropriation of the biblical text proves even more 'extraordinarily confident' than do his criticisms of papal simony. His transformations begin with the harlot herself; whereas in the biblical account the harlot seems intrinsically corrupt, in Dante's refashioning we must assume her to have been a woman who was originally good but who has become corrupt through the urging of another. If we link, for example, the harlot of lines 107–8 (*colei che siede sopra l'acque*) with the *bella donna* of line 57, whom Nicholas mentions to the pilgrim, mistaking him for Boniface, we see in both cases the image of a woman transformed through the demands of a male figure. In Nicholas's words, the church was originally a *bella donna*, whose corruption has come about through Boniface, who took her by deceit in his fraudulent deception of his predecessor in influencing him to abdicate.[52] This image of the virtuous woman corrupted is used by Dante in the culmination of his invective against Nicholas, as he transforms the image of the whore of Apocalypse 17. In the biblical text, the whore is not portrayed as corrupted, but as sitting upon a coloured beast, which has seven heads and ten horns, later interpreted within the same chapter as 'the seven mountains, upon which the woman sitteth: and they are seven kings' and 'ten kings' that 'shall fight with the Lamb.'[53] The generally negative view of these details is reinforced in the *Glossa ordinaria*, which reads the seven heads of the whore, for example, as 'the senses and then error, and finally the Antichrist, through which seven things the devil leads men into sin.'[54]

Dante, however, changes all of these details. First, he abandons the beast and replaces it with a husband, not found in the biblical text. Second, he moves the heads and horns, which in the Apocalypse appear on the beast, to the woman herself and gives them a positive value, a conclusion that follows from the fact that the woman received strength from them 'as long as virtue pleased her husband.' Most commentators, therefore, identify the 'diece corna' as the ten commandments and the 'sette teste' as the seven gifts of the Holy Spirit or the seven sacraments.[55] Some medieval commentators of Revelation 17 identified the woman's seven heads with the seven capital sins;[56] if Dante's purpose here is to create a positive value for the heads (at least until corruption sets in), identifying them with one of the sevens of medieval Christianity is plausible. Finally, he implicitly assigns to the husband the responsibility for the fornication of the woman. Given the fact that the language of fornication and prostitution has been used throughout the canto to signify papal simony, the most common identification of the husband – as the pope – is most likely correct, a likelihood reinforced by the link between Dante's language here and that directed by Nicholas toward Boniface at lines 55–7, and made more certain by the logic of Dante's words: the evangelist noted you (papal) pastors when he saw the woman sitting upon the waters. Likewise, the link between these lines strongly underscores the identification of the woman sitting upon the waters as the church, rather than the city of Rome, another difference between the text of the Apocalypse and Dante's use of it here.[57]

Some of these details can be found in one form or another in the Bible itself or in the commentary tradition of Apocalypse 17. The merging of the whore and the beast, for example, seems common enough. Olivi, for example, writes in his commentary that 'this woman, inasmuch as she is carnal and bestial is called a beast; truly, inasmuch as she was set above and ruled over the bestial peoples of the world and, furthermore, as she is lord over more bestial peoples that are placed under her, she is said to sit on the beast' (828).[58] Furthermore, Dante may have discovered the possibility that the whore of Apocalypse 17 was originally an innocent woman who has been corrupted by associating her with the woman who appears in Apocalypse 12. This woman is described as a 'great sign' (*signum magnum*), who is 'clothed with the sun, and the moon under her feet, and on her head a crown of twelve stars.' While she is in the travails of childbirth, a great dragon appears 'having seven heads and ten horns and on his heads seven diadems.' After taking the third part of the stars of heaven and casting them to the earth, he stands before the woman 'that, when she should be delivered, he might devour her son.' The woman delivers a child 'who was to rule the nations with an iron rod,' and he is 'taken up to God and to his throne.' The woman then flees to the wilderness, to a place prepared for her by God. This woman was usually identified, as she is the *Glossa ordinaria,* with the church, and the conflict between the woman and the dragon was read as representing the struggles of the early church. Dante seems to take this woman of Apocalypse 12 and to read her into the harlot of chapter 17, thereby creating the image of a church corrupted. The husband, however, cannot be accounted for by a reference to the biblical text.[59]

There remains one further way in which Dante's image of the whore relates to biblical images, especially to the Old Testament image of an unfaithful Israel: both images are related to idolatry. In the Old Testament, Israel's 'prostitution' most frequently refers to God's people forsaking him for the gods of other nations, an idolatry that could be manifested either in syncretic cultic practices or in political alliances that – for the prophets – demonstrated a lack of faith in Israel's God.[60] Dante links papal avarice to idolatry, since the popes treat riches as gods:

Fatto v'avete dio d'oro e d'argento;
e che altro è da voi a l'idolatre,
se non ch'elli uno, e voi ne orate cento?   (*Inf.* 19.112–14)

(You have made yourselves a god of gold and silver; and what difference
is there between you and an idolater, if not that that he worships one and
you a hundred gods?)

Dante likewise bases this tercet on a biblical text, Hosea 8.4: 'of their
silver, and their gold they have made idols to themselves.'[61] Dante's
final blaming of the Donation of Constantine for many of the woes of
the church may seem to deflect attention away from the idolatry of
papal simony, but that is not the case, as the two were firmly linked
in Dante's mind. In his only systematic discussion of the Donation,
found in *Monarchia* 3.10, Dante did not deny the document's authenticity but argued against it as legally binding for either Constantine or
Pope Sylvester. Constantine could not legally divest himself of control of the empire, since that would violate the very purpose of his office. The pope, on the other hand, was bound not to accept it, since
the 'Church was in any event not designed for the receiving of temporal things because of an express command of prohibition' found in
scriptural passages such as Matthew 10.9 cited above.[62] The problem
with the Donation is that it should never have been accepted in the first
place, but papal avarice has twisted Constantine's good intentions to
'so much evil' (*quanto male*).

What, then, are we to make of Dante's biblically charged discourse,
which uses the Bible in a way and to an extent that is unseen elsewhere
in the poem's first canticle? The key to this question lies, I suggest, in his
rewriting of Apocalypse 17 in lines 106–11. Biblical antecedents can be
found for most of Dante's changes, but what may be most remarkable
is Dante's insistence that his words are those of John himself – he opens
his rewriting of Apocalypse 17 with the assertion that he will simply
be reporting John's vision of the corrupt popes ('Di voi pastor s'accorse
il Vangelista') – even while, as I have tried to show, he imaginatively
recombines a number of biblical texts and images to form a new, and
different, version of Apocalypse 17. It is this marking of the text as biblical, his insistence that he summarizes what John saw, that sets Dante's
intertextual practice apart from that of other medieval writers who frequently rewrote the Bible in their works.[63] Evidently, as Dante sought
and failed to find a scriptural text that would unequivocally condemn

papal simony, he created one instead, writing of a wife who becomes a whore through the urging of her husband. This is not to say that Dante's message departs radically from the biblical text, as his more straightforward use of biblical examples shows. The whore of chapter 17 portrays the persecution of the church of Christ; Dante alters the text in order to preserve that message for his own day, as the greatest persecutor of the church of Christ in the early fourteenth century was the leadership of the church itself. Dante's reworking, in other words, seeks to preserve the 'originary' authority of the Bible and even to extend it to his own reworking of it, 'updating' the message of the Apocalypse to make it relevant to his contemporaries.[64]

He accomplishes this remarkable task by saturating the pilgrim's speech with biblical examples and allusions and by insisting that his own words that change the Apocalypse are actually those of John the Revelator. He then 'frames' his biblical alteration with another more or less straightforward translation of a biblical text. Dante's rewriting constitutes not a parody but an *appropriation* – an attempt to make the Bible his own so as to make it new, so that it speaks directly to what, in his mind, constitutes the most serious problem of the church. The fact that virtually none of Dante's near contemporaries even noted Dante's changes[65] – and that they have evoked little critical response since[66] – marks Dante's success, since his purpose was not to call attention to but to conceal the fact of transformation and thus preserve its biblical authority.

The Bible thus exists in the *Inferno* in at least two primary manifestations – the allusive misprision of scripture by the damned and Dante's appropriation of it here. Both uses are, in their way, miscitations, but their functions differ profoundly. In other places in hell, the damned reveal their ignorance of and yet rootedness in a world defined and delimited by the Bible. Dante's transformation in *Inferno* 19, on the other hand, is both conscious and willful, and it is ultimately paradoxical, at least on the surface, for he claims both the licence to change the Bible *and* the originary authority belonging to the word of God. Dante's freedom is authoritative. But this freedom arises only out of a profound meditation on the Bible and on its final book in particular. Dante seeks the meaning of the living Bible for himself and for his readers, and to bring that meaning to the surface he appropriates the text and makes it his own and thereby makes it new even while he retains its larger truth. The meaning of the Apocalypse in canto 19 relates not (or no longer) to the persecution of the early Christians; it refers now to the corruption at the church's highest levels, a danger far more potent than external harassment. In order to communicate the immediate reality of that danger to the church, he turns to the Bible, but changes it so as to reveal its enduring meaning anew.

The practice of intertextual citation in which a sacred text is miscited and yet retains its authority is itself biblical. Gerhard von Rad, for example, has shown that the biblical prophets both transformed and extended the traditions that they inherited so as to make room for their own message: 'the comfortable words of the tradition . . . are both called into question by the prophet's message of judgment and reconverted by him into an anti-typical new form of predication.'[67] Von Rad's analysis has been further confirmed and deepened by Michael Fishbane's account of what he calls 'inner-biblical exegesis,' the Bible's commentary on itself, which is often found in prophetic books. Jeremiah 17.21–2 serves as an apt example:

> Thus saith the Lord: Take heed to your souls and carry no burdens on the sabbath day: and bring them not in by the gates of Jerusalem. And do not bring burdens out of your houses on the sabbath day: neither do ye any work: sanctify the sabbath day, as I commanded your fathers.

Jeremiah seems to refer here to the prohibition of work on the Sabbath found in the Decalogue, specifically from its deuteronomic version (see Deuteronomy 5.12–14). The commandments that Jeremiah highlights, however, are nowhere to be found; the injunction against bearing burdens (and then selling them), for example, is absent. Fishbane's analysis of these verses throws light onto the intertextual methods of both Jeremiah and Dante:

> The more remarkable fact is that the divine voice adverts to the deuteronomic text ('as I commanded your forefathers') as if to emphasize the antiquity of the prohibition. For, by this means, the divine voice speaking through Jeremiah does not just reinforce the prohibition or merely cite Deut. 5.12 ('as YHWH . . . commanded you') but *uses* this quotation-tag to authorize the legal innovation and imply that the Sabbath rule now articulated – with its additions – is the very same that was taught at Sinai! The new teachings are authorized by a pseudo-citation from the Pentateuch, spoken with divine authority.[68]

Like Jeremiah, Dante uses a 'quotation-tag' ('Di voi pastor s'accorse il Vangelista') to authorize his prophetic revision and to imply that *his* innovation was actually intended and foreseen by the author of the sacred text.

Dante's 'violence' with the text here may perhaps be metaphorically anticipated by the famous and disputed autobiographical episode that he recalls earlier in the canto, when he briefly recounts his breaking of the baptismal structure in the Florence baptistery. He compares the holes in the *bolgia* to those in the baptistery:

> Non mi parean men ampi né maggiori
> che que' che son nel mio bel San Giovanni,
> fatti per loco d'i battezzatori;
>   l'un de li quali, ancor non è molt' anni,
> rupp'io per un che dentro v'annegava:
> e questo sia suggel ch'ogn' omo sganni.   (19.16–21)

(They did not appear to me less or more large than those that are in my beautiful San Giovanni, made as the place for the *battezzatori;* one of which, not many years ago, I broke for the sake of one who was drowning there; and let this be the seal that every man is undeceived.)

However one views the 'battezzatori' (whether as the priests who perform the baptisms or the holes in which the priests placed and baptized the infants),[69] the importance of the episode lies in what it reveals about Dante. External violence to the church is necessary in order to save the souls within it, just as his violence with respect to the scriptures serves a larger purpose in saving the church from papal avarice and in ultimately preserving the force of the scriptures themselves.

If we place this canto in opposition to the surrounding cantos, some interesting parallels emerge. Canto 18, for example, describes the first two pouches of the *Malebolge,* the seducers and the flatterers. Flattery obviously constitutes a sinful and deceitful use of language for personal gain, but Dante also portrays the seducers as being guilty primarily of a *linguistic* sin. When Virgil describes, for example, the reason for Jason's damnation, he notes that he successfully deceived the women he seduced through his *parole ornate* or 'accomplished words':

> Ivi con segni e con parole ornate
> Isifile ingannò, la giovinetta
> che prima avea tutte l'altre ingannate.   (18.91–3)

(There with signs and accomplished words he deceived Hypsipyle, the young woman who first had deceived all the others.)

In the following canto, however, Dante differentiates his words from those deceitful if accomplished words employed by Jason in his enterprise of seduction:

> I' credo ben ch'al mio duca piacesse,
> con sì contenta labbia sempre attese
> lo suon de le parole vere espresse.   (19.121–3)

(I believe that my words were well pleasing to my leader, he heard with such a contented face the sound of the true words.)

Dante's language in this canto, using words derived from and based upon the Bible, is specifically defined as true and differentiated from the fraudulent use of language found in the first and second *bolge* of the eighth circle.

Likewise, whereas in canto 19 Dante delivers a prophetic denunciation, in canto 20 he devotes his attention to the diviners and false prophets. The bulk of this canto, however, is given over to Virgil's extended account of his own, revised version of his native city's founding that corrects the account found in the *Aeneid*. Virgil finishes this account with this injunction to the pilgrim:

> Però t'assenno che, se tu mai odi
> originar la mia terra altrimenti,
> la verità nulla menzogna frodi.   (20.97–9)

(Therefore I urge you, if you ever hear of my land originating in another way, do not let any lie defraud the truth.)

As Teodolinda Barolini has argued, 'According to Vergil's own statement then, the *Aeneid* is a text that – like the false prophets of this *bolgia* – is capable of defrauding the truth.'[70] It is at this very moment that Dante has Virgil label the *Aeneid* a 'high tragedy' (*l'alta mia tragedìa* [20.113]), which he shortly thereafter juxtaposes with his own 'comedy,' naming it for the second time in the opening of the following canto (21.2). If in canto 20 Dante overtly corrects his pagan predecessor in order to assert the truth of his own poem and distance it from Virgil's 'menzogna,' he works in canto 19 to narrow the distance between his poem and the Bible.[71] Dante uses the sinners portrayed in the neighbouring cantos to define himself against them. Unlike the seducer Jason and the false prophets, Dante is immersed in the biblical text and speaks the truth out of the world of that book.[72]

Dante, then, works to present himself as a 'true' prophet, not one who has privileged access to the future but rather one who speaks *parole vere*. It is in this particular sense of 'prophet' that one may speak of Dante; for whatever else one may say about Dante's identity as a prophet,[73] he follows the prophetic model of citing sacred texts. As Dante himself noted, the ancient prophets wrote poetry,[74] and like them, he feels the call of God and the urgency to speak God's word to his readers. In order to do so, he, like biblical prophets, turns to texts sacred to his audience and changes them so that their underlying message is revealed anew. It turns out that we have lost sight of the sacred message, have relegated it to the past; only now can we understand how vital it is to our own time, how it contains the remedies for our spiritual illness. The word is both new and old; we have all heard this message of repentance before, but not in quite this way. Now it is directed to our own sins, our own failings, our own corruption, and it is we who must turn to God and live.

4 *Una nuova legge:*
The Beatitudes in the *Purgatorio*

If, as suggested in chapter 3, the Bible exists in the *Inferno* largely through the misprision, misallusion, and misunderstanding that characterizes the use of the Bible by the damned, we should – following the critical commonplace – expect with the resurrection of Dante's 'morta poesì' in the *Purgatorio* a corresponding redemption of biblical intertextuality. If the infernal shades by and large refer to scripture only obliquely, the souls on Mount Purgatory should reveal a profound grasp of the divine *verbum* and its relevance to their own situations. And indeed, with the first citation of the Latin Bible in the entire poem (which occurs in the second canto of *Purgatorio*), we encounter the unmediated biblical text. As Dante and Virgil watch a 'celestial nocchiero' ('celestial steersman') guide a boat with more than a hundred shades safely onto the shores of Mount Purgatory, they hear the passengers sing the 113th Psalm:

> '*In exitu Isräel de Aegypto*'
> cantavan tutti insieme ad una voce
> con quanto di quel salmo è poscia scripto.   (*Purg.* 2.46–8)

('*When Israel went out of Egypt*' all sang together in one voice with the rest of the Psalm that is written afterwards.)

The Psalm recounts the story of the exodus, which medieval exegetes found to be a pervasive *figura* or type: the exodus refers not only to the literal history of Moses leading the children of Israel out of bondage but also to the individual Christian soul and its forsaking the bondage of sin for the free, promised land of salvation offered by Christ. Indeed, Dante himself glossed the Psalm in precisely this way at the opening of the second book of the *Convivio*, where he makes the distinction between the allegories of the poets and of the theologians discussed in chapter 1. The Psalm, it will be recalled, serves to illustrate the anagogical sense:

> ... per le cose significate significa de le superne cose de l'etternal gloria: sì come vedere si può in quello canto del Profeta che dice che, ne l'uscita del popolo d'Israel d'Egitto, Giudea è fatta santa e libera. Che avvegna essere vero secondo la lettera sia manifesto, non meno è vero quello che spiritual- mente s'intende, cioè che ne l'uscita de l'anima dal peccato, essa sia fatta santa e libera in sua potestate. (*Conv.* 2.1.6–7)

> (... which signifies by the signified things the supernal matters of eternal glory, which can be seen in that song of the Prophet, which says that, in the exodus of the people of Israel from Egypt, Judah was made free and holy. While it is manifest that this is true according to a literal reading, that which is spiritually intended is no less true, that is, in the exodus of the soul from sin, it is made holy and free in its own power.)

Charles Singleton has argued that this typology (which actually implies two types of redemption – our redemption through Christ and the con- version of the soul) informs the entire poem.[1] The newly arriving souls thus aptly sing the song of exodus, celebrating their return home from the earthly life of bondage and exile.

This scriptural citation, in distinct contrast to what has come before in the *Inferno*, seems to correspond to the numerous indications that things are indeed markedly different here on Mount Purgatory. Dante's uncertain reference to 'una nuova legge' ('a new law') in line 106 of this same canto would seem to reinforce this sense of a new kind of inter- textuality at work.[2] Here the souls cite scripture knowingly, consciously applying it to themselves. This biblical citation may also be set against Dante's self-citation that occurs later in the same canto, when Casella sings the *Convivio* canzone, 'Amor che ne la mente mi ragiona.' Whereas the scriptural citation serves to illuminate the meaning of the journey of purgation that the souls arriving on Mount Purgatory will under- take, Dante's canzone refers to the past, to an earlier self preoccupied with his *donna gentile*, identified in the *Convivio* as philosophy. Casella's performance thus constitutes a regression, a nostalgic yearning for an earlier time enacted in the narrative when Casella's listeners become so enraptured by his performance that they provoke a rebuke from Cato. Robert Hollander has observed that the language of Cato's rebuke de- rives from a scriptural passage; 'Correte al monte a spogliarvi lo scoglio / ch'esser non lascia a voi Dio manifesto' ('Run to the mountain and strip yourselves of the slough that does not let God be manifest to you' [*Purg.* 2.122–3]) recalls Paul's exhortation to the Colossians: 'Lie not to one another: stripping yourselves (*expoliantes vos*) of the old man with his deeds, And putting on the new' (3.9–10).[3]

We find another Latin citation of the Bible in the fifth canto, when Dante and Virgil come across a group of souls chanting the fiftieth psalm:

> E 'ntanto per la costa di traverso
> venivan genti innanzi a noi un poco,
> cantando '*Miserere*' a verso a verso.   (*Purg.* 5.22–4)

(And along the opposite edge came people slowly toward us, singing *Miserere* verse by verse.)

Here again we see Dante cite a portion of the Vulgate's Latin text, after which he refers us to the rest of the Psalm, pointing to it without reproducing it within the poem. Both this citation and that of the 113th Psalm – in the fact that they are in Latin and that they point the reader outside the poem – stand out as scriptural texts separate from the rest of Dante's poem. We must turn away from the *Comedy* and open the Bible if we hope to read 'quanto di quel salmo è poscia scripto' ('the rest of that Psalm that is written afterward') or read the fiftieth psalm 'a verso a verso.' The Latin citations serve as linguistic markers, differentiating the Bible from the surrounding vernacular poetry and preserving its status as a sacred text, as if asserting its separateness from the poem in which it is cited.

These first biblical citations do not, however, fully account for the presence of the Bible in the *Purgatorio* and, as we have already seen, in the *Paradiso*. Above all, whereas Dante works in these citations to preserve and emphasize a distinction between the Bible and his own writing, at other moments he undermines that same distinction, adapting the Bible in creative ways to the demands of his poem.[4] The *Purgatorio* contains two key moments of this kind, which will form the basis for this chapter: Dante's rewriting of the Lord's Prayer in canto 11, and his recurring citation of the Beatitudes in the course of his ascent up the mountain.

The Lord's Prayer and Dante's 'O Padre nostro'

The Lord's Prayer was one of the most important biblical texts for the medieval church. Given by Jesus himself as a model to be emulated, the prayer became the basis for numerous commentaries and involved theological speculation concerning the proper role and form of prayer. Found in the middle of the Sermon on the Mount in the Gospel of Matthew, Jesus offers the prayer after having discussed common human motivations for praying, many of which depend upon the desire for earthly praise:

> And when ye pray, you shall not be as the hypocrites, that love to stand and pray in the synagogues and corners of the streets, that they may be seen by men: Amen I say to you, they have received their reward. But thou when thou shalt pray, enter into thy chamber, and having shut the door, pray to thy Father in secret: and thy Father who seeth in secret will repay thee. And when you are praying, speak not much, as the heathens. For they think that in their much speaking they may be heard. Be not you therefore like to them, for your Father knoweth what is needful for you, before you ask him.[5] (6.5–8)

The desire for earthly praise often outweighs our desire to be heard of God. Indeed, Jesus implies that words, strictly speaking, are unnecessary, because of God's foreknowledge of what we will ask. Patristic writers and medieval theologians paid particular attention to Jesus' admonition to be brief and to avoid 'much speaking.' In his commentary on Matthew, for example, Saint Jerome wrote that 'if the heathen multiplies words in his prayers, the Christian should speak few words, for "God hears not the words but the heart."'[6] Similarly, Saint Augustine tells us in his *De sermone Domini*, 'and thus it is that the heathen, that is the gentiles, consider that they are heard for their much speaking. And it is true that all manner of much speaking comes from the gentiles, who give greater attention to working their tongues than to cleansing their hearts.'[7] Augustine also treats this issue in his letter to Probas, when he suggests that prayers are most effective when we speak little but entreat much, using tears and sighs rather than words.[8] He advises in his treatise on the Sermon on the Mount that we commit the words of the Lord's Prayer to memory, although, he continues, 'we ought not, in order to obtain what we wish, direct words to God, but ideas which we carry in our minds, and by the exertion of our thoughts with pure delight and with artless feeling; but our Lord has taught us these very ideas in words, that we, having committed them to memory, may recall them at the hour of prayer.'[9] This commentary tradition posits an inverse relationship between words and sincerity. Words – a human form of communication – are used only to be heard of men; deeds and the intentions of our hearts, which God already knows, are much more effective tools of supplication than our tongues. And even when Augustine recognizes the necessity of words, he nevertheless places primary importance on the ideas in our minds, which Jesus' words help us to recall. And indeed there exists another tradition in which the Lord's Prayer, being spoken by the Lord himself, is too elevated for a prosaic exegesis. Chaucer's Parson, for example, says that he is unable to comment upon it, although he does allow for exegesis of it, provided that it is offered by one more qualified than he: 'The exposicioun of this hooly preyere, that is so excellent and digne, I bitake to thise maistres of theologie' (10.1042).[10]

Nevertheless, the insistence by these various commentators on the simplicity of the prayer is belied by the extensive commentary devoted to it. The Lord's words are simple on their face, but they reveal a profound organization that can only be elucidated through extensive exegesis. In addition, there existed alongside this interpretive tradition a tradition of exegetical paraphrase that expanded the prayer in order to elucidate it. The very brevity of the prayer seemed to necessitate expansion and interpretation. Saint Francis of Assisi, for example, is attributed with a reworking of the prayer in Latin. This *Expositio in Pater Noster* procedes phrase by phrase, inserting interpretive additions to the prayer. The reworking of the phrase requesting daily bread is one of the briefer sections but proves fairly typical:

(6) *Panem nostrum quotidianum:*
dilectum Filium tuum, Dominum nostrum Jesum Christum,
da nobis hodie:
in memoriam et intellegentiam et reverentiam amoris,
quem ad nos habuit,
et eorum, quae pro nobis dixit, fecit et sustulit.[11]

(*Our daily bread:* your beloved son the Lord Jesus Christ *give to us today:* in memory and understanding and reverence of the love, which he had for us, and of those things that he said, did, and bore for us.)

Francis thus reads the prayer for daily bread as a plea for spiritual nourishment, for Christ himself, perhaps as present in the Eucharist. Jacopone da Todi has a similar interpretive paraphrase in the vernacular. His version of the fourth petition recognizes three meanings of bread, one physical (referring literally to bread needed by our physical bodies) and two spiritual: devotion to God shown through charity to one's fellow creatures and the Eucharist, "l sacramento, / ne l'altare consecrate' ('the sacrament consecrated on the altar').[12] As noted in chapter 1, and as these two examples (and they could be multiplied)[13] demonstrate, paraphrases of the Lord's Prayer and of other biblical texts were frequent in the Middle Ages, though not universally accepted. Dante's use of the Lord's Prayer, therefore, should be understood within this context. Jesus gave the prayer as model ('Thus therefore shall you pray'), and patristic and medieval theologians devoted considerable attention to it; they found in it a model of simplicity and brevity, exemplary because of its lack of formal eloquence and authoritative because it was spoken by the Lord himself.

The pilgrim hears the prayer during his journey through Purgatory's first terrace, where the sin of pride is purged. Following his entrance into Purgatory proper in the previous canto, Dante notices the elaborate sculpted reliefs that line the wall of this terrace and that present positive examples of humility, encouraging the souls to become humble, as Mary, David, and Trajan demonstrated humility. He then notices some of the shades of the terrace approaching him, bent down because of the tremendous weights they are shouldering. As the tenth canto ends, they seem unable to continue, but the eleventh canto opens with the words of the prayer that these shades speak and that further exhorts them (as well as the pilgrim, Virgil, and Dante's readers) to humility.

The prayer occupies the first eight tercets of the canto, and it constitutes the only fully recited prayer in the canticle, a realm where prayers are prominent.[14] Purgatorial souls spend much of their time in prayer and become preoccupied not only with their own prayers, but also with those of their loved ones still alive on earth that may be offered to shorten their time in Purgatory. The frequency of the prayers together with Virgil's assertion – in contradiction of his own poem[15] – that the prayers of the righteous are able to move heaven point to the importance of prayers in Purgatory. The presence of an extended prayer in the middle of the first terrace should not surprise us; nevertheless, the fact that Dante reports it in its entirety (it extends to twenty-four lines), and that he opens the canto directly with the words of the prayer, only informing the reader afterwards that these words are actually spoken by the 'ombre' ('shades') that 'andavan sotto 'l pondo' ('move beneath the weight') (11.26), all work to draw the reader's attention to the prayer.

As has often been noted, Dante expands, translates, or paraphrases each phrase or request of the biblical prayer into a separate tercet in his poem. The first seven tercets of the eleventh canto correspond, that is, to the seven phrases of the prayer as recorded in the Sermon on the Mount in chapter 6 of Matthew's Gospel.[16] The eighth and final tercet of Dante's prayer has no biblical equivalent. By placing the two prayers side by side, we can gain a clearer understanding of how Dante expands and alters the prayer:

O Padre nostro, che ne' cieli stai,
non circunscritto, ma per più amore
ch'ai primi effetti di là sù tu hai,

Pater noster qui in caelis es,

laudato sia 'l tuo nome e 'l tuo valore
da ogne creatura, com' è degno
di render grazie al tuo dolce vapore.

sanctificetur nomen tuum.

Vegna ver' noi la pace del tuo regno,
ché noi ad essa non potem da noi,
s'ella non vien, con tutto nostro ingegno.

Veniat regnum tuum.

Come del suo voler li angeli tuoi
fan sacrificio a te, cantando *osanna*,
così facciano li uomini de' suoi.

Fiat voluntas tua sicut in caelo
et in terra.

Dà oggi a noi la cotidiana manna,
sanza la qual per questo aspro diserto
a retro va chi più di gir s'affanna.

Panem nostrum cotidianum[17]
da nobis hodie.

E come noi lo mal ch'avem sofferto
perdoniamo a ciascuno, e tu perdona
benigno, e non guardar lo nostro merto.

Et dimitte nobis debita
nostra, sicut et nos dimisimus
debitoribus nostris.

Nostra virtù che di legger s'adona,
non spermentar con l'antico avversaro,
ma libera da lui che sì la sprona.

Et ne inducas nos in tempta-
tionem. Sed libera nos a malo.

Quest' ultima preghiera, segnor caro,
già non si fa per noi, ché non bisogna,
ma per color che dietro a noi restaro.
(*Purg.* 11.1–24)

· [no equivalent in Matthew]

(Our father who art in the heavens, not circumscribed but for the greater love that you have for your first creations, /

(Our Father who art in heaven,

praised be your name and your worth by
every creature, as it is right to render thanks
to your sweet vapour. /

hallowed be thy name.

May the peace of your kingdom come to us,
as we cannot come to it of ourselves, if it
comes not, even with our whole genius. /

Thy kingdom come.

As your angels make sacrifice of their will
to You, singing *hosanna,* so may men do. /

Thy will be done on earth as it
is in heaven.

Give us today the daily manna, without
which those who most desire to progress
through this bitter wilderness go back. /

Give us this day our daily bread.

And as we pardon everyone the evil that
we have suffered, so you, merciful one,
pardon, and look not on our merit. /

And forgive us our debts, as
we also forgive our debtors.

Do not test our strength, which fails at
a small trial with the ancient adversary,
but deliver it from him who presses it. /
This last prayer, dear Lord, we do not
make for ourselves, who have no need,
but for those who remain behind us.)

And lead us not into temptation. But deliver us
from evil.

This comparison makes it clear that Dante rewrites the Lord's Prayer extensively and in significant ways, greatly expanding upon the original. Scholars have accounted for the differences between the *Pater noster* and Dante's *O Padre nostro* in various ways, from Tommaseo, who regrets the fact that Dante chose to paraphrase the prayer, to Mario Marti, who suggests that the daily liturgy forms Dante's real source here, and thus Dante is not really guilty of paraphrasing such a sacred text.[18] As we have seen, the fact that Dante paraphrases the Lord's Prayer is not in and of itself remarkable, as the practice of biblical paraphrase was fairly widespread; however, a more detailed look at the prayer is necessary in order to see to what degree Dante's rewriting corresponds to medieval notions about the prayer.

The initial address of the Lord's Prayer to 'our father' occasioned theological speculation regarding Jesus' use of the word 'noster.' The *Glossa ordinaria,* for example, suggests that this possessive adjective encourages us to proper feelings of fraternity. No one should call God *my* father unless he is his natural son; Jesus alone has the right to this form of address.[19] Dante, however, does not emphasize this idea in his rewriting; instead, he elaborates on the meaning of the Father's residence 'in heaven.' Saint Augustine explained that this phrase must be interpreted to mean that God dwells 'among the holy and just ones,' and not to imply that he is bound to live in one particular location. Furthermore, we should not assume that the higher one's residence the nearer one is to God, for then the birds would be considered nearer to God than the saints. Ultimately, the phrase 'is understood correctly to mean . . . in the hearts of the just, as in his holy temple.'[20] This last interpretation resembles that offered by Dante in his paraphrase, as his prayer tells us that God is not circumscribed in the heavens, though unlike Augustine he accounts for God's place of residence through the greater love that he has for his first creations, a humble acknowledgment for humans to make, since it recognizes the lesser place that they occupy within God's affections. The opening tercet of Dante's prayer thus offers a theological clarification of the meaning of God's residing 'in caelis,' but adds to traditional medieval commentary a recognition of man's place in the scheme of creation and his consequent need for humility.

Dante's transformation of the second phrase also has parallels in the commentary tradition. Jesus' plea that the Father's name be made holy seems superfluous, for is his name not sanctified already? Augustine had suggested that the petition to make God's name holy implies not that it lacks holiness now, but that it should be held holy among men. Dante echoes this interpretation and makes this, the prayer's first petition, an injunction for praise, though he expands the scope of the demand – not only men but all creatures should praise God – and seems to direct the petition to the creatures rather than the Creator, since he asks that God's name be praised by every creature, thus echoing, as Chiavacci Leonardi points out in her commentary, Saint Francis's 'Laudes creaturarum.'[21] The first two tercets of Dante's prayer thus insist upon the Father's greatness and the corresponding need for humble creatures to praise him. There is, however, more to the statement than this exhortation to humility. Many commentators, especially the earliest ones, saw in the triad *nome*, *valore*, and *vapore* of this tercet a reference to the Trinity, that is, to the Son, the Father, and the Holy Spirit respectively. Others see in this enumeration a reference in all three cases to the Father. Either way, however, Dante creates within his humble plea for all creatures to praise God a sophisticated, intricate praise of God.

According to Aquinas, the following two phrases of the Lord's Prayer are linked. The petition for the coming of God's kingdom constitutes a request 'for our admittance into the glory of his kingdom.' The phrase that follows, 'thy will be done on earth,' 'expresses the desire of meriting the goal [of entering into God's kingdom] through obedience ... The words "Thy will be done" rightly signify "May the commandments be obeyed on earth as in heaven, i.e., by men as well as by angels."'[22] Like Aquinas, Dante interprets the request *thy kingdom come* as representing an individual desire for salvation, for the peace of the kingdom of God. However, he adds two lines in order to explain that peace is necessary precisely because we are unable to attain it of ourselves, even with all of our intellect, 'con tutto il nostro ingegno.' In the following phrase, Dante – once again resembling Aquinas – indicates that God's will being done on earth means that men must do it; we must sacrifice our will to God's, as the angels do. In this tercet, however, he alters the formula he has employed up to this point. In the first three tercets, he translates or paraphrases the Vulgate text in the first line, and then offers two lines of commentary, filling out the meaning of the tercet's first line. In the fourth tercet, he does not divide things up so neatly, broadly combining paraphrase and commentary throughout the three lines. Yet Dante had already begun this process in the previous tercet, as its first line – *Vegna ver noi la pace del tuo regno* – both paraphrases and offers commentary on its biblical model, *veniat regnum tuum;* and, as we will observe, as the prayer continues, the dividing line between the original prayer and Dante's additions to it becomes increasingly difficult to find.

In both of the third and the fourth tercets, Dante nevertheless follows the medieval commentary tradition in his expansions and re-writings, if anything increasing the emphasis on humility implied in these phrases of the prayer, as he acknowledges the necessity of grace in the absence of human ability to attain God's kingdom and the importance of sacrificing the proud human will to God's design. His use of the word *ingegno* (in line 9) is particularly charged. Throughout the *Commedia*, Dante draws on the word's broad meaning,[23] as *ingegno* takes on a wide variety of connotations, from its first appearance in *Inferno* 2, when Dante invokes the muses and his own high genius to help him write ('O Muse, o alto ingegno, or m'aiutate' [7]) to its last in *Paradiso* 24, where Saint Peter refers derisively to the 'ingegno di sofista' ('the wit of the sophist' [81]). Dante both praises and censures human *ingegno*, as it can be both used in the service of poetic achievement and abused to create doctrinal confusion. According to the prayer, though, all of our intellectual capacities are insufficient to attain God's kingdom.

In the fifth tercet, Dante returns to his earlier practice of paraphrasing the prayer in the first line and then adding two lines of commentary or expansion, and this commentary follows the same basic pattern we have already seen. Aquinas, for example, drawing on Augustine's letter to Probas and Saint Jerome, argues that 'Panem nostrum cotidianum' refers primarily to the Eucharist, the sacramental bread of life – literally Christ himself – that provides us with essential spiritual nourishment. Dante incorporates this interpretation directly into his prayer, translating the neutral *panem* of the Vulgate with the theologically charged *manna*, referring not only to the nourishment miraculously provided to the children of Israel as they wandered in the barren margins of the promised land,[24] but also to the way that Jesus refers to this 'bread of heaven' in the sixth chapter of John's Gospel, where he spiritualizes the manna and identifies himself as the 'living bread which came down from heaven.' Dante endows the 'daily bread' of the Lord's Prayer with this Eucharistic meaning, thus emphasizing the necessity of the bread of life, for even the souls on Mount Purgatory not only fail to advance but actually fall back without the grace offered by and through Christ. Once again, of themselves, they can do nothing.

Dante's sixth tercet remains on the whole closest to the Vulgate text, as Dante uses all three lines for his interpretive translation, perhaps because the original biblical phrase is lengthier and thus leaves the poet less room for embellishment. He does make one significant addition at the conclusion of the tercet, and this addition, as we by now have come to expect, emphasizes humility; the souls ask not only that the Father pardon their sins, but also that he not consider their personal merit, which is obviously insufficient. The following seventh tercet – which translates the final phrase of the Lord's Prayer – likewise humbly admits to human limitations, noting that human *virtù* is easily seduced and is in need of divine deliverance from its ancient foe, finding in the Latin 'a malo' a reference to Satan as the embodiment of evil. But as the souls on Mount Purgatory's first terrace have no need to be liberated from temptation, the souls speak the prayer's final tercet, which has no source in the biblical text, as a kind of reversal of typical purgatorial prayer, in that on that terrace those in purgatory pray for those still alive.

The prayer thus constitutes an extended exhortation to humility, to disregard human merit and place one's hopes in grace. Dante's expansions and embedded commentary serve to highlight this aspect of the prayer. As Aquinas, quoting Augustine, says, 'the Lord's Prayer is the best of all because as Augustine says, *If we pray rightly and fittingly, we can say nothing but what is contained in the Lord's Prayer.*'[25] Dante's prayer thus seems to fit into this tradition of pious paraphrase, elaborated so as to emphasize the humility required for the long journey of purgation.

The context of this prayer, however, may work against such an easy interpretation. As Teodolinda Barolini has shown, throughout the first terrace Dante foregrounds questions of artistic representation and the relationship between human artistic and divine creation, raising questions regarding Dante's implicit artistic pride in his mimetic accomplishment and the overt exhortations to humility that fill the cantos of this terrace. Dante's reworking of the prayer proves analogous to his re-presentations of divine art in the surrounding cantos:

> Although the glosses added to the words of the prayer are exhortations to humility, the presence of the prayer in Canto XI ensures that the terrace's central canto will contain an instance of the Arachnean art that distinguishes Cantos X and XII: an instance of God's art (in this case, an instance of his verbal rather than visual art) elaborated, extended, commented on – in short, re-presented – by a man.[26]

Furthermore, the fact that God's art here reworked is not visual but verbal, and that Dante reworks a biblical text spoken by the Lord himself and identified by him as exemplary further highlights the artistic hubris Dante courts in this canto. In other words, while Dante elaborately describes the divine visual art contained in cantos 10 and 12, he actually changes the divine verbal art he reworks and places at the beginning of canto 11.

As we have seen, for patristic writers and the medieval theologians they influenced, Jesus' prayer in the Sermon on the Mount was purposefully simple. It is a humble prayer, but not because it contains exhortations to humility. Its humility consists, rather, in its humble language, which implicitly expresses the faith that God knows, far better than we do, what we need, and that he therefore does not need to hear an elaborate, formulaic prayer. Dante's rewriting of the prayer transforms its simple, straightforward language into a theologically sophisticated poetic achievement, which draws attention to itself as an artistic creation, a human artefact that takes Jesus' words and reworks them so as to meet the demands of Dante's poem. The biblical figure of David, who appears as one of the sculpted examples of humility in canto 10, serves to illustrate this paradoxical joining of pride and humility. We have already noted in chapter 2 that Dante is drawn to David as a figure of the inspired poet. In this purgatorial sculpture, David is shown dancing before the Ark of the Covenant while his wife Michal looks on with scorn (*Purg.* 10.55–69; the biblical story is found in 2 Sam. 6). David thus becomes the humble king, a paradox that Dante underscores in line 66 (*e più e men che re era in quel caso* ['and both more and less than king he was in that instance']) and that anticipates Christ's willing condescension through humility to bring about the sublime exaltation of the Incarnation (a conjunction of *humilitas* and *sublimitas*).[27] Dante's poem is similarly both more and less than vernacular poem, and Dante himself more and less than poet. He exhorts us to humility but does so through an elaborate rewriting of the Lord's Prayer that calls attention to its own artistry. Unlike the Latin citations of the Bible that Dante employs earlier in the canticle, citations that clearly are marked as separate from Dante's vernacular poem, Dante's rewriting of the prayer in the vernacular results in a much greater confusion, as it becomes difficult to discern where the Lord's Prayer ends and Dante's poem begins. By fusing the Bible and his poem in this way, Dante presents himself as an inspired writer, both more and less than poet. Less because he relies on the Bible, but more because he rewrites it in his poem, laying claim to the inspiration that animated the biblical prophets.

The Beatitudes and the Purgatorial Ascent

Another portion of Christ's Sermon on the Mount forms a key subtext on Mount Purgatory. When Dante and Virgil leave each terrace, they make a ritualistic transition to the following *cornice*. As they ascend, an angel erases one of the seven P's on the pilgrim's forehead, inscribed at the entrance to Purgatory proper, and one of Christ's Beatitudes is sung.[28] Although the use of the Beatitudes here seems to have no source in the liturgy, they do serve a liturgical function on the mountain, celebrating the progression of the individual soul by marking it with set actions and words.[29] Anna Maria Chiavacci Leonardi has argued that the Beatitudes undergird the structure of the second canticle, that 'all of *Purgatorio* rests – not only logically, but even in the innermost fibers of its language – on that which the Beatitudes in reality mean.'[30] It is true that the Beatitudes prove central to the second canticle in many ways, not only in terms of Purgatory's liturgical structure, but also by subtly commenting on the central questions Dante poses throughout this section of the poem. Before proceeding to a detailed investigation of the Beatitudes in Dante's *Purgatorio*, however, we need to understand the interpretive tradition in which Dante would have read them, as he draws on that tradition in interesting and creative ways.

Jesus opens the Sermon on the Mount (as found in Matthew 5.3–10) with the Beatitudes. Each Beatitude consists of two parts; in the first, the macarism, Christ declares a particular group defined by its behaviour to be blessed (μακάριοι [*makarioi*] in Greek and *beati* in Latin). In the second, he identifies the reward awaiting that group; this second part begins in each case in the Vulgate with *quoniam* (ὅτι in Greek). In Dante's use of them, he refers, with one exception, only to the first half of any given Beatitude.[31] Although nine consecutive sayings follow this structure, as we will see, in the ancient and medieval interpretive tradition, exegetes commonly identified seven Beatitudes. In fact, for ancient and medieval commentators, two interpretive issues became most prominent: order and number. Augustine, for example, was concerned with both of these issues; he found the ordering of the Beatitudes important because Christ intended through their concatenation to teach us how to attain perfection, which we gain by passing through humility and the other steps implicit in the Beatitudes until we gain the kingdom of God.[32] The numbering likewise proves to be important, for although the Sermon on the Mount begins with nine successive sayings that begin with the phrase 'blessed are,' Augustine ultimately counts seven Beatitudes. The ninth saying ('Blessed are ye when they shall revile you') should not be considered a Beatitude at all, since Christ speaks directly to his disciples, not following the impersonal structure of the eight Beatitudes that precede it. The eighth saying, 'Blessed are they that suffer persecution,' does fit the form of a Beatitude, but since it actually summarizes the first seven – a fact signalled by the return of its reward to that of the first Beatitude ('the kingdom of heaven') – it should be considered a summary and recapitulation of the others. Properly speaking, then, there are seven Beatitudes, an important point as it allows Augustine to find a correspondence between them and the 'sevenfold operation of the Holy Ghost.'[33]

Later authors became much more systematic in their attempts to link the Beatitudes to other significant lists in Christian doctrine, including prominent vices, such as those commonly identified as the seven deadly sins (more correctly referred to as the seven capital vices).[34] In this pairing, the Beatitudes were seen to provide a remedial effect, counteracting the vices. This trend is exemplified in Hugh of Saint Victor's *De quinque septenis*, in which Hugh lines up five groups of seven and shows how they relate to each other. Thus, the seven capital vices are seen to correspond to the seven petitions of the Lord's Prayer, the seven gifts of the Holy Spirit, the seven virtues, and the seven Beatitudes. These sevens emphasize the Beatitudes to a degree not immediately apparent, since the 'virtues' to which Hugh refers are not the traditional remedial virtues, nor the cardinal and theological virtues, but instead the macarisms that constitute the first half of each Beatitude.

Since the Beatitudes were seen both as remedies for vice and as providing a blueprint for moral improvement leading toward the perfection implicit in the ultimate beatitude, they became a locus for questions of moral theology. It should not surprise us, then, that the Beatitudes became a text of some interest with the rediscovery of Aristotle's *Nicomachean Ethics*, as philosophers and theologians sought ways of reconciling the newly authoritative views of Aristotle and traditional Christian ethics.[35] Indeed, the fundamental issues in the history of the exegesis of the Beatitudes relate directly to the issues of moral theology raised by the rediscovery of Aristotelian ethical thought. Three topics in particular gained importance.

First, Aristotle considers happiness only as it applies to this earthly life, whereas for Christians ultimate beatitude is possible only in the life to come. The debate concerning blessedness or happiness is well illustrated in a text that predates the complete translation of the *Ethics*, Abelard's *Dialogue of a Philosopher with a Jew and a Christian* (c. 1136), where Abelard has his Christian convince the Philosopher that one must look to the life to come in order to secure true blessedness, since all the good promised in this life reaches its perfection only in the 'supreme good of man or ... the goal of the good, in the blessedness of a future life, and the route thereto in the virtues.' This teaching was set down by the Lord Jesus himself, 'where he encouraged contempt for the world and the desire for this beatitude as well, saying, "Blest are the poor in spirit, for theirs is the kingdom of heaven" ... all prosperity is to be held in contempt or adversities tolerated out of hope for that highest and eternal life.'[36] It is telling that Abelard's Christian cites a Beatitude in order to 'prove' that ultimate blessedness resides only in the happiness of the kingdom of heaven.

Second, Christian theology traditionally held that charity, which is infused in the Christian soul by grace and not by any effort of the individual, is necessary for any virtuous action. For Aristotle, however, virtues can be learned through the development of habits and education of the mind. Saint Augustine was most influential in insisting that pagan virtue was no virtue at all since it was not based on charity, for actions that appear virtuous but lack charity actually consist of one vice (usually pride) overcoming another vice. 'Then, and only then, must those evil impulses be reckoned as defeated, when they are defeated by the love of God, which none but God himself can give; and he gives it only through the mediator between God and men, the man Christ Jesus.'[37]

And finally, Aristotle held that virtue was best defined as a mean between extremes. Dante, following Aristotle, states the idea in the *Convivio*: 'E ciascuna di queste vertudi ha due inimici collaterali, cioè vizii, uno in troppo e un altro in poco; e queste tutte sono li mezzi intra quelli.' ('each of these virtues has two collateral enemies, that is, vices, one in excess and another in deficiency; and these virtues are the means between those extremes' [4.17.7]). This 'moderate virtue' seems to contradict the ethics taught by Christ in the New Testament, which in many cases seem to embrace more extreme notions of virtue.[38]

Medieval Aristotelianism began to influence the ways in which exegetes read the Beatitudes well before Dante wrote the *Comedy*. A thorough attempt at reconciling the Beatitudes with the new moral philosophy can be found in Saint Thomas Aquinas, who devotes a question with four articles to a consideration of the Beatitudes in the *Summa theologiae*. His Aristotelian assumptions come to the fore in the third article of the question, where, in order to clarify why the 'list of Beatitudes is altogether appropriate,' he notes that 'there are three kinds of beatitude' after which people seek: the beatitude of a life of pleasure (*vita voluptuosa*), that of an active life (*vita activa*), and that of a contemplative life (*vita contemplativa*), a tripartite division derived from the beginning of the *Nicomachean Ethics* where Aristotle identifies the three most common perceptions of happiness: the life of pleasure (*vita voluptuosa*), the active life (*vita civilis*), and the contemplative life (*vita contemplativa*).[39] Thomas incorporates the standard interpretations of the Beatitudes as a narrative of ascent into this Aristotelian framework. Rather than reversing the progressively degenerative effects of sin, Aquinas, who accepts the standard enumeration of seven Beatitudes, sees the Beatitudes as counteracting the negative influence of incorrect notions of happiness. The first three Beatitudes 'eliminate the obstacle created by the happiness of pleasure.' The fourth and fifth teach the happiness of the active life, while the final two address the contemplative life, or 'the final beatitude itself,' which is the direct vision and contemplation of God enjoyed after this life.

Aquinas further weighs in on the issue of whether happiness can be obtained in this life, as Aristotle held, and it is here that we find Aquinas most resistant to Aristotle's conclusions. In an earlier article of this question, he writes, 'Beatitude is the last end of human life, as was said above. However, a person is said to have hold of the end already because of his hope in obtaining it. Hence according to Aristotle, boys are called happy out of hope; and Saint Paul says, "In hope we have been saved"' (1a.2æ. 69.1).[40] The conjunction of Paul and Aristotle provides an apt illustration of the Scholastic project of reconciliation, though Aquinas's use of Aristotle is problematic here when viewed against modern views of Aristotle's ethical thought.[41] The clearer Aquinas's definition becomes in the *Summa*, in fact, the further it moves away from Aristotle's notion of living well in this life according to reason and moral excellence. Ultimately, for Aquinas 'there can be no complete and ultimate happiness for us save in the vision of God.'[42] While Aquinas's emphasis on the happiness that obtains after death is, of course, foreign to Aristotle, Aquinas nevertheless uses the adult-child analogy in an Aristotelian fashion – the happiness of a mortal man for Aquinas is like that of a child for Aristotle; just as a child cannot be fully happy but can only anticipate an adult happiness, so can a mortal man only be imperfectly happy, anticipating that activity that defines happiness, but not being able to engage in it yet. Aquinas argues for the intermediary validity of the earthly notion of happiness found in the active life, while reserving ultimate happiness for the life to come. For while the beatitude of the life of pleasure is 'false and contrary to reason,' the beatitude of the active life 'disposes one for the beatitude which is to come' (1a.2æ.69.3).[43] For Aquinas, there can only be *one* happiness, since, as he states it in his commentary on the *Ethics*, there 'must be, indeed, one ultimate end for man precisely as man because of the unity of human nature.'[44]

Elsewhere in the *Summa*, Aquinas argues, against Augustine, that non-Christians can possess real moral virtues. As Bonnie Kent has shown, 'toward the end of the thirteenth century it became standard to distinguish between natural *moral* goodness, which makes one an admirable member of society in the present life, and supernatural, *meritorious* goodness, which makes one eligible for the perfect happiness of the afterlife.'[45] Aquinas uses this distinction to find a way to navigate between the ideas of happiness and moral virtue in Aristotle and those of Augustine in the earlier Christian tradition, while stopping short of embracing a fully Aristotelian notion of happiness. Full happiness for Aquinas is Christian blessedness.

Dante, then, inherited a rich interpretive tradition surrounding the Beatitudes, one that had fairly well-defined contours and limits but also some degree of variety based upon the theological and philosophical contexts in which the biblical text was interpreted. There was sufficient variety in the tradition to allow for a new Scholastic interpretation that could accommodate the Beatitudes into the context of medieval Aristotelian thought, but most interpreters took a great interest in the ordering of the sayings, finding in them a series of stages moving toward the ultimate beatitude of salvation and the contemplation of God. These stages were frequently seen to correspond to opposing lists of vices or equivalent lists of virtues, spiritual gifts, or other scriptural texts. They thus are ideally suited to the purpose for which Dante employs them – markers of the ascent of purgatorial souls toward the earthly paradise. And indeed, many commentators state as much. Tollemache, for example, notes that the seven Beatitudes enumerated by Saint Thomas correspond to the seven terraces of Mount Purgatory, and that they seem 'perfectly adapted to the ascetic demands of the *Purgatorio*, where the souls, intent on expiating their sins and on acquiring virtue, are supported by the hope of a future reward.'[46] He also argues for a precise analogy between Thomas's views on the Beatitudes and the use Dante makes of them. If we take even a cursory glance at how Dante employs them, however, we will see that things are not quite so straightforward.[47]

As we have seen, both Augustine and Aquinas are careful to stress the importance of the ordering of the Beatitudes (even though they differ on what that ordering reveals); for both, the enumeration forms a narrative of progressive ascent, with each Beatitude building on the one preceding it. Both also point to the fact that the Beatitudes were spoken by the Lord himself and hence must be correct as stated and in the order they are stated. Saint Thomas, for instance, considers three objections to the idea that the rewards of the Beatitudes are suitably enumerated, but states in the *sed contra* that 'on the other hand is the authority of the Lord himself who offered these rewards' (1a.2æ.69.4).[48] But while Dante orders the capital vices in accordance with one prominent strand of medieval thinking about them,[49] he does not even employ all of the Beatitudes; he omits the second ('Blessed are the meek') and instead divides the fourth ('Blessed are they that hunger and thirst after justice') between two terraces. He also treats their ordering with a fair degree of freedom, the degree of which we can illustrate by comparing it to Hugh of Saint Victor's traditional use of the Beatitudes in *De quinque septenis*. While Hugh and Dante both employ the same ordering of the vices and both associate the first Beatitude ('Blessed are the poor in spirit') with the first and foundational vice of pride, their juxtaposition does not coincide in any other case. Hugh takes care to use the Beatitudes in proper biblical order, associating the second Beatitude with the second vice, the third Beatitude with the third vice, and so on. Dante, however, disregards the traditional ordering completely, changing the sequence as follows:

second terrace (envious)	– fifth Beatitude ('Blessed are the merciful')
third terrace (wrathful)	– seventh Beatitude ('Blessed are the peacemakers')
fourth terrace (slothful)	– third Beatitude ('Blessed are they that mourn')
fifth terrace (avaricious)	– fourth Beatitude ('Blessed are they that hunger ... after justice')
sixth terrace (gluttonous)	– fourth Beatitude ('Blessed are they that ... thirst after justice')
seventh terrace (lustful)	– sixth Beatitude ('Blessed are the clean in heart')[50]

Even from this very broad overview, it is clear that Dante does not follow medieval convention as articulated by Aquinas, Augustine, or Hugh of Saint Victor.[51] He thus does not see in the ordering of the Beatitudes a concatenation of ascent, although the fact that the souls on Purgatory are literally ascending toward the blessed life would seem to call for an ordered use of them. Furthermore, he is not averse to making additions, subtractions, and alterations to the text of the Beatitudes, which he does to four of the six that he cites. In order to understand why he employs the Beatitudes so freely, we need to turn to a much more detailed consideration of each Beatitude, beginning with the first.

Noi volgendo ivi le nostre persone, 'Beati pauperes spiritu!' voci[52] cantaron sì, che nol diria sermone. (*Purg.* 12.109–11)

Beati pauperes spiritu, quoniam ipsorum est regnum caelorum. (Matt. 5.3)

(Turning ourselves in that direction, voices sung 'Beati pauperes spiritu' in such a way that it cannot be told.)

(Blessed are the poor in spirit: for theirs is the kingdom of heaven.)

This Beatitude marks the transition from the first terrace of pride to the second terrace of envy. As previously discussed, this terrace involves a dialectic of humility and pride, continuous exhortations to humility together with demonstrations of artistic pride. In this first Beatitude, however, the dialectic is absent; instead, Dante employs the beatitude in a straightforward, one might almost say humble, way. The 'poor in spirit' were understood by both Augustine and Aquinas to refer to those who have embraced humility and explicitly rejected those things of the world that are signs of pride. Augustine, for example, wrote that 'the poor in spirit are rightly understood as the humble and those fearing God, that is, not having a puffed-up spirit. Neither should blessedness begin at any other place, if it is to reach to the highest wisdom.'[53] Just as pride is the foundation of all other sins, so all spiritual progress begins with humility. Dante employs this Beatitude precisely according to this tradition; additionally, he does not alter the scriptural text but cites it in Latin.[54] Thus, if Dante's scriptural intertextuality may be seen to alternate between straightforward citations of the Bible, in which he 'humbly' makes room for the unmediated Word in the poem (as we see in *Purg.* 2.46), and much freer uses of scripture, in which he transforms the Bible to suit the needs of his poem (as in *Inf.* 19 or the opening of *Purg.* 11), this instance certainly falls into the first category. The Latin scripture stands out from its vernacular context, a point that Dante emphasizes by describing the singing of the Beatitude as such that it cannot be told in language. In the following tercet, he lingers on this purgatorial singing, noting how it differs from the ferocious laments of the underworld.[55] This Word of God exists beyond the literary skill of the poet, who can only include it in his poem.

His second Beatitude seems to follow the practice of the first, for as we leave the terrace of envy, we again hear the scriptural Latin of the Vulgate:

Noi montavam, già partiti di linci,
e 'Beati misericordes!' fue
cantato retro, e 'Godi tu che vinci!'
(*Purg.* 15.37–9)

Beati misericordes quia ipsi
misericordiam consequentur.
(Matt. 5.7)

(We were climbing, already having departed from there, and 'Beati misericordes!' was sung behind us, and' Rejoice, you who conquer!')

(Blessed are the merciful: for they shall obtain mercy.)

As previously noted, Dante does not follow the biblical ordering of the Beatitudes but jumps from the first to the fifth; since *misericordia* was commonly understood as a virtue opposed to the sin of envy,[56] Dante uses the Beatitude in praise of mercy to extol those who have purged away that vice. Here it becomes apparent, as already discussed, that he chooses not to adapt a progressive scheme such as Augustine, Hugh, and Aquinas proposed but instead must fit the Beatitudes into his delineation of the seven principal vices. Indeed, in the *Glossa ordinaria,* it is noted that the virtue of this fifth Beatitude – mercy – comes about from those four that preceded it. If one possesses true humility and a meek soul, mourns for one's sins, and hungers for righteousness, true mercy will be born.[57]

We saw that Dante cited the first Beatitude in Latin without adapting it; his use here appears similar, but he is already beginning to shift his intertextual practice. He cites the first part of the fifth Beatitude in Latin, but he also makes a vernacular addition, as the angel adds 'Godi tu che vinci' to the scriptural citation. The phrase alludes to a part of the Sermon on the Mount that immediately follows the Beatitudes, when Jesus calls blessed those disciples who will be persecuted for his sake. He speaks to them directly, encouraging them to rejoice at the persecution they will receive: 'Be glad and rejoice (*Gaudete et exultate*), for your reward is very great in heaven' (Matt. 5.12). Many commentators have suggested that this allusion is inserted here because Dante has just conquered the two most difficult sins, and as he progresses toward his reward in heaven he should rejoice. Whatever its meaning within the context of the pilgrim's purgatorial journey, however, we can sense in this vernacular addition (even if biblically inspired) a shift toward a freer use of the Beatitudes than Dante demonstrates in his first usage of them. As we shall see, this trend continues.

In the third instance, Dante follows the same practice: combining a Latin citation of the first half of the Beatitude with a vernacular addition, which this time directly follows the singing of the Beatitude:

senti'mi presso quasi un muover d'ala e ventarmi nel viso e dir: '*Beati pacifici*, che son sanz' ira mala!' (*Purg.* 17.67–9)

Beati pacifici, quoniam filii Dei vocabuntur. (Matt. 5.9)

(I felt close to me almost a wing's movement, and a wind in my face and words: '*Beati pacifici*, who are without evil wrath!')

(Blessed are the peacemakers: for they shall be called the children of God.)

Dante's addition draws on a common medieval distinction between righteous anger, often termed zeal (*zelus*), and anger or wrath (*ira*). Aquinas, for example, drawing on Saint Gregory, discusses the importance of the distinction at some length.[58] Dante is thus careful to point out that the *pacifici* are free of wrath but not necessarily of righteous indignation; as Grabher points out in his commentary, this distinction is certainly in accordance with Dante's temperament, whose wrath, motivated for love of justice or, as Aquinas wrote, 'in accordance with right reason' ('secundum rationem rectam'), is manifested throughout his poem. In the interest of pointing out the distinction between *ira mala* and zeal, however, the fact that Dante has made a direct vernacular addition to the seventh Beatitude is often lost. Furthermore, while mercy, as we have seen, was frequently linked to the sin of envy, medieval commentators did not usually make the connection between wrath and the seventh Beatitude.[59] Both Augustine and Aquinas treat the 'peace' of this Beatitude as that which comes from a contemplative life after one has cleansed oneself from worldly impurities. Thus, Dante's addition is necessary in order to bring the biblical text into agreement with his poem, and so Chiavacci Leonardi's reluctant appellation of the addition as a 'correction' seems accurate.[60] Gradually, Dante begins to change the Beatitudes to fit his poem, to make the biblical text more and more his own.

On the fourth terrace, souls purge the vice of sloth, which Dante terms 'little love' (*poco amor*), 'negligence' (*negligenza*), and 'acedia' (*accidia*), employing in this last instance the Greek word for sloth that had become standard in the Middle Ages. As Dante and Virgil leave this terrace they hear the angel pronounce the third Beatitude, though Dante recounts the Angel's words indirectly:

Mosse le pénne poi e ventilonne, '*Qui lugent*' affermando esser beati, ch'avran di consolar l'anime donne. (*Purg.* 19.49–51)	*Beati qui lugent, quoniam ipsi* *consolabuntur.* (Matt. 5.5)
(Then he moved his feathers and fanned us, affirming those '*Qui* *lugent*' to be blessed, for their souls will have consolation.)	(Blessed are they that mourn: for they shall be comforted.)

There is much to say about this passage, not the least of which is how Dante furthers the vernacularization of the Beatitudes that we have traced thus far. First, some consideration of the reason for Dante's choice

of the third Beatitude is in order. This Beatitude has traditionally troubled commentators, as it – unlike the previous Beatitudes – does not suit
its context; there is little correspondence to be seen between the blessed
mourners and the sin of sloth. The most common way of tying the two
together is to argue that the mourners will find consolation because they
mourn precisely for their sin of sloth and thus will find heavenly recompense. This reading has precedents in the exegetical tradition, with
Aquinas, for example, suggesting that those who forsake their sins must
willingly mourn for them, 'choosing voluntary sorrow' (*voluntarium luc-
tum assumendo*).[61] As Trucchi observes, however, when read in this way
the Beatitude applies to all the repentant souls on Mount Purgatory, not
just the slothful.[62] And while the Beatitude's relation to the sin of sloth is
not immediately apparent, if we note its more immediate context – it is
surrounded by the pilgrim's second purgatorial dream – we may begin
to understand its direct relevance to the canto.

Canto 19 opens with Dante's dream of the *femina balba* – the stuttering, lame woman who is transformed by Dante's gaze into a 'sweet
siren' (19) and who enraptures Dante just as she claims to have en-
tranced Ulysses. Her spell is broken, however, by the appearance of
a 'holy woman' (*donna ... santa*), who calls Virgil twice and asks him
'who is this woman?' before exposing the siren's belly. The resultant
smell awakens Dante, who then follows Virgil up to the terrace of the
avaricious, where, immediately following the angel's words of beatitude, we return to a discussion of the dream, with Virgil instructing
Dante to learn from it how to free himself from the dream's *antica strega*
by looking to the heavens for guidance. Dante's subsequent colloquy
with Pope Adrian V reinforces the meaning of this dream; we learn that
Adrian only learned to desire God after becoming pope and coming to
the realization that all earthly things fail to satisfy:

> La mia conversïone, omè!, fu tarda;
> ma, come fatto fui roman pastore,
> così scopersi la vita bugiarda.
>   Vidi che lì non s'acquetava il core,
> né più salir potiesi in quella vita;
> per che di questa in me s'accese amore.   (*Purg.* 19.106–11)

(My conversion was, alas, late: but, as I was made the Roman pastor I
thus discovered that life is deceitful. I saw that there my heart could not
come to rest, nor could I ascend further in that life; so for this life love was
ignited in me.)

Adrian's narrative further serves as an apt illustration of Virgil's discourse to the pilgrim in cantos 17 and 18 on human motivation, sin, and virtue, in which Dante has Virgil explain that all human action derives from love of some perceived good. The way to virtue and to God is to learn to place your love or desire on the proper goods. There are human goods that may be properly desired, but they are not the ultimate good, and all desires must finally be directed toward God. Thus, the first three terraces are dedicated to purging desires directed toward false goods; the middle terrace corrects the insufficient love for the ultimate good that characterizes sloth; and the final three terraces redirect desires for earthly things that are good but not the good that 'makes man happy' (*Purg.* 17.133). Adrian initially sought peace in an earthly good, and only on discovering that it failed to satisfy did he turn his love to God. Dante's dream in turn illustrates the process of desire in allegorical form. It is only through Dante's transformative gaze that the stuttering woman becomes the sweet siren, only when he directs his desire to her that he actually transforms her into an apparently beautiful and eloquent woman, a point made through the language he employs: 'lo sguardo mio le facea scorta / la lingua' ('my gaze straightened out her tongue' [*Purg.* 19.12–13]). Neither Dante nor Virgil is able to free Dante from the siren without the help of the holy woman who comes to reprimand Virgil and expose the siren. We learn later that Virgil had called Dante 'at least three times' (19.34) before he awakened from his dream, a reference, perhaps, to Virgil's inability to free Dante from the siren.

Dante held that certain moral virtues, the 'cardinal virtues,' as well as the happiness proper to this life could be obtained through solely earthly means, specifically through 'philosophical teachings' (*phylosophica documenta*) as he states it in book 3 of the *Monarchia*. We attain eternal happiness, however, through 'spiritual teachings that transcend human reason' (3.15.8).[63] While Dante, then, sides with the moderate Aristotelians such as Aquinas in arguing that real moral virtues are possible for non-Christians, he also maintained that certain moral virtues can only be attained through an infusion of grace that actually transforms our will, which, because of its fallen nature, cannot transform itself. With this context, if we read the 'holy woman' of Dante's dream as an agent of grace, a more complete allegorical reading of the dream emerges. Dante's fallen desires transform evils into apparent goods, so much so that he begins to follow after them. Virgil (or unaided reason?) is unable to free him from the grip of these desires, despite his attempts to call Dante back to himself. Only the 'holy woman,' or divine grace, can unmask the true nature of the apparent goods for the evils they are by correcting Dante's gaze so that he comes to see her rightly again. This sense of grace is reinforced by Dante when he has Virgil say to the pilgrim following his dream, 'Rise and come' (*Surgi e vieni* [19.35]), words that echo Christ's words in the Gospels to a paralytic man whom he heals, 'Rise ... and go' (*surge ... et vade;* Matt. 9.6). In this Gospel episode Christ had first forgiven the sins of a lame man, an action that aroused the anger of the scribes who witnessed it. Christ healed the man specifically to demonstrate the reality of the grace that he brings: 'that you may know that the Son of man hath power on earth to forgive sins.' Dante, in other words, associates himself with the paralytic from the Gospel episode, portraying himself as the recipient of miraculous, healing grace. His dream illustrates both the process of sinfully attaching our desires to false goods and the fact that grace is often necessary to change those desires.

Canto 19, then, occupies a central place in the moral order of the *Purgatorio*, illustrating both through Dante's dream and through his encounter with Pope Adrian V the nature of human motivation, sin, and reformation. The Beatitude spoken near the middle of the canto reinforces its message, as it declares blessed those who mourn for their sins, and it is ideally suited to this canto (if not to the particular sin of sloth) that portrays the dangerous seduction of worldly goods, and it also prepares the way for the final three terraces of Purgatory, which, as Virgil tells Dante, are devoted to the love that 'too much abandons itself' (*troppo s'abbandona* [*Purg.* 17.136]) to worldly goods.

We may also note, as do Bosco and Reggio, that only here is a complete Beatitude spoken, since line 51 represents the only time in the canticle that the second half of the Beatitude – the reward – is mentioned. Even though the first half of the Beatitude is in Latin (and it is not as complete as the Latin Beatitudes spoken in the previous instances, since it lacks *Beati*) and the second half in the vernacular, the vernacular translates – or at least paraphrases – the Latin *quoniam ipsi consolabuntur*. While it is thus in some ways the most complete of the Beatitudes spoken in Purgatory, nevertheless it also carries the gradual process of vernacularization that we have been tracing one step further. Whereas the earlier Beatitudes were all cited through direct discourse, with the poet citing the words of the angel, this Beatitude is reported indirectly, retold through the words of the poet, including even those Latin words from the Beatitude. Increasingly, then, as we progress through Purgatory Dante transforms the Latin text of the Vulgate into his own vernacular. He masks this process, however, by taking away with one hand what he gives with another. Only here does he provide in some version both halves of the Beatitude while he continues nevertheless to vernacularize the biblical texts he uses, adapting them to suit his own purposes. We see the process continue on the two following terraces.

The Beatitudes spoken at the end of the fifth and sixth terraces are actually different parts of the same Beatitude, the fourth ('Blessed are they that hunger and thirst after justice'). Dante divides the hunger from the thirst, and has thirst conclude the terrace of the avaricious, while hunger ends the terrace of the gluttonous. The choice of the fourth Beatitude is obviously appropriate for the sixth terrace, as gluttony involves immoderate hungering and thirsting, but it also proves suitable for the fifth terrace, since avarice was often described in terms of hungering and thirsting. In Richard of Saint Victor's words, for example, it involved hungering and thirsting after 'gold, silver, clothing, estates, lands, vineyards, houses, horses, and innumerable possessions.'[64] Souls on these terraces have immoderately desired worldly gain or food and drink and must learn to desire the things of God, which is summarized as hungering and thirsting for justice. From the perspective of medieval moral philosophy, this Beatitude is particularly interesting, since justice is one of the four cardinal virtues (along with prudence, fortitude, and temperance) not exclusive to Christians, and one discussed at length by Aristotle in book 5 of the *Ethics*. It was held by Aristotle and his Scholastic followers to be a virtue that was fully attainable by human beings without supernatural aid. In fact, before discussing the eleven Aristotelian virtues, including justice, Dante suggests in the *Convivio* that 'propiissimi nostri frutti sono le morali vertudi, però che da ogni canto sono in nostra podestate' ('fruits most proper to us are the moral virtues, since they are in every respect within our power' [4.17.2]). As we have just seen, however, Dante took some pains in canto 19 to suggest that grace was essential for finally overcoming certain vices and attaining virtue. One of the key questions we will need to ask, therefore, is to what degree the justice proclaimed in the fourth Beatitude is compatible with an Aristotelian conception of justice and the Beatitude proclaimed by Dante's angels at the end of the fifth and sixth terraces. We turn first to the fifth terrace.

The ascent from the fifth to the sixth terrace occurs during the initial encounter with Statius, a meeting that proves so engrossing that Dante actually seems to forget to narrate the encounter with the angel in its proper place; he must employ the pluperfect tense in order to describe the passage from terrace to terrace in retrospect, as having already occurred.

Già era l'angel dietro a noi rimaso,
l'angel che n'avea vòlti al sesto giro,
avendomi dal viso un colpo raso;
  e quei c'hanno a giustizia lor disiro
detto n'avea beati, e le sue voci
con 'sitiunt', sanz'altro, ciò forniro.
(*Purg.* 22.1–6)

Beati qui esuriunt et sitiunt
iustitiam, quoniam ipsi satura-
buntur. (Matt. 5.6)

(Already had the angel remained
behind us, the angel that had
turned us to the sixth terrace, having scraped a fault from my face;
and he declared those blessed who
have justice as their desire, and his
words with 'sitiunt,' without the rest,
concluded.)

(Blessed are they that hunger
and thirst after justice: for they
shall have their fill.)

The second tercet of canto 22 has frequently been considered obscure and its meaning has been debated from the earliest commentators.[65] My translation implicitly indicates my own reading of the lines, that they paraphrase the angel's words. The angel, as on previous terraces, cites one of the Beatitudes, declaring those souls blessed who *thirst* after justice, omitting the reference to hunger in the biblical original. The Latin *sitiunt* implies that Dante paraphrases a Latin original, which, if it followed the model of the first two Beatitudes, would read: *Beati qui sitiunt iustitiam*.

This retrospective account of the recitation of the Beatitude may remind us that Statius's account of his sin of prodigality causes us to revise our notion of the fifth terrace and its punishment of avarice. When Virgil expresses his surprise that a noble poet such as Statius should have fallen prey to a vice as base as avarice, Statius corrects him by confessing that his own sin was in fact prodigality – the opposite of avarice, and that 'avarizia fu partita / troppo da me' ('avarice departed too far from me') (*Purg.* 22.34–5), revealing an Aristotelian conception of the vice of prodigality, located at the opposite extreme of avarice, with liberality as the appropriately measured virtue in between the vicious extremes. Statius goes on to term his prodigality a *dismisura*, a lack of measure that echoes Aquinas's Aristotelian description of both avarice and prodigality. Following Statius's explanation, therefore, we realize in looking back that the fifth terrace was Aristotelian in its portrayal of vice and virtue. By including both avaricious and prodigal souls Dante portrayed vices that exist on the opposite ends of a virtue – representing attitudes toward wealth so extreme either in desiring it or in caring nothing for it that the souls suffering from either vice must learn virtue by coming to a virtuous mean. Originally, however, on a first reading of the terrace, the portrayal seemed completely one-sided. We met only two figures (Adrian V and the king Hugh Capet), and both were avaricious; we heard positive examples of those happy with virtuous poverty (Mary and the Roman consul Gaius Fabricius) and negative examples of avarice punished. The one exception to this portrayal was the third positive example – Saint Nicholas – whose virtue of generosity in providing dowries for an impoverished nobleman's three daughters hints at a proper, moderate, and Aristotelian attitude toward wealth. Dante's portrayal of Nicholas seems strongly influenced by the Aristotelian virtue of liberality, which Aristotle describes at the beginning of book 4 of the *Ethics*, and which Dante defines in the *Convivio* as 'moderatrice del nostro dare e del nostro ricevere le cose temporali' ('the mean between our giving and our receiving temporal goods' [4.17.4]). What seems wanted to remedy both sins is not an extreme virtue, i.e., poverty, such as many Christians including Saint Francis would embrace (for Statius, after all, avarice was *too far* from him), but a proper appetite for material goods, one that recognizes that they are good but does not mistake them for our final Good.

The justice, then, that the blessed are declared to desire at the end of the terrace must be understood in its Aristotelian sense, which in the *Convivio* Dante summarizes as 'amare e operare dirittura in tutte cose' ('loving and following rectitude in all things' [4.17.6]). Aristotle associates injustice with unfairness and inequality, and we have the implication that in thirsting after justice, the souls cured of avarice and prodigality now hunger fairly for material things, in a way that recognizes their worth without over- or under-estimating them, with the further implication that these souls would (were they alive) expend their riches fairly, as did Saint Nicholas, giving to each person his or her due.[66] One cannot help noticing, however, that the virtue thereby achieved is a resolutely earthly one, since riches, and the ability to distribute them, are not to be found in the afterlife. In addition, nowhere does Dante insist on the necessity of grace for the attaining of this virtue of justice. Indeed, when Statius tells Virgil and Dante how he came to repent of his prodigality, we learn that it was through reading Virgil's *Aeneid* that he began to appreciate that there was a proper or sacred hunger for gold that should restrain his spending: 'Per che non reggi tu, o sacra fame / de l'oro, l'appetito de' mortali?' ('Why do you not govern, o sacred hunger for gold, the appetite of mortals' [*Purg.* 22.40–1]).[67] In an Aristotelian and even an Augustinian context, there is, of course, a proper, ordinate, and even sacred hunger for all material goods. But it is striking that Statius attributes his newfound understanding to a reading of Virgil's poem. If we think back to Virgil's inability to unmask the siren in Dante's second purgatorial dream, Statius's learning of virtue through the study of the *Aeneid* presents a telling contrast. His virtue, it seems, comes about not through a supernatural infusion of grace, but through a reading of a pagan text that brings him to an understanding of Aristotelian ethical principles. We seem on the fifth terrace suddenly to be moving within an Aristotelian moral universe, a perhaps surprising development given Dante's emphasis on grace on the previous terrace.

If we examine the passage solely as a version of the biblical subtext, however, we will see that Dante has carried the gradual process of adaptation and vernacularization even further. Similar to his practice with the previous Beatitude, he gives us a vernacular paraphrase of the biblical text, spoken in his own voice and in indirect discourse. Indeed, the Latin word used to indicate which parts of the Beatitude Dante chooses to include serves primarily to underscore the difference between the Vulgate and Dante's Italian version, which words of the Beatitude the angel did *not* include. The sixth Beatitude on the mountain carries this process of vernacularization to its logical conclusion.

Dante recounts his ascent from the sixth to the seventh terrace at the end of the canto 24, and here he returns to a direct citation of the angel's words; in this instance, however, (and only here) the angel's words are spoken entirely in Dante's vernacular:

E senti' dir: 'Beati cui alluma   (see previous Beatitude)
tanto di grazia, che l'amor del gusto
nel petto lor troppo disir non fuma,
    esurïendo sempre quanto è giusto!'
(*Purg.* 24.151–4)

(And I heard him say: 'Blessed the ones whom grace illumines so that the love of

taste does not cause too much desire in their
breast, hungering always as much as is just!')

This passage limits the fourth Beatitude to those who hunger justly, just as that on the previous terrace referred only to those who thirst. And while Dante returns here to a direct citation of the angel's words, this Beatitude is farthest yet from the biblical text; it is the only instance where none of the Beatitude is spoken in Latin, and it constitutes a thorough rewriting of the original. Whereas the previous Beatitude, while paraphrasing and editing the biblical text, gave us a paraphrase close to the biblical original, this Beatitude completely rewrites it, expanding its message and altering its focus. First, we learn that the proper hunger comes from the illumination of grace, a detail absent from the original. Second, Dante changes the primary interest of the biblical text; whereas the Beatitude directs its attention to the *object* of hunger and thirst, the angel calls blessed those who hunger *in the proper measure*. It is not so much that they hunger after justice, but that they hunger justly ('*quanto* è giusto'). This rewriting accords more fully than does the biblical original with Virgil's explanation of the organization of Purgatory in canto 17. There, Dante groups the upper three *cornici* together, since they all purge sins that arise from an immoderate desire for something that while good is not the ultimate good ('L'amor ch'ad esso troppo s'abbandona'), which alone should receive our complete devotion. That is to say, Dante alters this Beatitude so that it more fully fits into the context established in the *Purgatorio*. Dante has thus completely transformed the original biblical text; its identity as Christ's fourth Beatitude is evident simply because of the pattern that Dante has previously established. Not only is this the only Beatitude rendered completely in Italian, it has also been altered to such a degree that it is no longer biblical so much as Dantean.

The reasons for his alterations can be found in the moral context of the sixth terrace. Gluttony is the vice purged on this terrace, and as on the previous terrace we have an Aristotelian virtue that was held to correct the vice: temperance. In the *Convivio*, temperance is listed among the Aristotelian virtues, and Dante defines it as the 'regola e freno de la nostra gulositade e de la nostra soperchievole astinenza ne le cose che conservano la nostra vita' ('rule and bridle of our gluttony and of our excessive abstinence from things that are necessary to life' [4.17.4]). The Aristotelian mean is implicit in this definition: we must restrain our gluttony, but we must also avoid excessive asceticism and endeavour to act like Aristotle's temperate man: 'such pleasures as conduce to health and bodily fitness he will try to secure in moderation.'[68] Coming as we have from the fifth terrace, we may well expect an Aristotelian virtue of temperance to be advocated on the sixth terrace and to see both gluttons and the excessively ascetic, just as we saw, at least in retrospect, the avaricious and the prodigal on the previous terrace. Instead, only the gluttonous are shown, and they purge their vice by desiring fruit that emits a sweet odour but hangs on an inaccessible, inverted tree. The result of their unrequited longing is complete emaciation. Dante tells us that the gluttonous are able to move rapidly because of their leanness as well as their 'voler leggera' ('light will' [*Purg.* 24.69]). Furthermore, certain famous ascetics (such as John the Baptist) are explicitly praised, undermining the sense that temperance is the virtue that the souls cultivate on this terrace.

Nevertheless, other aspects of the terrace suggest an Aristotelian framework. The method of purgation can also be read as having a kind of Aristotelian force. The extreme of one vice (gluttony) is purged and balanced by forcing the gluttonous over to the other extreme of complete abstinence from food, hoping thereby to create a properly temperate disposition.[69] It is in fact possible to view the purgative punishments of all of the terraces of Mount Purgatory, with their repetitive actions that are aimed at correcting the will, as fundamentally Aristotelian in that they are directed toward the establishment of virtuous habits.[70] And when we come to the pronouncement of the Beatitude at the end of the terrace, Dante transforms the fourth Beatitude into one that declares the temperate blessed, as the emphasis on hungering in just measure (*quanto è giusto*) identifies the virtue praised as temperance, even though it is not explicitly named.

Interestingly, two details indicate that the temperance praised both is and is not *Aristotelian* temperance. First, by proclaiming blessed those who *always* desire in the proper measure, the angel identifies the temperance of the blessed as Aristotelian. The thirteenth century witnessed a debate about the nature of temperance and the possibility of attaining it in this life. Aristotle made an important distinction between the temperate and the continent man; both act in the same way, but only the temperate man is truly virtuous. For Aristotle, the temperate man follows his own desires, but because those desires are virtuous, he perpetually acts in accordance with virtue. The continent man, however, has both good and bad desires, but because he is capable of recognizing the difference between the two, he refuses to act on his evil desires.[71]

Augustine had defined temperance in terms that resembled Aristotle's conception of continence; that is, Augustine's temperate man, like Aristotle's continent man, has disordered desires, since human desires are necessarily disordered because our fallen nature prohibits us from becoming fully temperate (in an Aristotelian sense) in this life. When Aristotle's *Ethics* was recovered and began to circulate widely in the thirteenth century, some of the more radical Aristotelians adopted Aristotle's view that continence is not essentially a virtue,[72] a position that opposed the teachings of Augustine and was specifically targeted by the Bishop of Paris, Étienne Tempier, in his Condemnation of 1277, which was aimed at radical Aristotelian teachings.[73]

Dante, then, identifies the temperance that the blessed learn on the sixth terrace as fully Aristotelian in that it constitutes a correction of their wills so that they no longer will or hunger in any measure but a just one. It is also, however, a Christian rather than an Aristotelian virtue because the souls attain it only through an infusion of grace (*Beati cui alluma / tanto di grazia*). Thus, whereas the Beatitude pronounced after the previous terrace made no mention of this necessity of grace in regulating the desires of the blessed, this Beatitude proclaims its necessity for the souls to obtain a supernatural virtue not attainable in this life and thus only suitable for the life to come.

The reason for the dissimilar Beatitudes of these two terraces (even though, we should remind ourselves, each is derived from the same biblical Beatitude) may well lie in Dante's conception (or – to be more accurate – conceptions) of happiness. As noted above, following the rediscovery of Aristotle a debate arose concerning the question of whether happiness was attainable in this life, as Aristotle held, or could be found only in the world to come (as the Beatitudes themselves seem to imply). As we have seen, while Aquinas made some movement in the direction of an Aristotelian conception, he stopped short of recognizing earthly happiness as true happiness, seeing in it only the anticipation of the blessedness that comes after this life in the vision of God. Dante's solution, however, is more radical; after detailing the Aristotelian virtues in the fourth book of the *Convivio*, Dante asserts that there are 'due felicitadi, secondo due diversi cammini, buono e ottimo, che a ciò ne menano: l'una è la vita attiva, e l'altra la contemplativa' ('two happinesses, according to two different paths, one good and one best, that lead to them. One is the active life, and the other is the contemplative' [4.17.9]). These two happinesses constitute Dante's shrewd attempt to reconcile the Christian view with the Aristotelian, since Aristotle too associates a real happiness with the active life that is inferior to the ultimate happiness of the contemplative life;[74] Dante adapts Aristotle's discussion so that the happiness of the contemplative life becomes perfected only in the complete beatitude of the life to come, which consists in the contemplation of God.[75] Nevertheless, for Dante the happiness of the active life is crucially important, more important than for many other Christian thinkers, including Aquinas, since Dante, unlike Augustine, considers the beatitude of this life important for God's providential ordering of history. In both the *Monarchia* and *Paradiso* 6–7, Dante argues that the divine ordering of history refers to both spiritual and temporal events; God willed both our salvation through Christ *and* the Roman Empire. Dante's well-known devotion to what he took to be the divinely ordained imperial order of Rome will be discussed at greater length in chapter 5, but here it may help explain why Dante creates an Aristotelian terrace specifically for the avaricious and the prodigal.

In Dante's ordering of the vices that structure Mount Purgatory, pride has pre-eminence as the first and foundation of all the other vices. While this ordering follows a medieval tradition inscribed in Gregory's *Moralia*, it is also true that in the later Middle Ages avarice had become a more prominent vice. Lester Little has argued that due to political and social change avarice had displaced pride as the root of all evil by Dante's day, because it was seen as particularly damaging to the political and social order of late medieval Europe.[76] While Dante keeps pride as the pre-eminent vice, he also spends a good deal of time criticizing avarice in all three canticles of the *Comedy*, largely because it upsets what he understands to be the divinely ordained order between church, empire, and local rulers.[77] Indeed, given Dante's abhorrence of avarice, the balanced, Aristotelian nature of the fifth terrace may come as something of a surprise. If we consider the life of Saint Francis recounted in *Paradiso* 11, we will recall that Dante there places particular emphasis on Francis's marriage to Lady Poverty, who had remained a widow since the death of Christ.[78] Indeed, Dante frequently and explicitly condemns popes and other ecclesiastical leaders who pervert the proper, spiritual role of the church by seeking after worldly things, a fact dramatized by Dante in his portrayal of the damned simonists in *Inferno* 19, among other places. Nevertheless, Dante does not hold up poverty as an ideal for all Christians.[79] In fact, the active life, which, as we have seen, Dante praises as a 'good' road to happiness, requires the proper, liberal use of wealth. Social problems arise when wealth is used improperly, either through avarice or prodigality, the results of which can be seen in certain local leaders, who, grasping as much as they can, make it more difficult for the divinely ordained political ruler of Christendom, the Roman Emperor, to gain his rightful place. Furthermore, these rulers also abuse ecclesiastical leaders, imprisoning and persecuting, for example, Boniface VIII in Anagni. Hugh Capet describes both of these corruptions on the terrace of the avaricious (see *Purg.* 20.43–90).

Avarice thus becomes for Dante not just a private vice for the individual soul to overcome, but an ecclesiastical and a political vice. The ecclesiastical vice of avarice requires an extreme solution – the church's willing divestment of worldly goods, after the manner of Saint Francis. Political avarice, however, requires a social remedy that can only be found through an Aristotelian virtue: justice. This virtue is appropriate for the active, earthly life in which we live, and is not limited to the life beyond, because our essential beatitude here on earth depends upon it.[80]

When we look back at the first six uses of the Beatitudes in the *Purgatorio*, we see a progression in more or less linear fashion from Latin to vernacular, from citation to transformation. After beginning with a Latin citation of the Vulgate, we progress through citations with vernacular additions, vernacular paraphrases that refer to the Latin original, and finally to a complete transformation of the biblical text into something barely recognizable as biblical in origin. He makes these alterations at least in part in order to better support his own beliefs concerning terrestrial and celestial happiness and the virtues appropriate for each, but his manipulations of the biblical text also have important implications for the poetic authority that Dante seeks to establish. As we turn to the next Beatitude, however, we may be surprised to observe Dante returning to the intertextual practice with which he began: direct citation of the Vulgate.

Fuor de la fiamma stava in su la riva,
e cantava '*Beati mundo corde!*'
in voce assai più ch la nostra viva.
(*Purg.* 27.7–9)

Beati mundo corde, quoniam ipsi
Deum videbunt. (Matt. 5.8)

(Outside the flames he stood on the bank and was singing '*Beati mundo corde!*' in a voice much more alive than ours.)

(Blessed are the clean of heart: for they shall see God.)

This Beatitude, like the others we have examined, seems appropriate to its context; as the souls leave Purgatory for the Earthly Paradise, all of their sins have been purged away and their hearts cleansed. And like the 'clean of heart,' they too shall see God as they ascend to Paradise. Indeed, both Augustine and Aquinas interpret this Beatitude as referring to those who are now fit for the contemplative life and the highest object of contemplation[81] – a characterization that fits the souls leaving the seventh terrace – and anticipates Dante's final purgatorial dream of Leah and Rachel, symbolizing the active and contemplative lives respectively. In terms of Dante's intertextual practice, however, we have come full circle; Dante's citation of the Vulgate text matches his biblical citation at the beginning of the purgatorial ascent. Just when we anticipate an irreversible pattern of rewriting and transformation, Dante returns to biblical citation. Dante's progressive reworking of the Beatitudes, in other words, is framed by 'straightforward' biblical citations, containing his translations and transformations within the Latin text of the Vulgate. What, then, are we to make of Dante's shifting practice?

In the previous chapter, we noted that within the *Inferno*, biblical reworkings generally take one of two forms. Either the reworking serves as an 'infernal' transformation of the Bible, where one of the damned unknowingly miscites the Bible in such a way that a moral and biblical world is evoked, which serves to condemn the sinner who inadvertently refers to it; or, in one significant case, the transformation of the Bible carries a prophetic import, as Dante rewrites the text in order to extend the force of biblical prophecy to his own day, to deliver an authoritative, 'originary' message grounded in the Bible even though the details of that message depart from the scriptural originals. Dante's reworking of the Lord's Prayer and the Beatitudes fits into neither of these categories. Rather, in these instances we see Dante turn to the Bible in order to punctuate his narrative and to illustrate the pilgrim's ascent toward Paradise. In both, the Bible (or rather Dante's use of it) serves – at least in part – a liturgical function. These citations and reminiscences of scripture mark the stages in the journey and celebrate the progress along that path. Indeed, we can see, in the case of the Beatitudes at any rate, an attempt by Dante to create a kind of purgatorial liturgy where the transitions from one terrace to the next attain a quasi-sacramental status. Aquinas, for example, noted that 'the term sacrament is properly applied to that which is designed to signify our sanctification,'[82] a definition that serves to describe Dante's Beatitudes, which serve as visible (or, in the case of the pilgrim, audible) signs of the soul's progress toward the Earthly Paradise. In Dante's hands, Purgatory, whose presence in the scriptures is marginal to say the least, is fitted into the biblical world. But this statement represents only half of the story, for as we have seen Dante also alters the scriptures so as to fit them into his own world and poem.

Dante's combination of reverent citation and free transformation ultimately confuses the status of the Bible within the poem. We move within a biblical world, but it is hard to know where the biblical world ends and Dante's begins, or – to be more accurate – to know how Dante has reimagined and extended the Bible in the course of creating his poem. The Beatitudes serve as an ideal case in point; we tend to glance over his alterations of the Bible because he sets up a pattern of biblical citation that we have come to rely on. When we examine it more closely, however, we realize that he has established this pattern to disrupt it so that he can adapt the biblical text for his own poetic purposes. As the repentant souls climb toward ultimate blessedness, Dante creatively employs the Beatitudes to remind us that our happiness on earth is also crucially important. The Beatitudes present, for the most part, images of a Christian blessedness brought about by a grace that enables the souls that receive it to ascend to the contemplation of God. On the terrace of avarice, however, Dante avoids descriptions of grace, instead proposing an Aristotelian virtue of justice that we can follow in our life here, insisting – as he does even in the *Paradiso* – on the necessity of our beatitude on earth as well as in heaven. Souls that pass through Purgatory will have their vices purged and their wills corrected through grace as they prepare to embark on the path that will lead them to the final happiness. We on earth must learn to follow justice in order to conquer avarice and follow the path of Aristotelian virtue to our properly terrestrial beatitude.

5 Dante's Apocalypse

Dante's poem begins *in mediis rebus*, but it is oriented toward the end time. For a late medieval poem this divided attention to present and future is not unexpected. The Middle Ages were saturated with visions and versions of the end, and one could often deduce a writer's ecclesiastical and political allegiances by how he understood the denouement of human history. In considering the events of his own time, a medieval writer would almost without thinking turn to the Bible's final book as a guide to understanding them. As Frank Kermode has suggested, the Apocalypse exerted a tremendous appeal because it offered a paradigm, an outline of the reach of cosmic history within which it was possible to place oneself and one's own historical moment. Even in our own day, 'there is still a need to speak humanly of life's importance in relation to [time] – a need in the moment of existence to belong, to be related to a beginning and to an end.'[1] The fascination of the book pointed to what Bernard McGinn has called 'the desire of the human soul to find a significant place for itself in the time process.'[2]

Despite our lingering apocalyptic framework, our unthinking historical scaffold of beginning and end, nowhere is the interpretive distance between medieval and modern readers of the Bible more apparent (with the possible exception of the Song of Songs) than in considerations of the Apocalypse, or Revelation, of Saint John.[3] For many educated modern readers, the Apocalypse seems surpassingly strange, even barbaric. Harold Bloom finds it 'a book without wisdom, goodness, kindness, or affection of any kind.'[4] Virtually all medieval readers of whom we have record, however, found in the Apocalypse a profound distillation of the meaning of history – God's blueprint for humankind, and, as part of that blueprint, a manifestation of God's, yes, goodness and kindness to his people. According to these medieval readers, the Apocalypse tells us that God has not forgotten his people but will intervene to restore justice on the earth.

It is certainly true that for many readers, both modern and medieval, John's arcane imagery proves impenetrable; the book appears to us especially, but also to our predecessors, in many ways 'a *coincidentia oppositorum,* a revelation that conceals.'[5] Our own disdain, however, has more to do with our underlying assumptions than our incomprehension of the opaque symbols of the vision. George Steiner has located our contempt of the apocalyptic in what he has called 'the eclipse of the messianic.' In our modern, secular era the longed-for hope of eternal peace and the rebirth of history have fallen dormant, whether we speak of the coming of a divine messiah or the end of history through the eventual but inevitable triumph of a Marxist revolution. 'Take away energizing anticipation, the luminous imperative of waiting, and these [future] tenses will be end-stopped. "Life-expectancy" is, then, no longer a messianic-utopian projection, but an actuarial statistic.'[6] For Steiner, the forward cast of the book is as much to blame as anything else, as it fails to energize us in our secular, consumerist complacency.[7]

Given this interpretive distance, we may begin to wonder how, precisely, a reader such as Dante would have read the Book of Revelation. Perhaps our easiest assumption – derived from our experience with fundamentalist literalism – is that Dante would have read the book 'historically,' that is, as referring (albeit extremely cryptically) to a series of events, cascading disasters poised on the near horizon, culminating in the battle of Armageddon, the second coming of Christ, and the final judgment. In fact, this method of reading the Apocalypse literally, in the modern sense, was far from the norm in the Middle Ages.

Early in the history of Christianity, however, such was the case. Fuelled by Jesus' own statement in the 'little Apocalypse' of the synoptic Gospels that 'this generation shall not pass till all these things be done' (Matt. 24.34), and pressured by imperial persecution to look for dramatic intervention to alter the course of human history, early Christians eagerly read the Apocalypse and other biblical apocalyptic texts as a guide for signs of the imminent end of the world. In *De civitate Dei,* on the other hand, Saint Augustine – following the lead of lay Donatist exegete and theologian Tyconius – rejected these interpretive practices. The crux of the matter depends upon a passage near the end of Revelation, in which John prophesies the binding of Satan and the simultaneous reign of the saints with Christ for one thousand years

(Apoc. 20.1–6). Most interpreters in his day gave a chiliastic or millennial interpretation of these verses, arguing that the 'first resurrection' mentioned in verse 6 refers to a bodily resurrection, and the 'thousand years' to a literal millennium at the beginning of which Christ will bind Satan and then create a utopian society, in which he will reign with his saints. Augustine admits that he 'also entertained this notion at one time,' but ultimately came to discard it. While he certainly believed in a bodily resurrection and a final judgment on the other side of the end of history, he refused to see in John's prophesied millennium a literal thousand-year utopia that will follow the second coming of Christ. For Augustine, the 'resurrection' discussed by Christ at John 5.25–6, whose hour 'cometh and now is,' refers not to the resurrection of the body, which is what is meant by the 'second resurrection' and 'which is to come at the end of the world,' but to the 'first resurrection' of the soul, which 'is here and now' and comes to all those who accept Christ and receive forgiveness. Similarly, the millennium refers to the state of the church now; the righteous already reign with Christ.

> ... the Church even now is the kingdom of Christ and the kingdom of heaven. And so even now his saints reign with him, though not in the same way as they will then reign [after the end of history]; and yet the tares do not reign with him, although they are growing in the Church side by side with the wheat.[8]

Augustine thus proposed an anti-millenarian reading of the Bible's final book, seeing in it instead a guide to the constant tribulations of the church, tribulations so widespread and diffused across history that it proved impossible to pin them down to specific historical events.[9] The result was an undermining of apocalyptic expectations as well as a debunking of the exegetical practice of turning the Apocalypse into a *roman à clef* in which interpreters offer competing identifications of the details of John's visions.

The Tyconian/Augstinian reading of the Apocalypse became normative for the medieval church, though millenarian and apocalyptic speculation and fears continued through other channels[10] until the twelfth century. As Ann Matter has written, the early medieval commentaries on the Apocalypse see the book as an allegory of the church; like the *Glossa ordinara* commentary from the early twelfth century that draws on them, most interpretations are 'far more ecclesiological than eschatological in their focus.'[11] In the twelfth century, though, millenarianism revived. The most influential statement of this new apocalypticism was by Joachim of Fiore – the Calabrian abbot who was, according to Dante, 'endowed with a prophetic spirit';[12] he proposed a new historical reading of the Apocalypse and argued that it outlined a definite, if somewhat vague, chronology. He also saw in the book an outline of a tripartite world history, which evolved from the age of God the Father (roughly the period of the Old Testament), to the age of God the Son (from the New Testament until the present day), to the promised age of the Holy Spirit (largely in the future though its beginnings were already visible to Joachim), which would result in a renewal of religious life.[13] Joachim's writings, however, remained controversial long after his death, especially when the Spiritual Franciscans appropriated them, seeing in them a reference to their own movement and its destiny.[14]

These competing visions of the Bible's final book did, however, share a common preoccupation: both saw in the Apocalypse the shape of history as God understands it. Confronted with the seemingly inexplicable unfolding of events, exegetes turned to the Apocalypse to gain a perspective, a context of a beginning and end in which they could situate and thus grasp their own present. Individuals were drawn to the Apocalypse not so much in reaction to a crisis, but because they sought understanding.[15] There is a danger, then, in overstating the shift from the Augustinian to the Joachite reading of the Apocalypse, since both treat the notion of an end time as one in which we can come to an understanding of the nature of history as well as the individual's place within that history. As we come to comprehend both the cosmic and the individual, we are forced to decide how the two coincide, where we will place ourselves. Augustine does this by distinguishing, as mentioned above, between what Jesus calls the 'first resurrection,' which Augustine interprets as referring to the 'resurrection of the soul,' and the 'second resurrection,' which is bodily. So when Jesus declares that 'the hour cometh, and now is, when the dead shall hear the voice of the Son of God, and they that hear shall live,' he does not refer to the end of the world and the bodily resurrection that occurs after the end of human history, but to the souls of those who are dead 'because of irreligion and wickedness,' who by hearing and obeying Jesus will be reborn to newness of life.[16] For Joachim, the nearness of the calamitous events of the end time should force the individual Christian to repent. In his widely circulated 'Letter to All the Faithful,' he delineates the destruction that awaits Christendom and urges his readers not to say that 'these times are not very clear' and so excuse themselves 'from understanding and personal involvement.' The fact that these things 'will not take place in the days of your children but in your own days, few and evil,' makes the task of repentance all the more urgent. He thus concludes his letter by pleading with his readers, 'Do penance now and be converted and live.'[17]

Bernard McGinn has argued that since, for the apocalypticist, history is moving quickly and inexorably to its divinely ordained end, the apocalyptic seer is not prophetic; he, 'unlike the prophet, issues no general call to repentance to turn the Lord from his anger (he is far too angry for that!).'[18] In Augustine's and in Joachim's hands, however, the Apocalypse becomes a prophetic text, not because it predicts the future but because it confronts the reader with the urgency of repentance, by making him or her feel the impending judgment of God, whether that judgment is simply our own realization, through hearing Jesus' voice, that our souls are dead and need to be reawakened, or whether it is the judgment of God that will soon be manifested through the imminent, physical destruction that awaits the wicked who refuse to repent.[19]

The Apocalypse, in the hands of Augustine and Joachim, thus provides an implicit injunction to repentance and change as well as a hermeneutic framework in which to understand human history and one's own moment within that history. We can see the interpretive function of the Apocalypse at work in Dante's poem if we return briefly to the use of the Apocalypse in *Inferno* 19 discussed in chapter 3. Dante's obvious disgust with those at the top of the church hierarchy is shown through his sarcasm and his careful use of biblical references. He holds up the biblical models of Christ and Peter and measures the simonist popes against them; not surprisingly, the popes are found wanting. Papal avarice and corruption 'saddens the world, crushing the good and raising the depraved' (*Inf.* 19.104–5). The question that immediately arises for one convinced of God's direction of human history, however, is how this state of affairs could come about. How could God have allowed the church to degenerate so rapidly? Dante turns to the Apocalypse not only to find a 'biblical' criticism of contemporary popes, as we have seen, but also to place the corruption within a context that will allow him and his readers to understand its place within the order of history. Since John the Revelator was aware of (*s'accorse*) 'you pastors,' it is clear that the corruption of the church is not an inexplicable occurrence manifesting an absent instead of a providential deity. God himself foresaw this eventuality and showed it to John. Dante's world view, even in his distaste for the corruption of his present age, is thoroughly apocalyptic rather than, say, Gnostic. Instead of dismissing human history as a hopelessly corrupt realm governed by demonic powers, Dante asserts God's knowledge of, and ultimate control over, all of human history, even over the corrupt present. The corruption, therefore, while not willed by God, is understood and will be addressed, it is implied, in the near future. Dante's invective serves both to provide a forceful critique of the church's temporal ambitions and to 'justify the ways of God to men.' Further, it constitutes a call to repentance to the papal simonists he criticizes so vigorously; when they confront the image of Peter and Paul, working in poverty to establish God's church, they may feel their own corruption and turn away from material goods toward God. When Dante next overtly and directly considers the corruption of the church at some length, at the summit of Mount Purgatory, he will do so once again within the context of Apocalyptic historiography.

The Apocalypse and Dante's Earthly Paradise

Dante's Earthly Paradise has many precedents and sources that the poet used to flesh out his vision of human origins and destiny, but the Apocalypse is chief among them. That is to say, Dante groups the final six cantos of the *Purgatorio* together, and he does so in a way that explicitly evokes the conventions of apocalyptic literature. I am not proposing that medieval writers had a clearly defined genre, 'apocalypse,' at their disposal, with well-established contours and characteristics. Indeed, it now seems likely that nothing like a full-blown genre theory existed in the west until the sixteenth century.[20] Nevertheless, as Tzvetan Todorov has argued, certain literary types become prominent in given historical periods, and these types are used by the public 'as keys (in the musical sense) for the interpretation of works; here the genre becomes, according to an expression of Hans Robert Jauss, a "horizon of expectation." The writer in turn internalizes his expectation; the genre becomes for him a "model of writing." '[21] Similarly, Claudio Guillèn has argued that individual texts can become so influential that they become classic or model texts; that is, they serve as an 'invitation to form' to poets hoping to create certain types of literature.[22] In the case of biblical texts, the invitation to form becomes even more powerful to a poet like Dante; the portrayal of a moment of revelation would seem for a Christian poet to require a biblical form, thus showing, as we have already seen at some length, a necessary continuity between the biblical message and Dante's own. A consideration, then, of the literary type of apocalyptic as found in biblical examples reveals similarities to the final cantos of Dante's *Purgatorio.*

Bernard McGinn briefly defines an 'apocalypse' as 'a mediated revelation of heavenly secrets to a human sage,' and he goes on to distinguish between 'two broad types': 'one based on a heavenly journey in which the seer receives his message in the celestial realm through the mediation of an angel, the other in which the message is conveyed on earth but also through the agency of some celestial figure.'[23] Dante's poem reflects both types identified by McGinn; in the *Purgatorio,* Dante receives a heavenly message mediated through a heavenly sage, but in the following canticle he will receive messages through the blessed. McGinn goes on to provide a more detailed description of the apocalyptic genre, which also resonates with Dante's Earthly Paradise.

> The secrets are revealed through both visual and auditory means. The heavenly journey type tends to be more interested in the revealing of cosmological and astronomical secrets and in the eventual fate of the soul; the other type is usually more concerned with the meaning of history, especially the approaching final drama of crisis and divine judgment. Nevertheless, the interest in the heavenly world and the concern for history and its end are frequently intermingled in Apocalypses ... Above all it is textual; something meant to be written down ... Later apocalypses ... built on earlier ones in complex ways. The Apocalypse of John is, at least in part, a reworking of the canonical apocalypse of Daniel and other traditional materials.[24]

Dante receives the apocalyptic message of the Earthly Paradise through both directly spoken messages and visual representations; like John before him, Dante is given his vision so as to understand the meaning of contemporary history, and he is assured that the seeming chaos of the present is actually ordered by God's providence; in addition, in the *Paradiso* the apocalyptic aspects of the poem take on the features of the heavenly journey model. And just as John experienced his vision orally and visually but then wrote it down so that it could circulate through the world, so Dante takes the visual details of the procession and allegorical tableau that the pilgrim sees and writes them down; the poem, like the biblical Apocalypse, is ultimately textual.[25] And finally, Dante's apocalypse, like John's, consists in large measure of reworkings of previous apocalyptic material.

This last characteristic is particularly interesting in Dante's case, especially when we examine Dante's metatextual consideration of his own intertextuality during the mystical procession of canto 29, when he describes the winged beasts surrounding the chariot by sending the reader off on a journey through the Bible in order to describe them.

> A descriver lor forme più non spargo
> rime, lettor; ch'altra spesa mi strigne,
> tanto ch'a questa non posso esser largo;
>   ma leggi Ezechïel, che li dipigne
> come li vide da la fredda parte
> venir con vento e con nube e con igne;
>   e quali i troverai ne le sue carte,
> tali eran quivi, salvo ch'a le penne
> Giovanni è meco e da lui si diparte.   (*Purg.* 29.97–105)

(To describe their appearance I no longer spend my verses, reader; for other concerns constrain me, so much so that I cannot be expansive with this; but read Ezekiel, who describes them as he saw them coming from the cold region with wind and cloud and fire, and as you find them in his pages, so were these, except for the wings, where John is with me and departs from him.)

Some critics have seen in this passage a very non-biblical example of Dante's art,[26] as in it the poet draws attention to himself as the maker of the text in a way that seems remote from biblical practices. It is true enough that Dante's overt rumination on his biblical sources (and where he lines up with them, or, to be more accurate, where they line up with him) is not biblical, but the pervasive intertextuality that the passage trumpets is directly in line with apocalyptic practice. Northrop Frye, in fact, has argued that the Book of Revelation is fundamentally a hermeneutic rather than a descriptive text: 'what the seer in Patmos had a vision of was primarily, as he conceived it, the true meaning of the scriptures, and his dragons and horsemen and dissolving cosmos were what he saw in Ezekiel and Zechariah, whatever or however he saw on Patmos.'[27]

Dante's following of apocalyptic convention, then, suggests that he was consciously constructing an apocalypse, because he wanted this section of his poem to serve an apocalyptic purpose: an uncovering, or revealing, of God's design for earthly history. This message was to be delivered to a seer designated and commissioned to speak to his contemporaries for God, providing both a judgment condemning the state of the world and the assurance that the reign of wickedness would soon end and justice would be restored to the earth. Indeed, the cantos at the end of the *Purgatorio* strike most readers as different from the rest of the poem – in particular, as more straightforwardly allegorical. Earlier in chapter 3, we noted what is now a fairly common critical observation, that the arrival of Virgil in the poem's opening canto signals a new kind of representational strategy, away from personification allegory – invoked in the first half of the canto and exemplified by the three beasts Dante encounters in his attempted ascent – to a new kind of allegory, often called figural and thought to be characteristic of a biblical rather than a poetic mode of signification. While the *lupa* may well be a fairly straightforward symbol of cupidity (though this too is debated), when Virgil appears he comes as, well, Virgil; he describes himself not as 'reason,' but as the poet who lived in the century before Christ and wrote the *Aeneid* (see *Inf.* 1.67–75). In the Earthly Paradise, however, we seem to return to the form of allegory seen in the poem's opening, one that calls for one-to-one correspondences between symbol and meaning. This may be viewed negatively, as by Benedetto Croce,[28] or more neutrally, as I propose to do here. As Ronald Herzman has stated this latter view, these cantos, 'in presenting as they do a series of pageants for Dante's instruction, function as a kind of play within a play and are therefore more open to the possibility of bringing in external references – allegorical correspondences – than are most other parts of the poem.'[29] Indeed, the Apocalypse was often read, especially after Joachim, as this kind of allegory, and it therefore should not surprise us that Dante employs it when constructing his own version of the Apocalypse.

Key to Dante's apocalyptic purpose is his location of the revelation in the Earthly Paradise, as well as his placing of the biblical Garden of Eden on the summit of Mount Purgatory, on the uninhabited side of the world, at the antipodes of Jerusalem. While this location may seem innovative, as Bruno Nardi demonstrated many years ago, there were strong precedents for a location out in the ocean, in proximity to either hell or purgatory (or both), and at the summit of a great mountain, which in some accounts extends up to the lunar sphere.[30] But as Nardi also points out, Dante's reasons for placing his Eden there appear to be largely theological – in seeing Eden and Jerusalem at opposite ends of the earth, he represents geographically the Pauline doctrine that Adam's sin is perfectly repaired and offset by Christ's crucifixion and resurrection; fall and redemption mirror one another.[31] In this view, Christ's salvific death works to repair the damage of Adam's fall; thanks to his grace, we are restored to the prelapsarian state in which God originally created us. Dante's location, then, of the Earthly Paradise as the culmination of his journey of purgation forces us to consider that journey as one of return, back to the Paradise for which humankind was originally destined.

Dante's Eden represents a new beginning for the pilgrim, the most overt reference to which is found in Virgil's final spoken words in the poem, which he delivers after the pilgrim's third purgatorial dream and immediately before he ventures off on his own into the *divina foresta*:

> Non aspettar mio dir più né mio cenno;
> libero, dritto e sano è tuo arbitrio,
> e fallo fora non fare a suo senno:
>   per ch'io te sovra te corono e mitrio.   (*Purg.* 27.139–42)

(Do not wait any longer for either my word or my gesture; free, upright, and healthy is your will, and it would be a fault not to act according to its impulse: thus I crown and mitre you ruler over yourself.)

Virgil's role as guide ends here, and the newness of Dante's journey is also signalled by Virgil's departure, simultaneous with, as Charles Singleton noted, the end of the pilgrim's journey toward Beatrice.[32] Here, Dante will leave Virgil behind just as Beatrice appears, and here as well his final purgation of sin will be enacted.[33] This new beginning constitutes a return to origins; we can only begin again by going back to where we started. Matelda notes that 'Qui fu innocente l'umana radice' ('Here was the human root innocent' [*Purg.* 28.142]), matching Dante's newfound sinlessness with that of our first parents. Nevertheless, there is a crucial difference. Dante's arrival in Eden is a return, a homecoming, rather than a first residence for a newly created being. And like all travellers who make homecomings, Dante retains the marks of his voyage, a fact that will be continuously apparent in the final six cantos of *Purgatorio*.

We begin this 'apocalypse' with what seems to be a pastoral account of the Earthly Paradise, for on a first reading the sections of cantos 28 and 29 that portray Eden do not appear to belong to any kind of apocalyptic discourse. The cantos' pastoral landscape as well as the stilnovistic exchange between the pilgrim and Matelda are remote from the stark imagery of John's Revelation (and Dante's 32nd canto). If we turn to the biblical examples of Apocalypse, for instance, we do not find any extensive description of the location in which the seer receives his revelation. John only identifies the setting for his vision as 'in the island, which is called Patmos,' where he was exiled 'for the word of God, and for the testimony of Jesus' (1.9); Ezekiel similarly tells us simply that when he was 'in the midst of captives by the river Chobar, the heavens were opened, and I saw the visions of God' (1.1). Dante, instead, spends many lines portraying the 'divina foresta' of Eden, a place seemingly removed from the realities of exile and history that characterize the biblical texts. Rather than a place of exile, the Earthly Paradise represents a homecoming for Dante, a return to the place where 'the human root was innocent,' a place that God gave to man 'in earnest of eternal happiness,' when he created him 'good and for the good' (28.142, 92–3). Furthermore, the Earthly Paradise seems to owe as much to classical traditions of the Golden Age as it does to Christian traditions of Eden, as Matelda tells Dante that pagan poets 'dreamed of this place' when they wrote of the 'age of gold and its happy state,' and Dante compares Matelda herself to the pagan goddesses Proserpina and Venus. Charles Singleton has argued that Matelda is Dante's analogue of Astraea, the pagan goddess of justice who lived on earth during the Golden Age.[34]

Of course, this syncretic conflation of biblical and classical myth is quintessentially typical of our poet, but Dante may have something more in mind here than simply combining the two traditions. Dante employs a classical genre – pastoral – as a way of portraying his Earthly Paradise, and his use of classical myth serves his larger purpose in using the conventions of that literary form. Dante follows Virgil in making the pastoral a locus not immune to history, as it is in the Greek poet Theocritus, but one in which the tensions and losses of life intrude noticeably, even if they are only there because our view of it is mediated by Dante.[35] The classical references to Proserpina and Venus, in fact, point to the intrusions of history into the Golden Age. Dante's Eden has the marks of history within it, and not only because those moving through it, like Dante himself, are fallen and redeemed creatures. Thus, when Dante first speaks to Matelda, he tells her

Tu mi fai rimembrar dove e qual era
Proserpina nel tempo che perdette
la madre lei, ed ella primavera.   (28.49–51)

(You cause me to remember where and what Proserpina was at the time when her mother lost her, and she lost spring.)

The reference, as virtually all of the commentators recognize, is to the myth of Ceres and Proserpina as told by Ovid (*Metamorphoses* 5.341–571). Dante specifies the time immediately before her rape by Dis, when Ceres' contentment in her daughter created one season of perpetual spring. It may well be true, as Peter Dronke has written, that Matelda 'herself remains the incarnation of an Arcadia that knows nothing of sin and has no need of pardon.'[36] Dante's description of this prelapsarian moment, however, emphasizes the loss (*perdette*), for Dante and for the rest of us, of that innocent state. As Cioffi points out, Matelda describes human innocence in the garden solely in the past tense: 'Qui *fu* innocente l'umana radice' ('Here *was* the human root innocent' [*Purg.* 28.142; my emphasis]).[37] We are, of course, in Eden, and just as in the valley of the princes we witnessed angels banish any threat of a fall, we will come to learn that there will be no reenactment of the fall here. Nevertheless, to use a Miltonic vocabulary, the memory of paradise lost seems as palpable here as the present reality of paradise regained.[38]

Thus, when Matelda goes on to describe the rivers of the Earthly Paradise that flow from the fountain at Eden's centre, she defines them by their function in redeeming the fallen human pilgrim:

> Da questa parte con virtù discende
> che toglie altrui memoria del peccato;
> da l'altra d'ogne ben fatto la rende.   (28.127–9)

(On this side it descends with power to take away the memory of sin; on the other side it returns the memory of every good deed.)

These rivers surely recall, as Durling and Martinez and other critics point out, the rivers of hell, which are described in *Inferno* 14, where Virgil informs the pilgrim that the Acheron, the Styx, and the Phlegethon derive from the tears of the *veglio di Creta*, who inhabits Mount Ida on Crete, and which Dante derived from the dream of King Nebuchadnezzar found in the Book of Daniel. The *veglio* has a head of gold, arms and a chest of silver, and a waist of brass. The lower part of his body is of iron, but his right foot is made of clay. The figure symbolizes, as does the biblical statue described in the book of Daniel, the progressive degeneration of human history, beginning with the age of gold and descending to the clay of the right foot, on which the *veglio* leans. Human history forms a narrative of deterioration, and the rivers that flow through hell derive directly from the tears of the *veglio* that seep through the fissure that runs through his entire body starting just below his head. These rivers represent spiritual states of corruption, as well as reflecting the course of human history. The rivers in the Earthly Paradise, of course, have a very different source, deriving from the 'sure and certain fountain' that flows according to the sustaining will of God (*fontana salda e certa, / che tanto dal voler di Dio riprende* [28.124–5]), but they nevertheless are also tied up in the vicissitudes of human history, as they must repair the effects of that history on the originally fallen but now redeemed men and women who pass through the Earthly Paradise on their way to the heavens.

Dante portrays the *divina foresta* as Paradise, but a postlapsarian Paradise, regained now but only after having been lost through 'the overreaching of Eve' (*l'ardimento d'Eva* [*Purg.* 29.24]). Each reference to the garden's prelapsarian state is marked by the memory of the fall into history. Dante's initial reaction to the Earthly Paradise is one of regret as well as delight. His experience of the joys of Eden serves to awaken his dissatisfaction over the loss of paradise through the transgression and fall into time that launches human history; had Eve proved faithful, he 'would have felt these ineffable delights earlier and for a longer time.'[39] Adam, Eve, and their posterity are banished from the garden, which in any case is preserved through its inaccessibility, and has thus been immune to the vicissitudes of climate and history that befell the rest of the world. Nevertheless, once the redeemed pilgrim regains paradise, he brings the marks of history with him. In a certain sense Dante regains the lost paradise, but in another sense it is not, and can never be, the same paradise. Since Dante has changed, has been marked by the fall and by his life in the world, he can only understand and experience that paradise differently. As Saint Augustine remarks of Eden and of the impossibility of regaining the perfect 'natural body' (*corpus animalis*) that Adam once possessed in paradise, there is a sense of loss that attends the fall, even after our redemption. '"So how," they ask, "are we said to be renewed if we don't get back what was lost by the first man, in whom we all sinned?" Clearly, there is a way in which we get this back, and there is a way in which we do not get this back.'[40]

We open the following canto in much the same way that canto 28 closes, with a reference to Matelda singing as a woman in love, in the manner of a woman from the *dolce stil nuovo*.

Cantando come donna innamorata,
continüò col fin di sue parole:
'*Beati quorum tecta sunt peccata!*'   (29.1–3)

(Singing as a woman in love, she continued after the end of her words,
'*Blessed those whose sins are covered!*')

In fact, as is widely recognized, the opening line recalls Cavalcanti's *pastorella*, 'In un boschetto,' where the speaker comes upon a 'pasturella' who 'cantava come fosse 'namorata.'[41] If we begin the canto within a pastoral context, through a reference to a poem that imagines a scene similar to the one in Dante's Earthly Paradise, but that moves toward a sensual climax in which the speaker finds 'gioia e dolzore' ('joy and sweetness' [line 25]), we quickly move toward a *biblical* context that once again evokes the predominant theme of individual sin and repentance, paradise lost and paradise regained. Matelda's first words in the canto come from the thirty-first Psalm, a penitential Psalm that emphasizes the wickedness and suffering of the speaker (traditionally held to be David) for his sins. The Psalm prepares the way for cantos 30 and 31, when Dante will be made to confess sorrowfully before being newly forgiven through a baptism in Lethe. It also reminds us, however, that this place, left behind at the fall, marks the long purgatorial process that leads souls such as Dante here. Its language, as Durling and Martinez remind us, forms 'a kind of summarizing allusion to the Beatitudes sung on the terraces of Purgatory.'[42] This reminder of the purgation experienced earlier and lower on the mountain also serves to recall the personal experiences of the souls passing through those terraces that were purged away, but that nevertheless left traces of themselves.

Juxtaposed with the sense of loss over the fall that permeates Eden is a suggestion of God's control over history, an optimistic assessment that can be seen even in Matelda's laughter. When Dante and Virgil seem puzzled by it, she directs them to the Psalms: 'ma luce rende il salmo *Delectasti*, / che puote disnebbiar vostro intelletto' (but the Psalm *Delectasti* brings light that can unfog your intellect' [*Purg.* 28.80–1]). Matelda's reference is to the fifth verse of the 91st Psalm, which reads, 'Quia delectasti me, Domine, in factura tua: et in operibus manuum tuarum exsultabo' ('For thou hast given me, O Lord, a delight in thy doings: and in the works of thy hands I shall rejoice'). The scriptures provide the hermeneutic guidance to understand Matelda's behaviour; the delight that she takes in the beauty of God's creations manifests itself in a laugh of joy, which recognizes the goodness of God's creation in spite of the fall, since he has found a way to remedy the loss of human history. This optimistic assessment is echoed in the Psalm Matelda cites; following the verse to which Matelda directly refers, the Psalm continues to praise God, but this time for his justice in punishing his enemies, concluding with the assertion that the redemption of the righteous 'may show, that the Lord our God is righteous, and there is no iniquity in him.'[43] This assertion of God's control over history and the consequent triumph of the righteous over the wicked anticipates the message of the Apocalypse, and Matelda's joyous laughter seems appropriate as a measure not only of the goodness of Eden, but ultimately of God's goodness in directing human history.

While canto 28 and the opening of canto 29, with their pastoral landscape and stilnovistic dialogue between the pilgrim and Matelda, often seem remote from the apocalyptic concerns to come, Dante shrewdly adapts the main features of pastoral so as to mark them with the traces of human history. The Earthly Paradise, as the origin and final destination of humanity, becomes an ideal location for a consideration of the meaning of time, containing within itself a beginning and an end to which we are all related. Dante's Eden, among other things, establishes a narrative context for the apocalyptic meditation that will shortly follow.

The Mystical Procession

In canto 29, in fact, we begin to see frequent, direct borrowings from the Apocalypse, as this is the biblical book from which the mystical procession that the pilgrim witnesses finds its direct inspiration, a fact evident from the very beginning, when Dante sees 'sette alberi d'oro' ('seven trees of gold' [29.43]), which he eventually perceives to be *candelabri* (29.50). Dante's candelabra are usually seen to derive from the fourth chapter of the Apocalypse where John receives a vision of heaven itself and sees the throne of God and 'seven lamps (*lampades*) burning before the throne, and round about the throne, which are the seven spirits of God' (4.5). Dante takes many details of the procession from this chapter of Revelation, but his use of the word *candelabri* suggests that he had a different source from the Apocalypse – the opening chapter – in mind. In fact, the candelabra are the first thing to appear to John while he is 'in the spirit on the Lord's day' – 'seven golden candlesticks (*septem candelabra aurea*)' (see Apoc. 1.10, 12), just as they are the first elements of the procession that Dante sees. If this reference is correct, we may also need to rethink the traditional interpretation of Dante's *candelabri* as the seven gifts of the Holy Spirit, an interpretation taken from the self-exegesis of the seven *lampades* in Apocalypse 4 (see verse 5). In chapter 1, the *candelabra* are interpreted to be 'the seven churches' in Asia (1.20), to which John is instructed to write letters, and which commentators commonly took to represent the universal church.[44] I am not suggesting here that we should take the *candelabri* (instead of the chariot to come) as representing the church; rather, Dante here is attempting to establish a visionary context for what follows. John the Revelator sees seven *candelabra* at the opening of his vision and is then instructed to write to each of the seven churches represented by the candlesticks, which medieval readers would have understood as messages delivered to the church as a whole, and not simply to the specific churches in Asia specified in chapters 2 and 3. Likewise, Dante sees seven *candelabri* and, following the procession and his personal confession and rebaptism, is also instructed specifically to write what he sees. The *candelabri*, then, link Dante's vision to John's; rather than forming a specific part of the procession, they set the stage for it and for the vision that follows, and establish this 'revelation' as destined for the church as a whole.

Indeed, as we proceed, it becomes clear that the procession is to be understood as a kind of prologue to what will occur in cantos 30–33. The procession, like canto 28, provides the context for the revelation to come. We are preparing for something, and here Dante assembles a procession that symbolizes God's word as he and his medieval readers understood it – as contained within the canonical Bible. Thus, Dante first sees 'ventiquattro seniori . . . coronati venien di fiordaliso' ('twenty-four elders . . . coming, crowned with lilies' [29.83–4]). He seems to have derived this symbolism, as many have noted, from Saint Jerome's preface to the four books of Kings (two books of Samuel and two books of Kings in the King James Version), the first preface to Jerome's translation of Old Testament texts, which Jerome named 'helmeted,' or *prologus galeatus*, because he intended it to protect his work against those who disputed his choice of books. Most of the preface, in fact, consists of a list of the works of the Old Testament that Jerome argued should be considered canonical. Following the Hebrew practice of dividing the Bible into three – Torah (Books of Moses), Prophets, and Writings – Jerome finds that the five books of Moses, the eight of the prophets (which include what we would normally consider the historical books of Judges and Kings, and which count the 'twelve minor prophets' as one book), and the eleven of the Writings or *Hagiographa*, make twenty-four books in all.

And these the Apocalypse of John represents by the twenty-four elders, who adore the Lamb, and with downcast looks offer their crowns, while in their presence stand the four living creatures with eyes before and behind, that is, looking to the past and the future, and with unwearied voice crying, Holy, Holy, Holy, Lord God Almighty, who wast, and art, and art to come.[45]

Jerome's reference is to the fourth chapter of the Apocalypse, where John sees 'four and twenty seats; and upon the seats, four and twenty ancients sitting, clothed in white garments, and on their heads were crowns of gold.' They worship God sitting on his throne, '[falling] down before him' and 'cast[ing] their crowns before the throne' and praising God (Apoc. 4.4, 10–11).[46] This scene of heavenly praise inspired visual representations as well. The mosaics on the apsidal arch in Santa Pressede in Rome and the relief sculptures that fill the tympanum of the south portal of the Clunaic Abbey Church of Saint Peter in Moissac, France represent the scene, with twenty-four elders surrounding four winged figures, representing the evangelists, and Christ (or, in the case of Santa Pressede, a lamb representing Christ) in the centre. Dante takes both the white-clad elders and their crowns from the Apocalypse as interpreted by Jerome, but adds his own detail of the lilies. Most commentators read the white colour of these flowers as referring to faith in Christ to come, imposing on the diversity of Old Testament books a unity that links them to the New Testament. He also changes the song sung by the twenty-four elders; in the Apocalypse they praise God, acclaiming both his holiness and the eternity of his existence, just as the 'one like to the son of man' declares to John that he is the 'first and the last.' Dante, however, gives his elders a song in praise of a woman:

> Tutti cantavan: '*Benedicta* tue
> ne le figlie d'Adamo, e benedette
> sieno in etterno le bellezze tue!'   (*Purg.* 29.85–7)

(All sang, 'Blessed are you among the daughters of Adam, blessed be your beauties in eternity!')

Virtually all commentators identify this language as deriving from Gabriel's annunciation to Mary, 'blessed art thou among women' (*benedicta tu in mulieribus* [Luke 1.28]), which in turn echoes the praise given to Judith (in Jth. 13.23 and 15.11), but there is some debate over the recipient of this praise, with most commentators identifying her as either Mary or Beatrice. Mary may well make the most sense here; as the mother of Christ, she gives birth to the Redeemer who undoes the effects of Adam's sin, and her bearing of the Messiah is the event toward which the Old Testament books look with anticipation. Through their crowns, then, they express their faith in Christ and praise Mary, through whom Christ will be born.[47]

Jerome finds in a detail of the Apocalypse a representation of the word of God in bodily form, and Dante seizes on it to provide a concrete embodiment of God's word that will serve to contextualize his own apocalyptic vision. He nevertheless alters it somewhat, transforming the apocalyptic image from one depicting twenty-four elders before the throne of God singing praises of God's eternal nature (and which represents the scriptures as an embodiment of the eternal *logos*)[48] to a procession of elders praising Mary for her role in the Incarnation, the entrance of the eternal *logos* into history. Indeed, Dante includes references to both the second and the first comings of Christ in the procession and in the events surrounding it. The light that flashes suddenly from the east (see 29.12, 16–18) as the procession begins, for example, recalls Jesus' statement in Matthew's Little Apocalypse that his own second coming would be like 'lightning coming out of the east' (Matt. 24.27). Dante's wondering at this light, 'che cosa è questa?' ('what thing is this?' [29.21]), alludes to the puzzled reactions of those who witnessed Christ's early miracles and the miraculous Pentacostal preaching of the apostles.[49] The singing of 'Hosanna' by the procession at line 51 reminds us of the voices that greeted Christ's triumphal entry, celebrated and liturgically reenacted on Palm Sunday. And indeed, we will see as we progress that, while Dante in some ways provides us with a processional, liturgical representation of the Bible that implies a static conception of God's word, he also includes details that historicize the scriptures, seeing them as similar to the Incarnation itself – the word of God made flesh by being embodied in particular moments in history.

Dante derives many further details from Apocalyptic imagery. Following the twenty-four elders, Dante sees four animals similar to those which John had seen with the twenty-four elders in his vision of the throne of God, and which Jerome mentions in his prologue: 'quattro animali, / coronati ciascun di verde fronda' ('four animals, each crowned with green branches' [29.92–3]). The green branches, most commentators agree, symbolize the hope of salvation; whereas the Old Testament scriptures looked forward with faith to the advent of Christ, the evangelists announce the reality of the hope of redemption through the birth and Passion of the Messiah. Dante then enriches his description: each of the animals has six wings, whose feathers are filled with eyes, which Dante describes by saying that if the eyes of Argus were real, they would be similar. But he goes on to refer us to Ezekiel for a fuller account (Ezekiel 1.4–14 contains a much more detailed portrayal of the creatures than Dante, or John, gives us), with a correction made by John. As discussed above, this intertextual journey is not foreign to apocalyptic convention, as these visionary texts frequently rework and elaborate on images and tropes from earlier visions, as John does with Ezekiel's. The difference for Dante is that he overtly advertises this intertextual relationship. He clearly wants us to notice that he is working within this biblical tradition, inheriting it from his New Testament predecessor, to whom he is closer than he is to Ezekiel. It is interesting, too, that Dante identifies the 'penne' as the source of difference between the Old Testament prophet and both John and himself.[50] Typically, this detail has been interpreted to mean that Dante's creatures possess six wings, as do John's (see Apoc. 4.8), while the creatures in Ezekiel's vision possess only four (see Ezek. 1.6). Dante specifies the difference between his account and Ezekiel's, however, not in wings, *ali*, but in feathers, *penne:* 'e quali i troverai ne le sue carte, / tali eran quivi, salvo ch'a le penne' (and as you find them in his pages, so were these, except with respect to the feathers' [*Purg. 29.103–4*]). The use of *penne* would seem to refer to the 'eyes' of the creatures, since he specifically mentions eyes with reference to *penne:* 'Ognuno era pennuto di sei ali; / le penne piene d'occhi' ('Each was feathered with six wings, the feathers full of eyes' [*Purg. 29.94–6*]). The 'eyes' prove to be important because, while John's creatures possess wings 'full of eyes,' Ezekiel's do not; instead, the wheels of Ezekiel's chariot are 'full of eyes,'[51] and so represent another difference between John and Ezekiel that Dante may well be pointing to here. As Teodolinda Barolini has observed of this passage, 'the issue is emphatically sight – what Argus sees, what the pilgrim sees, what Ezekiel sees, what John sees, what Dante sees.'[52] If this interpretation, which notes Dante's and John's difference from Ezekiel in both the number of the wings and the eyes found on the wings, is correct, it reinforces the sense we have that by moving from the pagan Ovid to the Old Testament Ezekiel to the New Testament John, with whom Dante aligns himself, we are increasing in vision and in sight, and Dante's own poem is like scripture, in that it has been written by one who has seen.

The next thing that catches Dante's attention – 'un carro, in su due rote, trïunfale, / ch'al collo d'un grifon tirato venne' ('a chariot, triumphal, on two wheels came, attached to the neck of a griffin' [*Purg.* 29.107–8]) – has no precedent in the Apocalypse, but is invented by Dante from other sources. E.R. Curtius points out, for example, that the 'allegorical car was a favorite motif in the twelfth and thirteenth centuries,' citing examples from Hildebert, Walter of Chatillon, John of Garland, and Alan of Lille.[53] Within the poem, Dante explicitly mentions the Roman triumphal chariots used to honour Scipio Africanus and Augustus; even the mythical chariot of the sun would seem poor next to it. The commentators almost universally identify this splendid chariot as the church, which, significantly, exists *within* the four animals that surround it: 'Lo spazio *dentro* a lor quattro contenne / un carro...' (*Purg.* 29.106–7; emphasis mine). Dante's statement in the third book of the *Monarchia* (discussed in chapter 1) that the Old and New Testaments exist *ante ecclesiam* and are therefore both temporally and authoritatively prior to the church itself reinforces this reading; the church is in some way dependent upon the scriptures, especially the Gospels, as the model for what the church should be.[54] Toward the end of the *Monarchia*, in fact, Dante asserts that the 'form of the Church is nothing other than the life of Christ, as much in his words as in his deeds.'[55] The Gospels that recount the life of Christ present for us the form that the church should follow. As we saw in chapter 3, it is the failure of contemporary popes to live up to the model of Christ's life as presented in the New Testament that condemns them in Dante's eyes.

In fact, most commentators find in Dante's discussion of the chariot of the sun a reference to the vengeance of God destined to come upon the church for its deviation from biblical models.

> quel del Sol che, svïando, fu combusto
> per l'orazion de la Terra devota,
> quando fu Giove arcanamente giusto.   (*Purg.* 29.118–20)

(that [chariot] of the Sun that, veering off course, was incinerated through the prayer of the devout Earth, when Jove was mysteriously just.)

We have already noticed one important Ovidian subtext in Dante's evocation of Argus; the reference to Phaeton constitutes the second, suggesting that next to the scriptures, the *Metamorphoses* provides the most important subtext for the procession, as Dante here evokes a figure already familiar to readers of the poem. Kevin Brownlee has argued that Phaeton figures here and throughout the *Commedia* as an inverted image of the pilgrim; whereas the simile suggests an awed Phaeton preparing – unwisely and presumptuously – to enter the chariot, the pilgrim here admires the chariot without daring to enter it.[56] The pilgrim's refusal to act as Phaeton and unwisely ascend into the ark recalls Dante's letter to the Italian Cardinals, in which he counters the charge that he is a rash layman who, like the Old Testament Uzzah, presumptuously 'steadies the ark' in levelling his criticism against the properly established leaders of the church, by claiming that he is not steadying the ark but trying to direct the stubborn animals leading the ark of God astray: '[Uzzah] paid attention to the ark, I to the recalcitrant oxen dragging [the ark] out of the path. He provides for the ark who opened his saving eyes on the fluctuating boat.'[57] This reference to cardinals as straying oxen together with the assertion of Christ's providence in attending to the ark himself parallels Dante's reference here to the chariot of the sun and Jove's mysterious justice. God's justice is now mysterious, as corruption in the church flourishes, but the promise contained in Dante's summary of Ovid's story as well as in the reference to Uzzah in his letter to the Italian Cardinals foresees the ultimate justice of God.

But while the meaning of the chariot has occasioned little debate, the identity of the griffin has provoked alternative views, especially within the last two decades or so. Peter Armour and John Scott make perceptive objections to the common reading and offer intriguing counter proposals, but the traditional view of the Griffin as Christ, whose dual nature of lion and eagle mirrors Christ's human and divine natures, still seems to me most persuasive.[58] As we have seen, Dante ties the 'form of the church' very closely to the life of Christ, and it is therefore appropriate that here, among the evangelists, the church take its meaning and direction from Christ himself.

The chariot and the griffin are interesting precisely because, like the seven *donne* that surround them, symbolizing the theological and cardinal virtues (see lines 121–32), they do not represent biblical books or authors, as do all the other figures from the procession. Peter Dronke sees the seven women as deriving from a biblical source – the seven stars in Apocalypse 1.6, where the figure seen by John is described as having 'in his right hand seven stars.'[59] Whatever the specific source of these details, Dante uses them in intriguing ways. As we have already seen, the church is seen in the midst of the evangelists to suggest the dependence of the church on the scriptures. The seven *donne* suggest the virtues that should attend the church at all times, but also, perhaps, the virtues that should follow the reading, and living, of the scriptures. The procession, in other words, does not solely represent the biblical word of God; it also represents the effect of the Word within the world, an idea that, as we saw in chapter 2, Dante explores extensively in the examination cantos of the *Paradiso*.

Following the description of the chariot, the griffin, and the seven dancing *donne*, Dante describes the remainder of the procession.

> Appresso tutto il pertrattato nodo
> vidi due vecchi in abito dispari,
> ma pari in atto e onesto e sodo.
> L'un si mostrava alcun de' famigliari
> di quel sommo Ipocràte che natura
> a li animali fé ch'ell' ha più cari;
> mostrava l'altro la contraria cura
> con una spada lucida e aguta,
> tal che di qua dal rio mi fé paura.
> Poi vidi quattro in umile paruta;
> e di retro da tutti un vecchio solo
> venir, dormendo, con la faccia arguta.   (*Purg.* 29.133–44)

(After the knot already described had completely passed, I saw two elders in diverse dress but alike in their behaviour – dignified and sober. The first seemed one of the disciples of that exalted Hippocrates, whom Nature made for the animals that she holds most dear; the other showed the opposite interest with a lucid, sharp sword so that even from the other side of the river he made me fear. Next I saw four in humble dress; and at the end of all, I saw an elder coming alone, sleeping, with a sharpened countenance.)

One of the intriguing things about this procession is that Dante alters the method of representation; for the Old Testament and the Gospels, he had used one figure to represent one book – twenty-four elders for twenty-four Old Testament books (even though, for example, Dante would have believed Moses to be the author of the first five books); four creatures for four Gospels. Here, however, the allegorical meaning of the figures seems to shift from the books themselves to their authors, since we see one figure of Paul to represent all twelve of his New Testament Epistles. The portrayal of the apostolic section of the New Testament in authors, nevertheless, is still not accomplished in an entirely consistent way. Luke is portrayed as the 'most dear physician,' as Paul calls him in his letter to the Colossians (4.14), which presumably is the source of the tradition of Luke's medical training.[60] The figure cannot represent Luke as the author of all of his New Testament works, as his Gospel had already been represented by one of the *quattro animali* that surround the chariot. Here, we must assume that he represents only the Book of Acts, the second half of his treatment of the origins of Christianity, which concerns the progress of the church following the resurrection and ascension of Christ, and which he links to his Gospel in the opening verses of the work.[61] Paul and Luke are linked, as Luke was Paul's missionary companion, and Acts devotes a good deal of space, most of the last two-thirds of the work, recounting the preaching and journeys of Paul. As I argued above, however, Dante wanted to present the canonical Gospels together as a group in order to emphasize the indebtedness of the church toward them, and so it was necessary for him to separate them out, even when their authors were held to be responsible for other works within the New Testament. These authors, including Luke and John, are therefore represented more than once.

Paul's carrying a sword derives ultimately from a passage in Ephesians, where Paul advises his readers to put on the 'armour of God,' including the 'sword of the Spirit (which is the word of God)' (see 6.11, 17), which also matches the common iconography of Paul. The portrait of Paul may also owe something to the portrayal of the 'one like to the Son of man,' described in the opening chapter of the Apocalypse with 'a sharp two edged sword' coming from his mouth (1.16), as well as to the description in Hebrews of the word of God, which is 'more piercing than any two edged sword; and reaching unto the division of the soul and the spirit, of the joints also and the marrow, and is a discerner of the thoughts and intents of the heart' (4.12). The fear that the sword induces in Dante from across the river thus has more to do with the power of the word of God that Paul speaks than to the threat of violence.

The four who follow Luke and Paul, briefly described as 'in umile paruta,' represent the Catholic Epistles, so called because each addresses the entire church. Once again, the figures represent the authors of the letters, rather than the letters themselves. While one Epistle is attributed to James and Jude each, two are assigned to Peter and three to John. The final figure, the 'vecchio solo... dormendo, con faccia arguta' continues the emphasis on representing biblical authors found at the end of the procession. As is the case with Luke, whom Dante represents with two figures to represent his Gospel and the Book of Acts, Dante actually employs three figures to account for all of the works attributed to John. One of the four animals stands in for John's Gospel, one of the four in humble attire represents his three general Epistles, and the sleeping elder becomes a figure for John the Revelator, who, Dante believed, was the same who authored the Gospel and the Epistles. Only in this last figure, however, does Dante individualize the figure to any degree. His age may refer to John's legendary long life, and his 'sleeping with a sharpened countenance' no doubt refers to his visionary abilities; while sleeping he nevertheless sees things invisible to mortal sight. A few critics have argued that we should see a figure of Dante himself in this *vecchio*, since he, like John, sees things others cannot see and reveals the truth of these hidden things to our mortal eyes.[62] We may speculate, in fact, that Dante's portrayal of the late New Testament biblical books – those that treat matters postdating the life of Christ – through their authors, culminating in John the Revelator, constitutes an attempt to provide an image for biblical, inspired authorship that he will draw on in the *Paradiso* in constructing his own identity as an inspired poet, one called to write the truth to an erring world.

These last seven figures wear crowns of red flowers so that 'giurato avria poco lontano aspetto / che tutti ardesser di sopra da' cigli' ('one not far removed would have sworn that all burned above their eyebrows') (*Purg.* 29.149–50). In this procession, then, Dante divides the biblical canon not into the two parts of Old and New Testament, as we would expect, but into three parts: Old Testament, Gospels, and other New Testament writings. Whereas the Old Testament figures wear crowns of white – the colour of faith, to represent their anticipation of Christ who would come to remedy the effects of the fall – and the animals representing the Gospels wore green crowns, noting their hope in Christ who has now come, these last figures are crowned in red, the colour of charity. As a whole, the figures representing the Bible are crowned with the colours that clothe the three women who dance next to the right-hand side of the chariot, representing the three theological virtues. The crowns serve to unite the scriptures, which, while they fit along a historical continuum that unfolds according to God's providential design, also are united within that overarching pattern. The Old Testament books look forward to Christ, the hope of whom is presented in the Gospels. The apostles then take that hope into the church and beyond, motivated by charity.

Dante presents us with a figuration of the Bible, as the word of God is personified, made flesh, and paraded before Dante, Statius, and Virgil.

If the procession is to be taken historically, as a chronological represen-tation of the unfolding of the word of God in time, the church must be understood, as suggested above, as the product of the Gospels and of the life of Christ that they recount. The later New Testament scriptures, then, come after the church, which is also seen as the product of divine providence and which has a dependent relationship to the scriptures, which surround and guide it. We come to grasp the significance of the church by recognizing its place within the world history recounted and foreseen in the word of God. Saint Bonaventure described this histori-cal function of the Bible in a passage that deserves to be cited at some length:

> And so the whole course of the universe is shown by the Scriptures to run in a most orderly fashion from beginning to end, like a beautifully com-posed poem in which every mind may discover, through the succession of events, the diversity, multiplicity, and justice, the order, rectitude, and beauty, of the countless divine decrees that proceed from God's wisdom ruling the universe. But as no one can appreciate the beauty of a poem unless his vision embraces it as a whole, so no one can see the beauty of the orderly governance of creation unless he has an integral view of it. And since no man lives long enough to observe the whole with his bodily eyes, nor can anyone by his own ability foresee the future, the Holy Spirit has given us the book of the Scriptures, whose length corresponds to the whole duration of God's governing action in the universe.[63]

This historical narrative is at this point only implicit, suggested through the unfolding of the procession in time as well as the pro-gressive symbolism of the crowns and other details. We have already seen that the Earthly Paradise is not only the place where human his-tory began and to which it seeks to return, it also bears within it the marks of that history, and it is therefore the place where human history can be viewed from a distance, contextualized, and understood. The scriptures for Dante are an integral part of that process of historical understanding.[64]

Cantos 30 and 31: Judgment and Redemption

We begin canto 30 with the first of several elaborate similes:

> Quando il settentrïon del primo cielo,
> che né occaso mai seppe né orto

né d'altra nebbia che di colpa velo,
   e che faceva lì ciascuno accorto
di suo dover, come 'l più basso face
qual temon gira per venire a porto,
   fermo s'affisse: la gente verace,
venuta prima tra 'l grifone ed esso,
al carro volse sé come a sua pace.   (*Purg.* 30.1–9)

(When the Septentrion of the first heaven, which has never known setting
nor rising nor the veil of another fog than that of guilt, and which there
made each aware of his duty, as the lower [Septentrion] does for the one
who turns the helm in order to come to port, came to a stop: the truthful
people who had come first between the griffin and it, turned themselves
to the chariot as if to their peace.)

At the conclusion of the previous canto, Dante informed us that the entire procession had come to a halt 'with the first standards' (*fermandosi
ivi con le prime insegne*) (*Purg.* 29.154), a baldly descriptive statement.
As we open the next canto, however, he repeats the same information
much more indirectly, as if illustrating an entirely different narrative
style. Here the candelabra are compared to the stars of the *ursa minor*
or little dipper – the constellation that, from the perspective of southern
Europe, never rises or sets, and that contains the pole star, by which
sailors navigated.[65] Like those stars, these lights never rise or set and
are only obscured by the veil of sin that obscures this heavenly guide
from the vision of mortals. The choice of describing the candelabra
through a constellation allows Dante to engage with the dialectic between time and eternity that has been operative throughout the Earthly
Paradise. Stars are heavenly and eternal, set above the sublunary realm
in the static world of the heavens. Nevertheless, through their motion,
time is measured on earth; Dante, following Aristotle, defined time in
the *Convivio* as a 'number of celestial movement.'[66] The *ursa minor,* by
including some of the few stars that never rise and set, approximates an
eternal motion, always visible in the night sky. Since it also contains the
pole star that orients sailors through a fixed point, a star that appears
to remain fixed in the heavens, it becomes like eternity itself, or, like
the end time that can force us to understand our own present moment.
Signalled by the candelabra, the twenty-four elders representing the
Old Testament turn to the chariot as if to their own peace, the peace that
ultimately comes only outside of time when we rest in God. The simile,

in other words, combines imagery of both motion and stasis, time and eternity, and therefore becomes an apt image of this Earthly Paradise which exists outside of human history and yet bears the traces of time within it.

This split attention to time and eternity is, as we have seen, the very definition of apocalyptic time, and Dante pushes that dialectic further as we proceed:

> e un di loro, quasi da ciel messo,
> *'Veni, sponsa, de Libano'* cantando
> gridò tre volte, e tutti li altri appresso.
>   Quali i beati al novissimo bando
> surgeran presti ognun di sua caverna,
> la revestita voce alleluiando:
>   cotali in su la divina basterna
> si levar cento, *ad vocem tanti senis,*
> ministri e messaggier di vita etterna.   (*Purg.* 30.10–18)

(and one of them, as if sent from heaven, 'Come, spouse, from Libanus!' singing, he cried three times, and all the others after him. Just as the blessed at the last call will rise instantly, each from his cavern, with his reclothed voice singing hallelujah: so on the divine chariot, at the voice of such an elder, there arose a hundred ministers and messengers of eternal life.)

First, the antiphonal exchange is worth noting. One of the elders, presumably the elder representing the Canticle of Canticles, speaks a slightly altered version of Cant. 4.8, which in the original reads, 'Veni de Libano sponsa, veni da Libano, veni' ('Come from Libanus, my spouse, come from Libanus, come'). He is then answered by all the others in the procession, who repeat his citation. Ann Matter has noted how the liturgical use of the Canticle alters the force of the text, transforming it from one in which God speaks into one in which human voices speak 'to heaven (to the Virgin Mary and to God) in praise and petition.'[67] This seems to be what we have here – a literal enactment of the New Testament's typological view of the Old Testament. The chanting elder, in this view, represents all the faithful who preceded Christ and who therefore looked forward with the eye of faith to fulfilment of the words of the Old Testament in the life and Passion of Christ. The verse he cites was, as was the entire Canticle of Canticles, commonly interpreted as an allegory in which Christ was seen as the bridegroom and the spouse was seen as the church, or the Christian soul, or, in many cases, the Virgin Mary.[68] It might seem, then, that the Virgin would be the object of the elder's scriptural plea. She makes sense within the biblical procession, as she represents the fulfilment of Old Testament prophecies in reversing the fall through the birth of her son, fulfilling, for example, the Lord's promise to Adam and Eve that the woman would crush the head of the serpent, commonly interpreted to refer to Mary's giving birth to Christ, who would defeat the devil. In the Coventry mystery play of the Annunciation, for example, Isaiah provides a prologue, in which he reminds his listeners of their dire state since a serpent gave them a mortal wound. Now, though, a maiden has come to conceive a child that will provide the remedy.[69] In terms of the unfolding of canto 30, however, Beatrice seems to make the most sense, as she will shortly appear in the chariot as the centre of the procession. As a *figura Christi*, someone who represents Christ for Dante, she too can be seen as an object of Old Testament longing. Indeed, with the rise of the cult of Mary, Beatrice's identity within the poem and within Dante's work as a whole no doubt draws from Mary and contemporary ideas of her. Dante creates a female figure who participates in the divine and serves as the intermediary between himself and God, drawing him to herself only to then draw him further towards God.[70]

Following this scriptural evocation, the procession is joined by 'a hundred' angels, who arise like the blessed at the winding up of history, leaving their graves behind and rejoicing in the Resurrection. We are placed, in other words, in an explicitly apocalyptic context, living through an anticipatory enactment of the end of time, complete with a resurrection, and, as we shall soon see, a judgment. These angels, though, refer back to the first coming of Christ through their citation of Latin texts, both scriptural and Virgilian:

> Tutti dicean: '*Benedictus qui venis!*'
> e, fior gittando e di sopra e dintorno,
> '*Manibus, oh, date lilïa plenis!*' (*Purg.* 30.19–21)

(All said, 'Blessed you who come!' and, throwing flowers both above and around, 'oh, give lilies with full hands!')

The first Latin citation comes, of course, from the Bible, originally from Psalm 117.26: 'Blessed be he that cometh in the name of the Lord,' a scriptural passage that was spoken by the multitudes to Christ during his triumphal entry into Jerusalem as a sign that they recognized him as the Davidic king. In Matthew's account, the crowd cries, 'Hosanna to the son of David: Blessed is he that cometh in the name of the Lord: Hosanna in the highest' (21.9).[71] As Grandgent noted, these 'are the last words sung by the assistants before the canon of the Mass; they express the expectation of the bodily coming of Christ.'[72] Dante changes the citation to the second person so as to address Beatrice directly, but he preserves the masculine ending of the adjective *benedictus,* reinforcing her identity as a *figura Christi.*

The second citation is more complex. It comes, as is well known, from the end of the sixth book of the *Aeneid* (and is the only Latin citation of the *Aeneid* in the poem), after Anchises has shown Aeneas his great progeny, destined to follow Aeneas's successful founding of the city that will become Rome. At the end of the procession of these shades, after the future shape of Roman history has become clear to Aeneas, one final shade approaches, but he does so with black night encircling his head in shadows (*nox atra caput tristi circumvolat umbra*).[73] When Aeneas asks his father the identity of the shade, Anchises tells him that he will be Marcellus, Augustus's adopted son, destined to an untimely death. Anchises then scatters lilies and 'scarlet flowers as well' – flowers of mourning for Virgil[74] – as an empty gift and a 'ritual of no avail' (*inani munere*) (6.885–6) in Fitzgerald's translation. Here, perhaps more than at any other place in Virgil's poem, we sense the disparity between public and private voices, between public triumph and private grief that, as Adam Parry observed in his famous essay, is frequently registered in the *Aeneid.*[75] For Virgil, public triumph cannot redeem the private tragedy of death, and even following the portrayal of the future glories of Rome and Augustus, Anchises offers Aeneas no comforting words of redemption for Marcellus's death; it is, instead, absolute.

When we return to examine the passage's appearance in the *Commedia,* however, we find something completely different. Dante has inserted Anchises' words, which mark a fruitless mourning, into a context of celebration, one in which we anticipate the arrival of Beatrice, whose coming is compared to that of Christ at both his triumphal entry into Jerusalem and his coming in glory at the final summons, *al novissimo bando,* anticipating the resurrection that he will bring. In this context the lilies, offered by Anchises as flowers of consolation and mourning, take on a Christian meaning as the flower of the Virgin Mary, who becomes the vehicle through whom God enters into human history to redeem it, and as the flower of the Resurrection, which seems to derive from the association of the 'Easter lily.'[76] Dante, that is to say, transforms Virgil's words of private tragedy into words of public *and* private triumph.

Shortly following this tercet, Dante recognizes Beatrice in the veiled woman who appears in the chariot in the midst of this profusion of angels and flowers, and he compares her appearance to the rising sun, another image frequently used of Christ. He turns to Virgil to tell him that his love remains alive: 'conosco i segni de l'antica fiamma' ('I recognize the signs of the old flame') (*Purg.* 30.48), a phrase that closely translates *Aeneid* 4.23, 'agnosco veteris vestigia flammae,' Dido's words to her sister Anna after she has fallen in love with Aeneas. Nevertheless, here again Dante has altered Virgil's meaning. At the opening of book 4, Dido, having fallen in love (at the connivance of Venus and Cupid) with Aeneas while he narrated his adventures, prepares to break her vow to her dead husband Sychaeus and take up with Aeneas in an uncontrolled, irrational love (which Virgil terms *furor*) that eventually leads to her death. Dante, however, remembers here his earliest beloved, the one to whom he should have been faithful but whom he abandoned following her death. As Beatrice herself tells Dante later in the canto, early in his life she had been able to lead him along the right path, but as soon as she died Dante left her for another (*e diessi altrui*) (*Purg.* 30.126).

> Quando di carne a spirto era salita,
> e bellezza e virtù cresciuta m'era,
> fu' io a lui men cara e men gradita;
>   e volse i passi suoi per via non vera,
> imagini di ben seguendo false,
> che nulla promession rendono intera.   (*Purg.* 30.127–32)

(When my soul had leapt from flesh to spirit, and my beauty and virtue had increased, I was less dear to him and less welcome; and he turned his steps on to an untrue path, following false images of good, which never entirely fulfil any promise.)

There is, of course, some debate about the identity of Dante's 'false images of good,' though most point to the *donna gentile* with whom Dante finds some consolation in the *Vita Nuova* following Beatrice's death, and whom he interprets in the *Convivio* as philosophy. While I would agree with this reading, the precise identification is not important for our purposes here. Dante's *antica fiamma,* unlike Dido's *vetus flamma,* represents a return to a purer, more divine love, one that, rather than driving him to a carnal death, will lead him to a newness of spiritual life. It is as if, here and in the previous citation, Virgil's text has been brought into the biblical world, and its images and words now take on the force of a biblical reality.

Dante's realization that Virgil has left him leads him to mourn his departure in the following tercet, in which he speaks the name of his guide three times:

> Ma Virgilio n'avea lasciati scemi
> di sé, Virgilio dolcissimo patre,
> Virgilio a cui per mia salute die'mi   (*Purg.* 30.49–51)

> (But Virgil had left us deprived of himself, Virgil, sweetest father, Virgil, to whom I gave myself for my salvation)

This double repetition alludes to yet another Virgilian text. Near the end of the fourth book of the *Georgics,* Proteus recounts the story of Orpheus and Eurydice. Devastated by the death of his wife, Orpheus makes his way to the underworld, where his poetry overcomes Pluto and death itself, and he leads his beloved Eurydice back to the surface. Just before he emerges, however, he looks back at her, and she is lost to him forever. Unable to move the dead again, he does nothing but lament his lost wife for seven months, until a group of bacchantes, upset with his perpetual dirge, tear him to pieces. Even in death, though, he continues to mourn:

> Eurydicen vox ipsa et frigida lingua,
> a miseram Eurydicen! anima fugiente vocabat:
> Eurydicen toto referebant flumine ripae.   (4.525–7)

> ('Eurydice,' that voice itself and his cold tongue called out, his soul fleeing, to wretched Eurydice: the river banks along the entire river echoed back 'Eurydice.')

This passage, like the earlier one from *Aeneid* 6, is one of mourning, a lament not only of death's power, but also of poetry's inability to redeem the loss imposed by death. Interestingly, this last, most distant allusion to a Virgilian text remains closest in meaning to the original.

Dante's lament for Virgil is heartfelt, as he realizes that, while his own sins will be forgiven and his life redeemed as he makes his way up to paradise, Virgil must return to the first circle of hell, eternally exiled from the heavenly Jerusalem, since he was, as he tells Dante at the very beginning of the poem, rebellious to God's law, and God does not want him in his city.[77] Just as the paradigmatic poet Orpheus was unable to rescue Eurydice through his song, not even Dante's poem can effect the redemption of the great Roman poet. His mourning of Virgil, like Orpheus's of Eurydice, appears hopeless.[78]

It is no accident that shortly following this moment, as John Freccero has observed, Beatrice appears and pronounces, for the only time in the poem, Dante's name.[79] Dante, that is to say, here makes a claim for his own poetic identity – as a Christian, comic poet who breaks free of his pagan, tragic predecessor.[80] Dante's loss of Virgil coincides with the appearance of Beatrice, his new guide and a figure of Christ, and, seen from the perspective of the *Vita Nuova*, the central figure of his own poetry. And if Beatrice as a figure of Christian poetry replaces Virgil in this canto, it seems that the Bible replaces the *Aeneid*, as the decreasing Virgilian textual presence, moving in the course of just a few lines from Latin citation to translation to echo, is balanced by an increasing biblical presence. We have already seen that in the same tercet in which Dante cites the Latin text of the *Aeneid*, he also cites (in slightly altered form) the Gospel of Matthew. Somewhat earlier, an elder from the Old Testament cites the Canticle of Canticles, also in Latin; later, the angels will sing the first eight verses of the thirtieth Psalm, to which Dante refers by citing the first line of the Vulgate text.[81] This canto, in other words, includes three separate Latin citations of the Vulgate Bible. Here, as we saw early in Purgatory, Dante seems to want to draw attention to the fact of scriptural presence within his poem, a presence that was literally enacted in the previous canto when the Word of God was personified and paraded before the pilgrim.

Following Beatrice's appearance, Dante becomes the focus of the procession, as she rebukes him for his sadness over Virgil's departure, pronouncing 'pianger' three times, as if the longing for Virgil expressed in Dante's three 'Virgils' had now to be transformed into repentance through mourning for his sins.[82] After noting the remarkable gifts that Dante had received, gifts that should have led to great things, Dante turned away from Beatrice after her death. She describes the seriousness of Dante's sins by stating that it was only through visiting hell that he was able to be rescued from his sinful state:

Tanto giù cadde, che tutti argomenti
a la salute sua eran già corti,
fuor che mostrarli le perdute genti.   (*Purg.* 30.136–8)

(He fell so far, that all arguments for his salvation were short to reach him,
outside of showing him the lost people.)

Charles Singleton has argued extensively that the procession culminating with the appearance of Beatrice presents us with an analogy of Christ's second coming, in which Beatrice serves as a *figura Christi*, whose coming not only anticipates Christ's second coming but also his role as judge, with her judgment of Dante serving as a precursor to the final judgment at the end of history,[83] which is described in the Apocalypse: 'And I saw the dead, great and small, standing in the presence of the throne, and the books were opened; and another book was opened, which is the book of life; and the dead were judged by those things which were written in the books, according to their works' (20.12). But while Singleton seeks to uncover what he calls the 'pattern at the center,' and the ways in which the *Vita Nuova* anticipates and to some degree projects into the *Comedy*, here I seek to emphasize Dante's use of an apocalyptic context as the culmination of his purgatorial journey. The pilgrim here confronts his own end time, a judgment that imposes a kind of closure on his life, so that he can grasp how fully he has strayed from the path that Beatrice marked out for him.

John Freccero has pointed out that Christian autobiography, especially as first practiced by Saint Augustine, seeks to solve a narratological problem that haunts the entire autobiographical enterprise. If autobiography seeks to gain and present a sense of the writer's life as a whole, it is marred by the impossibility for the writer to see that life completely, simply because an entire life can only be understood after death. In Saint Augustine's account of his early life, however, this problem is solved by the imposition of an end – conversion – that gives shape and order to the period of his life that led to that moment. As Saint Paul puts it, conversion and baptism bring about the death of our old self and the birth of a new self through our turning to God: 'we are buried together with him [Christ] by baptism into death; that as Christ is risen from the dead by the glory of the Father, so we also may walk in newness of life' (Rom. 6.4). There are thus two Augustines who appear in the *Confessions*. The second, post-conversion Augustine narrates the life of the earlier, now spiritually dead Augustine, whose life, which ends at conversion, can be understood whole by the later Augustine, who looks back on the story of his earlier self and recognizes in it a narrative shape of fall and redemption that ends famously in a garden. Of course, Dante's poem has a similar narrative structure – the poet recounts the conversion and journey to God of his earlier self; and as he also stands in a garden, he suddenly sees that self whole.[84] Thus, when the pilgrim responds to Beatrice's demand that he confess his sins and tell her why he strayed from her, his response avoids specifics but blames his straying on the appeal of 'present things': 'Le presenti cose / col falso lor piacer volser miei passi, / tosto che 'l vostro viso si nascose' ('present things with their false pleasure turned my steps, as soon as your face was hidden') (*Purg.* 31.34–6). Dante's language relates his earlier life to Purgatory's narrative of moral ascent, recalling, for example, Virgil's language describing sin in canto 17, as well as the second purgatorial dream (discussed above in chapter 4), which Beatrice explicitly recalls after Dante's confession, hoping that his current shame will render him stronger when he hears the sirens again ('udendo le serene') (*Purg.* 31.45]). Following his confession, Dante is brought through the river Lethe in a new baptism and then before Beatrice, where Dante anticipates his final state of blessedness, which he will taste briefly in Paradise, when Beatrice removes her veil. In his attempt to describe her unveiling, Dante employs language which anticipates that of the final canticle, portraying Beatrice's beauty by saying only how ineffable it is, how incapable he is of representing it (see *Purg.* 31.139–45).

In the Earthly Paradise cantos we have examined so far, then, Dante recapitulates the plot of the poem, a plot that itself recapitulates the archetypal human life. Beginning with the myth of the expulsion from Eden, we come to understand the nature of human life as fallen, and Dante as well is forced to see his own life in exile from Eden as one that is both fallen and sinful, but also as one that can be redeemed by his acceptance of the reality of divine intervention in his life – an intervention represented by Beatrice – and by his action on that sense of his life by turning to God in repentance. In other words, as he develops an understanding of his life within the shadow of an end time, and becomes aware of God's care for him, Dante comes to grasp the significance of his existence. My point here, however, is that this underlying narrative structure of conversion is fundamentally apocalyptic; just as the pilgrim is able through Beatrice to grasp the significance of his life by seeing it as a complete narrative that begins in sin and leads to the moment of judgment in the Earthly Paradise, it is by imposing an end time on human history that Dante is able, like John before him, to present to us his sense of human history.

We saw in chapter 3 that Dante employed the Apocalypse in the service of a vivid and forceful denunciation of church corruption, a not uncommon use of the final biblical book in late medieval Europe. In *Purgatorio* 32, he will again turn to John's Revelation for this reason, creating a visionary overview of church history in a structure and with imagery derived from the Apocalypse. The individual, personal judgment that he has undergone, however, proves to be an essential prelude to the global vision to come. Like Isaiah, Jeremiah, and other prophetic figures before him, Dante must confront his own personal history, must be cleansed and made fit to receive the vision and to transmit it to the 'world that lives badly.'[85]

Cantos 32 and 33: Toward the End of the World?

In the final two cantos of the *Purgatorio* we come to the apocalyptic vision for which Dante has been preparing. The biblical procession, the appearance of Beatrice, and the confession and baptism of Dante have all been important elements in creating the environment in which we can understand the vision of history that Dante will unfold. He now turns more fully to the Bible's final book for a perspective from which to view the history of the Christian church and, above all, the present and near future. Eschatology becomes a hermeneutic enterprise, a way of grasping the meaning of the present within the sweep of human history.

We thus begin canto 32 with a recapitulation of what has gone before. The procession resumes and proceeds back into the forest, which, Dante notes again, is empty because of Eve's fault. The fall is further illustrated as the procession approaches a tree of immense height, 'despoiled of leaves,' and all murmur 'Adam.' The tree represents, or actually *is*, the tree of knowledge of good and evil, whose fruit led to the fall, an identification we can make both because of the reference to Adam and because of its description as 'sweet to the taste' (*esto legno dolce al gusto*) (*Purg.* 32.44), a detail that recalls Genesis 3.6, where we are told that Eve 'saw that the tree was good to eat' (*vidit igitur mulier quod bonum esset lignum ad vescendum*). These references to the fall, however, are offset by the assertion of God's providential redemption, first, through an angelic song that accompanies Dante's thoughts of Eve, and, second, through the griffin, who, when he is tied to the tree, immediately causes the tree to break out in new foliage, a renewal that, in repairing the effects of the fall, figures the Incarnation of Christ. This brief representation of fall and redemption echoes the mystical procession, with its careful portrayal of Old Testament hope for Christ to come and New Testament faith in the salvation Christ brings at his first coming, as well as Dante's own individual enactment of this same narrative, when he is judged by Beatrice, repents, and is baptized.

The members of the procession next sing a hymn that is so sweet that it overcomes the pilgrim's senses, and he falls into a sleep, which he finds himself incapable of representing. He is awakened, however, by the coming of 'a brightness' (*un splendor*) and a voice that calls to him, 'Arise: what are you doing?' (*Surgi: che fai?*) (see *Purg*. 32.71–2). The poet describes that awakening with a simile that compares the pilgrim's experience with that of three biblical apostles:

> Quali a veder de' fioretti del melo
> che del suo pome li angeli fa ghiotti
> e perpetüe nozze fa nel cielo,
>   Pietro e Giovanni e Iacopo condotti
> e vinti, ritornaro a la parola
> da la qual furon maggior sonni rotti,
>   e videro scemata loro scuola
> così di Moïsè come d'Elia,
> e al maestro suo cangiata stola;
>   tal torna' io, e vidi quella pia
> sovra me starsi che conducitrice
> fu de' miei passi lungo 'l fiume pria.   (*Purg*. 32.73–84)

(Just as Peter and James and John were taken to see the flowers of that apple tree, whose fruit makes the angels hungry and causes continuous wedding feasts in heaven, and, overcome, returned at the word by which greater sleeps were broken, and saw their school reduced thus by Moses as well as by Elias, and their master's changed dress, so I returned, and I saw that compassionate woman standing over me, who earlier accompanied my steps along the river.)

The pilgrim's waking is seen as similar to that of Peter, James, and John after the Transfiguration on the Mount, recounted in Matthew 17.1–13.[86] The Transfiguration of Christ was an event that, as Dante tells us, was eschatological in a fundamental sense in that it gave to the apostles a glimpse of Christ's identity outside of history, and allowed them to anticipate the great wedding feast that follows the end time, as prophesied in Apocalypse 19.9, where the saints 'are called to the marriage of the Lamb.' Dante renders the event as the eating of a now accessible fruit, in contrast to the forbidden fruit whose 'mortal taste brought death into the world, and all our woe,' as Milton phrases it. Dante thus brings into the marriage of the Lamb a reminiscence of the fall, which is simultaneously remembered and redeemed in the act of eating the heavenly apple. Indeed, the Transfiguration was commonly interpreted eschatologically; in the *Glossa ordinaria,* for example, Christ's shining face is to be seen as an 'example of future beatitude and brightness.'[87] Interestingly, the Franciscan Spiritual Peter John Olivi in his commentary on the Gospel of Matthew also views this passage as key to understanding history, seeing the indication of the time of the Transfiguration's occurrence ('after six days Jesus taketh unto him Peter and James, and John his brother') as a prophecy that after six periods of church history, the church (or mystical body of Christ) will be transformed, and Francis as the new Elias will come to help effect this transformation.[88] While Dante's version of this biblical passage does not contain any of the specifically Franciscan reading of history that Olivi finds in it, it is nevertheless true that Dante uses it to mark a moment of eschatological unveiling. Dante places himself in the position of Christ's earliest apostles, ready to receive a revelation of God's purposes in history.

This aspect of the scene becomes clearer when Beatrice gives him a prophetic commission to observe and to write what he sees for the benefit of the erring world.

> Qui sarai tu poco tempo silvano;
> e sarai meco sanza fine cive
> di quella Roma onde Cristo è romano.
>   Però, in pro del mondo che mal vive,
> al carro tieni or li occhi, e quel che vedi,
> ritornato di là, fa che tu scrive.   (*Purg.* 32.100–5)

(Here you will be in the wood a short time; and you will be with me without end a citizen of that Rome where Christ is Roman. Therefore, on behalf of the world that lives badly, fasten your eyes on the chariot, and that which you see, once you have returned there, see that you write it.)

Beatrice's injunction both to observe and to write is itself a regular feature of apocalyptic revelations, as John is told at the beginning of his book by 'one like to the Son of man' to 'write therefore the things which thou hast seen' (1.13, 19). Unexpected is Beatrice's description of heaven in Roman terms and of Dante's membership among the blessed as a kind of Roman citizenship, as it represents a clear break from both apocalyptic and medieval precedent, which consistently refer to a heavenly Jerusalem rather than a heavenly Rome.[89] The reference to Rome, however, prepares us for the history of the church to come, as Dante sees that history as caught up in Rome (seen as both a city and an empire) in fundamental ways.

Following Beatrice's injunction, Dante witnesses a kind of sacred tableau, in which the chariot undergoes repeated modifications, the details of which are in many cases derived from the Apocalypse, and which represent the history of the church after the ascension of Christ. The stage for this tableau has already been set; prior to Beatrice's words, Dante learns that most members of the procession have followed the griffin in ascending to heaven, leaving only Beatrice and the seven virtues behind, a reference to the early life of the church following the resurrection of Christ, when it exists in its purity and is governed by virtue and by Beatrice, representing divine revelation or theology.[90] There is, of course, a good deal of debate surrounding the meaning of individual details in the apocalyptic drama,[91] but there is little question that for Dante the history of the church is one of gradual decline from the state of purity with which it begins. He represents the decline through seven stages, a very common division of church, and indeed world, history, given that the Apocalypse itself divided its narrative into sevens, with seven letters to seven churches, seven seals that are opened to reveal seven stages of history, and seven angels with seven vials containing plagues to be unleashed upon the world. Dante sees this pattern replicated in the history of the church, with each stage represented by a particular trial for the church.

The initial two trials strike the church, but do not seem to affect it permanently. The first (lines 109–17) comes at the hand of the Roman Empire; Jove's eagle, standing for the Roman Empire, falls through the tree and onto the cart, striking it 'di tutta sua forza; / ond' el piegò come nave in fortuna, / vinta da l'onda, or da poggia, or da orza' ('with all its force; whence it buckled like a ship in a storm, overcome by the waves, now to leeward, now to windward') (*Purg.* 32.115–17). The battering of the chariot by the eagle refers to the persecutions of the early church at the hands of Roman officials; it was common to describe the church as a ship, often as the 'ship of Peter,' which finds itself in danger of foundering because of the persecutions. The image also recalls Saint James's description of a man of insufficient faith who wavers, 'for he that wavereth is like a wave of the sea, which is moved and carried about by the wind' (1.6), an allusion that suggests that the ship's wavering may be due to insufficient faith as well as to external trial. The second stage (lines 118–23) is marked by heresy – an internal threat symbolized by a fox who, 'deprived of all good food,' feeds on pernicious doctrines. Beatrice puts the fox to flight, symbolizing, it seems, sound theology and philosophy that undermines and eventually destroys the heresies that surfaced in the early church.

The trial of the third stage also comes at the hand of the Roman Empire, but its effects prove to be much more long lasting.

> Poscia per indi ond' era pria venuta,
> l'aguglia vidi scender giù ne l'arca
> del carro e lasciar lei di sé pennuta;
> e qual esce di cuor che si rammarca,
> tal voce uscì del cielo e cotal disse:
> 'O navicella mia, com' mal se' carca!'   (*Purg.* 32.124–9)

(Then through the same path it had taken at first, I saw the eagle descend into the cart and leave it feathered with its own feathers; and as a voice escapes from a grieving heart, such a voice came out of the heavens and spoke in this way: 'O my little ship, how badly you are burdened!')

It is interesting that for Dante the third stage of his church history is limited to one event, whereas each of the other stages encapsulates relatively lengthy periods of history characterized by a given pattern (such as persecution or the fight against heresy). Here, apparently because of its far-reaching effects, the Donation of Constantine, which, as we saw in *Inferno* 19, Dante blames as the origin of church corruption, forms the only event of this 'stage.' Of course, Dante's attitude toward the Donation and its role in church history is not unprecedented; some mendicant commentators had an attitude that resembles Dante's. In a Dominican commentary on the Apocalypse that Robert Lerner attributes to Hugh of Saint Cher, for example, we find an indictment of the Donation in the exegesis of Apocalypse 12.15. We may recall from chapter 3 that Apocalypse 12 concerns the woman with child who is persecuted by the 'great red dragon,' and who was taken to represent the struggles of the early church against Roman persecutions. As the woman escapes to the wilderness, 'the serpent cast out of his mouth after the woman, water as it were a river; that he might cause her to be carried away by the river' (Apoc. 12.15). In Hugh's commentary, the water flowing from the dragon's mouth is interpreted as 'abundance of temporal goods . . . which the dragon sent into the church of God, when the western empire was given by Constantine to the church.' Hugh enriches this interpretation by a repetition of the legend that when the gift was given, angels' voices were heard saying, 'today poison has been poured into the church of God,'[92] a story that closely resembles Dante's account.

Following the third stage, each successive stage is marked by further trial and further decline. The fourth (lines 130–5), in which a dragon arises out of the earth and, piercing the chariot with its tail, carries off part of it, seems to refer to schism, perhaps through Mohammed, who was often seen as a Christian schismatic, an interpretation that is particularly favoured by the earliest commentators.[93] In the fifth stage (lines 136–41) Dante returns to the effects of the Donation, as the chariot, 'both wheels and the pole,' quickly becomes covered with feathers 'offered perhaps with healthy and benign intention.' This particular stage most likely refers to the increase of gifts and wealth that were given to the papacy during the Carolingian and (perhaps) Ottonian periods, but Dante's imagery of feathers implies that these latest gifts complete the materialization of the church begun by Consantine's gift. Similarly, the characterization of the feathers as 'offerta / forse con intenzion sana e benigna' echoes language that Dante uses elsewhere in reference to the Donation.[94] Dante, then, is careful to link this new stage to the Donation, because Constantine's gift opened the door to papal avarice. In Dante's view, avarice is insatiable and virtually unstoppable, and so the progressive corruption of the church was inevitable once it accepted the temporal goods offered by Constantine. We may recall, for example, Hugh Capet's narrative of his family's Capetian dynasty on the terrace of avarice. Hugh and his descendants were 'not worth much' at first, but they refrained from doing serious harm. It was only when 'the great dowry of Provence' came into the family through the marriage of Charles of Anjou to Beatrice, the daughter of Raymond Berenguer, that 'they began their plundering with force and fraud.' The introduction of wealth into the church leads its leaders only to grasp more and more, like the insatiable *lupa* Dante meets on the hill in the poem's opening canto.[95]

The chariot continues to transform in the sixth stage (lines 142–7), adding ten horns and seven heads, details derived from Apocalypse

12 and 17 (and which Dante used in *Inferno* 19), to its feathers. In Apocalypse 12, a woman is attacked by a dragon that has seven heads and ten horns. When we come to chapter 17, we see a woman identified as 'the great harlot' who sits upon a beast 'full of names of blasphemy, having seven heads and ten horns.' In chapter 3, I suggested that Dante sees these two women as the same woman – an image of the innocent church, attacked by a dragon (perhaps an image that suggested to Dante his image of the chariot attacked by the eagle), who becomes the corrupted harlot of chapter 17. The seven heads and ten horns carry a positive connotation in the *Inferno* (where they are usually interpreted to mean the seven sacraments or seven virtues and the ten commandments); here Dante's use is more in line with his biblical source, where the horns and heads mark the dragon and then the corrupt beast upon which the harlot sits, which are interpreted negatively both within the Apocalypse itself and within the exegetical tradition. Indeed, it has often been noted that Dante's use of apocalyptic imagery is inconsistent between *Inferno* 19 and *Purgatorio* 32, an issue we will explore at the conclusion of this chapter.[96]

Dante employs the remainder of the canto to narrate his seventh and final stage (lines 148–60) of church history, which is the only stage that, when seen from the fictional date of the journey, predicts the future in portraying the state of the church at the time Dante was writing. Once again, this scene reminds us of the apocalyptic language employed in *Inferno* 19, where Dante invented a husband for the harlot of Apocalypse 17 and associated her with the pope, blaming him for the corruption (*fin che virtute al suo marito piacque*), and used sexual language to refer to the straying, unfaithful church and the pope, who turns pimp in prostituting his wife (*la bella donna*), selling her to the highest bidder. Similarly, here Dante invents a giant, who is responsible for beating the *puttana sciolta* or 'ungirt harlot' and then, after the harlot casts her eyes on the pilgrim, beats her and carries her off away from the chariot and into the forest. Most commonly, commentators see in this episode an allusion to the relationship between the French monarchy and the papacy in the early fourteenth century, with the giant representing Philip the Fair.[97] There are numerous interpretations of what is meant by the harlot's wandering eye settling on Dante,[98] but whatever its meaning, it is an action that infuriates the giant, who beats her for it. The beating seems to be a reference to Philip's humiliation of Boniface VIII in Anagni, when he sent his envoys to force Boniface to accede to his demands. Most significant, however, is the dragging off of the chariot and harlot into the woods, which is almost universally interpreted as the inauguration of the 'Babylonian Captivity,' when the papacy was taken from Rome, eventually establishing itself in Avignon, an event to which Dante also alludes in *Inferno* 19 through Nicholas's prophecy of Clement V (*un pastor sanza legge*).

The allegorical tableau with which canto 32 concludes presents a unified narrative in which church history is configured as a series of seven trials that, following the second, result in a steady corruption and degeneration, culminating in the removal of the church from the tree, the divinely ordained location of Rome. Even seen within the context of late medieval criticisms of church corruption, this is an extraordinary view of church history. Dante at this point couches it within an allegorical framework, but later in the *Paradiso* he will not be so coy. In canto 27, Peter pulls no punches in criticizing the papacy and what it has done to the church, with Peter telling Dante that the current vicar of Christ is a usurper (*Quelli ch'usurpa in terra il luogo mio*) and is not recognized as the successor of Peter by the Son of God himself, as his actions please the devil rather than God (*onde 'l perverso / che cadde di qua sù, là giù si placa*) (*Par.* 27.22, 26–7).

Dante's view of church history is tied up with his political views: that the proper governance of the temporal world is as necessary to human happiness as the proper oversight of the church, and that these two institutions – the papacy and the world monarch – have distinct responsibilities that cannot be abrogated without significant consequences. Thus, the Donation of Constantine, while well intentioned, violated the divinely ordained order of world governance and led to the progressive corruption of the church so that the church became hopelessly caught up in the vicissitudes of worldly affairs. In order to communicate this vision, Dante draws on well-established images taken from the Apocalypse and the exegetical tradition devoted to it, but he combines them in a new way in order to illustrate his personal vision of the progression and degeneration of God's church on earth.

His originality can be seen at many points. The first stage of church history, for example, is most commonly seen as the primitive and innocent apostolic church. Dante indeed seems to include this part of church history (in lines 85–99), but he carefully excludes it from the tableau itself, since the tableau only begins *after* Beatrice's prophetic commission, which divides the allegorical depiction of the primitive church and the first stage of the tableau, marked by the rapid descent of the eagle into the chariot. In Dante's hands, the church's history is one of continual tribulation; in the initial two stages, it is true, the church survives intact, but the remaining five stages all portray a gradually disintegrating church. Second, he places an unexpected emphasis on the Donation of Constantine, making it one of the stages of church history and the catalyst for another. If we compare, for example, Dante's seven stages to those of Peter John Olivi – a Franciscan Spiritual who was no friend to the materialism of the church – we find that Olivi not only fails to identify the Donation with one of the stages, he sees materialism develop as a problem only much later in the church's history, in its fifth stage.[99] In addition, Dante ends his seven stages not with an apocalyptic resolution of the defeat of the Antichrist and a millennial reign of peace, the traditional sixth and seventh stages in medieval accounts of church history, but with the culmination of the church's corruption, ending inconclusively in the present (or in the near future when seen from the perspective of the fictional date of the journey).[100] Indeed, the irresolution of church history is perhaps the most deeply unsettling aspect of Dante's vision. As we have noted previously, the Apocalypse proved to be comforting to medieval readers precisely because it envisioned a providential resolution of earthly history.

In the final canto we do see an attempt to provide the kind of reassurance that most medieval readers found in the Apocalypse. This consolation, though, does not depend on our finding the definitive interpretation of Beatrice's prophecy of the 'five hundred, ten, and five,' but in the overall sense of history that the canto unfolds, which is revealed as early as the canto's opening lines:

> 'Deus, venerunt gentes,' alternando
> or tre or quattro dolce salmodia,
> le donne incominciaro, e lagrimando;
> e Bëatrice, sospirosa e pia,
> quelle ascoltava sì fatta, che poco
> più a la croce si cambiò Maria.   (Purg. 33.1–6)

('O God, the heathens are come,' the women began, alternating their sweet psalmody, now by three now by four, and weeping; and Beatrice, sighing and grieving, listened to them so that she became such that Mary at the cross changed little more.)

This is one of the few cantos that open with a citation, and a Latin citation at that.[101] The words are from the beginning of Psalm 78, which contains

Israel's lament over the conquest of Jerusalem and the destruction of the temple by King Nebuchadnezzar in 587 BCE; verse 1 continues, 'they have defiled thy holy temple: they have made Jerusalem as a place to keep fruit.' On the one hand, this Psalm appropriately recalls the Babylonian Captivity of ancient Israel as a commentary on the representation of the contemporary Babylonian Captivity we have just seen represented. But the Psalm has a much broader resonance as well; while it mourns the destruction that has just come upon Israel, it also foresees the near time of God's intervention and the restoration of a remnant of Israel to the Promised Land. Following the lament, for example, the psalmist pleads for vengeance ('Pour out thy wrath upon the nations that have not known thee'), asks for mercy ('Remember not our former iniquities'), and looks for a time when Israel will be restored to God's favour ('we thy people, and the sheep of thy pasture, will give thanks to thee forever'). This basic pattern of favour, followed by apostasy, punishment, mercy, and restoration is common to much Old Testament prophetic literature. The first chapter of Isaiah provides a compact example of the pattern. It opens with the Lord's declaration, 'I have brought up children, and exalted them: but they have despised me' (1.2). The Lord goes on to announce that his vengeance will soon fall upon Judah ('your land is desolate, your cities are burnt with fire: your country strangers devour before your face, and it shall be desolate as when wasted by enemies' [1.7]), but promises that a remnant or seed (*semen* in the Vulgate) will survive and be restored. This pattern is then repeated twice before the end of the chapter.[102]

New Testament writers also find this basic narrative structure in the life of Christ, and they support it with citations from the Old Testament. The pattern of birth, ministry, and popularity which turns to rejection and crucifixion, which is then followed by resurrection and redemption, fulfils within the life of Christ the type that the Old Testament prophets discerned within the history of Israel and Judah. Toward the end of Luke's Gospel, for example, there is the intriguing episode of the disciples on the road to Emmaus, where Jesus himself (unknown to the disciples he instructs) expresses impatience with his disciples' inability to comprehend this basic narrative structure and how it applies to his own life. When the disciples lament his crucifixion, Jesus responds: 'O foolish, and slow of heart to believe in all things which the prophets have spoken. Ought not Christ to have suffered these things, and so to enter into his glory? And beginning at Moses and all the prophets, he expounded to them in all the scriptures, the things that were concerning him' (Luke 24.25–7). Finally, we also see this basic pattern in the Apocalypse itself, with its narrative of wickedness, chastisement, and the ultimate triumph of God and the reward of the righteous in the heavenly Jerusalem, though the pattern can even be seen in the letters that John is instructed to write and deliver in chapters 2 and 3. Each of these seven letters (to the seven churches in Asia) follows a basic pattern: praise of the church being addressed, accusation and exhortation to repentance, and then a promise of blessings that will come to the penitent.[103]

When seen within this wider biblical context, the overall shape of Dante's sense of history as revealed in *Purgatorio* 32 and 33 emerges as quintessentially biblical. He begins with a period of divine favour in his portrayal of the primitive church, which is followed by the seven trials. Initially, the church withstands these tribulations, but eventually – with Constantine's gift – it gives way to corruption and is punished, stolen away as Judah was in the period of the Babylonian Captivity. Nevertheless, in canto 33 Beatrice promises divine vengeance and the return of the church – the modern Israel – to God's favour, even though the details of how this restoration will come about remain obscure (just as they are in the biblical texts that Dante may have had in mind when composing this section of the poem).

> Sappi che 'l vaso che 'l serpente ruppe,
> fu e non è; ma chi n'ha colpa, creda
> che vendetta di Dio non teme suppe.
> Non sarà tutto tempo sanza reda
> l'aguglia che lasciò le penne al carro,
> per che divenne mostro e poscia preda;
> ch'io veggio certamente, e però il narro,
> a darne tempo già stelle propinque,
> secure d'ogn' intoppo e d'ogne sbarro,
> nel quale un cinquecento diece e cinque,
> messo da Dio, anciderà la fuia
> con quel gigante che con lei delinque.   (*Purg.* 33.34–45)

(Know that the vessel that the serpent broke, was and is not; but for the one guilty of it, believe that the justice of God fears no hindrance. The eagle who left the feathers in the chariot will not be long without an heir, for which reason the chariot became a monster and then a prey; and I see certainly, and thus I tell it, stars already near, free from every delay and obstacle, will bring about a time in which a five hundred ten and five, sent by God, will kill the thief with that giant that sins with her.)

Beatrice calls her words a 'narrazion buia' ('dark narrative') and an 'enigma forte' ('stubborn enigma'), so it is no surprise that the interpretation of these lines has been the matter of some debate. Certain general issues, however, seem clear. The vengeance of God, for example, will be directed at the church and at the political leaders who collude with her in her temporal ambitions. If the most common interpretation of the giant as Philip the Fair is correct, we may extrapolate that Beatrice directs her words against the corrupt leaders of the church as well as against nationalist political leaders, both of whom resist what Dante sees as the rightful imperial rule in order to pursue their own avaricious interests. This interpretation also accords with Dante's fifth, sixth, and seventh epistles, all of which concern Dante's hopes that the new Holy Roman Emperor Henry VII will become a political saviour. Dante was not the first to see a divinely ordained emperor as the key to the apocalyptic unfolding of history; following Constantine's conversion, a tradition arose of a 'good Christian emperor who would come at the End of time to defeat the enemies of the Cross and usher in a period of peace and plenty.'[104] Beatrice's suggestion at lines 37–9 that the coming saviour is an heir to the empire reminds us of the 'good emperor' of apocalyptic legend. While it was the imperial gift of Constantine that led to the corruption of the church, so it will also be the heir to the eagle who kills the harlot that the church has become by assuming control over all of the temporal affairs of Europe, wresting them away from both the corrupt church and the kings who fornicate with her; a new Holy Roman Emperor, it seems, will be the agent simultaneously of vengeance and restoration. If we think back to the prophetic commission that Beatrice delivers to Dante just prior to the historical tableau, where she describes heaven itself as 'that Rome where Christ is Roman,' we are reminded just how inextricably church and empire were tied together in Dante's historical vision.

Of course, there are many other places where this vision becomes apparent; we may think of the second book of the *Monarchia* as well as the sixth and seventh cantos of the *Paradiso*, where Dante makes the case for a providential directing of imperial as well as salvation history. It is in the final canticle, however, with the words of Peter in canto 27, that we have the final assertion of history moving toward its divinely ordained end by the proper ordering of church and empire, in apocalyptic language that recalls both *Inferno* 19 and *Purgatorio* 32:

Non fu la sposa di Cristo allevata
del sangue mio, di Lin, di quel di Cleto,
per essere ad acquisto d'oro usata.   (*Par.* 27.40–2)

(The bride of Christ was not nourished by my blood, by that of Linus and
of Cletus, to be used for the purchase of gold.)

The imagery of the bride of Christ for the church who is bought and
sold with gold derives from the Canticle of Canticles as well as from
the woman and harlot that Dante takes from chapters 12 and 17 of the
Apocalypse. After cataloguing the degeneracy of the church here, Peter,
as does Beatrice in *Purgatorio* 33, prophesies the imminent intervention
of God to ensure that history will meet its proper end, and he does
so by associating divine providence with the progress of *Roman* rather
than Christian history.

Ma l'alta provedenza, che con Scipio
difese a Roma la gloria del mondo,
soccorrà tosto, sì com' io concipio.   (*Par.* 27.61–3)

(But providence from on high, that with Scipio defended the glory of the
world for Rome, will soon intervene, as I conceive.)

Dante's version of the unfolding of Christian history, tied up as it is
with his own view of Roman exceptionalism as well as with apocalyptic traditions of the 'angelic emperor,'[105] while deeply idiosyncratic
when seen from one perspective, is profoundly rooted in the biblical
tradition when looked at in terms of its overall shape. The details of
Beatrice's prophecy and the enigmatic reference to the 'five hundred,
ten, and five' should not blind us to the biblical pattern that underlies
the vision that Dante gives us in the final two cantos of the *Purgatorio*:
divine favour, followed by apostasy, divine vengeance, and ultimately
mercy and restoration. Marjorie Reeves has argued that Dante is most
likely indebted to Joachim of Fiore for his overall view of history as
containing two turning points – the first with the advent of Christ, and
the second with the *renovatio mundi* that would transform society so
that it was in accordance with God's will – as only Joachim 'propheti-
cally placed a second turning-point in history just ahead in time.'[106] But
this biblical pattern, when seen from the perspective of the Christian

church, posits a similar *renovatio,* or restoration. The church is, as was ancient Israel, favoured by God as long as it remains righteous. Now, because of its wickedness, it is soon to attract divine wrath; however, we can expect a return of God's favour once the punishment has passed and society has been restored to its proper place. Similarly, seen from this biblical perspective, *Inferno* 19, despite its difference in details from *Purgatorio* 32, follows this same pattern. The church, originally a 'bella donna' (see *Inf.* 19.57), becomes a prostitute, sold by the pope to the highest bidder. God's vengeance, though, will shortly follow, restoring the church to its original, poor, state. As Isaiah prophesied, 'Sion shall be redeemed in judgment, and they shall bring her back in justice' (1.27).[107]

The Righting of the Ship

As I argued at the beginning of this chapter, Dante modelled the earthly paradise cantos in significant ways on biblical apocalyptic discourse, filling them with images and motifs from the Bible's final book, as well as from Ezekiel, Daniel, Matthew, and other apocalyptic texts. Most critics who have examined this section of the poem have done so convinced that such extensive borrowing presupposes Dante's indebtedness – and even fidelity – to mainstream medieval apocalyptic traditions.[108] But if we examine Dante's apocalyptic achievement more closely, I think that his use of the Apocalypse, and his own apocalyptic imagination, proves to be more idiosyncratic than is generally believed.

What, then, is the evidence for Dante's traditional apocalypticism? Bernard McGinn has argued that apocalyptic writings present a 'new kind of redemption'; broader in scope, apocalyptic redemption 'expands outward from the national and innerhistorical perspective to a cosmic and transhistorical one.'[109] This broadened perspective frequently manifests itself in the insistence of the apocalyptic seer on the end of history and a focus on the heavenly Jerusalem to the exclusion of any earthly city. It would seem that Dante's Apocalypse offers a broadened vision of redemption in precisely these terms. The last third of the *Comedy,* after all, recounts Dante's escaping the earth – the 'little threshing floor' (*aiulo*) as it appears to him from the transcendent perspective of the heaven of the fixed stars (*Par.* 22.151), a perspective that allows him to laugh at the apparent chaos of earthly history. Furthermore, in *Paradiso* 30, Beatrice points to the paucity of seats that remain unfilled in the heavenly rose, which critics often take as evidence of Dante's traditional apocalypticism in anticipating the near end of the world.[110]

However, Dante has a harder time leaving the earth behind than our assumption of his traditional apocalyptic perspective would allow. As part of the same discourse in which she seems to point to the nearness of the end time, Beatrice devotes her final words to lamenting the fate of Henry VII, pointing to the empty throne that awaits him after he fails to redeem an Italy desperate for his help but unready to accept it, indicating a recognition that the divine intervention Dante had anticipated is being delayed. The historical tragedy of Henry's failure does not seem mitigated here by a cosmic perspective on the insignificance of earthly events. If we return to *Purgatorio* 33, we will find that Beatrice's exegetical discourse and concluding prophecy similarly lack the insistence on the end time characteristic of most apocalyptic works. Nevertheless, critics have seen in her words ties to medieval tradition. Robert Kaske, for example, finds in Beatrice's prophecy an anticipation of the 'time of peace beginning with the death of the Antichrist';[111] and Charles T. Davis likewise understands her words to refer to 'one final scene of history [that] apparently remains to be played out before the Last Judgment.'[112] Kaske's interpretation may be accurate, but he draws his conclusion not from any explicit statement within the poem, but from a comparison of the medieval tradition of the seven stages of church history with the details of Dante's poem, guided by his certainty that Dante's own apocalypticism must be close to that of other medieval thinkers. Davis's understanding of the Last Judgment as an implicit part of Beatrice's prophecy is also guided by his own expectations of apocalyptic discourse; Beatrice herself makes no mention of the final judgment. We have, of course, seen references, both implicit and explicit, to the Last Judgment in previous cantos; Dante's simile comparing the angels surrounding the chariot at the beginning of canto 30 to the blessed *al novissimo bando* comes to mind, as does Beatrice's judgment, standing as a *figura Christi*, of Dante later in that same canto. But where we would most expect her to expand her perspective 'outward from the national and innerhistorical perspective to a cosmic and transhistorical one,' Dante limits her words to the vaguest of hints.[113] Except for that brief moment in *Paradiso* 30, the end is not in view. Peter's prophecy in *Paradiso* 27, in fact, ends with the assertion that God will soon intervene so that history may be set right, not so that it may end. Thus, the implications of his imagery are that history will continue on into the future.

>   ... la fortuna che tanto s'aspetta,
>   le poppe volgerà u' son le prore,
>   sì che la classe correrà diretta;
>   e vero frutto verrà dopo 'l fiore.   (*Par.* 27.145–8)

(the fortune we wait for so anxiously will turn the poops where the sterns are, so that the fleet will run straight; and the true fruit will come after the flower.)

The ship will be set right (we may recall here Dante's comparison of the church to a ship at *Purgatorio* 32.115–17), and, we must conclude, resume its voyage, this time to its properly sanctioned port, along the 'strait' way that leads to life, as Christ tells us in the Sermon on the Mount (Matt. 7.14). The voyage continues, and the tree, rather than being cast into an apocalyptic fire, again bears fruit.

My purpose here is not to suggest that Dante was not apocalyptic, but rather that he was not traditionally so. His writings on the necessity of the world monarch and his hope for the restoration of that monarchy, tied as they are to his conception of the possibility and necessity of earthly happiness for the working out of God's purposes, imply that he envisioned not the imminent end of the world, but a restoration of the proper form of worldly government together with a cleansing of the church, so that, poor and free from avarice, it could function as Christ intended it to function in aiding Christians toward eternal life. If we want to see Virgil's prophecy of the 'Veltro' in *Inferno* 1, where the *lupa* of cupidity is chased back to hell, banished, it seems, from earthly life, as a prediction of a millennial period of earthly history, we may do so, but Dante nowhere makes that explicit. All we can say is that he anticipated the imminent intervention of God to restore earthly life to its proper, and just, functioning, and that he looked forward to that restoration; that is to say, he looks not for the end of history, but for the righting of the ship that would enable us to fulfil our divinely ordained purpose here on earth.

Marjorie Reeves has argued that Dante was indebted to Joachim for his notion of a renovation of society, but the differences between their two conceptions are as noteworthy as are the similarities.[114] While it is true that, like Joachim, Dante foresaw a transformation of society the profundity of which would rival that brought about by the initial advent of Christ, unlike Joachim, Dante does not see in this transformation a movement toward a new, unprecedented third stage of history. Dante's transformation, as I have argued, is better understood as a restoration – a return to a historical Golden Age when the Roman emperor rightly governed the world, to be joined now, though, by a properly functioning and poor church, free from cupidity. Human history must be transformed and once again set upon the proper path, not brought to an end.

Conclusion: Poet of the Biblical World

As we have seen throughout this study, Dante often uses the Bible freely at various moments in the *Commedia*, much as he does his other sources, both Christian and pagan. Nevertheless, unlike his treatment of most of his other sources, he also continually insists on the truth of the Bible, even as he treats it freely. But for Dante, most important is that the truths of the Bible are lived; if they do not have an existential force, he has little interest in the text's historical accuracy. He thus updates the Bible, brings it into his own day so that his readers may see it anew. He does not hope that his poem will replace the Bible; rather, he seeks to bring readers back to the sacred text through a reading of his poem. Only when they understand, personally and existentially, the truths of the scriptures will they again see the world as it really is, as defined in the Bible. Until that time, too many Christians are like those the pilgrim meets in hell – seeing the truth only incompletely and mistakenly, with tragic results.

Dante's intertextual practice thus not only draws on the Bible for the sake of his own poem; it also changes the way that we read key sections of the Bible. We have considered at some length that intertextuality is fundamentally hermeneutic; that is, the citation and appropriation of other texts *always* involves interpretation; the act of choosing another text and placing it within a new composition necessarily interprets and thereby transforms it. The subtext now forms part of another poem, and we read its original meaning (the meaning we ascribed to the text before knowing its place in a new text) against its context in the new work. We also, moreover, return to the subtext in its original context with a transformed view of its original meaning. Coming again to the end of the sixth book of the *Aeneid* after having read *Purgatorio* 30, we cannot help but sense the underlying sadness and tragedy of Anchises' lament for Marcellus more fully than we have before. But this is equally true for Dante's use of the Bible. Now when we turn to the beginning of Acts and read the account of the calling of Matthias to replace Judas as an apostle, following our reading of *Inferno* 19, we notice a palpable absence in the narrative – an absence of wealth, of simony, of corruption. When Peter tells a lame beggar, 'silver and gold I have none' (see Acts 3.6), we read not only about Peter, but also – by implication – about Nicholas, Boniface, and Clement.

Dante's use of the Bible thus has profound implications not only for his poem but also for the ways in which his readers will read the Bible when they return to it, as he hopes they will, following their reading of his poem. The twofold hermeneutic of Dante's intertextuality forces us to consider the Bible as we read his poem, and to remember his poem when we return to the Bible. We now more readily find in the Bible texts that vigorously criticize avarice and corruption, and that encourage the re-establishment of a poor church, divorced from temporal influence. Dante therefore fleshes out the biblical message and shows its meaning for his own time, drawing on the many interpretive traditions of the scriptures current in his day, but always bending and adjusting them for his own poetic designs. His purpose with respect to scripture, however, is ultimately conservative, though his conservatism is oriented toward the future. It is in the past, then, in the revelations given by God in previous moments in history, that we find, when we interpret them against the crisis of the current age, the significance of the present and an understanding of where to look in the future.

But there is more to Dante's attraction to the Bible even than this understanding of God's will for his contemporaries with its links to an overall, biblical sense of the shape of history. Harold Bloom has written that, unlike Milton, Dante was not haunted by the Bible, that 'the *Comedy*, for all its learning, is not deeply involved with the Bible.'[1] Bloom underestimates, however, how thoroughly Dante even as a poet moves within a biblical world, and how much the Bible taught him not only about theology, but also, it seems certain, about poetry and realistic narrative. Erich Auerbach, of course, did much to impress upon modern readers the *literary* qualities of the Bible, especially its underappreciated realism. As he writes in the opening chapter of *Dante: Poet of the Secular World*, 'the depth and scope of the naturalism in the story of Christ are unparalleled.'[2] Auerbach goes on to argue that the realism of biblical narrative, 'the mimetic content of the story of Christ,' went ignored for some time, 'more than a thousand years,' in fact, falling prey to 'Neo-Platonic Spiritualism and its Christian heresies.' More recently, however, scholars have convincingly questioned the traditional view of medieval Christianity as dualistic, devoted to an anti-materialist world view. It is now possible to argue not only that a simultaneous attachment to things heavenly and earthly, to the physical and the spiritual, is compatible with a medieval and biblical world view, but that such an attachment is also, at its heart, fundamentally inherent in both biblical and medieval thought.[3]

In *Poet of the Secular World*, Auerbach saw Dante the realistic poet as both conservative and progressive, pointing the way forward to a European literature and art that portrays human beings in their 'living historical reality, the concrete individual in his unity and wholeness,' but doing so by defending the 'physical, ethical, and political unity of the Scholastic Christian cosmos at a time when it was beginning to lose its ideological integrity' (175). Of course, Auerbach was right to see that the political and, for the most part, the theological ideology that Dante supports in his poem was soon to fragment and ultimately break apart and fade, and that for later poets and thinkers Dante's poem became a vital source that nourished a much more secular world and literature in spite of, rather than because of, his world view. Dante himself, however, seemed to sense that his journey was one out of time, or at least 'fuor del moderno uso' ('outside of modern usage') (*Purg.* 16.42), as he has the pilgrim tell Marco Lombardo on the purgatorial terrace of wrath. From this point of view, his journey and poem, with its accounts of miraculous, divine intervention as well as prophetic commissions to write, seem more biblical than Scholastic. In fact, it may well be that Dante's immersion in the world of the Bible goes farther in explaining his unprecedented realism than does any other literary precedent. To be sure, Dante calls Virgil 'lo mio maestro e 'l mio autore' ('my master and author') (*Inf.* 1.85), but he also takes pains to distance himself from his pagan predecessor, whom he defines as a tragic poet, in opposition to his own comic, Christian, prophetic, and ultimately realistic, poetic self.

From our current perspective, Dante can indeed seem paradoxical – as a poet who heralds a new realism through writing the fantastic, as a hard-headed political reactionary whose attachment to traditional Christianity does not prohibit his placing a nearly equal value on earthly happiness, as an apocalyptic Christian whose belief in divine judgment on the other side of human history goes hand in hand with a seemingly unbreakable attachment to the beauties and realities of earthly life. Yet Dante's apparent contradictions may perhaps be best understood as expressions of a fundamentally biblical outlook, albeit one updated and re-imagined for a later time. If we wish to be true to Dante's vision and poem, then, it may well be best to speak of him as the poet of the biblical world.

Notes

Introduction

1 Dante's words refer to John 20.3–10. He mistakes the biblical passage in two ways: first, in the Gospel account, John races ahead of Peter and beats him to the sepulchre (Dante's account of it in *Paradiso* 24 directly contradicts this detail); second, the beloved disciple is led to faith (Peter's faith, in contrast, is not mentioned) only *after* entering and seeing the empty sepulchre, 'for as yet they knew not the scripture, that he must rise again from the dead' (9). Dante refers correctly to the passage in *Monarchia* 3.19.6.

2 Edward Moore writes that he finds it 'unnecessary to stop to prove Dante's very great familiarity with, and unbounded reverence for, the Bible ... His quotations from it are most numerous.' See *Contributions to the Textual Criticism of the 'Divina Commedia'* (Cambridge: Cambridge University Press, 1889), 695. Similarly, Angelo Penna writes that 'senza dubbio la Bibbia costituisce la fonte citata più frequentemente o comunque utilizzata da Dante.' See his entry, 'Bibbia,' in *ED*, 1:626.

3 Amilcare A. Iannucci, for example, writes that the Bible is 'the only authority that Dante does not challenge in the *Commedia* ... and hence his appropriation of scriptural passages is fundamentally different from his way of engaging other (secular) texts.' See his Introduction to *Dante: Contemporary Perspectives*, ed. Amilcare A. Iannucci (Toronto: University of Toronto Press, 1997), xvi.

4 'A poet has not God's power and may not presume to write as He can. But he may *imitate* God's way of writing.' For Singleton, Dante imitates God's way of writing by constructing 'a literal historical sense ... in the make-believe of his poem, as God's literal sense is in His book ... And he will make his allegorical or mystic, his other sense, even as God's: a

sense concerning our journey, our way of salvation, here in this life.' See *Commedia: Elements of Structure* (Cambridge, MA: Harvard University Press, 1954), 15–16. Robert Hollander argues more extensively for the identification of Dante's allegory in the *Commedia* with the fourfold method of exegesis usually reserved for the Bible in *Allegory in Dante's 'Commedia'* (Princeton: Princeton University Press, 1969), 15–56.

5 The work of Christopher Kleinhenz and Peter Hawkins comes first to mind. Kleinhenz has written careful studies of the various ways in which Dante cites or alludes to biblical texts in the course of the poem. See, for example, 'Dante and the Bible: Intertextual Approaches to the *Divine Comedy*,' *Italica* 63 (1986): 225–36; 'Biblical Citation in Dante's *Divine Comedy*,' *Annali d'Italianistica* 8 (1990): 346–59; and 'Dante and the Art of Citation,' in *Dante Now*, ed. Theodore J. Cachey (Notre Dame: Notre Dame University Press, 1995), 43–61. Hawkins has written essays on how the Bible shaped Dante's poetic imagination. See especially *Dante's Testaments: Essays in Scriptural Imagination* (Stanford: Stanford University Press, 1999). See also the collection, *Dante e la Bibbia,* ed. Giovanni Barblan (Florence: Olschki, 1988).

6 Robert Alter's work on the Hebrew Bible is extensive. His most influential works include *The Art of Biblical Narrative* (New York: Basic Books, 1981); and *The Art of Biblical Poetry* (New York: Basic Books, 1985). Others who fruitfully use the tools of modern literary criticism in the service of biblical interpretation include: Frank Kermode, *The Genesis of Secrecy: On the Interpretation of Narrative* (Cambridge, MA: Harvard University Press, 1979); Meir Sternberg, *The Poetics of Biblical Narrative: Ideological Literature and the Drama of Reading* (Bloomington: Indiana University Press, 1985); Gabriel Josipovici, *The Book of God: A Response to the Bible* (New Haven: Yale University Press, 1988); Robert Alter and Frank Kermode, eds., *The Literary Guide to the Bible* (Cambridge, MA: Harvard University Press, 1987).

7 The terms that I use here are in accordance with the discipline of the academic study of literature rather than biblical studies; in the latter, 'literary criticism' usually refers to the study of the various layers of composition assumed to exist in a given biblical text.

8 James L. Kugel, *The Bible As It Was* (Cambridge, MA: Harvard University Press, 1997), xiv; emphasis Kugel's. Further reference to this book will be made in the text.

9 The kind of reaction I have in mind can be seen, for example, in Stephen A. Barney, '*Ordo paganis:* The Gloss on Genesis 38,' *South Atlantic Quarterly* 91 (1992): 929–43, who writes, in reference to medieval interpretive practices such as those found in the *Glossa ordinaria,* that 'the community of

interpretation as always is more important than the text it preserves' (940), as if the text and its interpretation were easily separable, just as Kugel assumes. For a discussion of Barney's position from the perspective of a scholar of the medieval Bible, see E. Ann Matter, 'The Bible in the Center: The *Glossa ordinaria,*' in *The Unbounded Community: Papers in Christian Ecumenism in Honor of Jaroslav Pelikan,* ed. William Caferro and Duncan G. Fisher (New York: Garland, 1996), 33–42.

10 I will treat allegory at greater length in chapter 1. Here, it is enough to note the widespread contemporary assumption of the hermeneutical il-legitimacy of allegory in biblical and theological studies, which predates the Romantic disdain of allegory. Andrew Louth, while attempting to re-claim patristic allegory as a legitimate form of theological interpretation, nevertheless notes the widespread rejection of the practice in *Discerning the Mystery: An Essay on the Nature of Theology* (Oxford: Clarendon Press, 1983), 96–7.

11 Hans Frei, *The Eclipse of Biblical Narrative: A Study in Eighteenth and Nineteenth Century Hermeneutics* (New Haven: Yale University Press, 1974), 41; further reference to this book occurs in the text. Willemien Otten makes a related observation in stating that for modern readers, 'knowledge of the Bible's compositional origin holds the key to unlocking its truths,' and that the truth resides in a 'shared faith in the accuracy of historical reconstruc-tion.' See 'Nature and Scripture: The Demise of a Medieval Analogy,' *The Harvard Theological Review* 88 (1995): 257–84.

12 This tendency is apparent in scholarly and in more popular discussions of the Bible. See, for example, Jeffrey L. Sheler, *Is the Bible True? How Modern Debates and Discoveries Affirm the Essence of the Scriptures* (San Francisco: HarperSanFrancisco, 1999). The question of the book's title (which Sheler answers with a qualified yes) is understood almost exclusively in historical terms. The Bible is worthy of credence insofar as it is historically accurate; faith in the Bible is understood as equivalent to gauging the trustworthi-ness of a document after the careful sifting of rational evidence. Similarly, the work of scholars who dispute the truth of the Bible as traditionally conceived (as in the case of the well-publicized Jesus Seminar) also appeal to historical analysis to buttress their claims. Both attackers and defenders of biblical truth, that is, work from the same set of assumptions concerning the importance of historical reliability. Sheler does write that his work is not concerned with 'theological' issues or truths, which he therefore leaves to one side. But this very division, I suggest, is one that Dante and other medieval thinkers would not have recognized. Frei, for example, has writ-ten that in the modern study of the Bible, 'literal and figurative reading

of the biblical narratives, once natural allies, not only came apart, but the successors looked with great unease at each other – historical criticism and biblical theology were different enterprises and made for decidedly. strained company' (8).

13 I wish here to acknowledge a general debt to my colleague James E. Faulconer's penetrating essay, 'Scripture as Incarnation,' in *Historicity and the Latter-day Saint Scriptures*, ed. Paul Y. Hoskisson (Provo, UT: Religious Studies Center, 2001), 17–61, which forced me to think much more seriously about the differences between pre-modern and modernist scriptural interpretation.

14 Beryl Smalley, *The Study of the Bible in the Middle Ages* (1952; Notre Dame: Notre Dame University Press, 1964), 356, 358. As we will see in chapter 1, Smalley's determination to find a narrative of progression toward a rejection of allegory and acceptance of the primacy of the literal sense coloured her reading of Dante's *Monarchia* as well.

15 See, for example, Carol Harrison, *Beauty and Revelation in the Thought of Saint Augustine* (Oxford: Clarendon Press, 1988); and David Dawson, 'Transcendence as Embodiment: Augustine's Domestication of Gnosis,' *Modern Theology* 10 (1994): 1–26; as well as Dawson's entry, 'Figure, Allegory,' in *Augustine through the Ages: An Encyclopedia*, ed. Allan D. Fitzgerald (Grand Rapids: Eerdmans, 1999), 365–8. An obvious example of the kind of misreading I refer to above can be found in Robin Lane Fox's introduction to the Everyman edition of Augustine's *Confessions* (New York: Knopf, 2001). Lane Fox describes Augustine's task in the last three books of the work as 'finding the wildest meanings in the opening of Genesis' (xxiv) and depicts Augustine the exegete as 'a meditator on the book of Genesis who has not the slightest clue of its origin and history and the evolutionary truth about the world' (xxv). No biblical interpretation, in other words, is worth our time that does not correspond to our own notions of scientific truth and does not recognize that the *real* meaning of a biblical text is limited to verifiable historical reference.

16 The *Grande dizionario della lingua italiana* lists Benivieni (1453–1542) as the earliest to use 'simbolo' in the sense of a concrete image or thing representing something else. In the *Ottimo commento*, a fourteenth-century commentary on the *Commedia*, we do find the phrase 'simbolo delli Apostoli,' but in this usage, 'simbolo' refers to one of the formulaic statements of the Christian faith.

17 See 'Symbolism,' in *DE*, 803–6.

18 A number of critics have also argued for the fruitfulness of considering Dante's poem and its interpretation within the light of modern, hermeneutical

thought. D.S. Carne-Ross, for example, in his review of Singleton's translation of and commentary on the poem, offered Gadamer's notion of understanding as a way of overcoming some of the contradictions that attend a reading of Dante such as Singleton's. See 'Dante Agonistes,' *New York Review of Books*, 1 May 1975. More recently, William Franke has sought more extensively to understand the *Commedia* within the light of modern hermeneutic thought in *Dante's Interpretive Journey* (Chicago: University of Chicago Press, 1996). See also Christine O'Connell Baur, *Dante's Hermeneutics of Salvation: Passages to Freedom in the 'Divine Comedy'* (Toronto: University of Toronto Press, 2007). I am indebted to these last two critics in my discussion of textual truth here and in chapter 2.

19 Baur, *Dante's Hermeneutics of Salvation*, 67.

20 Hans-Georg Gadamer, *Truth and Method*, 2nd ed., trans. revised by Joel Weinsheimer and Donald G. Marshall (New York: Continuum, 1989), 306; emphasis Gadamer's.

21 *Truth and Method*, 489.

22 Joel C. Weinsheimer, *Gadamer's Hermeneutics: A Reading of 'Truth and Method'* (New Haven: Yale University Press, 1985), 258.

23 *Truth and Method*, 303–4; emphasis mine.

24 *Confessions* 11.8. 'Quis porro nos docet nisi stabilis ueritas? Quia et per creaturam mutabilem cum admonemur, ad ueritatem stabilem ducimur, ubi uere discimus, cum stamus et audimus eum et gaudio gaudemus propter uocem sponsi, reddentes nos, unde sumus.' The Latin text is cited according to the *CCSL* edition (vol. 27), ed. Lucas Verheijen (Turnhout: Brepols, 1981). Translation is taken from *Confessions*, trans. Henry Chadwick (Oxford: Oxford University Press, 1992). I return to this passage in chapter 1.

25 Teodolinda Barolini, *Dante and the Origins of Italian Literary Culture* (New York: Fordham University Press, 2006), 15.

26 See, for example, Peter Hawkins, 'The Metamorphosis of Ovid,' in *Dante's Testaments*, 145–58.

27 On visual art, see, for example, Jeffrey Schnapp's chapter, 'Sant'Apollinare in Classe and Dante's Poetics of Martyrdom,' in *The Transfiguration of History at the Center of Dante's 'Paradise'* (Princeton: Princeton University Press, 1986), 170–238.

28 Jonathan Culler, 'Presupposition and Intertextuality,' in *The Pursuit of Signs: Semiotics, Literature, Deconstruction* (Ithaca: Cornell University Press, 1981), 103.

29 See, for example, Robert Hollander, *Il Virgilio dantesco: Tragedia nella 'Commedia'* (Florence: Olschki, 1983); Teodolinda Barolini, *Dante's*

Poets: Textuality and Truth in the 'Comedy' (Princeton: Princeton University Press, 1984); Rachel Jacoff and Jeffrey T. Schnapp, eds., *The Poetry of Allusion: Virgil and Ovid in Dante's 'Comedy'* (Stanford: Stanford University Press, 1991); Madison U. Sowell, ed., *Dante and Ovid: Essays in Intertextuality* (Binghamton, NY: Medieval & Renaissance Texts & Studies, 1991); Franke, *Dante's Interpretive Journey*, 191–232.

30 See Michael Fishbane, *Biblical Interpretation in Ancient Israel* (Oxford: Clarendon Press, 1988), 282. Jacob Neusner cautions against too wide-ranging and indiscriminate a conception of intertextuality in *Canon and Connection: Intertextuality in Judaism* (Lanham: University Press of America, 1987).

31 See Fishbane's discussion of the prophetic interpretation, or even appropriation, of the law in his chapter, 'Aggadic Exegesis of Legal Traditions in the Prophetic Literature,' in *Biblical Interpretation*, 292–317.

32 Gerald Bruns, 'Hermeneutics of Allegory and the History of Interpretation,' *Comparative Literature* 40 (1988): 392.

33 See *Monarchia* 3.4.16. I discuss this section of the treatise at greater length in chapter 1.

34 See, for example, Charles T. Davis, 'Education in Dante's Florence,' in *Dante's Italy and Other Essays* (Philadelphia: University of Pennsylvania Press, 1984), 137–65; and Peter Hawkins, *Dante's Testaments*, 23–30.

1. Dante's Idea of the Bible

1 *Confessions* 3.5.9. 'sed uisa est mihi indigna, quam Tullianae dignitati compararem.' 'Et ecce uideo rem non compertam superbis neque nudatam pueris, sed incessu humilem, successu excelsam et uelatam mysteriis.' As noted previously, the Latin text is cited from the *CCSL* edition (vol. 27), ed. Lucas Verheijen (Turnhout: Brepols, 1981), and translations are from *Confessions*, trans. Henry Chadwick (Oxford: Oxford University Press, 1992), though I have occasionally modified the translation.

2 For a consideration of the Romantic redefinition of, and consequent preference for, symbol over allegory, see Tzvetan Todorov, *Theories of the Symbol*, trans. Catherine Porter (Ithaca: Cornell University Press, 1982), 198–221. Rita Copeland and Stephen Melville have argued that the opposition between symbol and allegory has been replaced in the wake of deconstruction with an equally unhelpful distinction between allegory (works specifically composed as allegory) and allegoresis (allegorical interpretation). See 'Allegory and Allegoresis, Rhetoric and Hermeneutics,' *Exemplaria* 3 (1991): 159–87.

3 I am thinking in particular here of the first half of de Man's essay, 'The
Rhetoric of Temporality,' from *Blindness and Insight*, 2nd ed. (Minneapolis:
University of Minnesota Press, 1983), 187–208. De Man views allegory
sympathetically because allegory, unlike the symbol, 'designates primarily
a distance in relation to its own origin, and, renouncing the nostalgia and
the desire to coincide, it establishes its language in the void of this temporal difference' (207). The status of allegory has become increasingly problematic over the last few decades. While Paul de Man questioned what had
since the Romantics become a commonplace distinction between allegory
and symbol, more recently Gordon Teskey has revived the Romantic claim
that allegory represents an artificial imposition of meaning and radicalized
it, seeing allegory as a violent act, forcing meaning on a reality that is at
heart disordered and resistant to interpretation. See *Allegory and Violence*
(Ithaca: Cornell University Press, 1996). A recent and helpful review of
theories of allegory from the last fifty years, with specific reference to
medieval literature, can be found in Suzanne Conklin Akbari, *Seeing
through the Veil: Optical Theory and Medieval Allegory* (Toronto: University of
Toronto Press, 2004), 3–20. Copeland and Melville offer a useful consideration of the ways in which allegory and allegoresis are tied up together in
'Allegory and Allegoresis.' Andrew Louth, in his *Discerning the Mystery: An
Essay on the Nature of Theology* (Oxford: Clarendon Press, 1983), attempts
to reclaim allegory as a legitimate form of theological interpretation, while
noting that 'Patristic allegorization . . . sticks in the gullet of modern theology, and not just "modern theology" in some limited sense: at all levels
this allegorization is something deplored' (96–7). On the ancient allegorical tradition, see Robert L. Lamberton, *Homer the Theologian: Neoplatonist
Allegorical Reading and the Growth of the Epic Tradition* (Berkeley: University
of California Press, 1986); and Jon Whitman, *Allegory: The Dynamics of an
Ancient and Medieval Technique* (Cambridge, MA: Harvard University Press,
1987), both of whom attempt to see allegory differently, as a practice that
still has force for us as readers of texts, a fact recognized by Gerald Bruns's
perceptive review essay of these works, 'Hermeneutics of Allegory and
the History of Interpretation,' *Comparative Literature* 40 (1988): 384–95.
Bruns's comment concerning the logic of allegory is relevant here: 'what
seems strange or scandalous about any allegorical interpretation – what
seems irrational about it – is likely to derive from the historical situation in which it occurs, not from the logic or illogic of the practice itself'
(390). Indeed, it is worth keeping in mind that two of the most prominent
interpretive 'schools' of the twentieth century – the psychoanalytic and the
Marxist – were primarily allegorical in practice.

4 See, for example, R.A. Markus, *Signs and Meanings: World and Text in Ancient Christianity* (Liverpool: Liverpool University Press, 1996), 12.

5 For an overview of Augustine's life and thought, see the standard biography by Peter Brown, *Augustine of Hippo: A Biography*, rev. ed. (Berkeley: University of California Press, 2000); the best account of Augustine's development as a reader is Brian Stock, *Augustine the Reader: Meditation, Self-Knowledge, and the Ethics of Interpretation* (Cambridge, MA: Harvard University Press, 1996); a concise account is Thomas Williams, 'Biblical interpretation,' in *The Cambridge Companion to Augustine*, ed. Eleonore Stump and Norman Kretzmann (Cambridge: Cambridge University Press, 2001), 59–70.

6 See O'Donnell's entry, 'Bible,' in *Augustine through the Ages: An Encyclopedia*, ed. Allan D. Fitzgerald (Grand Rapids: Eerdmans, 1999), 99–100.

7 'Nihil enim fere de illis obscuritatibus eruitur, quod non planissime dictum alibi reperiatur' (*De doctrina christiana* 2.6.8). The Latin text is taken from the *CCSL* edition (vol. 32), ed. Joseph Martin (Turnhout: Brepols, 1962). English translation is taken from *On Christian Doctrine*, trans. D.W. Robertson, Jr (New York: Macmillan, 1958).

8 'Aut quis nisi tu, deus noster, fecisti nobis firmamentum auctoritatis super nos in scriptura tua diuina? . . . Neque enim nouimus alios libros ita destruentes superbiam, ita destruentes inimicum et defensorem resistentem reconciliationi tuae defendendo peccata sua. Non noui, domine, non noui alia tam casta eloquia, quae sic mihi persuaderent confessionem et lenirent ceruicem meam iugo tuo et inuitarent colere te gratis.'

9 See Hans-Georg Gadamer, *Truth and Method*, 303–4, and my discussion of Gadamer's notion of textual truth in the Introduction.

10 From Saint Augustine, *On Genesis*, trans. Edmund Hill (Hyde Park, NY: New City Press, 2002).

11 For extended considerations of the literal sense in ancient and medieval exegesis, see Henri de Lubac, *Exégèse médiévale: Les quatre sens de l'écriture*, 4 vols. in 2 parts (Paris: Aubier, 1959–64), 1.2: 425–87; and Gilbert Dahan, *L'exégèse chrétienne de la Bible en Occident médiévale: XIIe – XIVe siècle* (Paris: Éditions du Cerf, 1999), 239–97. Both authors note that medieval authors used *historia* and *littera* more or less interchangeably. See also Anthony Nemetz, 'Literalness and the *Sensus Litteralis*,' *Speculum* 34 (1959): 76–89, who carefully distinguishes between modern and medieval understandings of the literal sense and suggests that the '*sensus litteralis* is concerned with the signification of words and concepts,' though he identifies three different emphases in the *sensus litteralis* among medieval thinkers.

12 'Titulus horum librorum inscribitur *De Genesi ad litteram,* id est non secundum allegoricas significationes sed secundum rerum gestarum proprietatem.' *Retractiones* 2.24. Cited according to the *CCSL* edition (vol. 57), ed. Almut Mutzenbecher (Turnhout: Brepols, 1984).

13 'Introduction to *The Literal Meaning of Genesis,*' in *On Genesis,* 159.

14 'fieri enim potest, ut etiam ego aliam *his diuinae scripturae uerbis congruentiorem* fortassis inueniam.' *De Genesi ad litteram* 4.28; emphasis mine. Cited according to the *CSEL* edition, vol. 28, pt. 1 (1894; New York: Johnson Reprint Corp., 1970).

15 'Si tamen hujus vocabuli significatione largius utimur, nullum est inconveniens, ut scilicet "historiam" esse dicamus, non tantum rerum gestarum narrationem; *sed illam primam significationem cujuslibet narrationis, quae secundum proprietatem verborum exprimitur.* Secundum quam acceptionem omnes utriusque Testamenti libros . . . ad hanc lectionem secundum litteralem sensum pertinere puto' (*Didascalicon* 6.3; *PL* 176: 801a–b). English translation taken from *The Didascalicon of Hugh of St. Victor,* trans. Jerome Taylor (New York: Columbia University Press, 1961), 137–8; emphasis mine.

16 Frank Kermode, 'What Precisely Are the Facts?' in *The Genesis of Secrecy: On the Interpretation of Narrative* (Cambridge, MA: Harvard University Press, 1979), 110.

17 'sine uoluntate atque ullo appetitu significandi praeter se aliquid aliud ex se cognosci faciunt' (*De doctrina christiana* 2.1.2).

18 'At illa [mens prudens] comparauit haec uerba temporaliter sonantia cum aeterno in silentio uerbo tuo et dixit: "aliud est longe, longe aliud est. Haec longe infra me sunt nec sunt, quia fugiunt et praetereunt: uerbum autem dei mei supra me manet in aeternum."' Cf. also *De Genesi ad litteram* 8.27.

19 George Steiner's notion of 'understanding as translation' seems to be a modern analogue; see *After Babel: Aspects of Language and Translation,* 2nd ed. (Oxford: Oxford University Press, 1992), 1–50. On Augustine's theory of signs, see: B. Darrell Jackson, 'The Theory of Signs in St. Augustine's *De Doctrina Christiana,*' in *Augustine: A Collection of Critical Essays,* ed. R.A. Markus (New York: Doubleday, 1972), 93–147; R.A. Markus, 'St. Augustine on Signs,' in *Augustine,* 61–91; Eugene Vance, 'Saint Augustine: Language as Temporality,' *Mimesis: From Mirror to Method, Augustine to Descartes,* ed. John D. Lyons and Stephen G. Nichols, Jr. (Hanover: University Press of New England, 1982), 20–35; Marcia Colish, *The Mirror of Language: A Study in the Medieval Theory of Knowing,* rev. ed. (Lincoln: University of Nebraska Press, 1983), 7–54.

20 'Formata quippe cogitatio ab ea re quam scimus uerbum est quod in corde
    dicimus, quod nec graecum est nec latinum nec linguae alicuius alterius,
    sed cum id opus est in eorum quibus loquimur perferre notitiam aliquod
    signum quo significetur assumitur' (*De Trinitate* 15.10.19). Latin text cited
    from the *CCSL* edition, vol. 50A, ed. W.J. Mountain (Turnhout: Brepols,
    1968). English translation is taken from *The Trinity,* trans. Edmund Hill
    (Hyde Park, NY: New City Press, 1991).
21 'non dicitur sicuti est sed sicut potest uideri audiriue per corpus.'
22 'Quomodo venit, nisi quod *uerbum caro factum est et habitauit in nobis*? Sicuti
    cum loquimur' (*De doctrina christiana* 1.13.12).
23 See Carol Harrison, *Beauty and Revelation in the Thought of Saint Augustine*
    (Oxford: Clarendon Press, 1992), 54–67. In much of my discussion of
    Augustine and language, I owe a general debt to her analysis. Further ref-
    erences to this work occur in the text.
24 'uerbum quod foris sonat signum est uerbi quod intus lucet cui magis
    uerbi competit nomen . . . Ita enim uerbum nostrum uox quodam modo
    corporis fit assumendo eam in qua manifestetur sensibus hominum sicut
    uerbum dei *caro factum est* assumendo eam in qua et ipsum manifestaretur
    sensibus hominum.'
25 'fortassis autem aliis intrinsecus uel effabilibus uel ineffabilibus modis
    deus cum illis antea loquebatur, sicut etiam cum angelis loquitur ipsa
    incommutabili ueritate inlustrans mentes eorum' (11.33).
26 *Augustine the Reader,* 16.
27 'Signa corporaliter edita generationes aquarum propter necessarias causas
    carnalis profunditatis.'
28 Gadamer is drawn to Augustine's discussion of the human *verbum* and
    the divine *Verbum* in his consideration of language, and his conclusion,
    similar to Augustine's, is that the human word is not wholly arbitrary
    and cannot be separated into the Saussurian division of *langüe* and *parole.*
    See his chapter, 'The Development of the Concept of Language in the
    History of Western Thought,' in *Truth and Method,* 405–38, esp. 418–28. Joel
    Weinsheimer gives a lucid account of Gadamer's views of language in 'A
    Word Is Not a Sign,' in *Philosophical Hermeneutics and Literary Theory* (New
    Haven: Yale University Press, 1991), 87–123.
29 'Ipsum est uerbum tuum, quod et principium est, quia et loquitur nobis.
    Sic in euangelio per carnem ait, et hoc insonuit foris auribus hominum,
    ut crederetur et intus quaereretur et inueniretur in aeterna ueritate, ubi
    omnes discipulos bonus et solus magister docet. Ibi audio uocem tuam,
    domine, dicentis mihi . . . quis porro nos docet nisi stabilis ueritas? Quia
    et per creaturam mutabilem cum admonemur, ad ueritatem stabilem

ducimur, ubi uere discimus, cum stamus et audimus eum et gaudio gaudemus propter uocem sponsi, reddentes nos, unde sumus.'

30 Hans Frei, *The Eclipse of Biblical Narrative,* 3; further references to this book
in the present chapter occur in the text.

31 'Dum ergo quisque conatur id sentire in scripturis sanctis, quod in eis
sensit ille qui scripsit, quid mali est, si hoc sentiat, quod tu, lux omnium
ueridicarum mentium, ostendis uerum esse, etiamsi non hoc sensit ille,
quem legit, cum et ille uerum nec tamen hoc senserit?'

32 'Ego certe . . . sic mallem scribere, ut, quod ueri quisque de his rebus capere
posset, mea uerba resonarent, quam ut unam ueram sententiam ad hoc
apertius ponerem, ut excluderem ceteras, quarum falsitas me non posset
offendere.'

33 'Est vero sermo, nota aut imago rerum, & veluti quaedam perspicilla, per
quae res ipsas intuemur. Quare, si fermo sit, vel per se, vel nobis obscurus;
difficulter ex eo res ipsas cognosciumus.' Matthias Flacius Illyricus, *De ratione cognoscendi sacras literas: Über den Erkenntnisgrund der Heiligen Schrift,*
ed. Lutz Geldsetzer (Dusseldorf: Stern-Verlag Janssen, 1968), 6.

34 In fact, many Catholics attacked Flacius's work as derivative from the
church fathers, since he advocated the method of comparing 'clear' passages with 'obscure' ones, something that Augustine had advocated.
And while at times Flacius followed Luther in asserting scripture's self-
interpreting clarity, at others he discussed the obscurity of certain passages
and argued for two levels of meaning, one suited to the 'young' and others
to more mature readers. It is, however, Flacius's assumption of the ability of language to refer transparently to a single reality that differentiates
him from the church fathers he draws on and that marks his hermeneutics
as modernist, or at least as moving toward the assumptions of modern-
ism. See the brief discussion of Flacius's role in the history of interpretation in Jean Grondin, *Introduction to Philosophical Hermeneutics,* trans. Joel
Weinsheimer (New Haven: Yale University Press, 1994), 42–4.

35 A typical statement by a Dante scholar of the common view of Augustine's
hermeneutics as dualistic can be found in Guy Raffa, *Divine Dialectic:
Dante's Incarnational Poetry* (Toronto: University of Toronto Press, 2000),
in which Raffa asserts that 'the distinction between the spirit and the letter is the *sine qua non* of proper interpretation' for Augustine (129). He
finds justification for this position in Umberto Eco, *Interpretation and
Overinterpretation: Umberto Eco with Richard Rorty, Jonathan Culler, Christine
Brook-Rose,* ed. Stefan Collini (Cambridge: Cambridge University Press,
1992), 29–66, where Eco traces the development of a 'hermetic semiosis,'
which Raffa links to Augustine. Raffa's discussion is problematic both

because of his characterization of Augustine and his use of Eco, who never mentions Augustine specifically in this work, except to cite a passage from *De doctrina christiana* to support his model of how to *avoid* overinterpretation (and 'hermetic semiosis') (65). Nor does Eco mention Paul, another example for Raffa of interpretive dualism; in fact, Eco seems to me to exempt medieval hermeneutics from his discussion of overinterpretation. Lesley Smith, however, makes a point similar to the one I am making here: 'It is *not* the case that medieval interpreters had no historical sense, that they ignored etymology, philology, context, subtext, or change over time; but medieval interpreters proceeded by giving scripture a higher face value than academic theologians might today, and they acted accordingly. I would argue that that face value is Christ.' See 'The Theology of the Twelfth- and Thirteenth-Century Bible,' in *The Early Medieval Bible: Its Production, Decoration, and Use*, ed. Richard Gameson (Cambridge: Cambridge University Press, 1994), 226–7; emphasis Smith's.

36 *Homiliae in Hiezechihelem prophetam*, book 2, Homily 3.18. 'Si uero portam Scripturam sacram hoc in loco accipimus, ipsa quoque duo limina habet, exterius et interius, quia in littera diuiditur et allegoria. Limen quippe Scripturae sacrae exterius littera, limen uero eius interius allegoria. Quia enim per litteram ad allegoriam tendimus, quasi a limine quod est exterius, ad hoc quod est interius uenimus.' Latin text cited according to the *CCSL* edition (vol. 142), ed. Marcus Adriaen (Turnhout: Brepols, 1971), 250.

37 'Translata sunt, cum et ipsae res, quas propriis uerbis significamus, ad aliquid aliud significandum usurpantur.'

38 Erich Auerbach, 'Figura,' in *Scenes from the Drama of European Literature* (1959; Minneapolis: University of Minnesota Press, 1984), 53.

39 Markus, *Signs and Meanings*, 10. See also G.R. Evans, *The Language and Logic of the Bible: The Earlier Middle Ages* (Cambridge: Cambridge University Press, 1984), 51–9.

40 See the extended discussion of this couplet by Henri de Lubac in his introduction to *Exégèse médiévale* 1.1: 23–39.

41 Louth, in *Discerning the Mystery*, makes much of the order of the senses that the couplet encapsulates: 'For it is not just a list of senses, but an order or movement: we move from history to allegory, and within allegory we perceive first the dogmatic dimensions of the Christian mystery, then the response it calls for on our part (the moral sense), and then finally we are given a glimpse of the fruition of the mystery which calls on us (the anagogical sense)' (116).

42 *Events and Their Afterlife: The Dialectics of Christian Typology in the Bible and Dante* (Cambridge: Cambridge University Press, 1966), 58.

43　See Henri de Lubac, 'Typologie et allégorisme,' *Recherches de science religieuse* 34 (1947): 180–226, where he writes, 'Le scrupule relatif à l'*allegoria* est chose tout à fait récente.' See also Jean Pépin, who, in *Dante e la tradition de l'allégorie* (Montreal: Institut d'études médiévales, 1971), observes that typology is a modern term and that, with rare exceptions, was not preferred to allegory. Indeed, he asserts that 'les pères latins . . . sont unanimes à nommer "allégorie" ce que l'on entend aujourd'hui par typologie' (46–7). David Dawson notes that for Augustine, 'trying to sort out these terms [*allegoria, figura,* etc.] according to a set of systematically organized categories seems to be an especially futile enterprise.' See his entry, 'Figure, Allegory,' in *Augustine through the Ages,* 365–8. Similarly, it is interesting to note that the distinction between *symbol* and allegory, dear to Coleridge, Goethe, and many Dante critics, is not a distinction that Dante made; to him the word 'symbol' was unknown. See my entry on 'Symbolism' in *DE,* 803–6.

44　I translate from Rufinus's Latin rendering of the original Greek text: 'nisi quod sancta scriptura ab his non secundum spiritalem sensum, sed secundum litterae sonum intellegitur.' When discussing interpretation in the *De principiis,* he asserts that in the Old Testament, narratives that seem straightforward, concerning, for example, the begetting of children or marriage, are actually types (τύποι) (4.2.2). (In Rufinus's Latin translation, the narratives are described as forms and figures of hidden and sacred realities [*formae ac figurae . . . latentium sacrarumque rerum*]). Of course, given that the majority of Origen's extant work exists only in free Latin translations, any statement about his vocabulary must be made cautiously. Latin and Greek text cited from the *SC* edition of *De principiis:* Origen, *Traité des principes,* ed. Henri Crouzel and Manlio Simonetti, 5 vols. (Paris: Éditions du Cerf, 1978–84).

45　Henri de Lubac, *Exégèse médiévale* 1.2: 440. Beryl Smalley, on the other hand, argued that prior to the Scholastics, most 'Christian commentators had despised the letter and dwelt on "mysteries."' *The Study of the Bible in the Middle Ages* (1952; Notre Dame: University of Notre Dame Press, 1964), 295.

46　'Cuius operis et laboris prima obseruatio est, ut diximus, nosse istos libros etsi nondum ad intellectum, legendo tamen uel mandare memoriae uel omnino incognitos non habere . . . ut ad obscuriories locutiones illustrandas de manifestioribus sumantur exempla.'

47　He discusses at some length, for instance, the fact that each of the four evangelists made choices in deciding which material from the life of Christ to put into his Gospel and how to order that material, though he also is quick to argue that this human influence on the composition of the New

Testament does not adversely affect its truth value. See *De consensu evange-listarum* 2.12.28, 2.14.31, and 2.66.128.

48 'Thus the Holy Spirit has magnificently and wholesomely modulated the Holy Scriptures so that the more open places present themselves to hunger and the more obscure places may deter a disdainful attitude. Hardly any-thing may be found in these obscure places which is not found plainly said elsewhere' ('Magnifice igitur et salubriter spiritus sanctus ita scripturas sanctas modificauit, ut locis apertioribus fami occurreret, obscurioribus autem fastidia detergeret. Nihil enim fere de illis obscuritatibus eruitur, quod non planissime dictum alibi reperiatur' [2.6.8]).

49 *Discerning the Mystery*, 112.

50 For a brief but more traditional and linear account of the development of biblical interpretation in the later Middle Ages, see my entry 'Biblical Exegesis,' in *Medieval Italy: An Encyclopedia*, ed. Christopher Kleinhenz (New York and London: Routledge, 2004), 121–4.

51 Christopher Ocker provides a discussion of the different literary forms this new exegesis took in *Biblical Poetics before Humanism and Reformation* (Cambridge: Cambridge University Press, 2002), 8–14.

52 See the classic study of this tradition, Dom Jean Leclerq, *The Love of Learning and the Desire for God*, trans. Catherine Misrahi (New York: Fordham University Press, 1961). G.R. Evans provides a summary of the differences between biblical study in the monastery and the schools in *The Language and Logic of the Bible: The Earlier Middle Ages*, 13–36.

53 'Vobis, fratres, alia quam aliis de saeculo, aut certe aliter dicenda sunt . . . nisi frustra forte ex longo studiis estis caelestibus occupati, exer-citati sensibus, et in lege Dei meditati die ac nocte. Itaque parate fauces non lacti, sed pani.' Citations from Bernard are taken from the *SC* edition, *Sermons sur le Cantique*, ed. J. Leclerq et al., 5 vols. (Paris: Éditions du Cerf, 1996–2007), 1:60–2.

54 For the history of the *Glossa ordinaria*, see Beryl Smalley, *The Study of the Bible in the Middle Ages*, 49–66; and Guy Lobrichon, 'Une nouveauté: Les gloses de la Bible,' in *Le Moyen Âge et la Bible*, ed. Pierre Riché and Guy Lobrichon (Paris: Beauchesne, 1984), 95–114. A more recent summary of research on the *Glossa ordinaria* is E. Ann Matter, 'The Church Fathers and the *Glossa ordinaria*,' in *The Reception of the Church Fathers in the West: From the Carolingians to the Maurists*, 2 vols., ed. Irena Backus (Leiden: Brill, 1997), 1:83–111. Matter notes that, contrary to previous assumptions, 'the *Glossa ordinaria* to each book (or collection of books) to the Bible had an independent development, and therefore drew on different sources from earlier centuries of Christian biblical learning' (83).

55 E. Ann Matter, 'The Bible in the Center,' in *The Unbounded Community: Papers in Christian Ecumenism in Honor of Jaroslav Pelikan*, ed. William Caferro and Duncan G. Fisher (New York: Garland, 1996), 34.

56 M.T. Gibson has argued that the '*Glossa ordinaria* is the junction between traditional patristic exegesis and modern scholastic method.' See 'The Place of the *Glossa ordinaria* in Medieval Exegesis,' in *Ad Litteram: Authoritative Texts and Their Medieval Readers*, ed. Mark D. Jordan and Kent Emery, Jr (Notre Dame: University of Notre Dame Press, 1992), 5–27.

57 Studies considering the impact of Scholasticism on biblical interpretation include: Beryl Smalley, *The Study of the Bible*, 281–308; and 'The Bible in the Medieval Schools,' in *The West from the Fathers to the Reformation*, ed. G.W.H. Lampe, vol. 2 of *The Cambridge History of the Bible*, 3 vols. (Cambridge: Cambridge University Press, 1969), 197–220; Robert M. Grant with David Tracy, *A Short History of the Interpretation of the Bible*, 2nd ed. (Philadelphia: Fortress Press, 1984), 83–91; A.J. Minnis and A.B. Scott with the assistance of David Wallace, ed., *Medieval Literary Theory and Criticism c. 1100–1375: The Commentary Tradition*, rev. ed. (Oxford: Clarendon Press, 1991), 197–276; Giuseppe Cremascolli, 'Allegoria e dialettica: Sul travaglio dell'esegesi biblica al tempo di Dante,' in *Dante e la Bibbia*, ed. Giovanni Barblan (Florence: Olschki, 1988), 197–276; and Alessandro Ghisalberti, 'L'esegesi della scuola domenicana del secolo XIII,' in *La Bibbia nel medioevo*, ed. Giuseppe Cremascoli and Claudio Leonardi (Bologna: Edizioni Dehoniane, 1996), 291–304. For the view that the shift toward a more literal-minded exegesis is grossly exaggerated, see: D.H. Robertson, Jr, *A Preface to Chaucer: Studies in Medieval Perspectives* (Princeton: Princeton University Press, 1962); and Henri de Lubac, *Exégèse médiévale*, 2.4: 263–367. Similarly, R.W. Southern argues against what he calls the 'longest lasting misconception about scholastic thought'–that the Bible somehow diminished in importance during the Scholastic period. See *Scholastic Humanism and the Unification of Europe*, vol. 1, *Foundations* (Oxford: Blackwell, 1995), 102–33.

58 *Medieval Literary Theory and Criticism*, 110 and 105: 'quod pro mysteriorum significatione quae ex interpretationibus nominum percipitur factum esse'; 'solius Spiritus sancti instinctu sine omni exteriori adminiculo' (Latin text found in *PL* 191: 59, 55).

59 See Minnis and Scott, 199, 271–6. For a consideration of the Aristotelian prologue and its place in late medieval conceptions of authorship, see A.J. Minnis, *Medieval Theory of Authorship: Scholastic Literary Attitudes in the Later Middle Ages*, 2nd ed. (London: Scolar Press, 1988).

60 Minnis, *Medieval Theory of Authorship*, 84.

61 'Ad primum ergo dicendum quod multiplicitas horum sensuum non facit aequivocationem aut aliam speciem multiplicitatis, quia, sicut jam dictum est, sensus isti non multiplicantur propter hoc quod una vox multa significet, sed quia ipsae res significatae per voces aliarum rerum possunt esse signa. Et ita etiam nulla confusio sequitur in sacra Scriptura, cum omnes sensus fundentur super unum, scilicet litteralem. Ex quo solo potest trahi argumentum, non autem ex his quae secundum allegoriam dicuntur, ut Augustinus dicit in epistola contra Vincentium donatistam. Non tamen ex hoc aliquid deperit sacrae Scripturae, quia nihil sub spirituali sensu continetur fidei necessarium quod Scriptura per litteralem sensum alicubi manifeste non tradat.'

62 'Quis autem non impudentissime nitatur aliquid in allegoria positum pro se interpretari, nisi habeat et manifesta testimonia, quorum lumine illustrentur obscura.' *Epistolae* 93.8.24 (*PL* 33: 334).

63 Grant with Tracy, 90. Compare the account of Jacques Verger in 'L'exégèse de l'Université,' in *Le Moyen Âge et la Bible*, 199–232: 'Il en resort che saint Thomas n'entend nullement remettre en cause l'approche traditionelle de l'Écriture, dont il cite expressément les origines patristiques et spécialement augustiniennes, mais bien plutôt la préciser, la justifier en raison et, par suite, la protéger de certaines aberrations' (206).

64 'Quaedam enim sunt quae procedunt ex principiis notis lumine naturali intellectus ... quaedam vero sunt quae procedunt ex principiis notis lumine superioris scientiae ... Sacra doctrina credit principia revelata a Deo.'

65 'Quia vero sensus litteralis est quem auctor intendit, auctor autem sacrae Scripturae Deus est qui omnia simul suo intellectu comprehendit, non est inconveniens, ut Augustinus dicit XII *Confess.* si etiam secundum litteralem sensum in una littera Scripturae plures sint sensus.'

66 See, for example, James H. Morey, *Book and Verse: A Guide to Middle English Biblical Literature* (Urbana and Chicago: University of Illinois Press, 2000), 9–23.

67 Thomas H. Bestul, review of *Book and Verse: A Guide to Middle English Biblical Literature* by James H. Morey, *Speculum* 77 (2002): 609.

68 Morey, *Book and Verse*, 24–44.

69 Théophile Desbonnets, 'The Franciscan Reading of the Scriptures,' in *Francis of Assisi Today,* ed. Christian Duquoc and Casiano Floristán (New York: Seabury, 1981), 44, 42. See also Gian Luca Potestà, 'I frati minori e lo studio della Bibbia: Da Francesco d'Assisi a Nicolò di Lyre,' in *La Bibbia nel medioevo*, 269–90.

70 See Paolo Chiesa, 'Le traduzioni,' in *La Bibbia nel medioevo*, 30–1.

71 Gilbert Dahan identifies a different but related triad of ideas as forming
the 'hermeneutic assumptions' of a late medieval idea of the Bible: (1) the
belief in an inspired (and thus uniquely true) text, (2) a closed canon, but
with a developing interpretive tradition that results in (3) an 'evolving
text' defined by a multiplicity of interpretations, even an infinite horizon
of interpretive possibilities. See *L'exégèse chrétienne de la Bible en Occident
médiévale*, 37–73. For an exploration of the idea of infinite interpretation,
see Pier Cesare Bori, *L'interpretazione infinita: L'ermeneutica cristiana antica e
le sue trasformazioni* (Bologna: Mulino, 1987).

72 Dante mentions his attendance at religious schools and philosophical
debates at *Conv.* 2.12.7. 'E da questo imaginare cominciai ad andare là
dov'ella si dimostrava veracemente, cioè ne le scuole de li religiosi e a
le disputazioni de li filosofanti.' For attempts to reconstruct the educational
milieu in which Dante would have encountered and studied the scriptures, see Charles T. Davis, 'Education in Dante's Florence,' in *Dante's Italy
and Other Essays* (Philadelphia: University of Pennsylvania Press, 1984),
137–65; the notes on the passage in the Vasoli/De Robertis edition of the
Convivio on pages 205–10; and Peter Hawkins, *Dante's Testaments: Essays in
Scriptural Imagination* (Stanford: Stanford University Press, 1999), 23–30.

73 See See L. Negri, 'Dante e il testo della Vulgata,' *Giornale storico della letteratura italiana* 85 (1925): 288–307; for briefer treatments, see Hawkins, *Dante's
Testaments*, 39–40; and Angelo Penna's entry on 'Bibbia' in *ED*, 1:626–9.

74 Margaret T. Gibson, *The Bible in the Latin West* (Notre Dame: University of
Notre Dame Press, 1993), 12.

75 See the discussion and bibliography in Gilbert Dahan, *L'exégèse chrétienne
de la Bible en Occident médiévale*, 8–12.

76 See Foster's entry, 'Vernacular Scriptures in Italy,' in *The Cambridge History
of the Bible*, vol. 2, *The West from the Fathers to the Reformation*, ed. G.W.H.
Lampe (Cambridge: Cambridge University Press, 1969), 464.

77 In the *De vulgari eloquentia* (1.10.2), Dante refers to the French or 'lingua oïl'
Bible, while in the *Convivio* (1.7.14–17), he mentions the Latin translation of
the Psalter as evidence that translations of poetry lose the musical qualities
of the original texts.

78 'Vernacular Scriptures in Italy,' 464.

79 Dante's attempt to adjudicate between authorities was a necessary step,
since, as G.R. Evans has shown, he wrote during a time in which the issue
of which authorities were most authoritative was vexed and debated. See
'Exegesis and Authority in the Thirteenth Century,' in *Ad Litteram*, ed.
Jordan and Emery, 93–111.

80 Wicksteed proposes that Dante here uses *prius* and *post* in two ways, according to 'the first two ways enumerated by Aristotle' in the *Categories:* that is, temporal and causal priority or posteriority. In this sense, then, the Bible is both temporally and causally prior to the Church; the writings of the fathers together with the authoritative councils are written during the formation of the Church and contribute to its foundation; the Decretals, however, are subsequent to the Church's founding. See Dante Alighieri, *A Translation of the Latin Works of Dante Alighieri,* ed. and trans. A.G. Ferrers Howell and Philip H. Wicksteed (London: Dent, 1904), 233 ff. See also Vinay's discussion of the passage on pages 204–5 of his commentary: Dante Alighieri, *Monarchia,* ed. Gustavo Vinay (Florence: Sansoni, 1950).

81 Both the interlinear gloss, which identifies 'testamentum' as 'novum,' and the longer gloss ('testamentum novum eterna gratia consecratum') support this reading.

82 See Richard Kay, trans. with commentary, *Dante's 'Monarchia'* (Toronto: Pontifical Institute of Medieval Studies, 1998), 213.

83 'Vetus Testamentum continet legem, prophetas, agiographos. Novum autem Evangelium, apostolos, Patres ... In tertio ordine primum habent locum Decretalia, quos canones, id est regulas appellamus; deinde sanctorum Patrum, et doctorum scripta' (*PL* 176: 778–9); emphasis mine.

84 'Exceptis igitur divinis libris, & in summa quadam auctoritatis arce sepositis, primum post eos locum tenent Epistolæ decretales Romanorum Pontificium, & Canones generalium Conciliorum; opuscula quoque sacrorum Doctorum ... Utrumque ergo genus in primo auctoritatis gradu merito ponitur; quoniam ut excedentia & excessa tibi vicissim præferuntur. Illos autem sacros Doctores in eo gradu ponere volui, qui auctoritate Romanæ Ecclesiæ canonizati sunt, & eorum libri per Concilia Pontificum approbati ... Medium vero locum tenent Doctores cæteri, prudentes quidem & Catholici; sed non Canonizati ... tertium autem & infimum tenent gradum Philosophi, Doctoresque gentilium' ('Generalis Prologus,' chap. 12). Vincent de Beauvais, *Speculum quadruplex sive Speclum maius* (1624; Graz-Austria: Akademische Druck – u. Verlagsanstalt, 1964).

85 'O summum facinus ... ecterni Spiritus intentione abuti! Non enim peccatur in Moysen, non in David, non in Iob, non in Matheum, non in Paulum, sed in Spiritum Sanctum qui loquitur in illis. Nam quanquam scribe divini eloquii multi sint, unicus tamen dictator est Deus, qui beneplacitum suum nobis per multorum calamos explicare dignatus est.' Dante makes a similar statement at 3.1.4: 'Spiritus Patri et Filio coecternus aiat per os David.'

86 'Non igitur dicendum est quod quarto die Deus hec duo regimina fecerit; et per consequens intentio Moysi esse non potuit illa quam fingunt' (3.4.16).

87 'circa sensum misticum dupliciter errare contingit: aut querendo ipsum ubi non est, aut accipiendo aliter quam accipi debeat.'

88 Augustine's warnings, however, must be understood in context. Earlier in the same chapter he famously declares that anyone who finds a charitable meaning in the scriptures has read them correctly 'even though he has not said what the author may be shown to have intended in that place' and 'he has not been deceived' ('Quisquis vero talem inde sententiam duxerit ... quod ille quem legit eo loco sensisse probabitur, non perniciose fallitur nec omnino mentitur'). He goes on, however, to issue the warning cited by Dante, since deviating from the author's intention may lead to greater interpretive problems down the road.

89 For a brief discussion of the development of this doctrine and the practice of adducing Luke 22.38 in its support, see Yves Congar, 'La trop fameuse théorie des deux glaives,' in *Sainte Église: Études et approaches ecclésiologiques* (Paris: Éditions du Cerf, 1964), 411–16. Of course, Dante refers again to this debate at *Purg.* 16.106–14, altering the biblical language used by his opponents. Thus, he has Marco Lombardo declare that in fact Rome should have 'two suns' that govern the two roads of earthly life; and rather than possessing two swords, the Pope has joined the sword of temporal power with his pastoral staff ('ed è giunta la spada / col pasturale, e l'un con l'altro insieme / per viva forza mal convien che vada'). Dante goes on in this same canto to suggest a biblical precedent to support the separation of church and temporal power in the exemption of the tribe of Levi from its share of the inheritance in the Promised Land: 'or discerno perché dal retaggio / li figli di Levì furono essenti' (*Purg.* 16.131–2).

90 'Et ad hoc dicendum per interemptionem sensus in quo fundant argumentum.'

91 See, for example, Richard Kay's edition, where the passage is translated as follows: 'And I respond to this by denying the allegorical sense on which they base their argument'; and Nardi, who renders the passage: 'Anche a ciò va risposto negando l'interpretazione allegorica sulla quale l'argomento si fonda.'

92 *Didascalicon* 6.8. 'Expositio tria continet: litteram, sensum, sententiam' (*PL* 176: 806).

93 *L'exégèse de la Bible en Occident médiévale,* 240; he describes each of these steps at length at pages 242–97,

94 Dante does include Hugh in the heaven of the sun, where Bonaventure points him out in his circle of great church doctors.

95 See, for example, *Inf.* 3.12, 'Maestro, il senso lor m'è duro,' where the pilgrim cannot understand the meaning of the words engraved over the

gate of hell, and *De vulgari eloquentia* 2.12.6, where Dante refers to the *sensus* of certain canzoni under discussion in a context that suggests that Dante simply has the meaning of the poems in mind, and not a hidden or allegorical meaning. See also Alfonso Maierù's entry on 'senso' in *ED*, 5:166–68: 'senso ha il valore di "significato" di un termine o di una proposizione (secondo una tradizione fissata da testi molto noti nel Medioevo . . .).' In considering Dante's use of the word in *Monarchia* 3, he writes that 'il termine ha il valore di "interpretazione" di due passi della Scrittura.'

96 *The Study of the Bible*, 307.
97 'Et hoc etiam dicebat premonens eos pressuram futuram et despectum futurum erga eos' (3.9.7).
98 'Quod si verba illa Cristi et Petri typice sunt accipienda, non ad hoc quod dicunt isti trahenda sunt, sed referenda sunt ad sensum illius gladii de quo scribit Matheus sic: [citation of Matthew 10.34–5]. Quod quidem fit tam verbo quam opere; propter quod dicebat Lucas ad Theophilum "que cepit Iesus facere et docere." Talem gladium Cristus emere precipiebat, quem duplicem ibi esse Petrus etiam respondebat. Ad verba enim et opera parati erant, per que facerent quod Cristus dicebat se venisse facturum per gladium, ut dictum est.'
99 Michel Zink, in fact, argues that medieval writers made a 'very careful distinction between the composition of a work of fiction which conveys allegorical meaning, the allegorical commentary on a text whose literal level is true, such as the Bible, and the allegorical commentary on a text whose literal level is fictitious.' See 'The Allegorical Poem as Interior Memoir,' trans. Margaret Miner and Kevin Brownlee, *Yale French Studies* 79 (1986): 105. A more extensive consideration of the question is found in Armand Strubel, ' "Allegoria in factis" et "allegoria in verbis," ' *Poétique* 23 (1975): 342–57.
100 See, for example, the commentary on the *Aeneid* attributed to Bernardus Silvestris, who writes that Virgil's 'procedure is to describe allegorically by means of an integument (*in integumento describit*) what the human spirit does and endures while temporarily placed in the human body . . . The integument is a type of exposition which wraps the apprehension of truth in a fictional narrative, and thus it is also called an *involucrum*, a cover.' See *Commentary on the First Six Books of Virgil's 'Aeneid,'* trans. Earl G. Schreiber and Thomas E. Maresca (Lincoln: University of Nebraska Press, 1979), 5. Copeland and Melville perceptively consider the place of the *integumentum* in medieval allegory in 'Allegory and Allegoresis,' 169–71.

101 Of course, the resemblance to the discussion of the *Commedia*'s (and the Bible's) polysemous narrative in the Letter to Can Grande is also striking. 'Ad evidentiam itaque dicendorum sciendum est quod istius operis non est simplex sensus, ymo dici potest polisemos, hoc est plurium sensuum; nam primus sensus est qui habetur per litteram, alius est qui habetur per significata per litteram' (7.20). Another link between the *Convivio* passage and the letter is the use of the exodus typology in order to illustrate the spiritual senses. Because of debates concerning the letter's authenticity, I will not treat it here, though it is perhaps useful to bear in mind Umberto Eco's observation that whatever the proper attribution of the expository sections of the letter, they accord with medieval views of interpretation. See 'L'epistola XIII, l'allegorismo medievale, il simbolismo moderno,' in *Sugli specchi e altri saggi* (Milan: Bompiani, 1985), 215–41.

102 An examination of Dante's scriptural exegesis in the *Convivio* is beyond the scope of this chapter. It is interesting to note, however, that two scholars who have studied the *Convivio* in these terms find an increasing biblical presence in the course of the treatise, with a marked increase in biblical citations in book 4. See Maria Corti, *La felicità mentale: Nuove prospettive per Cavalcanti e Dante* (Torino: Einaudi, 1983), 129–33; and Cesare Vasoli, 'La Bibbia nel *Convivio* e nella *Monarchia*,' in *Dante e la Bibbia*, 19–27.

103 Bestul, 609; see also pages 34–5, and note 67, above.

104 In the *Convivio*, as noted above, he remarks that much of the poetic quality of the Hebrew psalms is lost in translation: 'E questa è la cagione per che li versi del Salterio sono sanza dolcezza di musica e d'armonia; ché essi furono transmutati d'ebreo in greco e di greco in latino, e ne la prima transmutazione tutta quella dolcezza venne meno' ('And this is the reason why the verses of the Psalter are without the sweetness of music and harmony; that they were translated from Hebrew into Greek and from Greek into Latin, and in the first translation all this sweetness was diminished' [1.7.15]).

105 'Tu es qui venturus es, an alium expectamus?'

106 'Ecce Agnus Dei, ecce qui tollit peccata mundi.'

107 'Nam et tu in regem sacratus es ut Amalech percutias et Agag non parcas, atque ulciscaris Illum qui misit te de gente brutali et de festina sua sollempnitate, que quidem et Amalech et Agag sonare dicuntur.'

108 'Eia itaque, rumpe moras, proles altera Isai, sume tibi fiduciam de oculis Domini Dei Sabaoth coram quo agis, et Goliam hunc in funda sapientie tue atque in lapide virium tuarum prosterne; quoniam in eius occasu nox et umbra timoris castra Philistinorum operiet: fugient Philistei et liberabitur Israel. Tunc hereditas nostra, quam sine intermissione deflemus

ablatam, nobis erit in integrum restituta; ac quemadmodum, sacrosanctę
Ierusalem memores, exules in Babilone gemiscimus, ita tunc cives et
respirantes in pace, confusionis miserias in gaudio recolemus' (7.8.29–30).
109 See John Larner, *Italy in the Age of Dante and Petrarch* (London and New
York: Longman, 1980), 24–25.
110 See Marjorie Reeves, *The Influence of Prophecy in the Later Middle Ages: A
Study of Joachimism* (Oxford: Clarendon Press, 1969), 149–54.
111 The letter must be dated after the death of Clement V (20 April 1314) and
before the Italian cardinals were excluded from the conclave (14 July of
the same year), or at least before Dante heard of their exclusion. For a
discussion of the events surrounding the composition of the letter, see
Arsenio Frugoni, 'Dante tra due conclavi: La lettera ai cardinali italiani,'
Letture classensi 2 (1969): 69–91; and Raffaelo Morghen, 'La lettera di Dante
ai Cardinali Italiani e la coscienza della sua missione religiosa,' in *Dante
profeta: tra la storia e l'eterno* (Milan: Jaca Book, 1983), 109–29.
112 Niccolò Mineo makes a compelling argument that Dante works to
identify himself with Paul as well as with Jeremiah in this letter. See
*Profestismo e Apocalittica in Dante: Strutture e temi profetico-apocalittici in
Dante: Dalla 'Vita Nuova' alla 'Divina Commedia'* (Catania: Università di
Catania, 1968), 145–7; Frugoni, in 'Dante tra due conclavi,' emphasizes
Dante's conscious assumption of a prophetic voice in the letter.
113 'Nec Oze presumptio quam obiectandam quis crederet, quasi temere
prorumpentem me inficit sui tabe reatus; quia ille ad arcam, ego ad boves
calcitrantes et per abvia distrahentes attendo' (11.5.12).
114 Marjorie Reeves, 'The Bible and Literary Authorship in the Middle Ages,'
in *Reading the Text: Biblical Criticism and Literary Theory,'* ed. Stephen
Prickett (Oxford: Blackwell, 1991), 18.
115 Erich Auerbach, *Mimesis: The Representation of Reality in Western Literature,*
trans. Willard R. Trask (Princeton: Princeton University Press, 1953), 15.

2. Biblical Truth in the *Paradiso*

1 Søren Kierkegaard, *Concluding Unscientific Postscript to 'Philosophical
Fragments,'* ed. and trans. Howard V. Hong and Edna H. Hong, 2 vols.
(Princeton: Princeton University Press, 1992), 1:28–9.
2 'Scio hominem in Christo ante annos quattuordecim, sive in corpore
nescio, sive extra corpus nescio, Deus scit, raptum eiusmodi usque ad tertium caelum. Et scio huiusmodi hominem, sive in corpore sive extra corpus nescio, Deus scit, quoniam raptus est in paradisum, et audivit arcana
verba quae non licet homini loqui.'

3 Paola Rigo, *Memoria classica e memoria biblica in Dante* (Florence: Olschki, 1994), 110–28. Rigo notes that although the Vulgate uses the verb *comedere* to describe Adam's and Eve's eating of the forbidden fruit, Augustine often used *gustare*.

4 Giuseppe Di Scipio, *The Presence of Pauline Thought in the Works of Dante* (Lewiston: Edwin Mellen Press, 1995). Paul puts forward his view of the new man most forcefully, perhaps, in Romans 5.1–10. Many critics have treated Paul's presence in Dante, though most have been preoccupied with the question of whether Dante knew the *Visio Pauli* and if it influenced his use of Paul. See, for example, Francesco D'Ovidio, 'Dante e San Paolo,' in *Studii sulla 'Divina Commedia'* (Milan: Remo Sandron, 1901), 326–55; and Giorgio Petrocchi, 'San Paolo in Dante,' in *Dante e la Bibbia,* ed. Barblan, 235–48. Petrocchi argues persuasively that it is unlikely that the *Visio* exercised any significant influence on Dante.

5 Manuele Gragnolati argues that the Ovidian passage glosses the Pauline reference, affirming that the pilgrim actually has his body with him, and describes what happens to it, as it is purified of mortal conditions. See *Experiencing the Afterlife: Soul and Body in Dante and Medieval Culture* (Notre Dame: University of Notre Dame Press, 2005), 172–3.

6 Kevin Brownlee explores this dialectic in 'Pauline Vision and Ovidian Speech in *Paradiso* I,' in *The Poetry of Allusion: Virgil and Ovid in Dante's 'Commedia,'* ed. Rachel Jacoff and Jeffrey T. Schnapp (Stanford: Stanford University Press, 1991), 202–13, arguing that 'the entire *Paradiso* may be seen as a new Pauline vision articulated by a new kind of authoritative voice: that of the Christian, vernacular *poeta*' (203). Other work on Dante and Paul includes Robert Hollander, 'Dante and Paul's Five Words with Understanding,' Center for Medieval and Early Renaissance Studies, Occasional Papers 1 (Binghamton, NY: Medieval & Renaissance Texts & Studies, 1992).

7 See Joseph Anthony Mazzeo, 'Dante and the Pauline Modes of Vision,' *Harvard Theological Review* 50 (1957): 275–306, who delineates the history of interpretation concerning Paul's vision and relates it to Dante's use of Paul. See also Giovanni Fallani, 'Analogie tra Dante e S. Paolo, come introduzione agli aspetti mistici del *Paradiso*,' in *Lectura Dantis Mystica: Il poema sacro alla luce delle conquiste psicologiche odierne* (Florence: Olschki, 1969), 444–60.

8 'O summum facinus . . . ecterni Spiritus intentione abuti! Non enim peccatur in Moysen, non in David, non in Iob, non in Matheum, non in Paulum, sed in Spiritum Sanctum qui loquitur in illis. Nam quanquam scribe divini eloquii multi sint, unicus tamen dictator est Deus, qui beneplacitum suum nobis per multorum calamos explicare dignatus est.'

9 Teodolinda Barolini, *Dante's Poets: Textuality and Truth in the 'Comedy'* (Princeton: Princeton University Press, 1984), 275–9; see also Robert Hollander, 'Dante's Use of the Fiftieth Psalm,' in *Studies in Dante* (Ravenna: Longo, 1980), 107–13.

10 There are two ways of reading this line, depending on whether one takes it for a subjective or objective genitive. That is, David may be the Singer of the Holy Spirit because he is inspired by that spirit (in other words, he is the Holy Spirit's singer – a subjective genitive), or he may be the singer of the Holy Spirit in that the Holy Spirit is his subject matter (objective genitive). Here I assume the former reading, as I think it makes the best sense within the context of the entire passage.

11 For this section I have borrowed freely from my entry, 'David,' in *DE*, 289–90.

12 'Talia sunt quippe quae restant, ut degustata quidem mordeant, interius autem recepta dulcescant' (*Consolatio philosophiae*, book 3, prose 1). Latin text and translation are taken from Boethius, *'Tractates' and' The Consolation of Philosophy,'* trans. S.J. Tester (Cambridge, MA: Harvard University Press, 1973).

13 Robert Hollander also notes the biblical context in his recent commentary (available at the Dartmount Dante Project – see the Note on Texts at the beginning of the book), referring to the passage from the Apocalypse discussed below.

14 'Tu autem, fili hominis, audi quaecumque loquor ad te: et noli esse exasperans sicut domus exasperatrix est, aperi os tuum et comede quaecumque ego do tibi. Et vidi et ecce manus missa ad me in qua erat involutus liber, et expandit illum coram me, qui erat scriptus intus et foris: et scriptae erant in eo lamentationes et carmen et vae. Et dixit ad me: fili hominis, quodcumque inveneris comede: comede volumen istud et vadens loquere ad filios Israhel. Et aperui os meum et cibavit me volumine illo. Et dixit ad me: fili hominis, venter tuus comedet, et viscera tua conplebuntur volumine isto, quod ego do tibi. Et comedi illud, et factum est in ore meo sicut mel dulce.'

15 'per librum quem accepit Scripturae sacrae paginae designantur' (*Homiliae in Hiezechihelem prophetam* 1:9.29). 'Lamentationes uidelicet, quia in eo scripta est paenitentia peccatorum' (1:9.34). Latin text cited according to the *CCSL* edition (vol. 142), ed. Marcus Adriaen (Turnhout: Brepols, 1971).

16 'Scriptura sacra cibus noster et potus est.'

17 'In eius quippe ore Scriptura sacra dulcis est, cuius uitae uiscera mandatis illius replentur . . . Nam sermo dulcedinem non habet, quem uita reproba intra conscientiam remordet' (10.13).

18 'Et vox quam audivi de caelo iterum loquentem mecum et dicentem, vade accipe librum apertum de manu angeli stantis supra mare et supra terram. Et abii ad angelum dicens ei ut daret mihi librum. Et dicit mihi, accipe et devora illum, et faciet amaricare ventrem tuum, sed in ore tuo erit dulce tamquam mel. Et accepi librum de manu angeli et devoravi eum. Et erat in ore meo tamquam mel dulce et cum devorassem eum amaricatus est venter meus. Et dicunt mihi, oportet te iterum prophetare populis et gentibus et linguis et regibus multis.'

19 'Id est ad Scripturam a Deo completam et fidelibus intimatam.'

20 'il rito dell'imposizione delle mani e la consacrazione al ministero Apostolico.' See *Discorso sul testo della 'Commedia' di Dante,* chapter 43 (more generally chapters 38–52). I have cited the edition presented in the *Edizione nazionale delle opere di Ugo Foscolo* (Florence: Le Monnier, 1979), vol. 9, *Studi su Dante,* 1.241.

21 Aquinas, for example, asserts that all definitions of faith derive from the Pauline definition found in Hebrews. See *Summa theologiae* 2a.2æ.4.1.

22 See *Monarchia* 3.4.11, and the discussion of the passage in chapter 1, above.

23 See *Summa theologiae* 2a.2æ.1.4 and 4.8. Giuseppe Mazzotta provides an informative discussion of the theological context of Dante's discussion of faith in the examination cantos in 'Theology and Exile,' in *Dante's Vision and the Circle of Knowledge* (Princeton: Princeton University Press, 1993), 174–96; Christian Moevs gives a perceptive reading of the dialectic between faith and reason in canto 24 in 'Miraculous Syllogisms: Clocks, Faith, and Reason in *Paradiso* 10 and 24,' *Dante Studies* 117 (1999): 59–84.

24 In its entirety, the verse reads 'ergo fides ex auditu; auditus autem per verbum Christi.' Paul implies, therefore, that faith comes through the hearing of the scriptures.

25 In the previously published article on which this part of this chapter is based, I wrote the following: 'Dante exploits this dialectic in his poem, continuously alluding to the fact that his faith has now been rendered superfluous by his journey to the heavens. Since he sees, he knows, and belief – which concerns true but *un*seen things – is no longer necessary ... His status as a knower thus renders much of the rest of the discussion concerning his own faith exemplary rather than personal.' See 'Biblical Truth in the Examination Cantos of Dante's *Paradiso,' Dante Studies* 115 (1997): 95. Since that time, however, I have revised this view and am now convinced that faith continues in Dante's Paradise, even for the blessed. I am currently finishing an article exploring the dialectic between faith and sight in the *Paradiso.*

26 See Deuteronomy 32.2: 'Concrescat in pluvia doctrina mea, fluat ut ros eloquium meum: quasi imber super herbam et quasi stillae super gramina' ('Let my doctrine gather as the rain, let my speech distill as the dew: as a shower upon the herb, and as drops upon the grass').

27 In the *Summa contra Gentiles*, Aquinas makes a similar point, arguing that the divine Wisdom 'reveals its own presence, as well as the truth of its teaching and inspiration, by fitting arguments (*convenientibus argumentis*); and in order to confirm those truths that exceed natural knowledge (*naturalem cognitionem*), it gives visible manifestation to works that surpass the ability of all nature (*opera visibiliter ostendit, quae totius naturae superant facultatem*' (1.6.1). Latin text from *Summae contra Gentiles*, 2 vols. (Rome: Forzanius et Socii, 1894). Translation from *Summa contra Gentiles, book 1: God,* trans. Anton C. Pegis (1955; Notre Dame: University of Notre Dame Press, 1975).

28 Dante treats the relationship between miracles and faith in the *Convivio* at 3.7.16 and at 3.14.14. Benedicta Ward has shown that theories of miracles underwent a change in the Middle Ages. Augustine considered the entire creation a miracle, as well as each natural process; at times, God creates unusual miracles to remind us, whose senses have been dulled through sin, of the continuous miracle that is the creation. In later periods, however, miracles were viewed in a much more limited fashion and were distinguished from the workings of nature on the one hand and the actions that arise from the will of men on the other. This last view of both miracles and nature seems to be the one adopted in these lines, though – as we will see – things soon get more complicated. See Benedicta Ward, 'The Theory of Miracles,' in *Miracles and the Medieval Mind: Theory, Record, and Event, 1000–1250* (Philadelphia: University of Pennsylvania Press, 1982), 3–19.

29 'et ut credatur unum incredibile, quod de carnis resurrectione atque in caelum ascensione dicitur, multorum incredibilium testimonia tanta congerimus et nondum ad credendum horrenda duritia incredulos flectimus. Si uero per apostolos Christi, ut eis crederetur resurrectionem atque ascensionem praedicantibus Christi, etiam ista miracula facta esse non credunt, hoc nobis unum grande miraculum sufficit, quod eam terrarum orbis sine ullis miraculis credidit.' Latin text from the *CCSL* edition, vols. 47–8, ed. Bernard Dombart and Alfons Kalb (Turnhout: Brepols, 1955). Translation taken from *The City of God,* trans. Henry Bettenson (London: Penguin, 1984), 1029.

30 'Haec autem tam mirabilis mundi conversio ad fidem christianam indicium certissimum est praeteritorum signorum, ut ea ulterius iterari necesse non sit, quum in suo effectu appareant evidenter.'

31 'Quibus animos mortalium assentire et maximum miraculum est, et manifestum divinae inspirationis opus, ut, contemptis visibilibus, sola invisi-
bilia cupiantur.'

32 'Quia cum homo assentiendo his quae sunt fidei elevetur supra naturam
suam, oportet quod hoc insit ei ex supernaturali principio interius
movente, quod est Deus. Et ideo fides quantum ad assensum, qui est prin-
cipalis actus fidei, est a Deo interius movente per gratiam.'

33 Here we may recall the discussion of textual truth in the Introduction, in
which I drew on the philosophical hermeneutics of Hans-Georg Gadamer,
who offers a discussion of textual truth similar to that given by Dante here.
Truth emerges, for Gadamer, through 'an encounter with something that
asserts itself as truth,' not through a demonstration in the manner of 'historical objectivism.'

34 I have emphasized the fact that the Bible refers only to John's belief,
as it is a point often glanced over. In his lectura of the canto, Giuseppe
Di Scipio, for example, summarizes the scriptural passage as '*they* saw
and believed' (emphasis mine). See 'XXIV,' in *Dante's 'Divine Comedy':
Introductory Readings III: 'Paradiso,'* special number of *Lectura Dantis* 16–17
(Spring – Fall 1995), 363.

35 Should we hear a pun in Dante's words? Are the 'più giovani piedi' both
younger and more Johanine?

36 Of the commentaries catalogued in the Dante Dartmouth Data Base, for
example, the following provide a reading similar to the one I have just
stated: L'Ottimo commentatore, Pietro di Dante, the Codice Cassinese,
Benvenuto, Serravalle, Daniello, Lombardi, Portirelli, Tommaseo, Torraca,
Grandgent, Mestica, Casini/Barbi, Trucchi, Pietrobono, and Sapegno.
Those who offer a different view (with the recognition that Dante's words
do not accord with their biblical source) include Venturi, Porena, Chimenz,
and Bosco/Reggio.

37 'Johannes significat Synagogam, quae prior venit ad monumentum sed
non intravit, quia prophetias de incarnatione et passione audivit, sed et
mortuum creder noluit. Petrus est ecclesia, quae cognovit carne mortuum
et viventem, credidit Deum, post quem et Judaea in fine intrabit.'

38 'I Comentatori [sic] s'ingengnano per sostenere che Dante non ha preso
granchio, come pare a prima vista ... Stimo ingenuità il dire: Dante qui ha
preso sbaglio.' See '*La Divina Commedia' di Dante Alighieri col comento* [sic]
del P. Pompeo Venturi, 3 vols. (Florence: Ciardetti, 1821), 3:334.

39 'Dicit etiam Iohannes ipsum [Petrum] introivisse subito, cum venit in
monumentum, videns alium discipulum cunctantem ad hostium.'

40 'ne quis in eis adtendat, quod sunt, sed potius, quod signa sunt, id est, quod significant' (*De doctrina christiana* 2.1.1). The Latin text is taken from the *CCSL* edition (vol. 32), ed. Joseph Martin (Turnhout: Brepols, 1962). Translation is taken from *On Christian Doctrine,* trans. D.W. Robertson, Jr (New York: Macmillan, 1958).

41 'propter hoc in terra sua duplicia possidebunt, laetitia sempiterna erit eis.'

42 As Anna Chiavacci Leonardi observes, the tradition of reading *terra* as the celestial home and *duplicia* as the double glory of the body and the soul was well established. See '"Le bianche stole": Il tema della resurrezione nel *Paradiso,*' in *Dante e la Bibbia,* 266.

43 'quia induit me vestimentis salutis et indumento iustitiae circumdedit me.'

44 'Post haec vidi turbam magnam quam dinumerare nemo poterat, ex omnibus gentibus et tribubus et populis et linguis stantes ante thronum et in conspectu agni amicti stolas albas, et palmae in manibus eorum.'

45 'et laverunt stolas suas et dealbaverunt eas in sanguine agni' (7.14).

46 'Innocentiam in baptismo acceptam vel corpora sua.' See also Genesis 49.11, in which Jacob blesses Judah that he will 'wash his robe in wine, and his garment in the blood of the grape,' which in the *Glossa ordinaria* is read as a reference to our redemption through Christ that is brought about through baptism.

47 ' . . . gloria corporis, quae secunda stola dicitur' (*Breviloquium* 7.7). This parallel is cited in Grandgent's commentary on the poem.

48 Manuele Gragnolati emphasizes the link between the appearance of John and the emphasis on the resurrection of the body earlier in canto 25. See *Experiencing the Afterlife,* 165–7.

49 'Si sic eum volo manere donec veniam, quid ad te?'

50 Rachel Jacoff explores these traditions and their relevance to the poem in 'Dante and the Legend(s) of St. John,' *Dante Studies* 117 (1999): 45–57.

51 'The reciprocity here seems continuous with the reraining which defines the process of *tëodia:* the *factor* is formed spiritually by Biblical texts and reciprocates in turn by producing texts.' William A. Stephany, 'XXV,' in *Dante's 'Divine Comedy': Introductory Readings III: 'Paradiso,'* a special number of *Lectura Dantis* 16–17 (Spring – Fall 1995): 379–81.

52 'non lingua confusionis, sed gratie frueretur' (*De vulgari eloquentia* 1.6.6).

53 See also Brenda Deèn Schildgen's reading of canto 26, 'Temporal Dispensations: Dante's "tëodia" and John's "alto preconio" in Canto 26, *Paradiso,*' *Stanford Italian Review* 11 (1991): 171–85; she also suggests that 'Adam's discussion of the mutability of human language, which changes with human pleasure, cannot fail to refer both to the durability of Dante's poem and even to the Holy Scriptures themselves, whose fluidity Dante

demonstrates by their openness to translation and reworking through interpretive, poetic, or literary transformations' (182).

54 They argue that since Dante must portray Peter as a paragon of faith, he 'adatta il testo sacro alle sue esigenze.' Dante, however, could have easily referred instead to other episodes in Peter's life (those recounted at the beginning of Acts, for example) that present him as a man of faith. See *'La Divina Commedia' con pagine critiche: Paradiso*, ed. Umberto Bosco and Giovanni Reggio (Florence: Le Monnier, 1988), 426.

3. The Bible in the *Inferno*: Misprision and Prophetic Appropriation

1 See John Freccero, 'The Sign of Satan,' in *Dante: The Poetics of Conversion*, ed. Rachel Jacoff (Harvard: Harvard University Press, 1986), 167–79; the complete hymn is cited in Charles Singleton's commentary to *Inf.* 34.1.

2 'Dies annorum nostrorum in ipsis septuaginta anni.'

3 See Anthony K. Cassell, *Lectura Dantis Americana: Inferno I* (Philadelphia: University of Pennsylvania Press, 1989), 7–8.

4 'viri impii non dimidiabunt dies suos, quia non implent opera virtutum, nec poenitendo emendant delicta.'

5 See *Esposizioni sopra la 'Comedia' di Dante*, ed. Giorgio Padoan, vol. 6 of *Tutte le opere di Giovanni Boccaccio*, ed. Vittore Branca (Verona: Mondadori, 1965), 63: 'Egli è il vero che le vie son molte, ma tra tutte non è che una che a porto di salute ne meni, e quella è esso Idio, il quale di sé dice nell'*Evangelio*: "*Ego sum via, veritas et vita.*"'

6 'Et hoc scientes tempus quia hora est iam nos de somno surgere, nunc enim propior est nostra salus quam cum credidimus. Nox praecessit dies autem adpropiavit. Abiciamus ergo opera tenebrarum et induamur arma lucis. Sicut in die honeste ambulemus, non in comesationibus et ebrietatibus, non in cubilibus et inpudicitiis, non in contentione et aemulatione, sed induite Dominum Iesum Christum, et carnis curam ne feceritis in desideriis.'

7 'Levavi oculos meos in montes, unde veniet auxilium meum.'

8 See Cassell, 45–76, for a detailed discussion of the beasts, their meaning, and the biblical subtexts relevant to them. The citation was taken from page 55.

9 The bibliography on Dante's allegory is enormous. The works that have most influenced me include: Charles S. Singleton, *'Commedia': Elements of Structure* (Cambridge, MA: Harvard University Press, 1954); Erich Auerbach, 'Figura,' in *Scenes from the Drama of European Literature* (1959; Minneapolis: University of Minnesota Press, 1984), 11–76; Robert

Hollander, *Allegory in Dante's 'Commedia'* (Princeton: Princeton University Press, 1969); Jean Pépin, *Dante e la tradition de l'allégorie* (Montreal: Institut d'études médiévales, 1971); Gian Roberto Sarolli, *Prolegomena alla 'Divina Commedia'* (Florence: Olschki, 1971); Giuseppe Mazzotta, 'Allegory: Poetics of the Desert,' in *Dante, Poet of the Desert: History and Allegory in the 'Divine Comedy'* (Princeton: Princeton University Press, 1979), 227–74; and Teodolinda Barolini, *The Undivine 'Comedy': Detheologizing Dante* (Princeton: Princeton University Press, 1992), 3–20.

10 Marjorie Reeves comments that Dante uses the historical figures with which he peoples the *Commedia* in a 'figural' sense, that is, in a way derived from medieval understanding of biblical figures, in which the figures present types or antitypes not only of Christ but also of contemporary history. Drawing on Hollander, *Allegory in Dante's 'Commedia'*, she provides a concise but wide-ranging discussion of such figures in 'The Bible and Literary Authorship in the Middle Ages,' in *Reading the Text: Biblical Criticism and Literary Theory*, ed. Stephen Prickett (Oxford: Blackwell, 1991), 12–63, esp. 38–50.

11 "nvidïosi son d'ogne altra sorte' (*Inf*. 3.48).

12 'Scio opera tua, quia nomen habes quod vivas: et mortuus es.'

13 'quia similes estis sepulchris dealbatis, quae a foris parent hominibus speciosa, intus vero plena sunt ossibus mortuorum et omni spurcitia.'

14 'Ecce quantus ignis quam magnam silvam incendit. Et lingua ignis est, universitas iniquitatis.'

15 'mitte Lazarum ut intinguat extremum digiti sui in aqua, ut refrigeret linguam meam.'

16 'Nescitis quod hii qui in stadio currunt, omnes quidem currunt, sed unus accipit bravium? Sic currite ut conprehendatis.'

17 This is a distinction that goes back to Aristotle, who, in his discussion of anger (*ira* in Latin translation) argues for an intermediate state, situated between excessive and insufficient anger (see *Nicomachean Ethics* 4.5 [1125b–1126a]). Aquinas follows Aristotle in identifying a deficiency of anger as a vice. See *Summa theologiae* 1a.2æ.46–8, and 2a.2æ.158.1.

18 '*Inferno* 8: The Passage Across the Styx,' *Lectura Dantis* 3 (1988): 34.

19 Kleinhenz states the point well: 'He [the pilgrim] thus falls victim yet another time to the snare of sin, yielding, as he did with Francesca, to his passions, to the excessive attraction of the human and earthly, albeit here in a totally different context, one of anger and rage and not of carnal passion' (34).

20 'The Poetics of Citation: Dante's *Divina Commedia* and the Bible,' in *Italiana 1988*, ed. Albert N. Mancini, Paolo A. Giordano, and Anthony J. Tamburri,

Rosary College Italian Studies 4 (River Forest, IL: Rosary College,
1990), 14.

21 See Joan Ferrante, 'Usi e abusi della Bibbia nella letteratura medievale,' in
Dante e la Bibbia, ed. Giovanni Barblan (Florence: Olschki, 1988), 216.

22 'Epicuro [e] tutti suoi seguaci, / che l'anima col corpo morta fanno'
('Epicurus [and] his followers who make the soul dead with the
body' [10.14–15]).

23 'scriptum est quia non in pane solo vivet homo, sed in omni verbo Dei.'

24 See 'Bestial Sign and the Bread of Angels,' in *Dante: The Poetics
of Conversion,* 152–66; the citation is found on page 163 (emphasis
Freccero's). As Freccero writes, 'a literalist who refuses to acknowledge the
spirit that animates the text reifies it as a cannibal reifies the human body.
The letter alone is dead' (166).

25 'Aut quis ex vobis homo quem si petierit filius suus panem numquid lapi-
dem porriget ei, aut si piscem petet, numquid serpentem porriget ei? Si
ergo vos cum sitis mali nostis bona dare filiis vestris, quanto magis Pater
vester qui in caelis est dabit bona petentibus se?' This biblical subtext was
first pointed out by Robert Hollander in '*Inferno* XXXIII, 37–74: Ugolino's
Importunity,' *Speculum* 59 (1984): 549–55.

26 'Petentibus Christum recta fide non datur lapis offensionis nec duritia
cordis. Ita si petieritis patrem vestrum caritatem sine qua nil sunt caetera,
ut sine pane inops est mensa, cui contraria est cordis duricia.'

27 '"Noi veggiam, come quei c'ha mala luce, / le cose," disse, "che ne son
lontano"' (10.100–1).

28 Marc Cogan, *The Design in the Wax: The Structure of the 'Divine Comedy' and
Its Meaning* (Notre Dame and London: University of Notre Dame Press,
1999), 38.

29 '"sed si quis ex mortuis ierit ad eos, paenitentiam agent." Ait autem illi,
"si Mosen et prophetas non audiunt, neque si quis ex mortuis resurrexerit
credent."'

30 For another view of how the Bible exists within the *Inferno,* see Raffaele
Manica, 'Lo spavento del sacro: Presenze bibliche nell'*Inferno*,' in *Memoria
biblica nell'opera di Dante,* ed. E. Esposito et al. (Rome: Bulzoni, 1996), 23–56.

31 In her commentary on the *Inferno* (Milan: Mondadori, 1991), Anna Maria
Chiavacci Leonardi notes the difference in tone: 'Questo canto si dis-
tanzia con forte distacco di tono, da tutti gli altri dedicati alle bolge, con
l'eccezione del XXVI, dove troveremo Ulisse' (1:561). On the relationship of the tone to the numerous biblical subtexts in the canto, see Paolo
Brezzi, 'Il canto XIX dell'*Inferno*,' *Nuove letture dantesche* 2, Casa di Dante in
Roma (Florence: Le Monnier, 1968), 161–82; Giorgio Varanini, 'Canto XIX

dell'*Inferno,' Lectura dantis neapolitana* (Naples: Loffredo, 1986), 15–19; and Barolini, *Undivine 'Comedy,'* 77–9.

32 See Alberto Chiari, 'Il canto dei Simoniaci,' *Nuove canti danteschi* (Varese: Magenta, 1966), 34. Richard K. Emmerson and Ronald B. Herzman discuss how important the figure of Simon Magus (especially as seen through the medieval traditions that surround this figure) is for this canto in 'Apocalypse, Church, and Dante's Conversion,' in *The Apocalyptic Imagination in Medieval Literature* (Philadelphia: University of Pennsylvania Press, 1992), 104–44.

33 In Acts 3.6, Peter claims, 'Silver and gold I have none,' a verse to which Dante refers in *Paradiso* 22.88: 'Pier cominciò sanz' oro e sanz' argento.' Dante also explicitly alludes to Peter's lack of silver and gold twice in canto 19.

34 See Ronald B. Herzman and William A. Stephany, ' "O miseri seguaci": Sacramental Inversion in *Inferno XIX*,' *Dante Studies* 96 (1978): 39–65, for an extensive and perceptive exploration of this facet of the canto.

35 For a general overview of the rise of simony, see Joseph H. Lynch, *Simoniacal Entry into Religious Life from 1000 to 1260* (Columbus: Ohio State University Press, 1976).

36 See Ann W. Astell, *The Song of Songs in the Middle Ages* (Ithaca: Cornell University Press, 1990); and Ann E. Matter, *The Voice of My Beloved: The Song of Songs in Western Medieval Christianity* (Philadelphia: University of Pennsylvania Press, 1990).

37 'Et transivi per te et vidi te, et ecce tempus tuum tempus amantium, et expandi amictum meum super te, et operui ignominiam tuam. Et iuravi tibi, et ingressus sum pactum tecum, ait Dominus Deus, et facta es mihi . . . Et egressum est nomen tuum in gentes propter speciem tuam, quia perfecta eras in decore meo quem, posueram super te, dicit Dominus Deus. Et habens fiduciam in pulchritudine tua, fornicata es in nomine tuo, et exposuisti fornicationem tuam omni transeunti ut eius fieres.'

38 'Cupiditatem unusquisque sibi duxit uxorem, quemadmodum et vos, que nunquam pietatis et equitatis, ut caritas, sed semper impietatis et iniquitatis est genetrix.' *Epistole* 11.7.14. Dante also employs this language of fornication, we should remember, in his discussion of the *lupa* of *Inferno* 1, where Virgil describes her as mating with several animals: 'Molti son li animali a cui s'ammoglia' (*Inf.* 1.100).

39 'Quod si de prelibato precipitio dubitatur, quid aliud declarando respondeam, nisi quod in Alcimum cum Demetrio consensistis?' (11.4.8).

40 Umberto Bosco, 'La "follia" di Dante,' in *Dante vicino* (Rome: Salvatore Sciascia, 1966), 55–75.

41 Other critics have made similar observations. See, for example, Paul Renucci, 'Le chant XIX de l'*Enfer*,' in *Letture dell'Inferno*, ed. Vittorio Vettori (Milan: Marzorati, 1963), 170: 'Dante fait mine de convertir sa témérité en doute, mais la "folie" de langage qu'il laisse entrevoir comme une excuse constitue le premier terme d'une prétérition.'

42 'Oportet ergo ex his viris qui nobiscum congregati sunt in omni tempore quo intravit et exivit inter nos Dominus Iesus, incipiens a baptismate Iohannis usque in diem qua absumptus est a nobis, testem resurrectionis eius nobiscum fieri unum ex istis.'

43 'Nolite possidere aurum neque argentum neque pecuniam in zonis vestris.'

44 I thus favour a more specific reading of lines 98–9–that they refer to Nicholas's receipt of Byzantine money in order to aid the rebellion that led to the Sicilian vespers. Though now considered a legend, it was believed in Dante's day. (It is, for example, narrated by Villani at *Cronica* 7.57.)

45 Peter Hawkins, *Dante's Testaments: Essays in Scriptural Imagination* (Stanford: Stanford University Press, 1999), 32.

46 William Franke, *Dante's Interpretive Journey* (Chicago: University of Chicago Press, 1996), 96.

47 'Et venit unus de septem angelis qui habebant septem fialas, et locutus est mecum, dicens: "veni, ostendam tibi damnationem meretricis magnae quae sedet super aquas multas, cum qua fornicati sunt reges terrae, et inebriati sunt qui inhabitant terram de vino prostitutionis eius." Et abstulit me in desertum in spiritu, et vidi mulierem sedentem super bestiam coccineam, plenam nominibus blasphemiae, habentem capita septem et cornua decem.'

48 For a concise account of Augustine's reading, see Paula Frederiksen, 'Tyconius and Augustine on the Apocalypse,' in *The Apocalypse in the Middle Ages*, ed. Richard K. Emmerson and Bernard McGinn (Ithaca: Cornell University Press, 1992), 20–37. I discuss the history of interpretation of the Apocalypse at greater length in chapter 5.

49 For a more detailed consideration of the relationship between the Spiritual Franciscans and Dante in *Inferno* 19 and elsewhere, see Nicholas Havely, *Dante and the Franciscans: Poverty and the Papacy in the 'Commedia'* (Cambridge: Cambridge University Press, 2004); and my study, 'Dante, Peter John Olivi, and the Franciscan Apocalypse,' in *Dante and the Franciscans*, ed. Santa Casciani (Leiden: Brill, 2006), 9–50.

50 'Vocatur ergo meretrix magna, quia a fideli cultu et a sincero amore et deliciis dei Christi sponsi sui recedens adheret huic seculo et divitiis et deliciis eius et diabolo propter ista et etiam regibus et magnatibus et

prelatis et omnibus aliis amatoribus huius mundi.' I cite the text of Olivi's commentary from the only modern edition of the work, edited by Warren Lewis and found in his University of Tübingen doctoral thesis, 'Peter John Olivi: Prophet of the Year 2000,' 1972. This cited passage is found on page 826; further references to this edition will occur in the text.

51 For a brief summary of Franciscan Spiritualist apocalypticism, with excerpts from major texts, see Bernard McGinn, *Visions of the End: Apocalyptic Traditions in the Middle Ages* (New York: Columbia University Press, 1998), 203–21.

52 According to the *Cronica fiorentina*, Cardinal Caetani (the future Boniface VIII) bribed the pope's attendants to allow him to hide himself in the pope's bed chamber and, speaking through a tube placed over the bed, impersonated an angel who commanded Celestine to renounce the papacy. See *Cronica fiorentina compilata nel secolo XIII*, in *Testi fiorentini del Dugento e dei primi del Trecento*, ed. Alfredo Schiaffini (Florence: Sansoni, 1954), 142. The relevant passage is cited in Singleton's commentary to *Inferno* 3.59–60 (Princeton: Princeton University Press, 1970), 50.

53 'septem capita, septem montes sunt super quos mulier sedet, et reges septem sunt . . . decem reges . . . cum agno pugnabunt.'

54 'Id est sensus, et postea errorem et tandem antichristum, per quae septem diabolus ducit homines ad peccatum.' The *Glossa* reads the ten horns according to the self exegesis of the work: 'id est, decem regna quae erunt tempore Antichristi, per quae alia intelliguntur.'

55 A noted exception to this reading is Richard Kay's interpretation, found in his 'The Pope's Wife: Allegory as Allegation in *Inferno* 19.106–11,' *Studies in Medieval Culture* 12 (1978): 105–11. Kay's major objection to the traditional view is that it contradicts the appearance of these same images in *Purgatorio* 32, a passage I will treat in chapter 5. Kay's view is that Dante here alludes to a text of canon law and to chapter 10 of the third book of Kings in order to criticize the Donation of Constantine.

56 See, for example, Saint Bernard, *Sententiae*, 3:89. Translation found in Bernard of Clairvaux, *The Parables and the Sentences*, ed. Maureen M. O'Brian (Kalamazoo, MI: Cistercian Publications, 2000), 284.

57 Charles T. Davis, in 'Canto XIX: Simoniacs,' *Lectura Dantis: Inferno*, ed. Allen Mandelbaum, Anthony Oldcorn, and Charles Ross (Berkeley: University of California Press, 1998), 262–74, and 'Rome and Babylon in Dante,' in *Rome and the Renaissance: The City and the Myth*, ed. P.A. Ramsey (Binghamton, NY: Medieval & Renaissance Texts & Studies, 1982), 19–40, finds numerous problems with this standard interpretation, though his major objections can be summarized as twofold: (1) so interpreted, the

image contradicts the use Dante makes of the same image in *Puragorio* 32; and (2) if we interpret Dante's use of Apocalypse 17, it goes against virtually the entire tradition of medieval exegesis of the book, and 'we know from *Monarchia* that he did not like gratuitous altering of the literal sense of Scripture' (269). As mentioned above, I will discuss the relation of the two uses of Apocalypse 17 in the final chapter of this study, where I will argue that the differences between them are only superficial. As to the second objection, I can only hope to show that, while I do believe that Dante alters the literal sense of scripture, he does not alter it gratuitously. Further, I am not persuaded by Davis's reading of the whore in canto 19 as the city of Rome rather than the church and of the husband as the emperor rather than the pope, which seems to me to ignore the numerous ties that link the image and the church at several other points in the canto.

58 'mulier ista in quantum est carnalis et bestialis dicitur bestia; in quantum vero quondam prefuit et regnavit super bestiales gentes mundi et adhuc super plures bestiales sibi subditas dominatur, dicitur sedere super bestiam.' Enrico Proto writes that 'tutti i commentatori finivano per confondere la donna con la bestia.' See *L'Apocalisse nella 'Divina Commedia'* (Naples: Luigi Piero, 1905), 9.

59 Cf. Davide Bolognesi, ' "Et mirror si iam non est": L'*Arbor vitae* di Ubertino da Casale nella *Commedia*,' *Dante Studies* 126 (2008): 57–88. Bolognesi argues that Dante's creation of the pope as the husband of the church is due to Ubertino da Casale, who specifically made the identification of the pope as husband of the church through an interpretation of Paul's discussion of marriage and the church in Ephesians 5. While Dante may well have derived the idea for the imagery he employs here from Ubertino, I would still argue that Dante's use of it in *Inferno* 19 is original and surprising. Ubertino, after all, makes his argument from a biblical passage that specifically mentions marriage, while Dante inserts it into a passage from the Apocalypse where no husband is mentioned.

60 For a brief overview of prostitution in the Old Testament, see Elaine Adler Goodfriend's entry, 'Prostitution: Old Testament,' in *The Anchor Bible Dictionary*, gen. ed. David Noel Freedman, 6 vols. (New York: Macmillan, 1992), 5:505–10.

61 'argentum suum et aurum suum fecerunt sibi idola.'

62 'Sed Ecclesia omnino indisposita erat ad temporalia recipienda per preceptum prohibitivum expressum, ut habemus per Matheum . . . ' (3.10.14).

63 On the frequent medieval practice of biblical transformation, see Joan Ferrante, 'Usi e abusi della Bibbia nella letteratura medievale,' in *Dante e la Bibbia*, ed. Barblan, 213–25; and 'The Bible as Thesaurus for Secular

Literature,' in *The Bible in the Middle Ages: Its Influence on Literature and Art*, ed. Bernard S. Levy (Binghamton, NY: Medieval & Renaissance Texts & Studies, 1992), 23–49. While Ferrante provides a valuable overview of the question, she does not sufficiently distinguish between works that subvert or parody biblical texts for secular purposes and those that modify them for religious ones.

64 Here, I use the term 'originary' in the sense in which it is employed by Rita Copeland in her *Rhetoric, Hermeneutics, and Translation in the Middle Ages* (Cambridge: Cambridge University Press, 1991), which derives from the writings of Derrida and Heidegger 'where it is not a synonym for "original" or "originating" but rather is construed in the sense of claiming the value (or attributing to something the value) of a fixed origin or foundational force' (230).

65 The one exception is Francesco da Buti, who makes the intriguing assertion that Dante 'aggiugne una autorità di San Giovanni Evangelistia, la quale è nell'Apocalissa, alla quale l'autore fa alcuna addizione per arrecarla a suo proposito, e questo si può fare: però che l'è profezia molto oscura.' *Commenta di Francesco da Buti sopra 'La Divina Commedia' di Dante Alighieri*, 3 vols. (Pisa: Nistri, 1858), 1:506.

66 Neither Peter Hawkins, in *Dante's Testaments*, nor William Franke, in *Dante's Interpretive Journey*, mention Dante's transformation in their discussions of the canto. Likewise, Ronald Herzman, in his valuable study of the Apocalypse in Dante, glances over Dante's alteration of the biblical text in *Inferno* 19. See 'Dante and the Apocalypse,' in *The Apocalypse in the Middle Ages*, ed. Emmerson and McGinn, 398–413.

67 Gerhard von Rad, *The Message of the Prophets* (San Francisco: HarperCollins, 1967), 101.

68 Michael Fishbane, 'Inner-Biblical Exegesis,' in *The Garments of Torah: Essays in Biblical Hermeneutics* (Bloomington and Indianapolis: Indiana University Press, 1989), 11. See also his more extensive treatment of the subject in *Biblical Interpretation in Ancient Israel* (Oxford: Clarendon Press, 1985), 281–317.

69 The most plausible explanation of this crux remains that of Vandelli, who, based on the authority of the Ottimo commentator and the drawing of the object in question that he provides, argues that that 'battezzatori' refer to the holes in which the baptism took place. See 'I "fori" del "bel San Giovanni,"' *Studi danteschi* 15 (1931): 55–66. Many other critics have noted that Dante's actions in the baptistery anticipate his actions in this canto. See, for example, Giuseppe Mazzotta, *Dante, Poet of the Desert*, 317–18. For the view that the episode should be understood solely in metaphorical terms,

see Susan Noakes, 'Dino Compagni and the Vow in San Giovanni: *Inferno* XIX, 16–21,' *Dante Studies* 86 (1968): 41–64. See also Rachel Jacoff, 'Dante, Geremia, e la problematica profetica,' in *Dante e la Bibbia*, ed. Barblan, 113–23, who argues that Dante here enacts the prophetic role of Jeremiah, whose life and actions also became a symbol of his message.

70 Teodolinda Barolini, *Dante's Poets: Textuality and Truth in the 'Comedy'* (Princeton: Princeton University Press, 1984), 217. See also Barolini's 'True and False See-ers in *Inferno* XX' *Lectura Dantis* 4 (1989): 42–54; and Robert Hollander, 'The Tragedy of Divination in *Inferno* XX,' in his *Studies in Dante* (Ravenna: Longo, 1980), 131–218.

71 Barolini notes also that there is a link between Virgil and Jason, since the same phrase – *parole ornate* – is used to describe the language of both. (Beatrice refers to Virgil's *parola ornata* at *Inf.* 2.67). See Barolini's extended discussion of Virgil in *Dante's Poets*, 201–56.

72 I thus disagree with both Robin Kirkpatrick, who argues that 'in this canto Dante's text proves inferior to the absolute force of the Scriptures,' and William Franke, who suggests – as noted above – that Dante steps aside here to let the Bible speak and then undermines his assumed prophetic identity through the portrayal of the false prophets in the following canto. Dante's manipulation of the scriptures and his insistence that he speaks true words suggests an appropriation of the Bible rather than an attempt simply to let the scriptures speak. See *Dante's 'Inferno': Difficulty and Dead Poetry* (Cambridge: Cambridge University Press, 1987), 255, and *Dante's Interpretive Journey*, 95–7, for Kirkpatrick and Franke respectively.

73 Too often we think of the model of a biblical prophet simply in terms of foretelling. Lawrence Rhu, for example, provides a summary of what most critics seem to understand by prophecy: '[It] . . . stands outside the temporality that defines narrative . . . Its privileged exemption from the flow of time makes it suspect in terms of mimetic norms that prize credible succession from one event to the next.' See 'After the Middle Ages: Prophetic Authority and Human Fallibility in the Renaissance Epic,' in *Poetry and Prophecy: The Beginnings of a Literary Tradition*, ed. James L. Kugel (Ithaca: Cornell University Press, 1990), 163–84. It is perhaps the 'unrealistic' aspect of prophecy that leads many critics to reject the label of prophet for this most realistic of poets. Biblical scholarship, however, has long questioned the notion that prophets are primarily predictors; rather than *foretelling* they *tell forth* – speaking forcefully and authoritatively to their contemporaries. Delivering the word of God to one's contemporaries meant translating the traditional, sacred word into language directly relevant to one's times, and often required the kind of 'inner-biblical exegesis' that Fishbane

describes. Any predictions that biblical prophets did make were based precisely on the 'credible succession from one event to the next,' on the prophet's sense of the progress of history taking shape because of the people's wickedness and God's judgment. If the children of Israel continue to disregard God's call, they will be destroyed. Prophecy as a discourse exists not to provide historical clues for later biblical literalists trying to peer into the future, but to urge action – specifically, repentance – in the present.

74 David is the pre-eminent example of someone whom Dante considers both poet and prophet. See, for example, *Convivio* 2.1.6 and *Paradiso* 20.38.

4. *Una nuova legge*: The Beatitudes in the *Purgatorio*

1 Charles S. Singleton, 'In Exitu Israel de Aegypto,' *Dante Studies* 78 (1960): 1–24. See also Peter Armour, 'The Theme of the Exodus in the First Two Cantos of the *Purgatorio*,' in *Dante Soundings: Eight Literary and Historical Essays*, ed. David Nolan (Totowa, NJ: Rowan & Littlefield, 1981), 59–99, who argues that 'the *Inferno* and the *Paradiso* do not actually refer to the Exodus, for the souls there are not going anywhere' (77); though one may point out that the pilgrim does go somewhere in those two canticles, even if the souls he meets are stationary. See also Carol V. Kaske, 'Mount Sinai and Dante's Mount Purgatory,' *Dante Studies* 89 (1971): 1–18.

2 Daniello's commentary on this line makes this same point: there is a 'nuova LEGGE, perche in Purgatorio non si canta cosa vane, & lascive; ma Hinni & Salmi in laude di Dio, & fasseli oratione.'

3 Robert Hollander, '*Purgatorio* II: Cato's Rebuke and Dante's *scoglio*,' in his *Studies in Dante* (Ravenna: Longo, 1979), 91–105; and '*Purgatorio* II: The New Song and the Old,' *Lectura Dantis* 6 (1990): 28–45. See also John Freccero, 'Casella's Song: *Purgatorio* 11, 112,' in *Dante: The Poetics of Conversion*, ed. Rachel Jacoff (Cambridge, MA: Harvard University Press, 1986), 186–94; and Teodolinda Barolini, *Dante's Poets: Textuality and Truth in the 'Comedy'* (Princeton: Princeton University Press, 1984), 31–40, for nuanced readings of the episode.

4 For a much more complete analysis of the variations in Dante's translations and citations of various texts, both Latin and vernacular, see Massimiliano Chiamenti, *Dante Alighieri traduttore* (Florence: Le Lettere, 1995), who suggests the following distinctions: transference (citation of the work in the original language), word-for-word or one-for-one translation, literal or faithful translation, modulated translation, and free translations of various sorts.

5 'Et cum oratis, non eritis sicut hypocritae, qui amant in synagogis et in angulis platearum stantes orare, ut videantur ab hominibus: amen dico

vobis, receperunt mercedem suam. Tu autem cum orabis intra in cubiculum tuum, et cluso ostio tuo, ora Patrem tuum in abscondito: et Pater tuus qui videt in abscondito reddet tibi. Orantes autem nolite multum loqui sicut ethnici. Putant enim quia in multiloquio suo exaudiantur. Nolite ergo adsmilari eis, scit enim Pater vester quibus opus sit vobis antequam petatis eum.'

6 'Si ethnicus in oratione multum loquitur, ergo qui christianus est debet parum loqui. *Deus* enim *non uerborum sed cordis auditor est*' (*Commentarium in Mattheum* 1.6.7). Cited according to the *SC* edition, vol. 242, ed. Émile Bonard (Paris: Éditions du Cerf, 1977), 128.

7 'ita ethnicorum, id est gentilium, in multiloquio se putare exaudiri. Et re uera omne multiloquium a gentilibus uenit, qui exercendae linguae potius quam mundando animo dant operam' (2.3.12). The Latin text is cited according to the *CCSL* edition, vol. 35: Saint Augustine, *De sermone Domini in monte libros duos,* ed. Almut Mutzenbecher (Turnhout: Brepols, 1967), 102.

8 'Absit enim ab oratione multa locutio, sed non desit multa precatio, si fervens perseverat intentio. Nam multum loqui, est in orando rem necessariam superfluis agere verbis. Multum autem precari, est ad eum quem precamur, diuturna et pia cordis excitatione pulsare. Nam plerumque hoc negotium plus gemitibus quam sermonibus agitur, plus fletu quam affatu' (9.20; *PL* 33: 502).

9 'Hic primo respondetur non uerbis nos agere debere apud deum, ut impetremus quod uolumus, sed rebus quas animo gerimus et intentione cogitationis cum dilectione pura et simplici affectu; sed res ipsas uerbis nos docuisse dominum nostrum, quibus memoriae mandatis eas ad tempus orandi recordemur' (2.3.13). Part of this passage is also cited in the *Glossa ordinaria* as a commentary on Matthew 6.8.

10 Citations of Chaucer refer to *The Riverside Chaucer,* ed. Larry D. Benson, 3rd ed. (Boston: Houghton Mifflin, 1987).

11 Text taken from the *SC* edition, François d'Assise, *Écrits* (Paris: Éditions du Cerf, 1981), 278.

12 Iacopone da Todi, *Laude,* ed. Franco Mancini (Rome-Bari: Laterza, 1974), 61.

13 See, for example, the reworking found in the final four stanzas of the medieval hymn *Deus, qui caeli lumen es,* the text of which is found in Clemens Blume, SJ, ed., *Die Hymen des Thesaurus Hymnologicus H.A. Davids,* vol. 51 of *Analecta hymnica medii aevi* (Leipzig: O.R. Reisland, 1908), 8.

14 Some commentators point to this prayer as the only fully recited prayer in the entire poem, though Bernard's prayer to the Virgin in *Paradiso* 33 is another.

15 See *Purgatorio* 6.25–48; the passage from Virgil's poetry is *Aeneid* 6.376.

16 I assume that Matthew's version of the prayer, and not Luke's abbreviated form of it (at 11.2–4), constitutes Dante's primary source.

17 Many Vulgate texts read *supersubstantialem* rather than *cotidianum* in this verse. The Douay-Rheims version renders the word as 'supersubantial,' while the King James Version has 'daily.' The translation, both into English and into Latin, depends upon the interpretation of the original Greek word, ἐπιούσιον, whose meaning is uncertain. Most scholars now believe that it means 'sufficient for the coming day,' as Liddell and Scott have it, but it seems that many earlier theologians took its meaning to be 'sufficient for physical necessity,' which is rendered by *supersubstantialem*. I am assuming, since Dante renders the word in Italian as 'cotidiana,' that the Vulgate text he knew contained the Latin cognate reading. Correspondingly, I have altered the Douay-Rheims translation below to 'daily' to accord with this Vulgate reading.

18 For Tommaseo, see *'Commedia' di Dante Alighieri*, con ragionamenti e note di Niccolò Tommaseo, 3 vols. (Milan: Francesco Pagnoni, 1869), 2:252: 'Difficile tradurre, più difficile commentare l'orazione insegnata di Cristo. La parafrasi non è indegna di Dante, ma è parafrasi.' For Marti, see 'L'effimero e l'eterno: La meditazione elegiaca di *Purgatorio* XI,' *Giornale storico della letteratura italiana* 161 (1984): 161–84. Enrico Panzacchi writes that 'In sostanza questa preghiera a me pare che qui, sopra tutto, abbia il significato di un atto di umiltà.' See 'Il canto XI del *Puragorio*,' in *Letture Dantesche*, ed. Giovanni Getto (Florence: Sansoni, 1962), 883–97. Chiamenti sees this 'translation' as a kind of paradigm that encompasses 'tutte le possibili modulazioni e tecniche della traduzione.' See *Dante Alighieri traduttore*, 115–17. According to Marianne Shapiro, the prayer occupies a key place in the artistic project of the *Purgatorio:* 'Yet the reading of the Lord's Prayer with its final *terzina* explicating the fiction of Purgatory, that its souls no longer require their own prayer, stakes out an unmistakable independence for the human word which alone interprets the divine.' '*Homo artifex:* A Rereading of *Purgatorio* XI,' *Lectura Dantis* 19 (1992): 59–69.

19 'Dum dicitur noster, fraternitatis admonemur, cum sit communis adoptio omnibus. Nemo dicat meus, quod proprie filio convenit, cui pater est per naturam.'

20 'PATER NOSTER QUI ES IN CAELIS, id est in sanctis et iustis; non enim spatio locorum continetur deus . . . Recte ergo intelligitur quod dictum est: PATER NOSTER QUI ES IN CAELIS, in cordibus iustorum esse dictum tamquam in templo sancto suo.' From *De sermone Domini* 2.5.17–18.

21 Saint Francis's poem reads, 'Laudato sie, mi' Signore, cum tucte le tue crea-
    ture.' See Dante Alighieri, *Commedia*, ed. and with a commentary by Anna
    Maria Chiavacci Leonardi, 3 vols. (Milan: Mondadori, 1991–7), 2:324.
22 *Summa theologiae* 2a.2æ.83.9. '*Adveniat regnum tuum*, per quam petimus ad
    gloriam regni ejus pervenire ... uno modo directe et principaliter, secun-
    dum meritum quo beatitudinem meremur Deo obediendo ... Quod autem
    dicitur, *Fiat voluntas tua*, recte intelligitur; ut obediatur praeceptis tuis; *sicut
    in caelo, et in terra*, idest, sicut ab Angelis, ita ab hominibus.'
23 The *Grande dizionario della lingua italiana* lists some seventeen different
    meanings for *ingegno*, most of which were current in Dante's time.
24 See, for example, Psalm 77, which summarizes the care that the Lord pro-
    vided for Israel in the wilderness, including the fact that he 'had rained
    down manna upon them to eat, and had given them the bread of heaven.
    Man ate the bread of angels: he sent them provisions in abundance'
    (verses 24–5).
25 'Dicendum quod oratio dominica perfectissima est, quia, sicut Augustinus
    dicit, *si recte et congruenter oramus, nihil aliud dicere possumus quam quod in
    ista oratione dominica positum est*' (*Summa theologiae* 2a.2æ.83.9). The citation
    of Augustine is from the Letter to Probas 130.12.
26 Barolini, *The Undivine 'Comedy': Detheologizing Dante* (Princeton: Princeton
    University Press, 1992), 122–42; citation found on page 141.
27 See my entry, 'David,' in *DE*, 289–90.
28 The only critic of whom I am aware who does not identify these passages
    as coming from the Beatitudes is Giuseppina Mezzadroli, who, in the
    entry 'Virtues and Vices,' in *DE*, 866–71, identifies these 'benedictions' as
    'taken from the Book of Psalms or from the hymns of the church.'
29 The fact that the Beatitudes are not included in the liturgy is noted by
    Evelyn Birge Vitz, 'The Liturgy and Vernacular Literature,' in *The Liturgy
    of the Medieval Church*, ed. Thomas J. Heffernan and E. Ann Matter
    (Kalamazoo: Medieval Institute Publications, 2001), 591–2.
30 See Anna Maria Chiavacci Leonardi, 'Le beatitudini e la struttura poetica
    del *Purgatorio*,' *Giornale storico della letteratura Italiana* 161 (1984): 1–29; the
    citation is taken from page 20. Chiavacci Leonardi's argument is that the
    uniqueness of the structure of the *Purgatorio* has largely gone unnoticed,
    convinced as critics are that Dante continues to rely here, as he does in the
    Inferno, on Aristotle. She suggests that while the first canticle is indeed
    founded on classical, especially Aristotelian, ethics and emphasizes justice,
    the second realm, with its exaltation of humility, meekness, and mercy,
    places its emphasis on love and derives this Christian ethics primarily

from the Beatitudes. Likewise, Giacalone in his commentary suggests that the Beatitudes in the *Comedy* 'appaiono nel pieno compimento figurale, rispetto alle parole di Gesù in terra.' As I hope to show, Chiavacci Leonardi and Giacalone insufficiently recognize the degree to which Dante adapts the Beatitudes for his own ends (a fact that is rhetorically signalled by Chiavacci Leonardi's contention that the *Purgatorio* is based on what the Beatitudes '*in realtà* significano'). Other treatments devoted to the Beatitudes include Frederigo Tollemache's entry on 'Beatitudini evangeliche' in the *ED*, 1:540–1; Richard Lansing's entry on 'Beatitudes' in the *DE*, 89; Sergio Cristaldi, 'Dalle beatitudini all'*Apocalisse:* Il Nuovo Testamento nella *Commedia,*' *Letture classensi* 17 (1988): 23–67; Mark Cogan, *The Design in the Wax* (Notre Dame: University of Notre Dame Press, 1999), 94–119; Peter S. Hawkins, *Dante's Testaments: Essays in Scriptural Imagination* (Stanford: Stanford University Press, 1999), 45–9; Patrick S. Boyde, *Human Vices and Human Worth in Dante's 'Comedy'* (Cambridge: Cambridge University Press, 2000), 106–10.

31 Peter Hawkins has argued that the absence of the rewards in citations of the Beatitudes suggests that 'the angel sings the versicle and the penitent soul *is* the response.' 'The Religion of the Mountain: Handling Sin in Dante's *Purgatorio*' (plenary address, 34th Annual Sewanee Medieval Coloquium, Sewanee, TN, 30–31 March 2007).

32 Earlier, Gregory of Nyssa, in what appears to be the earliest extended treatment of the Beatitudes, likewise found a narrative of ascent in them, which he illustrated through a comparison to a ladder: 'I think the arrangement of the Beatitudes is like a series of rungs, and it makes it possible for the mind to ascend by climbing from one to another.' See *Homilies on the Beatitudes: An English Version with Commentary and Support Studies*, ed. Hubertus R. Drobner and Alberto Viciano (Leiden: Brill, 2000), 32 (2.1). See also in the same volume, Judith L. Kovacs, 'Clement of Alexandria and Gregory of Nyssa on the Beatitudes,' 311–29, who notes that for the earlier Clement as well, 'the Beatitudes both enjoin and symbolize this gradual pursuit of perfection' (323).

33 Augustine, *De sermone Domini in monte*, book 1, 1.2–4.12.

34 Typically, medieval theologians defined sins as specific acts, while vices were held to be settled habits of sinful behaviour. In most Latin discussions, the 'seven deadly sins' were correspondingly referred to as *vitia*. For a brief discussion of the differences between sin and vice, see Boyde, *Human Vices*, 149–53.

35 Serious debate surrounding the *Ethics* began in the second half of the thirteenth century, as there was no complete translation of the text into Latin

until Robert Grosseteste's translation of 1246–47, though translations of the first three books did circulate prior to that time. For an overview of the reception and translation of the *Ethics* during this period, see R.A. Gauthier, 'L'Éthique à Nicomaque dans le Moyen Âge latin,' in *L'Éthique à Nicomaque: Introduction, traduction, et commentaire*, ed. Gauthier and J.Y. Jolif, 2nd ed., 2 vols. in 4 (Louvain: Publications Universitaires, 1970), 1:111–46; Georg Wieland, 'The Reception and Interpretation of Aristotle's *Ethics*,' in *The Cambridge History of Later Medieval Philosophy from the Rediscovery of Aristotle to the Disintegration of Scholasticism: 1100–1600*, ed. Norman Kretzmann, Anthony Kenny, and Jan Pinborg (Cambridge: Cambridge University Press, 1982), 657–72; and Bonnie Kent, *Virtues of the Will: The Transformation of Ethics in the Late Thirteenth Century* (Washington, DC: Catholic University of America Press, 1995), 39–93.

36 ' ... summum hominis bonum sive ipsum, ut dictum est, finem boni future vite beatitudinem et, qua illuc pervenitur, viam virtutes ponamus ... Dominus autem Ihesus ... ad contemptum mundi et ad huius beatitudinis desiderium pariter incitaret dicens: "Beati pauperes spiritu, quoniam ipsorum est regnum celorum" ... Et si diligenter adtendamus ad hec, universa eius precepta vel exhortationes adhibentur, ut spe illius superne et eterne vite omnia contempnantur prospera sive tolerentur adversa.' Latin text from Petrus Abaelardus, *Dialogus inter Philosophum, Iudaeum et Christianum*, ed. Rudolf Thomas (Stuttgart: Friedrich Frommann Verlag, 1970), 104–5. English translation from Peter Abelard, *Dialogue of a Philosopher with a Jew and a Christian*, trans. Pierre J. Payer (Toronto: Pontifical Institute of Medieval Studies, 1979), 95–6.

37 'Tunc itaque uicta uitia deputanda sunt, cum Dei amore uincuntur, quem nisi Deus ipse non donat nec aliter nisi per mediatorem Dei et hominum, hominem Christum Iesum' (*De civitate Dei* 21.16). Latin text from the *CCSL* edition, vols. 47–8, ed. Bernhard Dombart and Alfons Kalb (Turnhout: Brepols, 1955). English translation from *The City of God*, trans. Henry Bettenson (London: Penguin, 1984), 994.

38 In the Sermon on the Mount, for example, Jesus tells his disciples: 'Love your enemies; do good to them that hate you; and pray for them that persecute and calumniate you,' a teaching at variance with the spirit of Aristotle's ethical thought.

39 *Summa theologiae* 1a.2æ.69.3; Aristotle, *The Nicomachean Ethics*, trans. J.A.K. Thompson, rev. Hugh Tredennick (London: Penguin, 2004), 8–9 (1095b–1096a); though I cite this translation of the Greek, I have checked it against Grosseteste's Latin translation and note where there are important differences. Grosseteste's translation is available in *Ethica Nicomachea, translatio*

Roberti Grosseteste Lincolniensis, recensio pura, ed. R.A. Gauthier (Leiden: Brill, 1972).

40 'beatitudo est ultimus finis humanae vitae. Dicitur autem aliquis jam finem habere, propter spem finis obtinendi: unde et Philosophus dicit, in *Ethic.*, quod *pueri dicuntur beati propter spem;* et Apostolus dicit, *Rom.*, *Spe salvi facti sumus.'*

41 Aquinas alludes to Aristotle's discussion of happiness in chapter 9 of book 1. In Tredennick's translation, the passage reads, 'For the same reason no child is happy either, because its age debars it as yet from such activities; if children are so described, it is by way of congratulation on their future promise' (1100a.1–4). As I go on to argue below, in a way, Aquinas treats grown men and women as Aristotle does children, as being incapable in this life of true happiness but promised it in the life to come. Nevertheless, Aristotle never considers happiness after death, at least not in the way that Aquinas and other Christian Aristotelians treat it. In chapter 10 of book 1, Aristotle considers the question of whether a man can be counted happy only after this life, but for Aristotle, the question does not refer to the happiness of the afterlife, but only to the Greek assumption that misfortune late in life can nullify a man's earlier claim to happiness, as in Herodotus's account of Solon and Croesus in book 1 of the *Histories*. For Aristotle, *eudaimonia* is a resolutely terrestrial good.

42 *Summa theologiae* 1a.2æ.3.8: 'Dicendum quod ultima et perfecta beatitudo non potest esse nisi in visione divinae essentiae.'

43 'Nam beatitudo voluptuosa, quia falsa est et rationi contraria, impedimentum est beatitudinis futuræ. Beatitudo vero activae vitae dispositiva est ad beatitudinem futuram.'

44 'Necesse est enim unum esse ultimum finem hominis inquantum est homo, propter unitatem humanae naturae' (1.9.106). See also *Summa theologiae* 1a.2æ.1.5. Latin text is taken from *In X libros Ethicorum ad Nicomachum expositio,* in *Opera omnia,* 34 vols. (Paris, 1871–80), 25: 231–26: 88; English translation taken from Saint Thomas Aquinas, *Commentary on Aristotle's 'Nicomachean Ethics',* trans. C.J. Litzinger, OP (1964; Notre Dame: Dumb Ox Books, 1993).

45 *Virtues of the Will,* 30 (emphasis Kent's). See *Summa theologiae* 2a.2æ.10.4; 2a.2æ.23.7.

46 'beatitudini evangeliche,' in *ED,* 1:540.

47 Patrick Boyde also praises the way in which Dante combines 'homogeneous materials into a harmonious whole' in the *Purgatorio,* including Dante's use of the Beatitudes. 'There can be few more satisfying expressions in medieval art of the longing for order and synthesis which is so

characteristic of the high Middle Ages.' See *Human Vices*, 70. The fact of Dante's creativity in his use of the Beatitudes, however, was noticed as early as Edward Moore, 'Unity and Symmetry of Design in the *Purgatorio*,' in *Studes in Dante: Second Series: Miscellaneous Essays* (Oxford: Clarendon Press, 1899), 262–3.

48 'SED CONTRA est auctoritas ipsius Domini, praemia hujusmodi proponentis.'

49 The ordering Dante follows is often referred to, using the first letter of the Latin names of the vices, as SIIAAGL (superbia, invidia, ira, accedia, avaritia, gula, luxuria). As Richard Newhauser notes, this version of the capital vices had become the most common by the twelfth century. See *The Treatises on Vices and Virtues in Latin and the Vernacular* (Turnhout: Brepols, 1993), 190–1. Edward Moore explores Dante's ordering of the vices in relation to medieval tradition in *Studies in Dante: Second Series*, 182–209.

50 In addition, there is one final citation that fits into this pattern, though it comes from a different source. As Dante, Virgil, and Statius make their way through the earthly paradise, Dante tells us that Matelda sings '*Beati quorum tecta sunt peccata!*' (*Purg.* 29.3). These words are taken from the opening of Psalm 31, but they clearly echo the Beatitudes both in the words that are sung and in their liturgical function: Matelda sings these words as a way of marking the progress of Dante and Statius from the purging of the mountain into the Earthly Paradise, where they will soon witness the 'processione mistica.'

51 In his entry on the Beatitudes in the *DE*, Richard Lansing suggests that Dante may well have been influenced by Hugh's *De quinque septenis*, described above, since the work 'explicitly opposes the Beatitudes to the seven capital sins' (89). As the above list indicates, however, Dante follows Hugh only fitfully; his ordering, excepting the first Beatitude, is completely different and thus he pairs different Beatitudes with the sins in all but the first case.

52 The identity of the voice (or voices) that sings the first Beatitude, at *Purg.* 12.109–11, has been the subject of some debate since the earliest criticism of the poem. Since we are told that 'voci / cantaron' the Beatitude, many commentators have speculated that these words must have been spoken by the souls inhabiting either the terrace of pride that Dante and Virgil are leaving or that of the envious to which they are climbing. Benvenuto, for example, glossed the 'voci' as belonging to the proud souls ('illorum superborum'). Some read the 'voci' as referring to disembodied voices, circling the terrace. Since in the other instances the angel guarding the entrance to the following terrace is identified as singing the Beatitude, other contemporary commentators argue that an angel sings the first Beatitude

as well, and that Dante uses, in D'Ovidio's words, 'un plurale stilistico.' Others, also supporting the majority reading, understand 'voci' as 'words,' similar to the usage at *Purg.* 22.5. See, for example, Tozer and Trucchi.

53 'Quapropter recte hic intelleguntur pauperes spiritu humiles et timentes deum, id est non habentes inflantem spiritum. Nec aliunde omnino incipere oportuit beatitudinem, siquidem peruentura est ad summam sapientiam' (*De sermone Domini* 1.1.3).

54 As noted above, Dante almost always cites only the first half of the Beatitude, without any reference to the reward awaiting those whose blessedness is described in the macarism. Only in canto 19, his fourth use of a Beatitude, does he in some measure allude to the Beatitude's second part.

55 'Ahi quanto son diverse quelle foci / da l'infernali! ché quivi per canti / s'entra, e là giù per lamenti feroci' (*Purg.* 12.112–14).

56 See, for example, Aquinas, *Summa theologiae* 2a.2æ.36.3: 'invidia misericordiae opponitur et caritati.'

57 'Misericordia nascitur de praecedentibus, quia si praecesserit vera humilitas et animus mansuescat, et suos et aliorum casus fleat et justitiam esuriat, post nascitur vera misericordia.'

58 *Summa theologiae* 2a.2æ.158.1, 3. Saint Gregory considers the question in *Moralia in Job* 5.45.

59 There are related readings, however. Richard of Saint Victor, for example, in his *allegoriae in novum testamentum* (misattributed in *PL* to Hugh of Saint Victor) defines the *pacifici* as those who do not render evil for evil (*PL* 175: 765); similarly, the *Glossa ordinaria* states that the *pacifici* are those who have subjected every movement of the soul to reason (*ratio*).

60 Chiavacci Leonardi in her commentary links the 'correction' to Dante's personal motivation: 'Per questa profonda motivazione personale è qui introdotta la "correzione" alla beatitudine che crediamo tra tutte più vicina alle aspirazioni di Dante' (504).

61 *Summa theologiae* 1a.2æ.69.3. Singleton, based on Thomas's reading, argues in his commentary that 'this beatitude praises those who, unlike the slothful, have the fortitude to endure pain' (454).

62 In addition to Trucchi, other commentators who find no tie between purged sin and Beatitude include Tozer, Chimenz, and Bosco/Reggio.

63 'per documenta spiritualia que humanam rationem transcendunt.'

64 'Omnes homines esuriunt et sitiunt; sed alii esuriunt et sitiunt malum; alii esuriunt et sitiunt bonum. Alii etenim esuriunt et sitiunt aurum, argentum, vestes pretiosas, praedia, terras, vineas, domos, equos et possessiones innumeras.' *Allegoriae in Novum Testamentum, PL* 175: 764. Dante likewise

emphasizes this cumulative, increasingly rapacious nature of avarice in *Convivio* 4.12.14–19.

65 Part of the problem is textual; both 'n'avea' and 'n'avean' for the second word of line 5 have manuscript support, and *sitio* has much greater manuscript support than does Petrocchi's reading, *sitiunt*. The emendation is based on the fact that this passage obviously continues the convention established on the previous terraces of an angel's speaking a Beatitude. For a fuller consideration of the issue and a defence of the reading I assume here, see Tozer's commentary on these lines.

66 Richard Newhauser notes that this definition of justice, as 'a virtue allotting to each person that which is his/hers,' was very common in texts of the High Middle Ages. See 'Justice and Liberality: Opposition to Avarice in the Twelfth Century,' in *Virtue and Ethics in the Twelfth Century*, ed. István P. Bejczy and Richard G. Newhauser (Leiden: Brill, 2005), 295–316; citation on page 297.

67 My translation of 'sacra fame' as 'sacred hunger' is somewhat controversial in the history of commentary on this line. A majority of critics have historically translated the phrase as 'cursed hunger,' since that is what the phrase in the *Aeneid* means (see 3.56–7). My own sense of the context of the phrase in the *Comedy* as well as the fact that *sacro* means 'sacred' in all its other appearances in the poem lead me to support the translation I have provided. And indeed, most critics now read the line as 'sacred hunger.' See, for example, the commentaries of Bosco/Reggio (2:357) and Chiavacci Leonardi (2:664). My larger point, however, that Statius's reform resulted from the study of a pagan text, holds irrespective of how the phrase is translated. For a fuller consideration of these lines with justification of the reading I assume here (though for different purposes), see R.A. Shoaf, '"Auri sacra fames" and the Age of Gold,' *Dante Studies* 96 (1978): 195–9; Barolini, *Dante's Poets*, 256–69; and Ronald L. Martinez, 'La "sacra fame dell'oro" (*Purgatorio* 22, 41) tra Virgilio e Stazio: Dal testo all'interpretazione,' *Letture classensi* 18 (1989): 177–93. Interestingly, Shoaf reads 'sacra fame del'oro' not as an objective but as a subjective genitive, meaning 'the hunger belonging to or appropriate to gold,' with gold referring to the Golden Age. In this reading, Statius takes Virgil's text to advocate an appropriately moderate hunger, such as existed during the Golden Age as described in *Purg.* 22.148–50.

68 Aristotle, *Ethics* 1119a. 'Quecumque autem ad sanitatem sunt vel ad bonam habitudinem delectabilia existencia, hec appetet mensurate.'

69 There is an Aristotelian precedent for this idea; at the end of the second book of the *Ethics*, Aristotle suggests that since 'one of the extremes

is always more erroneous than the other,' a good rule of conduct is to 'choose the lesser of the evils.' See Aristotle, *Ethics* 1109a. This point is made even more strongly in Grosseteste's Latin translation where 'more erroneous' is rendered as the 'greater sin': 'Extremorum enim, hoc quidem est peccatum magis hoc autem minus.'

70 Marc Cogan has argued for the fundamentally Aristotelian nature of the structure of Purgatory in *The Design in the Wax*, 78–118.

71 See *Ethics* 7.9 (1151b–1152a).

72 See *Ethics* 4.9 (1128b).

73 See Kent, *Virtues of the Will*, 68–72, 209–10. For Augustine's views, see *De civitate Dei* 19.4.

74 See the *Ethics* 1.5 (1095b–1096a), 10.7 (1177a–1178a).

75 In this same passage of the *Convivio*, however, Dante refers to these two happinesses as possible 'in this life': 'noi potemo avere in questa vita due felicitadi, secondo . . .'

76 Lester K. Little, 'Pride Goes before Avarice: Social Change and the Vices in Latin Christendom,' *American Historical Review* 76 (1971): 16–49. Little as well as Alexander Murray, in *Reason and Society in the Middle Ages* (Oxford: Clarendon Press, 1978), 59–80, argue that the increased attention paid to avarice was linked to the rise of a money economy in the later Middle Ages. Richard Newhauser, though, has shown that avarice was viewed as the pre-eminent vice as early as the fifth century by a group of bishops in northern Italy. See *The Early History of Greed: The Sin of Avarice in Early Medieval Thought and Literature* (Cambridge: Cambridge University Press, 2000), 70–95. Of course, as Chaucer's Pardoner well knows, there is also scriptural support for the idea that avarice, or at least cupidity, is the root of all evil: 'radix malorum est cupiditas' (see 1 Timothy 6.10).

77 Murray argues that we should distinguish between the social prominence of a vice and its importance in Christian psychology. He thus notes that although Dante found more people damned for avarice than for any other sin (see *Inf.* 7.25), he nevertheless retained pride as the foundational vice in the moral structure of Purgatory. See *Reason and Society*, 436n62.

78 For a consideration of this episode, see Nick Havely, *Dante and the Franciscans: Poverty and the Papacy in the 'Commedia'* (Cambridge: Cambridge University Press, 2004), 130–52; and my 'Dante, Peter John Olivi, and the Franciscan Apocalypse,' in *Dante and the Franciscans*, ed. Santa Casciani (Leiden: Brill, 2006), 13–18.

79 Richard Newhauser traces the attempt, and ultimate failure, by the Spiritual Franciscans to make voluntary poverty a universal ideal of the Christian life in '*Avaritia* and *Paupertas*: On the Place of the Early

Franciscans in the History of Avarice,' in *In the Garden of Evil: The Vices and Culture in the Middle Ages,* ed. R. Newhauser (Toronto, Pontifical Institute of Medieval Studies, 2005), 324–48.

80 For a more detailed consideration of the multiple remedies Dante envisioned for avarice, see my 'Avarice, Justice, and Poverty in Dante's *Comedy,*' in *Laster im Mittelalter / Vices in the Middle Ages,* ed. Christoph Flüeler and Martin Rhode, *Scrinium Friburgense* 23 (Berlin: Walter de Gruyter, 2009), 201–29.

81 For Augustine, see *De sermone Domini* 2.8 and 3.10; for Aquinas, see *Summa theologiae* 1a.2æ.69.4.

82 *Summa theologiae* 3a.60.3: 'sacramentum proprie dicitur quod ordinatur ad significandam nostram sanctificationem.'

5. Dante's Apocalypse

1 Frank Kermode, *The Sense of an Ending: Studies in the Theory of Fiction* (Oxford: Oxford University Press, 1967), 4.

2 'Introduction: Apocalyptic Spirituality,' in *Apocalyptic Spirituality,* ed. Bernard McGinn (Mawhaw, NJ: Paulist Press, 1979), 1.

3 McGinn, one of the leading scholars of the history of the Apocalypse, also notes that the interpretive gap between 'academic readings carried on in schools of divinity and religion and in departments of English on the one hand and the mass of general readers on the other is probably greater now than ever before.' See 'Revelation,' in *The Literary Guide to the Bible,* ed. Robert Alter and Frank Kermode (Cambridge, MA: Harvard University Press, 1987), 539. E. Ann Matter treats the interpretive distance between modern and medieval readers of the Song of Songs in *The Voice of My Beloved: The Song of Songs in Western Medieval Christianity* (Philadelphia: University of Pennsylvania Press, 1990), 3–19; though she also points out that allegorical readings of the Song of Songs still form an important part of modern scholarly understanding of the book.

4 Harold Bloom, Introduction to *The Revelation of St. John the Divine,* ed. Harold Bloom (New York: Chelsea House, 1988), 4. See McGinn, 'Revelation,' for a brief history of the book's reception. It is perhaps not surprising, then, that the final cantos of the *Purgatorio,* which are so close to the Apocalypse, have received a mixed reception at best in modern Dante criticism. Benedetto Croce emphatically pointed to this section of the poem as 'non poesia,' since '[l]e immagini . . . non hanno in tal caso diretto valore di poesia, ma sono segni e mezzi per altra cosa.' See *La poesia di Dante* (Bari: Laterza, 1966), 129.

5 Richard K. Emmerson and Bernard McGinn, Preface to *The Apocalypse in the Middle Ages,* ed. Emmerson and McGinn (Ithaca: Cornell University Press, 1992), xi.

6 George Steiner, *Grammars of Creation* (New Haven: Yale University Press, 2001), 10.

7 Actually, utopianism thrives in certain limited circles, just not in places Steiner cares to look. Soon, we are told by various avatars of the technological future, for example, we will enjoy immortality, peace, and universal prosperity because of advances in computer and other technologies; and, like the Marxist future, the utopia soon to come is to be of our own making. Ray Kurzweil is probably the best-known techno-utopian who foresees an end of history, at least of human history. See, for example, *The Singularity Is Near: When Humans Transcend Biology* (London: Penguin, 2005), a book whose title betrays its eschatological import. Like Steiner, on the other hand, Caroline Walker Bynum and Paul Freedman wrote a few years ago that even in the face of environmental catastrophe, mindless technology, and other pervasive ills, 'we are neither very apocalyptic, nor very eschatological, nor even very scared. Not, perhaps, as much as we ought to be.' See Introduction to *Last Things: Death and the Apocalypse in the Middle Ages,* ed. Caroline Walker Bynum and Paul Freedman (Philadelphia: University of Pennsylvania Press, 2000), 17.

8 'Nondum de secunda resurrectione, id est corporum, loquitur, quae in fine futura est, sed de prima, quae nunc est' (*De civitate Dei* 20.6). 'Ergo et nunc ecclesia regnum Christi est regnumque caelorum. Regnant itaque cum illo etiam nunc sancti eius, aliter quidem, quam tunc regnabunt; nec tamen cum illo regnant zizania, quamuis in ecclesia cum tritico crescant' (*De civitate Dei* 20.9). Latin text cited from the *CCSL* edition, vols. 47–8, ed. Bernhard Dombart and Alfons Kalb (Turnhout: Brepols, 1955). English translation from Saint Augustine, *City of God,* trans. Bettenson, 904, 915.

9 For a concise account of Augustine's reading, see Paula Frederiksen, 'Tyconius and Augustine on the Apocalypse,' in *The Apocalypse in the Middle Ages,* ed. Emmerson and McGinn, 20–37; and Frederiksen's entry, 'Apocalypticism,' in *Augustine through the Ages: An Encyclopedia,* ed. Allan D. Fitzgerald (Grand Rapids, MI: Eerdmans, 1999), 49–53. In this last entry, she concludes: 'He created a third way, reading *ad litteram* – historically but *not* literally – and thus affirmed the historical realism of Christian redemption while renouncing any terrestrial eschatology' (53). Frederiksen here uses 'literally' in its modern rather than its ancient sense (which was precisely to read *ad litteram*).

10 See Richard Landes, 'Lest the Millennium Be Fulfilled: Apocalyptic Expectations and the Pattern of Western Chronography, 100–800 CE,' in *The Use and Abuse of Eschatology in the Middle Ages,* ed. Walter Verbeke et al. (Leuven, Belgium: Leuven University Press, 1988), 137–211.

11 E. Ann Matter, 'The Apocalypse in Early Medieval Exegesis,' in *The Apocalypse in the Middle Ages,* 38–50; the citation is from page 50.

12 'il calavrese abate Giovacchino / di spirito profetico dotato' (*Par.* 12.140–1).

13 On Joachim, see: Marjorie Reeves, *The Influence of Prophecy in the Latter Middle Ages: A Study in Joachimism* (Oxford: Clarendon Press, 1969), 1–132; Bernard McGinn, *The Calabrian Abbot: Joachim of Fiore in the History of Western Thought* (New York: Macmillan, 1985); and Gian Luca Potestà, *Il tempo dell'Apocalisse: Vita di Gioacchino da Fiore* (Rome: Laterza, 2004). Concise accounts include E. Randolph Daniel, 'Joachim of Fiore: Patterns of History in the Apocalypse,' in *Apocalypse in the Middle Ages,* 72–88; and Richard K. Emmerson and Ronald B. Herzman, 'The Apocalypse and Joachim of Fiore: Keys to the Medieval Apocalyptic Imagination,' in *The Apocalyptic Imagination in Medieval Literature* (Philadelphia: University of Pennsylvania Press, 1992), 1–35.

14 For an extended treatment of how Dante's use of the Apocalypse compares to that of the Spirituals, particularly the most influential Spiritualist exegete of the Apocalypse, Peter John Olivi, see my 'Dante, Peter John Olivi, and the Franciscan Apocalypse,' in *Dante and the Franciscans,* ed. Santa Casciani (Ledien: Brill, 2006), 9–50.

15 Norman Cohn and others have argued that a sense of crisis is primarily what motivates apocalyptic movements. See Cohn, *The Pursuit of the Millennium: Revolutionary Millenarians and Mystical Anarchists of the Middle Ages,* rev. ed. (London: Temple Smith, 1970). I find Bernard McGinn's notion, however – that those who turn to apocalyptic thought do so in order to make sense of the present – more persuasive. See, for example, his Introduction to *Apocalyptic Spirituality,* 8: 'The apocalyptic mentality is a particular form of pre-understanding rather than a mere way of responding. More sensitive to change than the mass of their fellows, apocalypticists are more in need of a religious structure within which to absorb and give meaning to the anxieties that always accompany existence and change.'

16 See *De civitate Dei* 20.6.1–2.

17 Citations are from the translation by Bernard McGinn in *Apocalyptic Spirituality,* 115, 117. McGinn notes that 'this letter was one of Joachim's more popular works to judge by the number of ms. copies that survive' (291n1).

18 McGinn, 'Introduction: John's Apocalypse and the Apocalyptic Mentality,' in *The Apocalypse in the Middle Ages*, 8

19 In spite of McGinn's argument that we must distinguish between the apocalyptic seer and the prophet in that the seer avoids general calls to repentance, McGinn notes similarly that apocalyptic texts 'invite the reader to place him- or herself in an apocalyptic situation in which present action is determined by reference to, and in light of, the coming final events. A kind of "psychological imminence" is always part of apocalyptic eschatology.' See 'John's Apocalypse and the Apocalyptic Mentality,' ibid., 9. Similarly, Emmerson and Herzman argue that one of the key aspects of the 'apocalyptic imagination' is the understanding of the personal and individual in universal terms. See *The Apocalyptic Imagination*, 3–34. Amilcare I. Iannucci has provided a perceptive reading of how Dante's eschatology fits into this prophetic framework in 'Already and Not Yet: Dante's Existential Eschatology,' in *Dante for the New Millennium*, ed. Teodolinda Barolini and H. Wayne Storey (New York: Fordham University Press, 2003), 334–48.

20 See, in particular, Daniel Javitch's work on genre theory in the Italian Renaissance, e.g., 'The Emergence of Poetic Genre Theory in the Sixteenth Century,' *MLQ* 59 (1998): 139–69.

21 Tzvetan Todorov, *Introduction to Poetics*, trans. Richard Howard (Minneapolis: University of Minnesota Press, 1981), 62. For Jauss's discussion of a 'horizon of expectation,' see *Toward an Aesthetic of Reception*, trans. Timothy Bahti (Minneapolis: University of Minnesota Press, 1982), especially the chapters 'Literary History as a Challenge to Literary Theory' and 'Theory of Genres and Medieval Literature.'

22 On the idea of genre as an invitation to form, see Claudio Guillèn, 'On the Uses of Literary Genre,' in *Literature as System: Essays toward the Theory of Literary History* (Princeton: Princeton University Press, 1971), 107–34; and Alistair Fowler, *Kinds of Literature: An Introduction to the Theory of Genres and Modes* (Cambridge, MA: Harvard University Press, 1982).

23 See Bernard McGinn, 'Introduction: John's Apocalypse and the Apocalyptic Mentality,' 5–6. John J. Collins offers a similar definition: '"Apocalypse" is a genre of revelatory literature with a narrative framework, in which a revelation is mediated by an otherworldly being to a human recipient, disclosing a transcendent reality which is both temporal, insofar as it envisages eschatological salvation, and spatial insofar as it involves another, supernatural world.' See 'Introduction: Towards the Morphology of a Genre,' in *Apocalypse: The Morphology of a Genre*, ed. John J. Collins, *Semeia* 14 (1979): 9. Collins argues that his own study and that of his collaborators leads to the conclusion that 'it is in fact possible

to identify a coherent and recognizable literary genre, which may appropriately be labeled "apocalypse" in the light of common scholarly terminology' (18). Bernard McGinn has argued elsewhere that the view that apocalypse does not constitute a distinctive literary genre 'can scarcely be maintained in the light of recent research.' See 'Early Apocalypticism: The Ongoing Debate,' in *The Apocalypse in English Renaissance Thought and Literature*, ed. C.A. Patrides and Joseph Wittreich (Manchester: Manchester University Press, 1984), 3. The question of the genre of medieval apocalyptic literature is nevertheless a vexed one. Morton Bloomfield's *Piers Plowman as a Fourteenth-Century Apocalypse* (New Brunswick, NJ: Rutgers University Press, 1962) is perhaps the best-known attempt to define the genre of medieval apocalypse and apply it to a canonical work of medieval literature, even though he admits that 'it is doubtful that such a literary form existed' (9). Richard Emmerson has criticized the desire to define a medieval apocalyptic genre, arguing that the attempt deflects interest from the more central question of the influence of the Apocalypse in medieval culture. See, in particular, 'The Apocalypse in Medieval Culture,' in *The Apocalypse in the Middle Ages*, ed. Emmerson and McGinn, 295–300; and his review of *Boethian Apocalypse: Studies in Middle English Vision Poetry*, by Michael D. Cherniss, in *Studies in the Age of Chaucer* 10 (1988): 134–7. I am arguing here, however, that Dante looked not to any medieval examples of apocalyptic literature, but to the biblical originals in his attempt to understand the Apocalypse. Peter Armour similarly argues for identifying Dante's final five cantos in the *Purgatorio* as an Apocalypse in *Dante's Griffin and the History of the World: A Study of the Earthly Paradise* (Oxford: Clarendon Press, 1989). Emmerson and Herzman assert that 'no work of literature, let alone medieval literature, so consistently and energetically evokes the Christian apocalyptic imagination as do the concluding cantos of the *Purgatorio*,' in *The Apocalyptic Imagination*, 141. James Nohrnberg has argued that the poem as a whole can be considered an apocalypse; see 'The First-Fruits of the Last Judgment: The *Commedia* as a Thirteenth-Century Apocalypse,' *Sewanee Medieval Studies* 12 (2002): 111–58. Similarly, Nicolò Mineo details similarities between the *Commedia* as a whole and the characteristics of biblical apocalyptic literature in *Profetismo e Apocalittica in Dante: Strutture e temi profetico-apocalittici in Dante: Dalla 'Vita Nuova' alla 'Divina Commedia'* (Catania: Università di Catania, 1968), 94–100.

24 McGinn, 'John's Apocalypse and the Apocalyptic Mentality,' 6–7.

25 McGinn elaborates: 'apocalyptic revelation is part of a broad movement away from the word of God conveyed in oral proclamation and tradition

and toward the word of God fixed in written texts. The apocalypses are the product of a learned elite.' See 'John's Apocalypse,' (6).

26 See, for example, Peter Hawkins, *Dante's Testaments: Essays in Scriptural Imagination* (Stanford: Stanford University Press, 1999), 63: 'One looks in vain to Dante's biblical precursors for anything even remotely like this.'

27 Northrop Frye, *The Great Code: The Bible and Literature* (New York: Harcourt, Brace, Jovanovich, 1982), 135.

28 See note 4, above.

29 Ronald B. Herzman, review of *Dante and Medieval Latin Traditions,* by Peter Dronke, *Studies in the Age of Chaucer* 9 (1987): 211.

30 See Bruno Nardi, 'Il mito dell'Eden,' in *Saggi di filosofia dantesca,* 2nd ed. (1930; Florence: La Nuova Italia, 1967), 311–40. See also Peter Armour's entry, 'Earthly Paradise,' in *DE,* 330–4, and bibliography there. Alison Morgan suggests that Dante's choice of the location for his Purgatory was found 'in the learned traditions of Eden and of Jerusalem.' See *Dante and the Medieval Other World* (Cambridge: Cambridge University Press, 1990), 160.

31 See Paul's joining of Adam and Christ at Romans 5.11–15 and 1 Cor. 15.21–2.

32 See the second volume of Singleton's *Dante Studies, Journey to Beatrice,* 2nd ed. (1958; Baltimore: Johns Hopkins University Press, 1977).

33 A. Bartlett Giamatti discusses how Dante's descriptions of landscape in the *Inferno* and *Purgatorio* anticipate the Earthly Paradise in *The Earthly Paradise and the Renaissance Epic* (Princeton: Princeton University Press, 1966), 94–105.

34 The references are to *Purg.* 28.139–41, 49–51, and 64–6. Singleton makes the argument about Astraea in 'Virgo or Justice,' in *Dante Studies 2: Journey to Beatrice,* 184–203. Caron Cioffi describes Matelda as 'a pagan nature deity,' in her entry on the figure in *DE,* 599.

35 Caron Ann Cioffi has persuasively argued that 'Dante's characterization of Eden as seemingly innocent yet fraught with erotic attractiveness, as serene yet shattered by violence, pain, and loss, and as timeless yet integrally bound up with history owes much to the way in which Virgil shaped his own pastoral vision.' See ' "Il cantor de' bucolici carmi": The Influence of Virgilian Pastoral on Dante's Description of the Earthly Paradise,' in *Lectura Dantis Newberryana,* vol. 1, ed. Paolo Cherchi and Antonio C. Mastrobuono (Evanston: Northwestern University Press, 1988), 94. My understanding of *Purgatorio* 28 has also been strongly influenced by Kyle Anderson's unpublished MA thesis, 'Dante and the Pastoral in Eden,' Brigham Young University, December 2005.

36 Peter Dronke, 'The Procession in Dante's *Purgatorio,' Deutsches Dante-Jahrbuch* 53–54 (1978–79): 21. Singleton similarly argues that 'Matelda exemplifies human nature as it was before sin and as it would have been had there been no sin.' See *Dante Studies 2,* 209.

37 Cioffi, 'Virgilian Pastoral,' 103.

38 Giuseppe Mazzotta sees this movement between memory of the fall and present redemption as key to the entire canticle: 'The memory of the fall, in a real sense, stands at the very heart of the representation of the new beginning of history, and the whole of *Purgatorio* enacts a steady oscillation between the memory of the fallen world and the longing for the new.' *Dante, Poet of the Desert: History and Allegory in the 'Divine Comedy'* (Princeton: Princeton University Press, 1984), 45–6.

39 'se divota fosse stata, / avrei quelle ineffabili delizie / sentite prima e più lunga fiata' (*Purg.* 29.28–30).

40 Saint Augustine, *De Genesi ad litteram* 6.24: 'Quomodo ergo, inquiunt, renouari dicimur, si non hoc recipimus, quod perdidit primus homo, in quo omnes moriuntur? hoc plane recipimus secundum quendam modum et non hoc recipimus secundum quendam modum.' Cited according to the *CSEL* edition, vol. 28, pt. 1. (1894; New York: Johnson Reprint Corp., 1970). English translation taken from Saint Augustine, *On Genesis,* trans. Edmund Hill (Hyde Park, NY: New City Press, 2002), 321. This passage is cited by Charles S. Singleton in *Dante Studies 2: Journey to Beatrice,* 218. In much of his chapter, 'Matelda,' Singleton makes a point similar to the one I am making here.

41 Cited according to the text in *Poeti del duecento,* 2 vols., ed. Gianfranco Contini (Milan: Ricciardi, 1960), 2:555–6.

42 In their commentary on Durling's translation of the *Purgatorio* (Oxford: Oxford University Press, 2003), 502.

43 'Quoniam ecce inimici tui, Domine; quoniam ecce inimici tui peribunt: et dispergentur omnes qui operantur iniquitatem. Et exaltabitur sicut unicornis cornu meum, et senectus mea in misericordia uberi. Et despexit oculus meus inimicis meis, et insurgentibus in me malignantibus audiet auris mea. Iustus ut palma florebit: ut cedrus Libani multiplicabitur. Plantati in domo Domini in atriis Dei nostri florebunt. Adhuc multiplicabuntur in senecta uberi, et bene patientes erunt, ut adnuntient quoniam rectus Dominus Deus noster et non est iniquitas in eo.'

44 In the *Glossa ordinaria* reading of 1.4, for example, the seven churches are said to represent *universae ecclesiae.* Similarly, Hugh of Saint Cher, in his commentary on the Apocalypse, writes of this same passage, 'per illas septem Ecclesias intelliguntur universae mundi Ecclesiae.' This commentary

was traditionally ascribed to Thomas Aquinas and can be found in his *Opera omnia,* 34 vols. (Paris, 1871–80), 31:469–32:86. The citation here is from 31:473.

45 'quos sub numero viginti quatuor seniorum Apocalypsis Joannis inducit adorantes Agnum, et coronas suas prostratis vultibus offerentes, stantibus coram quatuor animalibus oculatis et retro et ante, id est, et in praeteri-tum et in futurum respicientibus, et indefessa voce clamantibus, Sanctus, Sanctus, Sanctus, Dominus Deus omnipotens, qui erat, et qui est, et qui venturus est' (*PL* 28: 600). Translation from Saint Jerome, *Letters and Select Works,* trans. W.H. Fremantle, vol. 6 of *A Select Library of Nicene and Post-Nicene Fathers of the Christian Church* (New York: Christian Literature, 1893), 490.

46 'Et in circuitu sedis sedilia viginti quattuor; et super thronos, viginti quat-tuor seniores sedentes, circumamictos vestimentis albis, et in capitibus eorum coronas aureas . . . procident viginti quattuor seniores ante sed-entem in throno, et adorabunt viventem in saecula saeculorum, et mittent coronas suas ante thronum dicentes, dignus es Domine et Deus noster . . . '

47 Of course, it is possible that Dante wishes us both to recall Mary and, on a second reading, to see in the words an anticipation of Beatrice, who becomes a *figura Christi* for Dante, serving as an intermediary to lead him to repentance and God. In this reading as well, Beatrice serves not as an atemporal symbol of divine grace, but as an embodied creature through whom Dante can sense God's grace entering into history and into his own life.

48 Drawing on comments by J.S.P. Tatlock in 'The Last Cantos of the *Purgatorio,'* *Modern Philology* 32 (1934): 113–23, Durling and Martinez in their commentary note that, while the Apocalyptic scene of the elders sur-rounding the Lamb portrays a 'circular figure of eternity,' Dante's 'cross-shaped pageant' proceeds in a 'linear distension' (624) that reinforces the sense of Dante's portrayal of the scriptures as unfolding in time.

49 In the Gospel of Mark, for example, men in a synagogue witness the casting out of a demon, and ask among themselves, 'what thing is this?' (*quidnam est hoc?*) (1.27). In Acts 2.12, the Jews and proselytes who hear the miraculous preaching of the apostles ask, 'what meaneth this?' (*quidnam hoc vult esse?*).

50 This is not the only difference between the animals in the two visions, however. The most obvious difference other than the number of wings is that in Ezekiel's vision, the animals *each* have four faces: 'there was the face of a man, and the face of a lion on the right side of all the four: and the face of an ox, on the left side of all the four: and the face of an eagle

over all the four' (Ezek. 1.10). Even though Jerome preserves this aspect of the Hebrew text in his Vulgate translation, in the patristic exegetical tradition, Ezekiel's creatures are also treated as if they each had one face. Dante does not mention the faces of the creatures, nor does he differentiate among them. For a discussion of Ezekiel's vision and the patristic history of its interpretation, see Angela Russell Christman, *'What did Ezekiel See?'*: *Christian Exegesis of Ezekiel's Vision of the Chariot from Irenaeus to Gregory the Great* (Leiden: Brill, 2005). John's six winged-creatures may have been influenced by the theophany recounted in Isaiah 6.

51 'John's description of the creatures as *full of eyes* is derived from the Septuagint translation of Ezekiel 1.18, which puts the eyes on the creatures rather than on the wheel's rims' (Christman, *'What did Ezekiel See?'* 10n23). In addition, Ezekiel 10.12 describes the creatures as also full of eyes.

52 Teodolinda Barolini, 'Arachne, Argus, and St. John: Transgressive Art in Dante and Ovid,' in *Dante and the Origins of Italian Literary Culture* (New York: Fordham University Press, 2006), 168.

53 Ernst R. Curtius, *European Literature and the Latin Middle Ages,* trans. Willard R. Trask (Princeton: Princeton University Press, 1973), 120n34.

54 There is an interesting parallel between Dante's image of the chariot among the evangelists and an illustration of Honorius Augustodunensis's commentary on the Canticle of Canticles. As Ann Matter describes the illustration, 'the Sunamita [one of the manifestations of the bride in Honorius's interpretation] . . . rides in a chariot shaped like a tower; the four wheels are actually the four Evangelists: a man, an ox, a lion, an eagle; the cart is pulled by apostles and prophets.' See *The Voice of My Beloved,* 65; the illustration is reproduced on page 67. Lino Pertile explores more broadly the parallels between Honorius's commentary and Dante's procession in *La puttana e il gigante: Dal Cantico dei Cantici al Paradiso Terrestre di Dante* (Ravenna: Longo, 1998), esp. pages 36–42.

55 'Forma autem Ecclesie nichil aliud est quam vita Cristi, tam in dictis quam in factis comprehensa.' See *Monarchia* 3.14.3.

56 Kevin Brownlee, 'Phaeton's Fall and Dante's Ascent,' *Dante Studies* 102 (1984): 135–44; see also Maria Cristina Meschiari, 'Un idolo poetico: Fetonte nella *Commedia,'* *Studi e problemi di critica testuale* 45 (1992): 93–102.

57 'ille ad arcam, ego ad boves calcitrantes et per abvia distrahentes attendo. Ille ad arcam proficiat qui salutiferos oculos ad naviculam fluctuantem aperuit' (*Epistole* 11.5.12).

58 Many commentators credit Isidore of Seville as Dante's source, since he identifies the griffin as composed of the natures of the lion and eagle and elsewhere posits these two animals as appropriate symbols of Christ. See

Etymologiae 12.2.17 and 7.2.43–4 (*PL* 82: 436, 267). Peter Dronke (in 'The Procession'), Peter Armour, and John A. Scott, however, all point out that the griffin itself was not seen as a symbol of Christ by Isidore, or by anyone else for that matter. As Armour states it, 'the overwhelming evidence in Latin and in the vernacular tradition, backed by the authority of the Bible, is that the griffin was a large and fierce predator and that, when interpreted symbolically, it represented not Christ but evil and opposition to Christ: avarice; the devil; cruelty, persecution, and tyranny.' See *Dante's Griffin and the History of the World: A Study of the Earthly Paradise ('Purgatorio,' cantos xxix – xxxiii)* (Oxford: Clarendon Press, 1989), 43. See also Scott, *Dante's Political Purgatory* (Philadelphia: University of Pennsylvania Press, 1996), 187–9. Other details, however, support the traditional identification, notably the echoes of the Song of Songs in the description of the colours of the Griffin: 'le membra d'oro avea quant' era uccello, / e bianche l'altre, di vermiglio miste' (*Purg.* 29.113–14). These colours are echoed in the description of the bridegroom, traditionally seen as Christ, in Song of Sol. 5.10–11. For a detailed consideration of the identity of the Griffin that supports the traditional identification, see Pertile, *La puttana e il gigante,* 143–62. I agree with Pertile that the identification of the Griffin as Christ by the vast majority of Dante's earliest commentators suggests that the idea that Christ could be symbolized as a Griffin must have been acceptable to Dante's contemporaries.

59 Dronke sees this interpretation suggested in canto 31, where the women identify themselves: 'Noi siam qui ninfe e nel ciel siamo stelle; / pria che Beatrice discendesse al mondo, / fummo ordinate a lei per sue ancelle' (106–8). See 'The Procession,' 33–4.

60 Dante does not specify how Luke seems to be (literally, 'shows himself') a physician, and most commentators do not speculate about it. In his commentary, Singleton, following a few earlier commentators, suggests that Dante means us to understand that Luke is 'wearing the robes of a physician' (724).

61 See Luke 1.1–4 and Acts 1.1–2.

62 See, for example, Dronke, 'The Procession in Dante's *Purgatorio*'; and Barolini, 'Arachne, Argus, and St. John,' in *Dante and the Origins of Italian Literary Culture.*

63 'Sic igitur totus ille mundus ordinatissimo decursu, a Scriptura sacra describitur procedere, a principio usque ad finem, ad modum cujusdam pulcherrimi carminis ordinati, ubi potest quis speculari, secundum decursum temporis, varietatem, et multiplicitatem et aequitatem, et ordinem, rectitudinem et pulchritudinem multorum divinorum judicorum,

procedentium a sapientia Dei gubernante mundum. Unde sicut nullus potest videre pulchritudinem carminis, nisi aspectus ejus feratur super totum versum; sic nullus videt pulchritudinem ordinationis et regiminis universi, nisi eam totam speculetur. Et quia nullus homo tam longaevus est, quod totam possit videre oculis carnis suae, nec futura potest per se praevidere; providit nobis Spiritus sanctus librum Scripturae sacrae, cujus longitudo commetitur se decursui regiminis universi' (prologue, 2). Latin text from Saint Bonaventure, *Opera omnia*, 15 vols. (Paris, 1864–71), 7:243–4. English translation from *The Breviloquium*, vol. 2 of *The Works of Bonaventure: Cardinal, Seraphic Doctor, and Saint*, trans. José de Vinck, 4 vols. (Patterson, NJ: Anthony Guild Press, 1963), 11–12.

64 Harold Bloom, determined to find a 'gnostic' and heterodox Dante, argues that he employs the 'books of the two Testaments' in the procession 'not to rely on them, but to get them out of his way.' See *The Western Canon: The Books and School of the Ages* (New York: Harcourt Brace, 1994). As I have tried to argue, however, Dante's freedom with the biblical text means that he can adapt it for his own purposes without in any way seeking to get it 'out of the way.' The point of his adaptation is to return to the Bible.

65 Alison Cornish notes that these stars were also themselves compared to the tiller of a ship by Statius. See *Reading Dante's Stars* (New Haven: Yale University Press, 2000), 81.

66 'Lo tempo, secondo che dice Aristotile nel quarto de la Fisica, è "numero di movimento, secondo prima e poi"; e "numero di movimento celestiale"' (4.2.6).

67 E. Ann Matter, *The Voice of My Beloved*, 168.

68 For a history of the Canticle of Canticles, see Matter, *The Voice of My Beloved* (for the treatment of Mary, see esp. pages 151–77); and Ann W. Astell, *The Song of Songs in the Middle Ages* (Ithaca: Cornell University Press, 1990; for Mary, see pages 42–72).

69 'For though Adam be deemed to death / With all his children, as Abel and Seth, / Yet *Ecce, virgo concipiet*–/ Lo, where a remedy shall rise! / Behold a maiden shall conceive a child / And get us more grace than ever men had.' Text cited from A.C. Cawley, ed., *Everyman and Medieval Miracle Plays* (London: J.M. Dent, 1993), 67.

70 This point is further reinforced by the fact that Saint Bernard replaces Beatrice as Dante's guide at the end of the journey, only to direct Dante to the Virgin Mary. Following Bernard's prayer to the Virgin, however, Dante finally abandons all intermediaries to seek the vision of God directly.

71 'Osanna Filio David, benedictus qui venturus est [*or* venit, *which is also an attested reading*] in nomine Domini osanna in altissimis.'

72　C.H. Grandgent, ed. and annot., *La Divina Commedia,* by Dante Alighieri, rev. Charles S. Singleton (Cambridge, MA: Harvard University Press, 1972), 584. There are variations in the accounts of Mark (11.9–10) and Luke (19.38), though Matthew seems to have become the standard account.

73　*Aeneid* 6.866. Citations of the *Aeneid* are from Oxford Classical Text, ed. R.A.B. Mynors (Oxford: Oxford University Press, 1969).

74　Richmond Lattimore notes that Latin funerary epitaphs frequently represent 'a request on the part of the dead person that flowers be laid on the grave,' citing this passage from Virgil as 'a good literary precedent.' See *Themes in Greek and Latin Epitaphs* (Urbana: University of Illinois Press, 1962), 135. Drawing on other uses of lilies in ancient literature, A.G. Austin suggests that lilies are 'perhaps symbolic of a short life.' See Vergil, *Aeneidos: Liber sextus,* commentary by R.G. Austin (Oxford: Oxford University Press, 1986), 272.

75　Adam Parry, 'The Two Voices of Virgil's *Aeneid,' Arion* 2 (1963): 66–80.

76　See Louis Réau, *Iconographie de l'art chrétien,* 3 vols. (Paris: Presses Universitaires de France, 1955), 1:133.

77　'perch' i' fu' ribellante a la sua legge, / non vuol che 'n sua città per me si vegna' (*Inf.* 1.125–6).

78　There have been critics, though, who have argued that Dante in fact hopes for Virgil's salvation. See, for example, Mowbray Allan, 'Does Dante Hope for Vergil's Salvation?' *MLN* 104 (1989): 193–205.

79　John Freccero, 'Manfred's Wounds and the Poetics of the *Purgatorio,'* in *Dante: The Poetics of Conversion,* ed. Rachel Jacoff (Cambridge, MA: Harvard University Press, 1986), 195–208, esp. pages 206–8.

80　The contrast between Virgil as tragic poet and Dante as comic poet is dramatized at the end of *Inferno* 20 and the beginning of *Inferno* 21. As discussed in chapter 3, at the end of canto 20, Dante has Virgil define his poem as 'l'alta mia tragedìa' (line 113), while at the beginning of canto 21, Dante names his poem (for only the second time), as a comedy: 'la mia comedìa' (line 2). For an extended consideration of how Dante's poetic identity both depends on and ultimately moves beyond Virgil, see Teodolinda Barolini, *Dante's Poets: Textuality and Truth in the 'Comedy'* (Princeton: Princeton University Press, 1984), 201–86. In my view, Franco Masciandaro's argument in *Dante as Dramatist: The Myth of the Earthly Paradise and Tragic Vision in the 'Divine Comedy'* (Philadelphia: University of Pennsylvania Press, 1991), that Dante's poem should be considered tragic rather than comic, relies too much on his own sense, and that of modern critics, of the meaning of tragic, and underestimates Dante's determination to create his own 'comic' genre that he works to distinguish from the 'tragic' *Aeneid.*

81 'e li angeli cantaro / di sùbito '*In te, Domine, speravi*'; / ma oltre '*pedes meos*' non passaro' (*Purg.* 30.82–4). For a consideration of this Psalm and its relationship to Psalm 50 in the poem, see Robert Hollander, 'Dante's Use of the Fiftieth Psalm (A Note on *Purg.* XXX, 84),' in *Studies in Dante* (Ravenna: Longo, 1980), 107–13.

82 'Dante, perché Virgilio se ne vada, / non pianger anco, non piangere ancora; / ché pianger ti conven per altra spada' (*Purg.* 30.55–7).

83 See, in particular, Singleton, 'The Pattern at the Center,' in *Dante Studies 1: 'Commedia': Elements of Structure* (1954; Cambridge, MA: Harvard University Press, 1970), 45–60; and 'Advent of Beatrice,' in *Dante Studies 2: Journey to Beatrice*, 2nd ed. (Cambridge, MA: Harvard University Press, 1977), 72–85. Durling and Martinez also point out that Beatrice presents 'the case against the pilgrim as if arguing before a court ... this aspect of the episode is a particularly clear figure of the Last Judgment' (527).

84 See, for example, 'The Prologue Scene,' in *Dante: The Poetics of Conversion*, 1–28.

85 Isaiah's prophetic call is recounted in Isaiah 6, where a seraphim takes a coal off the altar and touches the prophet's lips with it, saying, 'thy iniquities shall be taken away, and thy sin shall be cleansed.'

86 The Transfiguration is recounted in each of the synoptic Gospels. See, in addition to Matthew 17, Mark 2.2–9 and Luke 9.28–36. Matthew, though, seems to be the most likely source of the three for Dante's simile, as the question that awakens the pilgrim in line 72, 'Surgi: che fai,' refers to Matthew's account, where, following the Transfiguration, Jesus tells his three apostles, 'Arise, and fear not' (*surgite et nolite timere*) (see verse 7). Matthew's account is the only one of the three that recounts Jesus' statement.

87 'In exemplum futurae beatitudinis et claritatis, quam videbunt iusti, prius sublatis impiis.'

88 For a discussion of this passage in the *Lectura super Matthaeum*, see Kevin Madigan, *Olivi and the Interpretation of Matthew in the High Middle Ages* (Notre Dame: University of Notre Dame Press, 2003), 89–91.

89 The idea of the 'heavenly Jerusalem' derives from the Apocalypse, where John recounts seeing 'the holy city Jerusalem coming down out of heaven from God' (21.10). Charles T. Davis has made the most systematic attempt to understand Dante's view of Rome. See especially *Dante and the Idea of Rome* (Oxford: Clarendon Press, 1957); and 'Rome and Babylon in Dante,' in *Rome and the Renaissance: The City and the Myth*, ed. P.A. Ramsey (Binghamton, NY: Medieval & Renaissance Texts & Studies, 1982), 19–40.

90 R.E. Kaske argues that this section of the canto actually represents Dante's first stage of church history, because it accords with common medieval

portrayals of the seven stages of church history. See 'The Seven *Status Ecclesiae* in *Purgatorio* XXXII and XXXIII,' in *Dante, Petrarch, Boccaccio: Studies in the Italian Trecento In Honor of Charles S. Singleton,* ed. Aldo S. Bernardo and Anthony L. Pellegrini (Binghamton, NY: Medieval & Renaissance Texts & Studies, 1983), 89–113.

91 The bibliography on *Purgatorio* 32 is enormous, and so I list only the studies that have most influenced my reading here: R.E. Kaske, 'Dante's *Purgatorio* XXXII and XXXIII: A Survey of Christian History,' *University of Toronto Quarterly* 43 (1974): 193–214; Kaske, 'The Seven *Status Ecclesiae*,' (ibid.); Kenelm Foster, '*Purgatorio* XXXII,' in *Cambridge Readings in Dante's 'Comedy',* ed. Foster and Patrick Boyde (Cambridge: Cambridge University Press, 1981), 138–54; Peter Hawkins, 'Transfiguring the Text: Ovid, Scripture, and the Dynamics of Allusion,' *Stanford Italian Review* 5 (1985): 115–39; Sergio Cristaldi, 'Dalle beatitudini all'*Apocalisse*,' 45–63; Armour, *Dante's Griffin;* Scott, *Dante's Political Purgatory;* Pertile, *La puttana e il gigante;* Nick Havely, *Dante and the Franciscans* (Cambridge: Cambridge University Press, 2004), 109–22.

92 'Vel per aquam fluminis signifcatur abundantia terrenorum . . . abundantiam quam misit draco Domino permittente in Ecclesiam Dei, quando a Constantino datum est ei imperium occidentalis Ecclesiae . . . Unde tunc audita fuit vox Angelorum in aere dicentium, "Hodie infusum est venenum in Ecclesia Dei," sicut legitur in Apocryphis Sylvestri.' As mentioned in note 44, above, this commentary can be found in the collection of Aquinas's complete works, 31:622–3. For a consideration of the commentary, its attribution, and the views on the Donation presented in it, see Robert E. Lerner, 'Poverty, Preaching, and Eschatology in the Revelation Commentaries of Hugh of St Cher,' in *The Bible in the Medieval World,* ed. Katherine Walsh and Diana Wood (Oxford: Basil Blackwell, 1985), 157–89. This legend of the angel's voice was widespread, and is repeated, for example, by Langland in *Piers Plowman* (B. 15.555–9), as Emmerson and Herzman have noted. See *The Apocalyptic Imagination,* 133–4.

93 Jacopo della Lana, one of the earliest commentators, for example, wrote that 'Lo drago che uscì dalla terra fra due ruote significa Maometto, il quale ne portò a sua legge grande parte de' fideli della chiesa, e picciola parte ne rimase al carro.'

94 See *Monarchia* 2.11.8, where Dante refers to Constantine's gift as having a 'pious intention' (*pia intentio*); and *Par.* 20.56 refers to the act as having been made 'under a good intention that bore evil fruit' (*sotto buona intenzion che fé mal frutto*).

95 'Mentre che la gran dota provenzale / al sangue mio non tolse la ver-
gogna, / poco valea, ma pur non facea male. / Lì cominciò con forza e con
menzogna / la sua rapina' (*Purg.* 20.61–5). I have attempted to describe
Dante's conception of avarice much more extensively in 'Avarice, Justice,
and Poverty in Dante's *Comedy*,' in *Laster im Mittelalter / Vices in the Middle
Ages*, ed. Christoph Flüeler and Martin Rhode, *Scrinium Friburgense* 23
(Berlin: Walter de Gruyter, 2009), 201–29.

96 Richard Kay and Charles Davis have explored these contradictions, seeking to find a way to reconcile them. See Kay, 'The Pope's Wife: Allegory
as Allegation in *Inferno* 19.106–11,' *Studies in Medieval Culture* 12 (1978):
105–11; and Davis, 'Rome and Babylon in Dante.'

97 Kaske sees in the giant a more generic figure of the Antichrist, 'who appears prominently as a giant in almost all medieval commentary on the
famous number 666 in Apocalypse 13.18' ('The Seven *Status Ecclesiae*,'
100). Emmerson and Herzman find in Dante's portrayal of the simonist
popes of *Inferno* 19 forerunners of the Antichrist. See *The Apocalyptic
Imagination*, 104–44.

98 The ancient commentators generally see Dante as a representative of the
Christian or the Italian people; there are a variety of interpretations by
modern commentators, including the possibility that Dante represents the
imperial ideal, Florence as an object of papal design, Boniface's attempts
to make alliances with other monarchs, or simply the rupture between
Boniface and Philip that led to the episode in Anagni.

99 For a detailed consideration of Olivi's commentary, see David Burr, *Olivi's
Peaceable Kingdom: A Reading of the Apocalypse Commentary* (Philadelphia:
University of Pennsylvania Press, 1993); for a much more detailed exami-
nation of Olivi's reading of the Apocalypse in relation to Dante's, see my
'Dante, Peter John Olivi, and the Franciscan Apocalypse.'

100 Kaske, in 'The Seven *Status Ecclesiae*,' argues for a much more traditional
portrayal of church history than I find. He identifies lines 85–99 (Dante's
portrayal of the primitive church) as the first stage, and he finds no place
at all for the gift of the eagle's feathers in the seven stages. Finally, he
also merges what I have identified as the fifth and sixth stages into
one stage – the fifth, which enables him to see the episode with the giant
and the harlot as the sixth stage. He then counts Beatrice's prophecy in
canto 33 as Dante's seventh stage, which, according to Kaske, announces
'the time of peace beginning with the death of the Antichrist' (106).

101 The only other instances of Latin citations beginning cantos are found in
Inferno 34 ('Vexilla Regis prodeunt inferni'), which actually qualifies as a

miscitation; and perhaps *Paradiso* 7 ('Osanna, sanctus Deus sabaòth . . . '),
though this opening tercet represents a brief hymn of Dante's own composition, made from Hebrew and Latin liturgical words. *Purgatorio* 11 begins, of course, with Dante's paraphrase of the Lord's Prayer. It therefore
seems that *Purgatorio* 33 constitutes the only case of a canto beginning
with an untransformed citation of any kind.

102 See the following: accusation of apostasy (11–14), promise of vengeance
(15), plea for repentance (16–18), promise of restoration if there is repentance (19); accusation of apostasy (21–3), promise of vengeance (24–5),
promise of restoration (26–31). For a discussion of the prophetic view of
history in the Old Testament, see Abraham J. Heschel, *The Prophets* (1962;
New York: Harper, 1991), 202–37.

103 The first letter, for example, contains praise (2.2–3), accusation (2.4–6),
and promise (2.7).

104 McGinn, *Visions of the End*, 33.

105 There has been some debate about Dante's indebtedness to these traditions; Charles T. Davis has pointed to the later version of Pietro di Dante's
commentary, where he links the *Veltro* prophecy of *Inferno* 1 with the DXV
prophecy in *Purgatorio* 33 and suggests that his father may have been
thinking of the *Rex Christianorum* prophesied by Methodius, which refers
to the prophecy of the Last World Emperor by the writer now identified as Pseudo-Methodius. See 'Dante's Vision of History,' *Dante Studies*
93 (1975): 143–60; selections from Pseudo-Methodius's prophecy can be
found in McGinn, *Visions of the End*, 75–6.

106 Marjorie Reeves, 'Dante and the Prophetic View of History,' in *The
World of Dante: Essays on Dante and His Times*, ed. Cecil Grayson (Oxford:
Clarendon Press, 1980), 44–60; citation is from page 57.

107 'Sion in iudicio redimetur, et reducent eam in iustitia.'

108 This is clearest in the case of Kaske. See, in addition to 'Seven *Status
Ecclesiae*' and 'Dante's *Purgatorio* XXXII and XXXIII,' his 'Dante's "DXV"
and "Veltro,"' *Traditio* 17 (1961): 185–252.

109 McGinn, 'John's Apocalypse and the Apocalyptic Mentality,' 9.

110 'vedi li nostri scanni sì ripieni, / che poca gente più ci sì disira' (*Par.* 30.131–2).

111 'The Seven *Status Ecclesiae*,' 106.

112 'Dante's Vision of History,' 151.

113 When, for example, she tells Dante that he is to write to those whose
life is a race to death: 'segna a' vivi / del viver ch'è un correre a la morte'
(*Purg.* 33.53–4).

114 See Reeves, 'Dante and the Prophetic View of History'; and 'The Third
Age: Dante's Debt to Gioacchino da Fiore,' in *L'età dello spirito e la fine dei*

tempi in Gioacchino da Fiore e nel gioachimismo medievale, ed. Antonio Crocco (San Giovane in Fiore: Centro Internazionale di Studi Gioachimiti, 1986), 125–39. Similarly, John Scott sees in Beatrice's words in canto 33 the influence of Joachim in anticipating the replacement of the *ecclesia carnalis* with the *ecclesia spiritualis.* See *Dante's Political Purgatory,* 203.

Conclusion: Poet of the Biblical World

1 Harold Bloom, *Ruin the Sacred Truths: Poetry and Belief from the Bible to the Present* (Cambridge, MA: Harvard University Press, 1989), 47.

2 Erich Auerbach, *Dante: Poet of the Secular World,* trans. Ralph Manheim (1961; New York: New York Review of Books, 2007), 15. Further reference to this work occurs in the text. Also crucial to understanding Auerbach's sense of biblical realism, of course, are the opening two chapters of *Mimesis: The Representation of Reality in Western Literature,* trans. Willard R. Trask (Princeton: Princeton University Press, 1953).

3 See, for example, A.N. Williams's correction of contemporary notions of Christianity: 'Christianity has of late apparently acquired a reputation for being hostile to the notion of the goodness of the body (a view with which Augustine is often, and inexplicably, associated), but in its doctrine of creation (in virtue of which all matter exists explicitly by the will of God), its doctrine of the Incarnation (the assertion that God became human), its sacramental theology (which indicates how grace is received via the body), and its doctrine of the Resurrection (identifying salvation with the eternal maintenance of our embodied state), Christianity is in an important sense deeply materialistic.' See 'The Theology of the *Comedy,*' in *The Cambridge Companion to Dante,* 2nd ed., ed. Rachel Jacoff (Cambridge: Cambridge University Press, 2007), 208.

Works Cited

Primary Sources

NOTE: Citations in the text and notes of commentators on the *Commedia* without bibliographic information refer to their commentaries as presented in the online archive, the Dartmouth Dante Project (http://dante. dartmouth.edu).

Abelard, Peter. *Dialogus inter Philosophum, Iudaeum et Christianum.* Ed. Rudolf Thomas. Stuttgart: Friedrich Frommann Verlag, 1970.
– *Dialogue of a Philosopher with a Jew and a Christian.* Trans. Pierre J. Payer. Toronto: Pontifical Institute of Medieval Studies, 1979.
Alighieri, Dante. *'La Commedia' seconda l'antica vulgata.* Ed. Giorgio Petrocchi. Milan: Montadori, 1966–67.
– *The Divine Comedy.* Trans. Charles Singleton. 3 vols. Princeton: Princeton University Press, 1970–75.
– *Convivio.* Ed. Cesare Vasoli and Domenico De Robertis. In *Dante Alighieri: Opere minori.* Vol. 2, parts 1 and 2. 1988. Milan: Ricciardi, 1995.
– *De vulgari eloquentia.* Ed. Pier Vincenzo Mengaldo. In *Dante Alighieri: Opere minori.* Vol. 3, part 1. 1979. Milan: Ricciardi, 1996.
– *Epistole.* Ed. Arsenio Frugoni and Giorgio Brurdi, 1996.
– *Monarchia.* Ed. Bruno Nardi. In *Dante Alighieri: Opere minori.* Vol. 3, part 1. 1979. Milan: Ricciardi, 1996.
Aquinas, Saint Thomas. *In X libros Ethicorum ad Nicomachum expositio.* In *Opera omnia,* 34 vols., 25:231–26:88. Paris, 1871–80.
– *Summa contra Gentiles, book 1: God.* Trans. Anton C. Pegis. 1955. Notre Dame: University of Notre Dame Press, 1975.
– *Summa theologiae.* 61 vols. New York: McGraw Hill, 1964–81.

– *Summae contra Gentiles.* 2 vols. Rome: Forzianius et Socii, 1984.
– *Commentary on Aristotle's 'Nicomachean Ethics.'* Trans. C.J. Litzinger, OP. 1964. Notre Dame: Dumb Ox Books, 1993.
Aristotle. *Ethica Nicomachea, translatio Roberti Grosseteste Lincolniensis, recensio pura.* Ed. R.A. Gauthier. Leiden: Brill, 1972.
– *The Nicomachean Ethics.* Trans. J.A.K. Thompson, rev. Hugh Tredennick. London: Penguin, 2004.
Augustine, Saint. *De civitate Dei. CCSL,* vols. 47–8. Ed. Bernhard Dombart and Alfons Kalb. Turnhout: Brepols, 1955.
– *On Christian Doctrine.* Trans. D.W. Robertson, Jr. New York: Macmillan, 1958.
– *De doctrina christiana. CCSL,* vol. 32. Ed. Joseph Martin. Turnhout: Brepols, 1962.
– *De sermone Domini in monte libros duos. CCSL,* vol. 35. Ed. Almut Mutzenbecher. Turnhout: Brepols, 1967.
– *De Trinitate. CCSL,* vol. 50A. Ed. W.J. Mountain. Turnhout: Brepols, 1968.
– *De Genesi ad litteram. CSEL,* vol. 28, pt. 1. 1894. New York: Johnson Reprint Corp., 1970.
– *Confessiones. CCSL,* vol. 27. Ed. Lucas Verheijen. Turnhout: Brepols, 1981.
– *Concerning the City of God against the Pagans.* Trans. Henry Bettenson. London: Penguin, 1984.
– *Retractiones. CCSL,* vol. 57. Ed. Almut Mutzenbecher. Turnhout: Brepols, 1984.
– *The Trinity.* Trans. Edmund Hill. Hyde Park, NY: New City Press, 1991.
– *Confessions.* Trans. Henry Chadwick. Oxford: Oxford University Press, 1992.
– *On Genesis.* Trans. Edmund Hill. Hyde Park, NY: New City Press, 2002.
Bernard of Clairvaux, Saint. *Sermons sur le Cantique.* Ed. J. Leclerq et al. 3 vols. Paris: Éditions du Cerf, 1996.
– *The Parables and the Sentences.* Ed. Maureen O'Brian. Kalamazoo, MI: Cistercian Publications, 2000.
Bernardus Silvestris. *Commentary on the First Six Books of Virgil's 'Aeneid.'* Trans. Earl G. Schreiber and Thomas E. Maresca. Lincoln: University of Nebraska Press, 1979.
Boethius. *'Tractates' and 'The Consolation of Philosophy.'* Trans. S.J. Tester. Cambridge, MA: Harvard University Press, 1973.
Bonaventure, Saint. *Breviloquium.* In *Opera omnia,* 15 vols., 7:240–343. Paris, 1864–71.
– *The Breviloquium.* Vol. 3 of *The Works of Bonaventure: Cardinal, Seraphic Doctor, and Saint.* Trans. José de Vinck. 4 vols. Patterson: Anthony Guild Press, 1963.

Blume, Clemens, SJ, ed. *Die Hymen des Thesaurus Hymnologicus H.A. Davids.* Vol. 51 of *Analecta hymnica medii aevi.* Leipzig: O.R. Reisland, 1908.

Cawley, A.C., ed. *Everyman and Medieval Miracle Plays.* London: J.M. Dent, 1993.

Chaucer, Geoffrey. *The Riverside Chaucer.* Ed. Larry D. Benson. 3rd ed. Boston: Houghton Mifflin, 1987.

Contini, Gianfranco, ed. *Poeti del duecento.* 2 vols. Milan: Ricciardi, 1960.

Cronica fiorentina compilata nel secolo XIII. In *Testi fiorentini del Dugento e dei primi del Trecento,* ed. Alfredo Schiaffini, 82–150. Florence: Sansoni, 1954.

Flacius Illyricus, Matthias. *De ratione cognoscendi sacras literas: Über den Erkenntnisgrund der Heiligen Schrift.* Ed. Lutz Geldsetzer. Dusseldorf: Stern-Verlag Janssen, 1968.

Francis of Assisi. *Écrits.* Ed. Théophile Desbonnets. Paris: Éditions du Cerf, 1981.

Gregory of Nyssa. *Homilies on the Beatitudes: An English Version with Commentary and Support Studies.* Ed. Hubertus R. Drobner and Alberto Viciano. Leiden: Brill, 2000.

Gregory the Great, Saint. *Moralia in Job.* PL 75: 509–76: 782.

– *Homiliae in Hiezechihelem prophetam. CCSL,* vol. 142. Ed. Marcus Adriaen. Turnhout: Brepols, 1971.

Hugh of Saint Cher. *In Apocalypsim.* In *Opera omnia,* by Thomas Aquinas, 34 vols., 31:469–32:86. Paris, 1871–1880.

Hugh of Saint Victor. *Didascalicon. PL* 176: 739–838.

– *The Didascalicon of Hugh of St. Victor.* Trans. Jerome Taylor. New York: Columbia University Press, 1961.

– *De quinque septenis.* In *Six Opuscules Spirituels,* ed. Roger Baron, 100–19. Paris: Éditions du Cerf, 1969.

Iacopone da Todi. *Laude.* Ed. Franco Mancini. Rome-Bari: Laterza, 1974.

Isidore of Seville. *Etymologiae. PL* 82: 73–728.

Joachim of Fiore. 'Letter to All the Faithful.' In *Apocalyptic Spirituality,* ed. McGinn, 113–17. Mahwah, NJ: Paulist Press, 1979.

Jerome, Saint. 'Prologus galeatus.' *PL* 28: 593–604.

– *Letters and Select Works.* Trans. W.H. Fremantle. Vol. 6 of *A Select Library of Nicene and Post-Nicene Fathers of the Christian Church.* New York: Christian Literature, 1893.

– *Commentaire sur Saint Matthieu.* Ed. Émile Bonard. 2 vols. Paris: Éditions du Cerf, 1977.

Olivi, Peter John. *Lectura super Apocalipsim.* In Warren Lewis, 'Peter John Olivi: Prophet of the Year 2000.' PhD diss., University of Tübingen, 1972.

Origen, *Traité des principes.* Ed. Henri Crouzel and Manlio Simonetti. 5 vols. Paris: Éditions du Cerf, 1980.

Richard of Saint Victor. *Allegoriae in Novum Testamentum*. *PL* 175: 751–924.
Vincent de Beauvais. *Speculum quadruplex sive Speculum maius*. 1624. Graz-
    Austria: Adademische Druck–u. Verlagsanstalt, 1964.
Vergil. *Opera*. Ed. R.A.B. Mynors. Oxford: Oxford University Press, 1969.

Secondary Sources

Akbari, Suzanne Conklin. *Seeing through the Veil: Optical Theory and Medieval
    Allegory*. Toronto: University of Toronto Press, 2004.
Allan, Mowbray. 'Does Dante Hope for Vergil's Salvation?' *MLN* 104
    (1989): 193–205.
Alter, Robert. *The Art of Biblical Narrative*. New York: Basic Books, 1981.
– *The Art of Biblical Poetry*. New York: Basic Books, 1985.
Alter, Robert, and Frank Kermode, eds. *The Literary Guide to the Bible*.
    Cambridge, MA: Harvard University Press, 1987.
Anderson, Kyle. 'Dante and the Pastoral in Eden.' MA thesis, Brigham Young
    University, 2005.
Armour, Peter. 'Earthly Paradise.' In *DE*, 330–4. New York: Garland, 2000.
– 'The Theme of Exodus in the First Two Cantos of the *Purgatorio*.' In *Dante
    Soundings: Eight Literary and Historical Essays*, ed. David Nolan, 59–99.
    Totowa, NJ: Rowan & Littlefield, 1981.
– *Dante's Griffin and the History of the World: A Study of the Earthly Paradise
    ('Purgatorio,' cantos xxix–xxxiii)*. Oxford: Clarendon Press, 1989.
Astell, Ann W. *The Song of Songs in the Middle Ages*. Ithaca: Cornell University
    Press, 1990.
Auerbach, Erich. *Mimesis: The Representation of Reality in Western Literature*.
    Trans. Willard R. Trask. Princeton: Princeton University Press, 1953.
– 'Figura.' In *Scenes from the Drama of European Literature*, 11–76. 1959.
    Minneapolis: University of Minnesota Press, 1984.
– *Dante: Poet of the Secular World*. Trans. Ralph Manheim. 1961. New York:
    New York Review of Books, 2007.
Austin, R.G., ed. *Aeneidos: Liber sextus*, by Vergil. Oxford: Oxford University
    Press, 1986.
Barblan, Giovanni, ed. *Dante e la Bibbia*. Florence: Olschki, 1988.
Barney, Stephen A. '*Ordo paganis*: The Gloss on Genesis 38.' *South Atlantic
    Quarterly* 91 (1992): 929–43.
Barolini, Teodolinda. *Dante's Poets: Textuality and Truth in the 'Comedy.'*
    Princeton: Princeton University Press, 1984.
– 'True and False See-ers in *Inferno* XX.' *Lectura Dantis* 4 (1989): 42–54.

– *The Undivine 'Comedy': Detheologizing Dante*. Princeton: Princeton University Press, 1992.

– *Dante and the Origins of Italian Literary Culture*. New York: Fordham University Press, 2006.

Baur, Christine O'Connell. *Dante's Hermeneutics of Salvation: Passages to Freedom in the 'Divine Comedy'*. Toronto: University of Toronto Press, 2007.

Benfell, V. Stanley. 'Biblical Truth in the Examination Cantos of Dante's *Paradiso.' Dante Studies* 115 (1997): 89–109.

– 'David.' In *DE*, 289–90. New York: Garland, 2000.

– 'Symbolism.' In *DE*, 803–6. New York: Garland, 2000.

– 'Biblical Exegesis.' In *Medieval Italy: An Encyclopedia*, ed. Christopher Kleinhenz, 121–4. New York and London: Routledge, 2004.

– 'Dante, Peter John Olivi, and the Franciscan Apocalypse.' In *Dante and the Franciscans*, ed. Santa Casciani, 9–50. Leiden: Brill, 2006.

– 'Avarice, Justice, and Poverty in Dante's *Comedy.' In Laster im Mittelalter / Vices in the Middle Ages*, ed. Christoph Flüeler and Martin Rhode, 201–29. *Scrinium Friburgense* 23. Berlin: Walter de Gruyter, 2009.

Bestul, Thomas H. Review of *Book of Verse: A Guide to Middle English Biblical Literature*, by James H. Morey. *Speculum* 77 (2002): 608–10.

Bloom, Harold. Introduction to *The Revelation of St. John the Divine*, ed. Bloom, 1–5. New York: Chelsea House, 1988.

– *Ruin the Sacred Truths: Poetry and Belief from the Bible to the Present*. Cambridge, MA: Harvard University Press, 1989.

– *The Western Canon: The Books and School of the Ages*. New York: Harcourt Brace, 1994.

Bloomfield, Morton. *Piers Plowman as a Fourteenth-Century Apocalypse*. New Brunswick, NJ: Rutgers University Press, 1962.

Boccaccio, Giovanni. *Esposizioni sopra la 'Comedia' di Dante*. Ed. Giorgio Padoan. Vol. 6 of *Tutte le opere di Giovanni Boccaccio*, ed. Vittore Branca. Verona: Mondadori, 1965.

Bori, Pier Cesare. *L'interpretazione infinita: L'ermeneutica Cristiana antica e le sue trasformazioni*. Bologna: Mulino, 1987.

Bosco, Umberto. *Dante vicino*. Rome: Salvatore Sciascia, 1966.

Bosco, Umberto, and Giovanni Reggio, eds. *'La Divina Commedia' con pagine critiche*, by Dante Alighieri. 3 vols. Florence: Le Monnier, 1988.

Boyde, Patrick. *Human Vices and Human Worth in Dante's 'Comedy.'* Cambridge: Cambridge University Press, 2000.

Brezzi, Paolo. 'Il canto XIX dell'*Inferno.'* In *Nuove letture dantesche* 2, 161–82. Casa di Dante in Roma. Florence: Le Monnier, 1968.

Brown, Peter. *Augustine of Hippo: A Biography*. Rev. ed. Berkeley: University of California Press, 2000.

Brownlee, Kevin. 'Phaeton's Fall and Dante's Ascent.' *Dante Studies* 102 (1984): 135–44.

– 'Pauline Vision and Ovidian Speech in *Paradiso* I.' In *The Poetry of Allusion*, ed. Jacoff and Schnapp, 202–13. Stanford: Stanford University Press, 1991.

Bruns, Gerald. 'Hermeneutics of Allegory and the History of Interpretation.' *Comparative Literature* 40 (1988): 384–95.

Burr, David. *Olivi's Peaceable Kingdom: A Reading of the Apocalypse Commentary*. Philadelphia: University of Pennsylvania Press, 1993.

da Buti, Francesco. *Commenta di Francesco da Buti sopra 'La Divina Commedia' di Dante Alighieri*. 3 vols. Pisa: Nistri, 1858.

Bynum, Caroline Walker, and Paul Freedman, eds. *Last Things: Death and the Apocalypse in the Middle Ages*. Philadelphia: University of Pennsylvania Press, 2000.

Carne-Ross, D.S. 'Dante Agonistes.' *New York Review of Books*, 1 May 1975.

Cassell, Anthony K. *Lectura Dantis Americana: Inferno I*. Philadelphia: University of Pennsylvania Press, 1989.

Charity, A.C. *Events and Their Afterlife: The Dialectics of Christian Typology in the Bible and Dante*. Cambridge: Cambridge University Press, 1966.

Chiamenti, Massimiliano. *Dante Alighieri traduttore*. Florence: Le Lettere, 1995.

Chiavacci Leonardi, Anna Maria. 'Le beatitudini e la struttura poetica del *Purgatorio*.' *Giornale storico della letteratura Italiana* 161 (1984): 1–29.

– '"Le bianche stole": Il tema della resurrezione nel *Paradiso*.' In *Dante e la Bibbia*, ed. Barblan, 249–71. Florence: Olschki, 1988.

Chiavacci Leonardi, Anna Maria, ed. *La Divina Commedia*, by Dante Alighieri. 3 vols. Milan: Mondadori, 1991–97.

Chiari, Alberto. 'Il canto dei Simoniaci.' In *Nuove canti dantesche*, 31–68. Varese: Magenta, 1966.

Chiesa, Paolo. 'Le traduzioni.' In *La Bibbia nel medioevo*, ed. Cremascoli and Leonardi, 15–27. Bologna: Edizioni Dehoniane, 1996.

Christman, Angela Russell. *'What did Ezekiel See?': Christian Exegesis of Ezekiel's Vision of the Chariot from Irenaeus to Gregory the Great*. Leiden: Brill, 2005.

Cioffi, Caron Ann. '"Il cantor de' bucolici carmi": The Influence of Virgilian Pastoral on Dante's Description of the Earthly Paradise.' In *Lectura Dantis Newberryana*, vol. 1, ed. Paolo Cherchi and Antonio C. Mastrobuono, 93–122. Evanston: Northwestern University Press, 1988.

– 'Matelda.' In *DE*, 599. New York: Garland, 2000.

Cogan, Marc. *The Design in the Wax: The Structure of the 'Divine Comedy' and Its Meaning*. Notre Dame: University of Notre Dame Press, 1999.

Cohn, Norman. *The Pursuit of the Millennium: Revolutionary Millenarians and Mystical Anarchists of the Middle Ages.* Rev. ed. London: Temple Smith, 1970.

Colish, Marcia. *The Mirror of Language: A Study in the Medieval Theory of Knowing.* Rev. ed. Lincoln: University of Nebraska Press, 1983.

Collins, John J., ed. *Apocalypse: The Morphology of a Genre.* Special issue of *Semeia* 14 (1979).

Congar, Yves. 'La trop fameuse théorie des deux glaives.' In *Sainte Église: Études et approches ecclésiologiques,* 411–16. Paris: Éditions du Cerf, 1964.

Copeland, Rita. *Rhetoric, Hermeneutics, and Translation in the Middle Ages.* Cambridge: Cambridge University Press, 1991.

Copeland, Rita, and Stephen Melville. 'Allegory and Allegoresis, Rhetoric and Hermeneutics.' *Exemplaria* 3 (1991): 159–87.

Cornish, Alison. *Reading Dante's Stars.* New Haven: Yale University Press, 2000.

Corti, Maria. *La felicità mentale: Nuove prospettive per Cavalcanti e Dante.* Torino: Einaudi, 1983.

Cremascolli, Giuseppe. 'Allegoria e dialettica: Sul travaglio dell'esegesi biblica al tempo di Dante.' In *Dante e la Bibbia,* ed. Barblan, 197–276. Florence: Olschki, 1988.

Cremascolli, Giuseppe, and Claudio Leonardi, eds. *La Bibbia nel medioevo.* Bologna: Edizioni Dehoniane, 1996.

Cristaldi, Sergio. 'Dalle beatitudini all'*Apocalisse*: Il Nuovo Testamento nella *Commedia*.' *Letture classensi* 17 (1988): 23–67.

Croce, Benedetto. *La poesia di Dante.* Bari: Laterza, 1966.

Culler, Jonathan. *The Pursuit of Signs: Semiotics, Literature, Deconstruction.* Ithaca: Cornell University Press, 1981.

Curtius, Ernst R. *European Literature and the Latin Middle Ages.* Trans. Willard R. Trask. Princeton: Princeton University Press, 1973.

Dahan, Gilbert. *L'exégèse chrétienne de la Bible en Occident médiévale: XIIe–XIVe siècle.* Paris: Éditions du Cerf, 1999.

Daniel, E. Randolph. 'Joachim of Fiore: Patterns of History in the Apocalypse.' In *The Apocalypse in the Middle Ages,* ed. Emmerson and McGinn, 72–88. Ithaca: Cornell University Press, 1992.

Davis, Charles T. *Dante and the Idea of Rome.* Oxford: Clarendon Press, 1957.

– 'Dante's Vision of History.' *Dante Studies* 93 (1975): 143–60.

– 'Rome and Babylon in Dante.' In *Rome and the Renaissance: The City and the Myth,* ed. P.A. Ramsey, 19–40. Binghamton, NY: Medieval & Renaissance Texts & Studies, 1982.

– *Dante's Italy and Other Essays.* Philadelphia: University of Pennsylvania Press, 1984.

- 'Canto XIX: Simoniacs.' In *Lectura Dantis: Inferno,* ed. Allen Mandelbaum, Anthony Oldcorn, and Charles Ross, 262–74. Berkeley: University of California Press, 1998.

Dawson, David. 'Transcendence as Embodiment: Augustine's Domestication of Gnosis.' *Modern Theology* 10 (1994): 1–26.

- 'Figure, Allegory.' In *Augustine through the Ages: An Encyclopedia,* ed. Allan D. Fitzgerald, 365–8. Grand Rapids: Eerdmans, 1999.

de Man, Paul. 'The Rhetoric of Temporality.' In *Blindness and Insight,* 187–228. 2nd ed. Minneapolis: University of Minnesota Press, 1983.

Desbonnets, Théophile. 'The Franciscan Reading of the Scriptures.' Trans. L.H. Ginn. In *Francis of Assisi Today,* ed. Christian Duquoc and Casiano Floristán, 37–45. Concilium 149. New York: Seabury, 1981.

Dronke, Peter. 'The Procession in Dante's *Purgatorio.'* *Deutsches Dante-Jahrbuch* 53–54 (1978–79): 18–45.

Durling, Robert M., ed. and trans. *The Divine Comedy of Dante Alighieri.* With Introduction and Notes by Ronald L. Martinez and Robert M. Durling. 2 vols. Oxford: Oxford University Press, 1996–2003.

Eco, Umberto. 'L'epistola XIII, l'allegorismo medievale, il simbolismo moderno.' In *Sugli specchi e altri saggi,* 215–41. Milan: Bompiani, 1985.

- *Interpretation and Overinterpretation: Umberto Eco with Richard Rorty, Jonathan Culler, Christine Brook-Rose.* Ed. Stefan Collini. Cambridge: Cambridge University Press, 1992.

Emmerson, Richard K. Review of *Boethian Apocalypse: Studies in Middle English Vision Poetry,* by Michael D. Cherniss. *Studies in the Age of Chaucer* 10 (1988): 134–7.

- 'The Apocalypse in Medieval Culture.' In *The Apocalypse in the Middle Ages,* ed. Emmerson and McGinn, 293–332. Ithaca: Cornell University Press, 1992.

Emmerson, Richard K., and Ronald B. Herzman. *The Apocalyptic Imagination in Medieval Literature.* Philadelphia: University of Pennsylvania Press, 1992.

Emmerson, Richard K., and Bernard McGinn, eds. *The Apocalypse in the Middle Ages.* Ithaca: Cornell University Press, 1992.

Evans, G.R. *The Language and Logic of the Bible: The Earlier Middle Ages.* Cambridge: Cambridge University Press, 1984.

- 'Exegesis and Authority in the Thirteenth Century.' In *Ad Litteram,* ed. Jordan and Emery, 93–111. Notre Dame: University of Notre Dame Press, 1992.

Fallani, Giovanni. 'Analogie tra Dante e S. Paolo, come introduzione agli aspetti mistici del *Paradiso.'* In *Lectura Dantis Mystica: Il poema sacro alla luce delle conquiste psicologiche odierne,* 444–60. Florence: Olschki, 1969.

Faulconer, James E. 'Scripture as Incarnation.' In *Historicity and the Latter-day Saint Scriptures,* ed. Paul Y. Hoskisson, 17–61. Provo, UT: Religious Studies Center, 2001.

Ferrante, Joan. 'Usi e abusi della Bibbia nella letteratura medievale.' In *Dante e la Bibbia,* ed. Barblan, 213–25. Florence: Olschki, 1988.

– 'The Bible as Thesaurus for Secular Literature.' In *The Bible in the Middle Ages: Its Influence on Literature and Art,* ed. Bernard S. Levy, 23–49. Binghamton, NY: Medieval & Renaissance Texts & Studies, 1992.

Fiedrowicz, Michael. 'Introduction to *The Literal Meaning of Genesis.*' In *On Genesis,* by Saint Augustine, trans. Hill, 155–66. Hyde Park, NY: New City Press, 2002.

Fishbane, Michael. *Biblical Interpretation in Ancient Israel.* Oxford: Clarendon Press, 1985.

– *The Garments of Torah: Essays in Biblical Hermeneutics.* Bloomington: Indiana University Press, 1989.

Fitzgerald, Allan D., ed. *Augustine through the Ages: An Encyclopedia.* Grand Rapids: Eerdmans, 1999.

Foscolo, Ugo. *Discorso sul testo della 'Commedia' di Dante.* In *Studi su Dante.* Vol. 9 of *Edizione nazionale delle opere di Ugo Foscolo.* Florence: Le Monnier, 1979.

Foster, Kenelm. 'Vernacular Scriptures in Italy.' In *The Cambridge History of the Bible,* vol. 2, ed. Lampe, 452–65. Cambridge: Cambridge University Press, 1969.

– 'Purgatorio XXXII.' In *Cambridge Readings in Dante's 'Comedy,'* ed. Foster and Patrick Boyde, 138–54. Cambridge: Cambridge University Press, 1981.

Fowler, Alistair. *Kinds of Literature: An Introduction to the Theory of Genres and Modes.* Cambridge, MA: Harvard University Press, 1982.

Franke, William. *Dante's Interpretive Journey.* Chicago: University of Chicago Press, 1996.

Freccero, John. *Dante: The Poetics of Conversion.* Ed. Rachel Jacoff. Cambridge, MA: Harvard University Press, 1986.

Frederiksen, Paula. 'Tyconius and Augustine on the Apocalypse.' In *The Apocalypse in the Middle Ages,* ed. Emmerson and McGinn, 20–37. Ithaca: Cornell University Press, 1992.

– 'Apocalypticism.' In *Augustine through the Ages: An Encyclopedia,* ed. Allan D. Fitzgerald, 49–53. Grand Rapids, MI: Eerdmans, 1999.

Freedman, David Noel, ed. *The Anchor Bible Dictionary.* 6 vols. New York: Macmillan, 1992.

Frei, Hans. *The Eclipse of Biblical Narrative: A Study in Eighteenth and Nineteenth Century Hermeneutics.* New Haven: Yale University Press, 1974.

Frugoni, Arsenio. 'Dante tra due conclavi: La lettera ai cardinali italiani.' *Letture classensi* 2 (1969): 69–91.

Frye, Northrop. *The Great Code: The Bible and Literature.* New York: Harcourt, Brace, Jovanovich, 1982.

Gadamer, Hans-Georg. *Truth and Method.* 2nd ed. Trans. revised by Joel Weinsheimer and Donald G. Marshall. New York: Continuum, 1989.

Gauthier, R.A. '*L'Éthique à Nicomaque* dans le Moyen Âge latin.' In *L'Éthique à Nicomaque: Introduction, traduction, et commentaire,* ed. Gauthier and J.Y. Jolif, 2nd ed., 2 vols. in 4, 1:111–46. Louvain: Publications Universitaires, 1970.

Ghisalberti, Alessandro. 'L'esegesi della scuola domenicana del secolo XIII.' In *La Bibbia nel medioevo,* ed. Cremascoli and Leonardi, 291–304. Bologna: Edizioni Dehoniane, 1996.

Giamatti, A. Bartlett. *The Earthly Paradise and the Renaissance Epic.* Princeton: Princeton University Press, 1966.

Gibson, Margaret T. 'The Place of the *Glossa ordinaria* in Medieval Exegesis.' In *Ad Litteram,* ed. Jordan and Emery, 5–27. Notre Dame: University of Notre Dame Press, 1992.

– *The Bible in the Latin West.* Notre Dame: University of Notre Dame Press, 1993.

Goodfriend, Elaine Adler. 'Prostitution: Old Testament.' In *The Anchor Bible Dictionary,* gen. ed. David Noel Freedman, 6 vols., 5:505–10. New York: Macmillan, 1992.

Gragnolati, Manuele. *Experiencing the Afterlife: Soul and Body in Dante and Medieval Culture.* Notre Dame: University of Notre Dame Press, 2005.

Grandgent, C.H., ed. *La Divina Commedia,* by Dante Alighieri. Rev. Charles S. Singleton. Cambridge, MA: Harvard University Press, 1972.

Grant, Robert, with David Tracy. *A Short History of the Interpretation of the Bible.* 2nd ed. Philadelphia: Fortress Press, 1984.

Grondin, Jean. *Introduction to Philosophical Hermeneutics.* Trans. Joel Weinsheimer. New Haven: Yale University Press, 1994.

Guillèn, Claudio. *Literature as System: Essays toward the Theory of Literary History.* Princeton: Princeton University Press, 1971.

Harrison, Carol. *Beauty and Revelation in the Thought of Saint Augustine.* Oxford: Clarendon Press, 1992.

Havely, Nick. *Dante and the Franciscans: Poverty and the Papacy in the 'Commedia.'* Cambridge: Cambridge University Press, 2004.

Hawkins, Peter S. 'Transfiguring the Text: Ovid, Scripture, and the Dynamics of Allusion.' *Stanford Italian Review* 5 (1985): 115–39.

– *Dante's Testaments: Essays in Scriptural Imagination.* Stanford: Stanford University Press, 1999.

- 'The Religion of the Mountain: Handling Sin in Dante's *Purgatorio.*' Plenary address, annual meeting of Sewanee Medieval Colloquium, Sewanee, TN, 30–31 March 2007.

Herzman, Ronald B. Review of *Dante and Medieval Latin Traditions,* by Peter Dronke. *Studies in the Age of Chaucer* 9 (1987): 209–212.

- 'Dante and the Apocalypse.' In *The Apocalypse in the Middle Ages,* ed. Emmerson and McGinn, 398–413. Ithaca: Cornell University Press, 1992.

Herzman, Ronald B., and William A. Stephany. 'O miseri seguaci: Sacramental Inversion in *Inferno* XIX.' *Dante Studies* 96 (1978): 39–65.

Heschel, Abraham J. *The Prophets.* 1962. New York: Harper, 1991.

Hollander, Robert. *Allegory in Dante's 'Commedia.'* Princeton: Princeton University Press, 1969.

- *Studies in Dante.* Ravenna: Longo, 1980.

- *Il Virgilio dantesco: Tragedia nella 'Commedia.'* Florence: Olschki, 1983.

- '*Inferno* XXXIII, 37–74: Ugolino's Importunity.' *Speculum* 59 (1984): 549–55.

- '*Purgatorio* II: The New Song and the Old.' *Lectura Dantis* 6 (1990): 28–45.

- 'Dante and Paul's Five Words with Understanding.' Center for Medieval and Early Renaissance Studies, Occasional Papers 1. Binghamton, NY: Medieval & Renaissance Texts & Studies, 1992.

Iannucci, Amilcare A., ed. *Dante: Contemporary Perspectives.* Toronto: University of Toronto Press, 1997.

- 'Already and Not Yet: Dante's Existential Eschatology.' In *Dante for the New Millennium,* ed. Teodolinda Barolini and H. Wayne Storey, 334–48. New York: Fordham University Press, 2003.

Jackson, B. Darrell. 'The Theory of Signs in St. Augustine's *De doctrina christiana.*' In *Augustine: A Collection of Critical Essays,* ed. Markus, 93–147. New York: Doubleday, 1972.

Jacoff, Rachel. 'Dante, Geremia e la problematica profetica.' In *Dante e la Bibbia,* ed. Barblan, 113–23. Florence: Olschki, 1988.

- 'Dante and the Legend(s) of St. John.' *Dante Studies* 117 (1999): 45–57.

Jacoff, Rachel, ed. *The Cambridge Companion to Dante.* 2nd ed. Cambridge: Cambridge University Press, 2007.

Jacoff, Rachel, and Jeffrey T. Schnapp, eds. *The Poetry of Allusion: Virgil and Ovid in Dante's 'Commedia.'* Stanford: Stanford University Press, 1991.

Javitch, Daniel. 'The Emergence of Poetic Genre Theory in the Sixteenth Century.' *MLQ* 59 (1998): 139–69.

Jauss, Hans Robert. *Toward an Aesthetic of Reception.* Trans. Timothy Bahti. Minneapolis: University of Minnesota Press, 1982.

Jordan, Mark D., and Kent Emery, Jr, eds. *Ad Litteram: Authoritative Texts and Their Medieval Readers.* Notre Dame: University of Notre Dame Press, 1992.

Josipovici, Gabriel. *The Book of God: A Response to the Bible*. New Haven: Yale University Press, 1988.

Kaske, Carol V. 'Mount Sinai and Dante's Mount Purgatory.' *Dante Studies* 89 (1971): 1–18.

Kaske, R.E. 'Dante's "DXV" and "Veltro."' *Traditio* 17 (1961): 185–252.

– 'Dante's *Purgatorio* XXXII and XXXIII: A Survey of Christian History.' *University of Toronto Quarterly* 43 (1974): 193–214.

– 'The Seven *Status Ecclesiae* in *Purgatorio* XXXII and XXXIII.' In *Dante, Petrarch, Boccaccio: Studies in the Italian Trecento in Honor of Charles S. Singleton*, ed. Aldo S. Bernardo and Anthony L. Pellegrini, 89–113. Binghamton, NY: Medieval & Renaissance Texts & Studies, 1983.

Kay, Richard. 'The Pope's Wife: Allegory as Allegation in *Inferno* 19.106–11.' *Studies in Medieval Culture* 12 (1978): 105–11.

Kay, Richard, ed. *Dante's Monarchia*, by Dante Alighieri. Toronto: Pontifical Institute of Medieval Studies, 1998.

Kent, Bonnie. *Virtues of the Will: The Transformation of Ethics in the Late Thirteenth Century*. Washington, DC: Catholic University of America Press, 1995.

Kermode, Frank. *The Sense of an Ending: Studies in the Theory of Fiction*. Oxford: Oxford University Press, 1967.

– *The Genesis of Secrecy: On the Interpretation of Narrative*. Cambridge, MA: Harvard University Press, 1979.

Kirkpatrick, Robin. *Dante's 'Inferno': Difficulty and Dead Poetry*. Cambridge: Cambridge University Press, 1987.

Kleinhenz, Christopher. 'Dante and the Bible: Intertextual Approaches to the *Divine Comedy*.' *Italica* 63 (1986): 225–36.

– '*Inferno* 8: The Passage across the Styx.' *Lectura Dantis* 3 (1988): 23–40.

– 'Biblical Citation in Dante's *Divine Comedy*.' *Annali d'Italianistica* 8 (1990): 346–59.

– 'The Poetics of Citation in Dante's *Divina Commedia* and the Bible.' In *Italiana 1988*, ed. Albert N. Mancini, Paolo A. Giordano, and Anthony J. Tamburri, 1–21. Rosary College Italian Studies 4. River Forest, IL: Rosary College, 1990.

– 'Dante and the Art of Citation.' In *Dante Now*, ed. Theodore J. Cachey, 43–61. Notre Dame: Notre Dame University Press, 1995.

Kleinhenz, Christopher, ed. *Medieval Italy: An Encyclopedia*. New York: Routledge, 2004.

Kovacs, Judith L. 'Clement of Alexandria and Gregory of Nyssa on the Beatitudes.' In *Homilies on the Beatitudes: An English Version with Commentary and Support Studies*, by Gregory of Nyssa, ed. Hubertus R. Drobner and Alberto Viciano, 311–29. Leiden: Brill, 2000.

Kretzmann, Norman, Anthony Kenny, and Jan Pinborg, eds. *The Cambridge History of Later Medieval Philosophy from the Rediscovery of Aristotle to the Disintegration of Scholasticism: 1100–1600*. Cambridge: Cambridge University Press, 1982.

Kugel, James L. *The Bible As It Was*. Cambridge, MA: Harvard University Press, 1997.

Kurzweil, Ray. *The Singularity Is Near: When Humans Transcend Biology*. London: Penguin, 2005.

Lamberton, Robert L. *Homer the Theologian: Neoplatonist Allegorical Reading and the Growth of the Epic Tradition*. Berkeley: University of California Press, 1986.

Lampe, G.W.H., ed. *The Cambridge History of the Bible*. Vol. 2, *The West from the Fathers to the Reformation*. Cambridge: Cambridge University Press, 1969.

Landes, Richard. 'Lest the Millennium Be Fulfilled: Apocalyptic Expectations and the Pattern of Western Chronography, 100–800 CE.' In *The Use and Abuse of Eschatology in the Middle Ages*, ed. Walter Verbeke, Daniël Verhelst, and Andries Welckenhuysen, 137–211. Leuven: Leuven University Press, 1988.

Lane Fox, Robin. Introduction to *Confessions*, by Saint Augustine. New York: Knopf, 2001.

Lansing, Richard. 'Beatitudes.' In *DE*, 89. New York: Garland, 2000.

Larner, John. *Italy in the Age of Dante and Petrarch*. London and New York: Longman, 1980.

Lattimore, Richmond. *Themes in Greek and Latin Epitaphs*. Urbana: University of Illinois Press, 1962.

Leclerq, Dom Jean. *The Love of Learning and the Desire for God*. Trans. Catherine Misrahi. New York: Fordham University Press, 1961.

Lerner, Robert E. 'Poverty, Preaching, and Eschatology in the Revelation Commentaries of Hugh of St Cher.' In *The Bible in the Medieval World*, ed. Katherine Walsh and Diana Wood, 157–89. Oxford: Basil Blackwell, 1985.

Little, Lester K. 'Pride Goes before Avarice: Social Change and the Vices in Latin Christendom.' *American Historical Review* 76 (1971): 16–49.

Lobrichon, Guy. 'Une nouveauté: Les gloses de la Bible.' In *Le Moyen Âge et la Bible*, ed. Riché and Lobrichon, 95–114. Paris: Beauchesne, 1984.

Louth, Andrew. *Discerning the Mystery: An Essay on the Nature of Theology*. Oxford: Clarendon Press, 1983.

de Lubac, Henri. 'Typologie et allégorisme.' *Recherches de science religieuse* 34 (1947): 180–226.

– *Exégèse médiévale: Les quatre sens de l'Écriture*. 4 vols. in 2 parts. Paris: Aubier, 1959–64.

Lynch, Joseph H. *Simoniacal Entry into Religious Life from 1000 to 1260.* Columbus: Ohio State University Press, 1976.

Madigan, Kevin. *Olivi and the Interpretation of Matthew in the High Middle Ages.* Notre Dame: University of Notre Dame Press, 2003.

Maierù, Alfonso. 'Senso.' In *ED*, 5:166–8. Rome: Istituto dell'Enciclopedia italiana, 1970–78.

Manica, Raffaele. 'Lo spavento del sacro: Presenze bibliche nell'*Inferno.*' In *Memoria biblica nell'opera di Dante*, ed. E. Esposito, R. Manca, N. Longo, and R. Scrivano, 23–56. Rome: Bulzoni, 1996.

Markus, R.A. *Signs and Meanings: World and Text in Ancient Christianity.* Liverpool: Liverpool University Press, 1996.

– 'St. Augustine on Signs.' In *Augustine*, ed. Markus, 61–91. New York: Doubleday, 1972.

Markus, R.A., ed. *Augustine: A Collection of Critical Essays.* New York: Doubleday, 1972.

Marti, Mario. 'L'effimero e l'eterno: La meditazione elegiaca di *Purgatorio* XI.' *Giornale storico della letteratura italiana* 161 (1984): 161–84.

Martinez, Ronald L. 'La "sacra fame dell'oro" (*Purgatorio* 22, 41) tra Virgilio e Stazio: Dal testo all'interpretazione.' *Letture classensi* 18 (1989): 177–93.

Masciandaro, Franco. *Dante as Dramatist: The Myth of the Earthly Paradise and Tragic Vision in the 'Divine Comedy.'* Philadelphia: University of Pennsylvania Press, 1991.

Matter, E. Ann. *The Voice of My Beloved: The Song of Songs in Western Medieval Christianity.* Philadelphia: University of Pennsylvania Press, 1990.

– 'The Apocalypse in Early Medieval Exegesis.' In Emmerson and McGinn, eds., *The Apocalypse in the Middle Ages*, 38–50. Ithaca: Cornell University Press, 1992.

– 'The Bible in the Center: The *Glossa ordinaria.*' In *The Unbounded Community: Papers in Christian Ecumenism in Honor of Jaroslav Pelikan*, ed. William Caferro and Duncan G. Fisher, 33–42. New York: Garland, 1996.

– 'The Church Fathers and the *Glossa ordinaria.*' In *The Reception of the Church Fathers in the West: From the Carolingians to the Maurists*, 2 vols., ed. Irena Backus, 1:83–111. Leiden: Brill, 1997.

Mazzeo, Joseph Anthony. 'Dante and the Pauline Modes of Vision.' *Harvard Theological Review* 50 (1957): 275–306.

Mazzotta, Giuseppe. *Dante, Poet of the Desert: History and Allegory in the 'Divine Comedy.'* Princeton: Princeton University Press, 1979.

– *Dante's Vision and the Circle of Knowledge.* Princeton: Princeton University Press, 1993.

McGinn, Bernard. 'Introduction: Apocalyptic Spirituality.' In *Apocalyptic Spirituality*, ed. McGinn, 1–16. Mahwah, NJ: Paulist Press, 1979.

- 'Early Apocalypticism: The Ongoing Debate.' In *The Apocalypse in English Renaissance Thought and Literature*, ed. C.A. Patrides and Joseph Wittreich, 2–39. Manchester: Manchester University Press, 1984.
- *The Calabrian Abbot: Joachim of Fiore in the History of Western Thought.* New York: Macmillan, 1985.
- 'Revelation.' In *The Literary Guide to the Bible*, ed. Alter and Kermode, 523–41. Cambridge, MA: Harvard University Press, 1987.
- 'Introduction: John's Apocalypse and the Apocalyptic Mentality.' In *The Apocalypse in the Middle Ages*, ed. Emmerson and McGinn, 3–19. Ithaca: Cornell University Press, 1992.
- *Visions of the End: Apocalyptic Traditions in the Middle Ages.* New York: Columbia University Press, 1998.

McGinn, Bernard, ed. *Apocalyptic Spirituality.* Mahwah, NJ: Paulist Press, 1979.

Meschiari, Maria Cristina. 'Un idolo poetico: Fetonte nella *Commedia.*' *Studi e problemi di critica testuale* 45 (1992): 93–102.

Mezzadroli, Giuseppina. 'Virtues and Vices.' In *DE*, 866–71. New York: Garland, 2000.

Mineo, Niccolò. *Profetismo e Apocalittica in Dante: Strutture e temi profetico-apocalittici in Dante: Dalla 'Vita Nuova' alla 'Divina Commedia.'* Catania: Università di Catania, 1968.

Minnis, A.J. *Medieval Theory of Authorship: Scholastic Literary Attitudes in the Later Middle Ages.* 2nd ed. London: Scolar Press, 1988.

Minnis, A.J., and A.B. Scott with David Wallace, eds. *Medieval Literary Theory and Criticism c. 1100–1375: The Commentary Tradition.* Rev. ed. Oxford: Clarendon Press, 1991.

Moevs, Christian. 'Miraculous Syllogisms: Clocks, Faith, and Reason in *Paradiso* 10 and 24.' *Dante Studies* 117 (1999): 59–84.

Moore, Edward. *Contributions to the Textual Criticism of the 'Divina Commedia.'* Cambridge: Cambridge University Press, 1889.

- *Studies in Dante: Second Series: Miscellaneous Essays.* Oxford: Clarendon Press, 1899.

Morey, James H. *Book and Verse: A Guide to Middle English Biblical Literature.* Urbana and Chicago: University of Illinois Press, 2000.

Morgan, Alison. *Dante and the Medieval Other World.* Cambridge: Cambridge University Press, 1990.

Morghen, Raffaelo. *Dante profeta: Tra la storia e l'eterno.* Milan: Jaca Book, 1983.

Murray, Alexander. *Reason and Society in the Middle Ages.* Oxford: Clarendon Press, 1978.

Nardi, Bruno. *Saggi di filosofia dantesca.* 1930. 2nd ed. Florence: La Nuova Italia, 1967.

Negri, L. 'Dante e il testo della Vulgata.' *Giornale storico della letteratura italiana* 85 (1925): 288–307.

Nemetz, Anthony. 'Literalness and the *Sensus litteralis.' Speculum* 34 (1959): 76–89.

Neusner, Jacob. *Canon and Connection: Intertextuality in Judaism.* Lanham: University Press of America, 1987.

Newhauser, Richard. *The Treatise on Vices and Virtues in Latin and the Vernacular.* Turnhout: Brepols, 1993.

– *The Early History of Greed: The Sin of Avarice in Early Medieval Thought and Literature.* Cambridge: Cambridge University Press, 2000.

– 'Justice and Liberality: Opposition to Avarice in the Twelfth Century.' In *Virtue and Ethics in the Twelfth Century,* ed. István P. Bejczy and Newhauser, 295–316. Leiden: Brill, 2005.

– '*Avaritia* and *Paupertas:* On the Place of the Early Franciscans in the History of Avarice.' In *In the Garden of Evil: The Vices and Culture in the Middle Ages,* ed. Newhauser, 324–48. Toronto: Pontifical Institute of Medieval Studies, 2005.

Noakes, Susan. 'Dino Compagni and the Vow in San Giovanni: *Inferno* XIX, 16–21.' *Dante Studies* 86 (1968): 41–64.

Nohrnberg, James. 'The First-Fruits of Last Judgment: The *Commedia* as a Thirteenth-Century Apocalypse.' *Sewanee Medieval Studies* 12 (2002): 111–58.

Ocker, Christopher. *Biblical Poetics before Humanism and Reformation.* Cambridge: Cambridge University Press, 2002.

O'Donnell, James J. 'Bible.' In *Augustine through the Ages: An Encyclopedia,* ed. Allan D. Fitzgerald, 99–100. Grand Rapids: Eerdmans, 1999.

Otten, Willemien. 'Nature and Scripture: The Demise of a Medieval Analogy.' *Harvard Theological Review* 88 (1995): 257–84.

D'Ovidio, Francesco. 'Dante e San Paolo.' In *Studii sulla 'Divina Commedia,'* 326–55. Milan: Remo Sandron, 1901.

Panzacchi, Enrico. 'Il canto XI del *Purgatorio.*' In *Letture Dantesche,* ed. Giovanni Getto, 883–97. Florence: Sansoni, 1962.

Parry, Adam. 'The Two Voices of Virgil's *Aeneid.' Arion* 2 (1963): 66–80.

Penna, Antonio. 'Bibbia.' In *ED,* 1:626–9. Rome: Istituto dell'Enciclopedia italiana, 1970–78.

Pépin, Jean. *Dante e la tradition de l'allégorie.* Montreal: Institut d'études médiévales, 1971.

Pertile, Lino. *La puttana e il gigante: Dal Cantico dei Cantici al Paradiso Terrestre di Dante.* Ravenna: Longo, 1998.

Petrocchi, Giorgio. 'San Paolo in Dante.' In *Dante e la Bibbia,* ed. Barblan, 235–48. Florence: Olschki, 1988.

Potestà, Gian Luca. 'I frati minori e lo studio della Bibbia: Da Francesco d'Assisi a Nicolò di Lyra.' In *La Bibbia nel medioevo*, ed. Cremascoli and Leonardi, 269–90. Bologna: Edizioni Dehoniane, 1996.

– *Il tempo dell'Apocalisse: Vita di Gioacchino da Fiore*. Rome: Laterza, 2004.

Proto, Enrico. *L'Apocalisse nella 'Divina Commedia.'* Naples: Luigi Piero, 1905.

Raffa, Guy. *Divine Dialectic: Dante's Incarnational Poetry*. Toronto: University of Toronto Press, 2000.

Réau, Louis. *Iconographie de l'art chrétien*. 3 vols. Paris: Presses Universitaires de France, 1955.

Reeves, Marjorie. *The Influence of Prophecy in the Later Middle Ages: A Study in Joachimism*. Oxford: Clarendon Press, 1969.

– 'Dante and the Prophetic View of History.' In *The World of Dante: Essays on Dante and His Times*, ed. Cecil Grayson, 44–60. Oxford: Clarendon Press, 1980.

– 'The Third Age: Dante's Debt to Gioacchino da Fiore.' In *L'età dello spirito e la fine dei tempi in Gioacchino da Fiore e nel gioachimismo medievale*, ed. Antonio Crocco, 125–39. San Giovane in Fiore: Centro Internazionale di Studi Gioachimiti, 1986.

– 'The Bible and Literary Authorship in the Middle Ages.' In *Reading the Text: Biblical Criticism and Literary Theory*, ed. Stephen Prickett, 12–63. Oxford: Blackwell, 1991.

Renucci, Paul. 'Le chant XIX de l'*Enfer*.' In *Letture dell'Inferno*, ed. Vittorio Vettori, 155–81. Milan: Marzorati, 1963.

Rhu, Lawrence. 'After the Middle Ages: Prophetic Authority and Human Fallibility in the Renaissance Epic.' In *Poetry and Prophecy: The Beginnings of a Literary Tradition*, ed. James L. Kugel, 163–84. Ithaca: Cornell University Press, 1990.

Riché, Pierre, and Guy Lobrichon, eds. *Le Moyen Âge et la Bible*. Paris: Beauchesne, 1984.

Rigo, Paula. *Memoria classica e memoria biblica in Dante*. Florence: Olschki, 1994.

Robertson, Jr, D.H. *A Preface to Chaucer: Studies in Medieval Perspectives*. Princeton: Princeton University Press, 1962.

Sarolli, Gian Roberto. *Prolegomena alla 'Divina Commedia.'* Florence: Olschki, 1971.

Schildgen, Brenda Deen. 'Temporal Dispensations: Dante's "tëodia" and John's "alto preconio" in canto 26, *Paradiso*.' *Stanford Italian Review* 11 (1991): 171–85.

Schnapp, Jeffrey. *The Transfiguration of History at the Center of Dante's 'Paradise.'* Princeton: Princeton University Press, 1986.

Di Scipio, Giuseppe. *The Presence of Pauline Thought in the Works of Dante*. Lewiston: Edwin Mellen Press, 1995.

– 'XXIV.' In Dante's 'Divine Comedy': Introductory Readings III: 'Paradiso.'
Special number of Lectura Dantis 16–17 (Spring–Fall 1995): 352–70.

Scott, John A. Dante's Political Purgatory. Philadelphia: University of Pennsylvania Press, 1996.

Shapiro, Marianne. 'Homo artifex: A Rereading of Purgatorio XI.' Lectura Dantis
19 (1992): 59–69.

Sheler, Jeffrey L. Is the Bible True? How Modern Debates and Discoveries Affirm
the Essence of the Scriptures. San Francisco: HarperSanFrancisco, 1999.

Shoaf, R.A. '"Auri sacra fames" and the Age of Gold.' Dante Studies 96
(1978): 195–9.

Singleton, Charles S. Dante Studies 1: 'Commedia': Elements of Structure. 1954.
Cambridge, MA: Harvard University Press, 1970.

– Dante Studies 2: Journey to Beatrice. 1958. 2nd ed. Baltimore: Johns Hopkins
University Press, 1977.

– 'In Exitu Israel de Aegypto.' Dante Studies 78 (1960): 1–24.

Singleton, Charles S., ed. and trans. The Divine Comedy, by Dante Alighieri.
3 vols. Princeton: Princeton University Press, 1970–75.

Smalley, Beryl. The Study of the Bible in the Middle Ages. 1952. Notre Dame:
University of Notre Dame Press, 1964.

– 'The Bible in the Medieval Schools.' In The Cambridge History of the Bible,
vol. 2, ed. Lampe, 197–220. Cambridge: Cambridge University Press, 1969.

Smith, Lesley. 'The Theology of the Twelfth- and Thirteenth-Century Bible.'
In The Early Medieval Bible: Its Production, Decoration, and Use, ed. Richard
Gameson, 223–32. Cambridge: Cambridge University Press, 1994.

Southern, R.W. Scholastic Humanism and the Unification of Europe. Vol. 1,
Foundations. Oxford: Blackwell, 1995.

Sowell, Madison U., ed. Dante and Ovid: Essays in Intertextuality. Binghamton,
NY: Medieval & Renaissance Texts & Studies, 1991.

Steiner, George. After Babel: Aspects of Language and Translation. 2nd ed.
Oxford: Oxford University Press, 1992.

– Grammars of Creation. New Haven: Yale University Press, 2001.

Stephany, William A. 'XXV.' In Dante's 'Divine Comedy': Introductory Readings
III: 'Paradiso.' Special number of Lectura Dantis 16–17 (Spring–Fall
1995): 371–87.

Sternberg, Meir. The Poetics of Biblical Narrative: Ideological Literature and the
Drama of Reading. Bloomington: Indiana University Press, 1985.

Stock, Brian. Augustine the Reader: Meditation, Self-Knowledge, and the Ethics of
Interpretation. Cambridge, MA: Harvard University Press, 1996.

Strubel, Armand. '"Allegoria in factis" et "allegoria in verbis."' Poétique 23
(1975): 342–57.

Tatlock, J.S.P. 'The Last Cantos of the *Purgatorio.' Modern Philology* 32 (1934): 113–23.

Teskey, Gordon. *Allegory and Violence.* Ithaca: Cornell University Press, 1996.

Todorov, Tzvetan. *Introduction to Poetics.* Trans. Richard Howard. Minneapolis: University of Minnesota Press, 1981.

– *Theories of the Symbol.* Trans. Catherine Porter. Ithaca: Cornell University Press, 1982.

Tollemache, Frederigo. 'Beatitudini evangeliche.' In *ED*, 1:540–1. Rome: Istituto dell'Enciclopedia italiana, 1970–78.

Tommaseo, Niccolò, ed. *'Commedia' di Dante Alighieri.* 3 vols. Milan: Francesco Pagnoni, 1869.

Vance, Eugene. 'Saint Augustine: Language as Temporality.' In *Mimesis: From Mirror to Method, Augustine to Descartes,* ed. John D. Lyons and Stephen G. Nichols, Jr, 20–35. Hanover: University Press of New England, 1982.

Vandelli, Giuseppe. 'I "for" del "bel San Giovanni."' *Studi danteschi* 15 (1931): 55–66.

Varanini, Giorgio. 'Canto XIX dell'*Inferno.'* In *Lectura Dantis Neapolitana,* 323–40. Naples: Loffredo, 1986.

Vasoli, Cesare. 'La Bibbia nel *Convivio* e nella *Monarchia.'* In *Dante e la Bibbia,* ed. Barblan, 19–27. Florence: Olschki, 1988.

Venturi, P. Pompeo, ed. *'La Divina Commedia' di Dante Alighieri col comento del P. Pompeo Venturi.* 3 vols. Florence: Ciardetti, 1821.

Verger, Jacques. 'L'exégèse de l'Université.' In *Le Moyen Âge et la Bible,* ed. Riché and Lobrichon, 199–232. Paris: Beauchesne, 1984.

Vinay, Gustavo, ed. *Monarchia,* by Dante Alighieri. Florence: Sansoni, 1950.

Vitz, Evelyn Birge. 'The Liturgy and Vernacular Literature.' In *The Liturgy of the Medieval Church,* ed. Thomas J. Heffernan and E. Ann Matter, 551–618. Kalamazoo: Medieval Institute Publications, 2001.

von Rad, Gerhard. *The Message of the Prophets.* San Francisco: HarperCollins, 1967.

Ward, Benedicta. *Miracles and the Medieval Mind: Theory, Record, and Event, 1000–1250.* Philadelphia: University of Pennsylvania Press, 1982.

Weinsheimer, Joel. *Gadamer's Hermeneutics: A Reading of 'Truth and Method.'* New Haven: Yale University Press, 1985.

– *Philosophical Hermeneutics and Literary Theory.* New Haven: Yale University Press, 1991.

Whitman, Jon. *Allegory: The Dynamics of an Ancient and Medieval Technique.* Cambridge, MA: Harvard University Press, 1987.

Wicksteed, Philip H., ed. and trans. *De Monarchia,* by Dante Alighieri. In *A Translation of the Latin Works of Dante Alighieri,* ed. and trans. A.G. Ferrers Howell and Philip H. Wicksteed, 127–292. London: Dent, 1904.

Wieland, Georg. 'The Reception and Interpretation of Aristotle's *Ethics.*' In
  The Cambridge History of Later Medieval Philosophy, ed. Kretzmann et al.,
  657–72. Cambridge: Cambridge University Press, 1982.
Williams, A.N. 'The Theology of the *Comedy.*' In *The Cambridge Companion to
  Dante,* ed. Rachel Jacoff, 201–17.
Williams, Thomas. 'Biblical Interpretation.' In *The Cambridge Companion to
  Augustine,* ed. Eleanore Stump and Norman Kretzmann, 59–70. Cambridge:
  Cambridge University Press, 2001.
Zink, Michel. 'The Allegorical Poem as Interior Memoir.' Trans. Margaret
  Miner and Kevin Brownlee. *Yale French Studies* 70 (1986): 100–26.

Citations of Dante's Works

Biblical and Apocryphal Citations

Index

Adam, 24, 40, 54, 75, 151–2, 155, 159–60, 170, 177, 221n3, 252n31, 257n69; language of, 75

Aeneas, 95, 171–2

allegoresis, 14, 29, 42, 204n2, 205n3

allegorical sense, 8, 27–8, 30, 32–3, 41–2

allegory, 6, 8, 14, 19, 29, 45, 169, 201n10, 205n3, 211n43; of the *Commedia*, 82, 151, 227–8n9; patristic, 30; of the poets, 29, 44–6; of the theologians, 29, 44–6, 82

Alter, Robert, 5

anagogical sense, 28–9, 44–5

Ananias, 53–4

Anchises, 171, 195

anger. *See* wrath

appropriation, rewriting as, 77, 98, 102, 194

Apocalypse, 60, 73, 97, 101–2, 151, 153, 157, 159, 180, 185, 187, 190; interpretive history of, 97–8, 143–8

apocalypse, genre of, 148–51, 250–1n23

Apollo, 53, 57

Aquinas, Thomas, 15, 28, 33–4, 63, 68, 115–16, 118, 122–3, 125–6, 128, 130, 138, 141, 242n41; on the literal sense, 33; *Summa contra Gentiles,* 67, 224n27; *Summa theologiae,* 33, 45, 67, 122–3

Aristotelian prologue, 32

Aristotle, 31–3, 82, 121–3, 132–4, 137–9, 168, 228n17, 242n41, 245–6n69; *Nicomachean Ethics,* 82, 121–3

Armour, Peter, 163

Astraea, 153

Auerbach, Erich, 28–9, 49, 195–6

Augustine, Saint, 8, 21, 22, 24, 28, 34, 38, 49, 68, 110–11, 115, 117, 118, 120, 121, 123, 126, 138, 141, 155, 175–6; on the Apocalypse, 97–8, 144–7; biblical hermeneutics of, 7, 19–31, 34; on language, 23–7, 72, 208n28; *Confessions,* 10, 20, 23, 24, 25, 26, 34, 81, 175–6; *De civitate Dei,* 40, 66–7, 144; *De doctrina christiana,* 20, 27, 28, 30, 33, 40; *De Genesi ad litteram,* 21, 24, 155; *De Trinitate,* 23, 24

authority: biblical, 3, 11, 21, 34, 35, 36, 37–9, 41, 46, 77, 102–3; Dante's, 48, 58, 95, 140; of the Decretals, 37; ecclesiastical, 94; of non-biblical writings, 38; of world monarch, 37, 47